MCSE

Exam
70-223

Microsoft® Windows® 2000
Advanced Server Clustering Services

Training Kit

IT Professional

PUBLISHED BY
Microsoft Press
A Division of Microsoft Corporation
One Microsoft Way
Redmond, Washington 98052-6399

Library of Congress Cataloging-in-Publication Data
    MCSE Training Kit : Microsoft Windows 2000 Advanced Server Clustering Services /
    Microsoft Corporation.
        p. cm.
    Includes index.
    ISBN 0-7356-1293-5
      1. Operating systems (Computers)   2. Microsoft Windows (Computer file)   I. Title:
    Microsoft Windows 2000 Advanced Server Clustering Services.   II. Microsoft Corporation.

    QA76.76.O63 M427 2001
    005.7'13769--dc21   2001030140

Printed and bound in the United States of America.

1 2 3 4 5 6 7 8 9   QWT   6 5 4 3 2 1

Distributed in Canada by Penguin Books Canada Limited.

A CIP catalogue record for this book is available from the British Library.

Microsoft Press books are available through booksellers and distributors worldwide. For further information about international editions, contact your local Microsoft Corporation office or contact Microsoft Press International directly at fax (425) 936-7329. Visit our Web site at mspress.microsoft.com. Send comments to *tkinput@microsoft.com*.

Acquisitions Editor: Thomas Pohlmann
Project Editor: Marzena Makuta
Technical Editor: Marzena Makuta
For Training Associates:
Project Manager: Dave Perkovich
Subject Matter Experts: Thomas Ingoglia, Dawn Golsarry, Wade Harding
Senior Technical Editor: Scott Schnoll
Technical Reviewers: Randy A. Hinders, Roland Fritsch, Don Shirah, James Stella, Bob Withers
Graphic Artist/Multimedia Developer: Stephanie Ingoglia

Body Part No. X08-04973

Contents

About This Book

Welcome to the *MCSE Training Kit: Microsoft Windows 2000 Advanced Server Clustering Services*. This Microsoft Press self-paced training kit is designed to provide you with comprehensive information about using Microsoft clustering technologies on Windows 2000 Advanced Server. This training kit also maps to the objectives presented by Microsoft for the Microsoft Certified System Engineer (MCSE) Exam 70-223. In addition to the exam material, this training kit presents useful information about Network Load Balancing.

Note For more information on becoming a Microsoft Certified Systems Engineer, see the section titled "The Microsoft Certified Professional Program" later in this chapter.

Each chapter in this book is divided into lessons. Most lessons include hands-on procedures that allow you to practice or demonstrate a particular concept or skill. Each chapter ends with a short summary of all chapter lessons and a set of review questions to test your knowledge of the material.

The "Getting Started" section of this chapter provides important setup instructions that describe the hardware and software requirements to complete the procedures in this course. It also provides information about the networking configuration necessary to complete some of the hands-on procedures. Read through this section thoroughly before you start the lessons.

Intended Audience

This book was developed for information technology (IT) professionals who need to design, plan, implement and support Microsoft clustering technologies or who plan to take the related Microsoft Certified Systems Engineer Exam 70-223, *Installing, Configuring, and Administering Microsoft Clustering Services by Using Microsoft Windows 2000 Advanced Server*.

Prerequisites

This course requires that students meet the following prerequisites:

- Install and configure Microsoft Windows 2000 Advanced Server.
- Manage users and security on a Windows 2000 domain.
- Install and configure Active Directory on a Windows 2000 server.
- List the differences between Microsoft Windows 2000 Server, Windows 2000 Advanced Server, and Windows 2000 Datacenter Server.

Reference Materials

You might find the following reference materials useful:

- Microsoft TechNet
- Windows 2000 Server Resource Kit

About the CD-ROM

The Supplemental Course Materials CD contains a variety of informational aids that may be used throughout this book. This includes sample files required to complete practices in this book and multimedia presentations to help you understand the concepts presented. For more information regarding the contents of this CD, see the section titled "Getting Started" later in this introduction.

The multimedia presentations supplement some of the key concepts covered in the book. You should view these presentations when suggested, and then use them as a review tool while you work through the material. A complete version of this book is also available online with a variety of viewing options. For information about using the online book, see the section "About the Online Book" later in this introduction.

The Supplemental Course Materials CD also contains files required to perform the hands-on procedures, and information designed to supplement the lesson material. These files can be used directly from the CD-ROM or copied onto your hard disk. The files include demonstrations of key concepts, and practice files for the exercises.

Features of This Book

Each chapter opens with a "Before You Begin" section, which prepares you for completing the chapter.

The chapters are then divided into lessons. Whenever possible, lessons contain practices that give you an opportunity to use the skills being presented or explore the part of the application being described. All practices offer step-by-step procedures that are identified with an icon like the one to the left of this paragraph.

The "Review" section at the end of each chapter allows you to test what you have learned in the lessons.

Appendix A, "Questions and Answers" contains all of the book's questions and corresponding answers.

Notes

Several types of Notes appear throughout the lessons.

- Notes marked **Tip** contain explanations of possible results or alternative methods.
- Notes marked **Important** contain information that is essential to completing a task.
- Notes marked **Note** contain supplemental information.
- Notes marked **Caution** contain warnings about possible loss of data.

Conventions

The following conventions are used throughout this book.

Notational Conventions

- Characters or commands that you type appear in *italic* type.
- *Italic* in syntax statements indicates placeholders for variable information. *Italic* is also used for book titles.
- Names of files and folders appear in Title Caps, except when you are to type them directly. Unless otherwise indicated, you can use all lowercase letters when you type a file name in a dialog box or at a command prompt.
- File name extensions appear in all lowercase.

- Acronyms appear in all uppercase.

- Monospace type represents code samples, examples of screen text, or entries that you might type at a command prompt or in initialization files.

- Square brackets [ ] are used in syntax statements to enclose optional items. For example, [*filename*] in command syntax indicates that you can choose to type a file name with the command. Type only the information within the brackets, not the brackets themselves.

- Braces { } are used in syntax statements to enclose required items. Type only the information within the braces, not the braces themselves.

- Icons represent specific sections in the book as follows:

Icon	Represents
	A multimedia presentation. You will find the applicable multimedia presentation on the book's accompanying CD-ROM.
	A hands-on practice. You should perform the practice to give yourself an opportunity to use the skills being presented in the lesson.
	Chapter review questions. These questions at the end of each chapter allow you to test what you have learned in the lessons. You will find the answers to the review questions in Appendix A, "Questions and Answers," at the end of the book.

Keyboard Conventions

- A plus sign (+) between two key names means that you must press those keys at the same time. For example, "press ALT+TAB" means that you hold down ALT while you press TAB.

- A comma (,) between two or more key names means that you must press each of the keys consecutively, not together. For example, "press ALT, F, X" means that you press and release each key in sequence. "Press ALT+W, L" means that you first press ALT and W together, and then release them and press L.

- You can choose menu commands with the keyboard. Press the ALT key to activate the menu bar, and then sequentially press the keys that correspond to the highlighted or underlined letter of the menu name and the command name. For some commands, you can also press a key combination listed in the menu.

- You can select or clear check boxes or option buttons in dialog boxes with the keyboard. Press the ALT key, and then press the key that corresponds to the underlined letter of the option name. Or you can press TAB until the option is highlighted, and then press the spacebar to select or clear the check box or option button.
- You can cancel the display of a dialog box by pressing the ESC key.

Chapter and Appendix Overview

This self-paced training course combines hands-on procedures, notes, multimedia presentations, and review questions to teach you how to implement and manage Microsoft clustering technologies. It is designed to be completed from beginning to end, but you can choose a customized track and complete only the sections that interest you. (See the next section, "Finding the Best Starting Point for You" for more information.) If you choose the customized track option, see the "Before You Begin" section in each chapter. Any hands-on procedures that require preliminary work from preceding chapters refer to the appropriate chapters.

The book is divided into the following chapters:

The "About This Book" section contains a self-paced training overview and introduces the components of this training. Read this section thoroughly to get the greatest educational value from this self-paced training and to plan which lessons you will complete.

Chapter 1, "Introduction to Microsoft Clustering Technologies," will introduce you to the two primary cluster technologies included with Windows 2000 Advanced Server, Cluster Service and Network Load Balancing.

Chapter 2, "Preparing Windows 2000 Server for Cluster Service," describes the necessary hardware and software required before installing the Microsoft Cluster Service.

Chapter 3, "Installing and Configuring Cluster Service," provides detailed information, including a step-by-step practice, for installing and configuring Cluster Service on two computers running Windows 2000 Advanced Server.

Chapter 4, "Administering and Managing a Cluster," describes common administrative tasks for managing and supporting a cluster.

Chapter 5, "Managing and Supporting a Cluster," describes how to implement common network solutions on a cluster such as file and printer sharing.

Chapter 6, "Implementing Applications and Network Services on a Cluster," describes how to implement advanced cluster solutions, such as deploying cluster-aware applications, common network services such as DHCP and WINS, and how to cluster Web sites using Internet Information Services (IIS).

Chapter 7, "Troubleshooting Cluster Service," lists common problems associated with managing a cluster and the necessary troubleshooting steps to correct the problems.

Chapter 8, "Installing and Supporting Exchange Server 2000 in a Clustered Environment," describes how to cluster Microsoft Exchange 2000 and includes a detailed step-by-step practice to help you deploy a clustered implementation of Microsoft's messaging system.

Chapter 9, "Installing and Supporting SQL Server 2000 in a Clustered Environment," describes how to cluster Microsoft SQL Server 2000 and includes a detailed step-by-step practice to help you deploy a clustered implementation of Microsoft's database system.

Chapter 10, "Introduction to Network Load Balancing," changes the focus of the training kit from the Cluster Service and introduces you to the second Microsoft clustering technology supported by Windows 2000 Advanced Server, Network Load Balancing (NLB).

Chapter 11, "Implementing Network Load Balancing," describes how to implement NLB on a network. The chapter also includes a detailed step-by-step practice to help you deploy a network load balanced Web site.

Appendix A, "Questions and Answers," lists all of the review questions from the book, showing the page number where the question appears and the correct answer or answers.

Appendix B, "Cluster.exe Command Reference," lists the primary and secondary commands associated with managing a cluster using the Cluster.exe command line utility.

Appendix C, "Error Messages," lists the various event messages that can appear in the Windows 2000 Event Log associated with the Cluster Service.

The Glossary lists the terminology related to both clustering technologies.

Finding the Best Starting Point For You

Because this book is self-paced, you can skip some lessons and revisit them later. But note that you must complete the procedures in Chapter 3, "Installing and Configuring Microsoft Cluster Service" before you can perform procedures in the other chapters. Use the following table to find the best starting point for you:

If you	Follow this learning path
Are preparing to take the Microsoft Certified Systems Engineer Exam 70-223, *Installing, Configuring, and Administering Microsoft Clustering Services by Using Microsoft Windows 2000 Advanced Server.*	Read the "Getting Started" section. Then work through Chapters 1 through 3. Work through the remaining chapters in any order.
Are reviewing information about specific topics from the exam.	Use the "Where to Find Specific Skills in This Book" section that follows this table.

Where to Find Specific Skills in This Book

The following tables provide a list of the skills measured on certification exam 70-223, *Installing, Configuring, and Administering Microsoft Clustering Services by Using Microsoft Windows 2000 Advanced Server.* The tables also tell you where in this book you will find the lesson relating to each skill.

Note Exam skills are subject to change without prior notice and at the sole discretion of Microsoft.

Skill Being Measured	Location in Book
Configuring Windows 2000 Advanced Server for the Cluster Service installation	
Configure and troubleshoot the software components of a network before an installation. Components include binding protocols, Internet Protocols (IP), single point of failure, and network infrastructure services.	Chapter 2, Lesson 1; Chapter 2, Lesson 2
Configure and troubleshoot the physical components of a network before an installation. Components include hardware, crossover cables, network adapters, hubs, routers, and switches.	Chapter 2, Lesson 2
Configure and troubleshoot volumes before an installation.	Chapter 2, Lesson 3
Configure and troubleshoot external storage subsystem before an installation. Hardware includes SCSI, host adapters, and the Fibre Channel device.	Chapter 2, Lesson 3
Installing, configuring, and troubleshooting Cluster Service	
Install and configure the Cluster Service software.	Chapter 3, Lesson 1
Upgrade an operating system on a clustered server.	Chapter 3, Lesson 3
Configure an automated deployment of a cluster.	Chapter 3, Lesson 1
Verify the Cluster Service installation, and troubleshoot cluster storage issues, SCSI configuration, name resolution, file system configuration, and partition and "Physical Disk resource" configuration.	Chapter 3, Lesson 2; Chapter 4, Lesson 1

(continued)

Skill Being Measured *continued*	**Location in Book**
Installing, configuring, and troubleshooting services and applications on a cluster	
Install, configure, and troubleshoot file shares and distributed file system (Dfs) on a cluster.	Chapter 5, Lesson 1
Configure and troubleshoot print services for a cluster.	Chapter 5, Lesson 2
Install, configure, and troubleshoot applications and services on a cluster.	Chapter 4, Lesson 1; Chapter 4, Lesson 2; Chapter 6, Lesson 1
Manage resources and applications on a cluster.	Chapter 4, Lesson 2; Chapter 4, Lesson 3; Chapter 6, Lesson 1
Configure and troubleshoot resource dependencies and virtual servers.	Chapter 4, Lesson 2
Troubleshoot applications and services, including failed applications, file and print services access, the Registry, cluster logs, and Resource Monitor.	Chapter 7
Managing cluster resources	
Configure and add clustering resources by using Cluster Service command-line utilities, scripting, and the graphical user interface (GUI).	Chapter 4
Remove, replace, evict, and add cluster nodes.	Chapter 4, Lesson 3
Configure advanced resource properties, including general properties and resource-specific properties.	Chapter 4, Lesson 2
Manage and monitor cluster storage.	Chapter 5, Lesson 3
Configure administrative access to a cluster.	Chapter 4, Lesson 3
Implement load balancing and failback for resource groups.	Chapter 4, Lesson 2
Troubleshooting, monitoring, and optimizing clustered services	
Optimize resource groups for failover.	Chapter 4, Lesson 1; Chapter 4, Lesson 2
Troubleshoot failure on a cluster and the Cluster Service.	Chapter 7, Lesson1; Chapter 7, Lesson 3
Manage and optimize cluster performance.	Chapter 1, Lesson 4; Chapter 4, Lesson 3
Implement disaster recovery methods.	Chapter 7, Lesson 5

Getting Started

This self-paced training course contains hands-on procedures to help you learn about Microsoft clustering technologies.

To complete these procedures, you must have two networked computers. Both computers must be capable of running Windows 2000 Advanced Server.

Caution Several exercises may require you to make changes to your servers. This may have undesirable results if you are connected to a larger network. Check with your Network Administrator before attempting these exercises.

Hardware Requirements

Each computer must have the following minimum configuration. All hardware should be on the Microsoft Cluster Service Hardware Compatibility List (HCL).

- Pentium II 300
- PCI 2.1 bus
- 256 megabytes (MB) of RAM
- 4-gigabyte (GB) hard disk
- 256-kilobyte (KB) L2 cache
- DVD or CD-ROM drive (12x or greater)
- Non-ISA network adapter
- 4-MB video adapter
- Super VGA (SVGA) monitor (17 inch)
- Microsoft Mouse or compatible pointing device
- Sound card with speakers
- One external hard drive approved for use with the clustering technologies
- Two non-ISA network adapters and a crossover network cable.

Software Requirements

The following software is required to complete the procedures in this course.

- Microsoft Windows 2000 Advanced Server
- Microsoft Windows 2000 Server Resource Kit
- Microsoft Exchange Server 2000 (optional)
- Microsoft SQL Server 2000 Enterprise Edition (optional)

Caution The 120-day Evaluation Edition software provided with this training kit is not the full retail product and is provided only for the purposes of training and evaluation. Microsoft Technical Support does not support these evaluation editions. For additional support information regarding this book and the CD-ROMs (including answers to commonly asked questions about installation and use), visit the Microsoft Press Technical Support Web site at *www.mspress.microsoft.com/support/*. You can also email tkinput@microsoft.com, or send a letter to Microsoft Press, Attn: Microsoft Press Technical Support, One Microsoft Way, Redmond, WA 98502-6399.

Setup Instructions

The following information is a checklist of the tasks that you need to perform to prepare your computer to install the evaluation software. If you do not have experience installing Windows 2000 or another network operating system, you may need help from an experienced network administrator. Step-by-step instructions for each task follow.

- Create Windows 2000 Advanced Server setup disks
- Run the Windows 2000 Advanced Server Pre-Copy and Text Mode Setup Routine
- Run the GUI mode and gathering information phase of Windows 2000 Advanced Server Setup
- Complete the Installing Windows Networking Components phase of Windows 2000 Advanced Server Setup
- Complete the hardware installation phase of Windows 2000 Advanced Server Setup

Note The installation information provided in this section will help you prepare a computer to run the evaluation software. It is not intended to teach you installation.

To prepare your cluster for the installation, do the following:

1. Install 2 network interface cards (NICs) in each computer. Be sure to verify that you are using the same 2 slots in each computer.
2. Connect one NIC to your local area network (LAN) and connect the second card with the crossover cable.

3. Repeat this network configuration on the second computer so that both computers are connected directly to one another with the crossover cable. Be sure to connect both computers with the crossover cable using the same NIC in each computer. For example, if you place the network cards in slots 3 and 4, verify that the crossover cable is connecting to the NIC in slot 4 in each computer.

Installing Windows 2000 Advanced Server

You should install Windows 2000 Advanced Server on a computer with no formatted partitions. During installation, you can use the Windows 2000 Advanced Server Setup program to create a partition on your hard disk, on which you install Windows 2000 Advanced Server as a stand-alone server in a workgroup.

To create Windows 2000 Advanced Server setup disks

Complete this procedure on a computer running MS-DOS or any version of Windows with access to the Bootdisk directory on the Windows 2000 Advanced Server installation CD-ROM. If your computer is configured with a bootable CD-ROM drive, you can install Windows 2000 without using the Setup disks. To complete this procedure as outlined, bootable CD-ROM support must be disabled in the BIOS.

Important This procedure requires four formatted 1.44-MB disks. If you use disks that contain data, the data will be overwritten without warning.

---

1. Label the four blank, formatted 1.44-MB disks as follows:
   - Windows 2000 Advanced Server Setup Disk #1
   - Windows 2000 Advanced Server Setup Disk #2
   - Windows 2000 Advanced Server Setup Disk #3
   - Windows 2000 Advanced Server Setup Disk #4

2. Insert the Microsoft Windows 2000 Advanced Server CD-ROM into the CD-ROM drive.

3. If the Windows 2000 CD-ROM dialog box appears prompting you to install or upgrade to Windows 2000, click No.

4. Open a command prompt.

5. At the command prompt, change to your CD-ROM drive. For example, if your CD-ROM drive name is E, type *e:* and press Enter.

6. At the command prompt, change to the Bootdisk directory by typing *cd bootdisk* and pressing Enter.

7. If you are creating the setup boot disks from a computer running MS-DOS or a Windows 16-bit operating system, type *makeboot a:* (where A: is the name of your floppy disk drive) and press Enter. If you are creating the setup boot disks from a computer running Windows NT or Windows 2000, type *makebt32 a:* (where a: is the name of your floppy disk drive), then press Enter. Windows 2000 displays a message indicating that this program creates the four setup disks for installing Windows 2000. It also indicates that four blank, formatted, high-density floppy disks are required.

8. Press any key to continue. Windows 2000 displays a message prompting you to insert the disk that will become the Windows 2000 Setup Boot Disk.

9. Insert the blank formatted disk labeled Windows 2000 Advanced Server Setup Disk #1 into the floppy disk drive and press any key to continue. After Windows 2000 creates the disk image, it displays a message prompting you to insert the disk labeled Windows 2000 Setup Disk #2.

10. Remove Disk #1, insert the blank formatted disk labeled Windows 2000 Advanced Server Setup Disk #2 into the floppy disk drive, and press any key to continue. After Windows 2000 creates the disk image, it displays a message prompting you to insert the disk labeled Windows 2000 Setup Disk #3.

11. Remove Disk #2, insert the blank formatted disk labeled Windows 2000 Advanced Server Setup Disk #3 into the floppy disk drive, and press any key to continue. After Windows 2000 creates the disk image, it displays a message prompting you to insert the disk labeled Windows 2000 Setup Disk #4.

12. Remove Disk #3, insert the blank formatted disk labeled Windows 2000 Advanced Server Setup Disk #4 into the floppy disk drive, and press any key to continue. After Windows 2000 creates the disk image, it displays a message indicating that the imaging process is done.

13. At the command prompt, type *exit* and then press Enter.

14. Remove the disk from the floppy disk drive and the CD-ROM from the CD-ROM drive.

Running the Windows 2000 Advanced Server pre-copy and text mode Setup routine

It is assumed for this procedure that your computer has no operating system installed, the disk is not partitioned, and bootable CD-ROM support, if available, is disabled.

1. Insert the disk labeled Windows 2000 Advanced Server Setup Disk #1 into the floppy disk drive, insert the Windows 2000 Advanced Server CD-ROM into the CD-ROM drive, and restart your computer.

   After the computer starts, Windows 2000 Setup displays a brief message that your system configuration is being checked, and then the Windows 2000 Setup screen appears.

Notice that the gray bar at the bottom of the screen indicates that the computer is being inspected and that the Windows 2000 Executive is loading, which is a minimal version of the Windows 2000 kernel.

2. When prompted, insert Setup Disk #2 into the floppy disk drive and press Enter.

   Notice that Setup indicates that it is loading the HAL, fonts, local specific data, bus drivers, and other software components to support your computer's motherboard, bus, and other hardware. Setup also loads the Windows 2000 Setup program files.

3. When prompted, insert Setup Disk #3 into the floppy disk drive and press Enter.

   Notice that Setup indicates that it is loading disk drive controller drivers. After the drive controllers load, the setup program initializes drivers appropriate to support access to your disk drives. Setup might pause several times during this process.

4. When prompted, insert Setup Disk #4 into the floppy disk drive and press Enter.

   Setup loads peripheral support drivers, like the floppy disk driver and file systems, and then it initializes the Windows 2000 Executive and loads the rest of the Windows 2000 Setup program.

   If you are installing the evaluation version of Windows 2000, a Setup notification screen appears, informing you that you are about to install an evaluation version of Windows 2000.

5. Read the Setup Notification message and press Enter to continue.

   Setup displays the Welcome To Setup screen. Notice that, in addition to the initial installation of Windows 2000, you can use Windows 2000 Setup to repair or recover a damaged Windows 2000 installation.

6. Read the Welcome To Setup message and press Enter to begin the installation phase of Windows 2000 Setup. Setup displays the License Agreement screen.

7. Read the license agreement, pressing Page Down to scroll down to the bottom of the screen.

8. Select I Accept the Agreement by pressing F8.

   Setup displays the Windows 2000 Server Setup screen, prompting you to select an area of free space or an existing partition on which to install Windows 2000. This stage of setup provides a way for you to create and delete partitions on your hard disk.

If your computer does not contain any disk partitions (as required for this exercise), you will notice that the hard disk listed on the screen contains an existing unformatted partition.

9. Make sure that the Unpartitioned space partition is highlighted and then type **c**.

   Setup displays the Windows 2000 Setup screen, confirming that you've chosen to create a new partition in the unpartitioned space and informing you of the minimum and maximum sizes of the partition you might create.

10. Specify the size of the partition you want to create (at least 2048 MB) and press Enter to continue.

    Setup displays the Windows 2000 Setup screen, showing the new partition as C: New (Unformatted).

Note Although you can create additional partitions from the remaining unpartitioned space during setup, it is recommended that you perform additional partitioning tasks after you install Windows 2000. To partition hard disks after installation, use the Disk Management console.

---

11. Make sure the new partition is highlighted and press Enter.

    You are prompted to select a file system for the partition.

12. Use the arrow keys to select Format The Partition Using The NTFS File System and press Enter.

    The Setup program formats the partition with NTFS. After it formats the partition, Setup examines the hard disk for physical errors that might cause Setup to fail and then copies files to the hard disk. This process will take several minutes.

    Eventually, Setup displays the Windows 2000 Advanced Server Setup screen. A red status bar counts down for 15 seconds before Setup restarts the computer.

13. Remove the Setup disk from the floppy disk drive.

Important If your computer supports booting from the CD-ROM drive and this feature was not disabled in the BIOS, the computer could boot from the Windows 2000 Advanced Server installation CD-ROM after Windows 2000 Setup restarts. This will cause Setup to start again from the beginning. If this happens, remove the CD-ROM and then restart the computer.

Setup copies additional files and then restarts your machine and loads the Windows 2000 Setup Wizard.

Running the GUI mode and gathering information phase of Windows 2000 Advanced Server Setup

This procedure begins the graphical portion of Setup on your computer.

1. On the Welcome To The Windows 2000 Setup Wizard page, click Next to begin gathering information about your computer.

   Setup configures NTFS folder and file permissions for the operating system files, detects the hardware devices in the computer, and then installs and configures device drivers to support the detected hardware. This process takes several minutes.

2. On the Regional Settings page, make sure that the system locale, user locale, and keyboard layout are correct for your language and location, then click Next.

   Note You can modify regional settings after you install Windows 2000 by using Regional Options in Control Panel.

   Setup displays the Personalize Your Software page, prompting you for your name and organization name. Setup uses your organization name to generate the default computer name. Many applications that you install later will use this information for product registration and document identification.

3. In the Name field, type your name; in the Organization field, type the name of an organization; then click Next.

   Note If the Your Product Key screen appears, enter the product key, located on the sticker attached to the Windows 2000 Advanced Server, Evaluation Edition, CD sleeve bound into the back of this book.

   Setup displays the Licensing Modes page, prompting you to select a licensing mode. By default, the Per Server licensing mode is selected. Setup prompts you to enter the number of licenses you have purchased for this server.

4. Select the Per Server Number of concurrent connections button, type 5 for the number of concurrent connections, then click Next.

   Important Per Server Number of concurrent connections and 5 concurrent connections are suggested values to be used to complete your self-study. You should use a legal number of concurrent connections based on the actual licenses that you own. You can also choose to use Per Seat instead of Per Server.

   Setup displays the Computer Name And Administrator Password page.

Notice that Setup uses your organization name to generate a suggested name for the computer.

5. In the Computer Name field, type *NodeA*.

Windows 2000 displays the computer name in all capital letters regardless of how it is typed.

Warning If your computer is on a network, check with the network administrator before assigning a name to your computer.

---

6. In the Administrator Password field and the Confirm Password field, type *password* (all lowercase) and click Next. Passwords are case-sensitive, so make sure you type *password* in all lowercase letters.

For the labs in this self-paced training kit, you will use "password" for the Administrator account password. In a production environment, you should always use a complex password for the Administrator account (one that others cannot easily guess). Microsoft recommends mixing uppercase and lowercase letters, numbers, and symbols (for example, Lp6*g9).

Setup displays the Windows 2000 Components page, indicating which Windows 2000 system components Setup will install.

7. On the Windows 2000 Components page, click Next.

You can install additional components after you install Windows 2000 by using Add/Remove Programs in Control Panel. Make sure to install only the components selected by default during setup. Later in your training, you will be installing additional components.

If a modem is detected in the computer during setup, Setup displays the Modem Dialing Information page.

8. If the Modem Dialing Information page appears, enter an area code or city code and click Next.

The Date And Time Settings page appears.

Important Windows 2000 services perform many tasks whose successful completion depends on the computer's time and date settings. Be sure to select the correct time zone for your location to avoid problems in later labs.

---

9. Enter the correct Date and Time and Time Zone settings, then click Next.

The Network Settings page appears and Setup installs networking components.

Completing the installing Windows networking components phase of Windows 2000 Advanced Server Setup

Networking is an integral part of Windows 2000 Advanced Server. There are many selections and configurations available. In this procedure, basic networking is configured. In a later exercise, you will install additional network components.

1. On the Networking Settings page, make sure that Typical Settings is selected, then click Next to begin installing Windows networking components.

   This setting installs networking components that are used to gain access to and share resources on a network and configures Transmission Control Protocol/Internet Protocol (TCP/IP) to automatically obtain an IP address from a DHCP server on the network.

   Setup displays the Workgroup or Computer Domain page, prompting you to join either a workgroup or a domain.

2. On the Workgroup Or Computer Domain page, make sure that the button No, This Computer Is Not On A Network Or Is On A Network Without A Domain is selected, and that the workgroup name is WORKGROUP, then click Next.

   Setup displays the Installing Components page, displaying the status as Setup installs and configures the remaining operating system components according to the options you specified. This will take several minutes.

   Setup then displays the Performing Final Tasks page, which shows the status as Setup finishes copying files, making and saving configuration changes, and deleting temporary files. Computers that do not exceed the minimum hardware requirements might take 30 minutes or more to complete this phase of installation.

   Setup then displays the Completing The Windows 2000 Setup Wizard page.

3. Remove the Windows 2000 Advanced Server CD-ROM from the CD-ROM drive, then click Finish.

   Windows 2000 restarts and runs the newly installed version of Windows 2000 Advanced Server.

Completing the hardware installation phase of Windows 2000 Advanced Server Setup

During this final phase of installation, any Plug and Play hardware not detected in the previous phases of Setup will be detected.

1. At the completion of the startup phase, log on by pressing Ctrl+Alt+Delete.

2. In the Enter Password dialog box, type *administrator* in the User Name field and type *password* in the Password field.

3. Click OK.

If Windows 2000 detects hardware that was not detected during Setup, the Found New Hardware Wizard screen displays, indicating that Windows 2000 is installing the appropriate drivers.

4. If the Found New Hardware Wizard screen appears, verify that the Restart The Computer When I Click Finish check box is cleared and click Finish to complete the Found New Hardware Wizard.

   Windows 2000 displays the Microsoft Windows 2000 Configure Your Server dialog box. From this dialog box, you can configure a variety of advanced options and services.

5. Select I Will Configure This Server Later, then click Next.

6. From the next screen that appears, clear the Show This Screen At Startup check box.

7. Close the Configure Your Server screen.

   You have now completed the Windows 2000 Advanced Server installation and are logged on as Administrator. Perform the same installation process on the second computer in your cluster. Name it NodeB.

Note To properly shutdown Windows 2000 Advanced Server, click Start, choose Shut Down, and then follow the directions that appear.

Caution If your computers are part of a larger network, you *must* verify with your network administrator that the computer names, domain name, and other information used in setting up Windows 2000 Advanced Server as described in this section do not conflict with network operations. If they do conflict, ask your network administrator to provide alternative values and use those values throughout all of the exercise in this book.

Creating a domain and connecting the external drive

1. Using dcpromo, create a new domain and add each computer to the domain as a domain controller.

2. Connect the shared external hard drive to each computer. In the case of a SCSI drive, be sure to terminate the SCSI bus based on the SCSI card manufacturer's instructions.

3. Instructions will be provided in Chapters 2 and 3 on how to configure the NICs and the shared external hard drive for use with Microsoft Cluster Service.

The Exercise Files

The Supplemental Course Materials CD-ROM contains a set of exercise files that you will need to install on your hard disk drive to complete many of the exercises in this book. Specific instructions are provided with each exercise.

The Media Files

The Supplemental Course Materials CD-ROM contains audiovisual demonstration files that you can view by running the files from the CD-ROM. You will find a prompt within the book indicating when each demonstration should be run. You must have installed Windows Media Player 7 and an Internet browser on your computer to view these files. (Microsoft Internet Explorer and Windows Media Player are included on the companion CD for this purpose. To install either of these software products, see the installation instructions in the Readme.txt files on the CD.)

To view the demonstration

1. Insert the Supplemental Course Materials CD-ROM into your CD-ROM drive.
2. Select Run from the Start menu on your desktop and type *D:\Media\demonstration_filename* (where *D* is the name of your CD-ROM drive).

About The Online Book

The CD also includes an online version of the book that you can view on-screen using Microsoft Internet Explorer 4.01 or later.

To use the online version of this book

1. Insert the Supplemental Course Materials CD-ROM into your CD-ROM drive.
2. Select Run from the Start menu on your desktop, and type *D:\Ebook\Setup.exe* (where *D* is the name of your CD-ROM disk drive). This will install an icon to for the online book to your Start menu.
3. Click OK to exit the Installation Wizard.

Note You must have the Supplemental Course Materials CD-ROM inserted in your CD-ROM drive to run the online book.

The Microsoft Certified Professional Program

The Microsoft Certified Professional (MCP) program provides the best method to prove your command of current Microsoft products and technologies. Microsoft, an industry leader in certification, is on the forefront of testing methodology. The exams and corresponding certifications are developed to validate your mastery of critical competencies as you design and develop, or implement and support, solutions with Microsoft products and technologies. Computer professionals who become Microsoft certified are recognized as experts and are sought after industry-wide.

The Microsoft Certified Professional program offers eight certifications, based on specific areas of technical expertise:

- *Microsoft Certified Professional (MCP).*   Demonstrated in-depth knowledge of at least one Microsoft operating system. Candidates may pass additional Microsoft certification exams to further qualify their skills with Microsoft BackOffice products, development tools, or desktop programs.

- *Microsoft Certified Systems Engineer (MCSE).*   Qualified to effectively plan, implement, maintain, and support information systems in a wide range of computing environments with Microsoft Windows NT Server and the Microsoft BackOffice integrated family of server software.

- *Microsoft Certified Database Administrator (MCDBA)*   Individuals who design physical databases, develop logical data models, create physical databases, create data services by using Transact-SQL, manage and maintain databases, configure and manage security, monitor and optimize databases, and install and configure Microsoft SQL Server.

- *Microsoft Certified Solution Developer (MCSD).*   Qualified to design and develop custom business solutions with Microsoft development tools, technologies, and platforms, including Microsoft Office and Microsoft BackOffice.

- *Microsoft Certified Trainer (MCT).*   Instructionally and technically qualified to deliver Microsoft Official Curriculum through a Microsoft Certified Technical Education Center (CTEC).

Microsoft Certification Benefits

Microsoft certification, one of the most comprehensive certification programs available for assessing and maintaining software-related skills, is a valuable measure of an individual's knowledge and expertise. Microsoft certification is awarded to individuals who have successfully demonstrated their ability to perform specific tasks and implement solutions with Microsoft products. Not only does this provide an objective measure for employers to consider; it also provides guidance for what an individual should know to be proficient. And as with any skills-assessment and benchmarking measure, certification brings a variety of benefits to the individual and to employers and organizations.

Microsoft Certification Benefits for Individuals

As a Microsoft Certified Professional, you receive many benefits:

- Industry recognition of your knowledge and proficiency with Microsoft products and technologies.

- Access to technical and product information directly from Microsoft through a secured area of the MCP Web site.

- MSDN Online Certified Membership that helps you tap into the best technical resources, connect to the MCP community, and gain access to valuable resources and services. (Some MSDN Online benefits may be available in English only or may not be available in all countries.) See the MSDN Web site for a growing list of certified member benefits.

- Logos to enable you to identify your Microsoft Certified Professional status to colleagues or clients.

- Invitations to Microsoft conferences, technical training sessions, and special events.

- A Microsoft Certified Professional certificate.

- Subscription to Microsoft Certified Professional Magazine (North America only), a career and professional development magazine.

Additional benefits, depending on your certification and geography, include

- A complimentary one-year subscription to Microsoft TechNet Technical Plus, providing valuable information on monthly CD-ROMs.

- A one-year subscription to the Microsoft Beta Evaluation program. This benefit provides you with up to 12 free monthly CD-ROMs containing beta software (English only) for many of Microsoft's newest software products.

Microsoft Certification Benefits for Employers and Organizations

Through certification, computer professionals can maximize the return on investment in Microsoft technology. Research shows that Microsoft certification provides organizations with the following benefits:

- Excellent return on training and certification investments by providing a standard method of determining training needs and measuring results.

- Increased customer satisfaction and decreased support costs through improved service, increased productivity and greater technical self-sufficiency.

- Reliable benchmark for hiring, promoting, and career planning.

- Recognition and rewards for productive employees by validating their expertise.

- Retraining options for existing employees so they can work effectively with new technologies.

- Assurance of quality when outsourcing computer services.

To learn more about how certification can help your company, see the backgrounders, white papers and case studies available on *www.microsoft.com/mcp/ mktg/bus_bene.htm*

- Financial Benefits to Supporters of Microsoft Professional Certification, IDC white paper (1998wpidc.doc 1,608K)

- Prudential Case Study (prudentl.exe 70K self-extracting file)
- The Microsoft Certified Professional Program Corporate Backgrounder (mcpback.exe 50K)
- A white paper (mcsdwp.doc 158K) that evaluates the Microsoft Certified Solution Developer certification.
- A white paper (mcsestud.doc 161K) that evaluates the Microsoft Certified Systems Engineer certification.
- Jackson Hole High School Case Study (jhhs.doc 180K)
- Lyondel Case Study (lyondel.doc 21K)
- Stellcom Case Study (stellcom.doc 132K)

Requirements for Becoming a Microsoft Certified Professional

The certification requirements differ for each certification and are specific to the products and job functions addressed by the certification.

To become a Microsoft Certified Professional, you must pass rigorous certification exams that provide a valid and reliable measure of technical proficiency and expertise. These exams are designed to test your expertise and ability to perform a role or task with a product, and are developed with the input of professionals in the industry. Questions in the exams reflect how Microsoft products are used in actual organizations, giving them "real-world" relevance.

Microsoft Certified Product Specialists are required to pass one operating system exam. Candidates may pass additional Microsoft certification exams to further qualify their skills with Microsoft BackOffice products, development tools, or desktop applications.

Microsoft Certified Systems Engineers are required to pass a series of core Microsoft Windows operating system and networking exams, and BackOffice technology elective exams.

Microsoft Certified Database Administrators are required to pass three core exams and one elective exam that provide a valid and reliable measure of technical proficiency and expertise.

Microsoft Certified Solution Developers are required to pass two core Microsoft Windows operating system technology exams and two BackOffice technology elective exams.

Microsoft Certified Trainers are required to meet instructional and technical requirements specific to each Microsoft Official Curriculum course they are certified to deliver. In the United States and Canada, call Microsoft at (800) 636-7544 for more information on becoming a Microsoft Certified Trainer or visit *www.microsoft.com/train_cert/mct/*. Outside the United States and Canada, contact your local Microsoft subsidiary.

Technical Training for Computer Professionals

Technical training is available in a variety of forms, with instructor-led classes, online instruction, or self-paced training available at thousands of locations worldwide.

Self-paced Training

For motivated learners who are ready for the challenge, self-paced instruction is the most flexible, cost-effective way to increase your knowledge and skills.

A full line of self-paced print and computer-based training materials is available direct from the source—Microsoft Press. Microsoft Official Curriculum courseware kits from Microsoft Press, designed for advanced computer system professionals, are available from Microsoft Press and the Microsoft Developer Division. Self-paced training kits from Microsoft Press feature print-based instructional materials, along with CD-ROM–based product software, multimedia presentations, lab exercises, and practice files. The Mastering Series provides in-depth, interactive training on CD-ROM for experienced developers. Both of these kits are great ways to prepare for Microsoft Certified Professional (MCP) and Microsoft Certified Systems Engineer (MCSE) exams.

Online Training

For a more flexible alternative to instructor-led classes, turn to online instruction. It's as near as the Internet and it's ready whenever you are. Learn at your own pace and on your own schedule in a virtual classroom, often with easy access to an online instructor. Without ever leaving your desk, you can gain the expertise you need. Online instruction covers a variety of Microsoft products and technologies. It includes options ranging from Microsoft Official Curriculum to choices available nowhere else. It's training on demand, with access to learning resources 24 hours a day. Online training is available through Microsoft Certified Technical Education Centers.

Microsoft Certified Technical Education Centers

Microsoft Certified Technical Education Centers (CTECs) are the best source for instructor-led training to help you prepare to become a Microsoft Certified Professional or a Microsoft Certified Systems Engineer. The Microsoft CTEC program is a worldwide network of qualified technical training organizations that provide authorized delivery of Microsoft Official Curriculum courses by Microsoft Certified Trainers to computer professionals.

For a listing of CTEC locations in the United States and Canada, visit *www.microsoft.com/CTEC/default.htm.*

Technical Support

Every effort has been made to ensure the accuracy of this book and the contents of the companion CD. If you have comments, questions, or ideas regarding this book or the companion CD, please send them to Microsoft Press using either of the following methods:

E-mail:

tkinput@microsoft.com

Postal Mail:

Microsoft Press
Attn: *MCSE Training Kit: Microsoft Windows 2000 Advanced Server Clustering Services* Editor
One Microsoft Way
Redmond, WA 98052-6399

Microsoft Press provides corrections for books through the World Wide Web at the following address:

//mspress.microsoft.com/support/

Please note that product support is not offered through the above mail addresses. For further information regarding Microsoft software support options, please connect to *www.microsoft.com/support/* or call Microsoft Support Network Sales at (800) 936-3500.

Evaluation Edition Software Support

The Evaluation Edition of Microsoft SQL Server 7 included with this book is not supported by either Microsoft or Microsoft Press, and should not be used on a primary work computer. For online support information relating to the full version of Microsoft SQL Server 7 that might also apply to the Evaluation Edition, you can connect to

//support.microsoft.com/

For information about ordering the full version of any Microsoft software, please call Microsoft Sales at (800) 426-9400 or visit *www.microsoft.com*. Information about any issues relating to the use of the Evaluation Edition with this training kit is posted to the Support section of the Microsoft Press Web site (*www.mspress.microsoft.com/support/*).

C H A P T E R   1

Introduction to Microsoft Clustering Technologies

About This Chapter

This chapter introduces the two Microsoft clustering technologies supported by Microsoft Windows 2000: Microsoft Cluster Service and the Network Load Balancing (NLB) service. You'll learn how to use Cluster Service to provide greater availability for applications and services and how to use NLB to complement Cluster Service. In addition, you'll learn about the operating system and hardware requirements for using Cluster Service.

Before You Begin

To complete this chapter, you must have

- Completed the lessons in the Microsoft Press, *MCSE Training Kit: Microsoft Windows 2000 Server* or have equivalent knowledge
- Completed the lessons in the Microsoft Press, *MCSE Training Kit: Microsoft Windows 2000 Network Infrastructure Administration* or have equivalent knowledge

Lesson 1: Overview of Windows Clustering Technologies

To provide administrators with advanced capabilities for managing enterprise and commercial network servers, Microsoft has integrated clustering technologies into the Windows 2000 operating system. This lesson will introduce you to Cluster Service and NLB. Although both technologies provide solutions for increased server availability and efficiency, they are complementary technologies. This lesson explains when you might implement one service over the other and when you might consider implementing both.

Before you implement a clustering technology, you must decide on an appropriate operating system. Not all of the Windows 2000 operating systems support the clustering technologies. This lesson describes some of the key differences among the Windows 2000 family of servers in regard to clustering support.

After this lesson, you will be able to

- List the two Windows clustering technologies
- Describe when to use Cluster Service and when to use NLB
- List which Windows 2000 operating systems support Cluster Service
- Describe how Windows 2000 Advanced Server and Windows 2000 Datacenter Server differ in regard to clustering support

Estimated lesson time: 30 minutes

Cluster Service and NLB

In Windows NT Server Enterprise Edition, Microsoft introduced a technology that allowed organizations to increase the availability of servers that hosted mission-critical applications by grouping servers. If one server failed, another one would assume its responsibilities. This technology was called Microsoft Clustering Server, or MSCS. MSCS was designed to group multiple physical servers that had access to a shared drive array, so that they could act as a single network server. Clients would access the applications using a single computer name as if the cluster were a normal server. The MSCS service would monitor the health of each server, or node, within the cluster. If one were to fail, MSCS would move the responsibility for hosting an application to another node. Since network clients would be using a server name managed by MSCS, they would not have to be reconfigured each time an application was moved from a one node to another.

In Windows 2000, MSCS has been updated and renamed Microsoft Cluster Service. Cluster Service provides added benefits and is easier to install.

Microsoft Windows NT Enterprise Edition also came with Windows Load Balancing (WLB) technology, which allowed administrators to group many servers so that each could respond to client requests. For example, a large commercial Web site that handles millions of client requests is actually a group of servers responding to these requests. WLB was designed to provide this functionality across many servers. In Windows 2000, WLB has been updated and renamed Network Load Balancing.

When to Implement a Cluster

Clustering can be beneficial in a number of scenarios. You should consider a cluster when your network services require a high degree of availability, such as when you have an e-commerce site that processes live transactions based on customer orders. Here are some of the possible reasons to implement a cluster:

- To reduce downtime due to routine maintenance or unplanned failures
- To perform upgrades to nodes, resources, and applications without interrupting client access
- To perform rolling upgrades (operating system upgrades that do not interrupt client access)
- To increase server availability for mission-critical applications and network services
- To take advantage of cluster-aware applications such as Microsoft Exchange Server or Microsoft SQL Server

The following table lists some specific scenarios and the clustering technology you can use in each.

Cluster Scenarios

Scenario	Cluster Service	NLB
Web server farm	No	Yes
File/print server	Yes	No
Database/messaging application	Yes	No
E-commerce site	Yes	Yes

You should consider using NLB for a Web server farm because it allows for rapid expansion. File and print servers and database or messaging applications should use Cluster Service because these require a high level of availability. Many e-commerce sites can benefit from both clustering technologies because they require a high level of availability, performance, and expandability.

Choosing an Operating System

Not all Windows 2000 operating systems support clustering. In order to support clustering, the operating system must be able to

- Create and delete network names and addresses dynamically
- Modify the file system to close open files during a drive dismount
- Modify the I/O subsystem to share disks and volume sets among multiple servers, or nodes, in the cluster

Currently, only Windows 2000 Advanced Server and Windows 2000 Datacenter Server provide all three of these capabilities. Windows 2000 Server, which supports up to four microprocessors and 4 GB of physical memory, is intended as a general-purpose server operating system, so it does not support advanced features such as Cluster Service or NLB.

Windows 2000 Advanced Server

Windows 2000 Advanced Server provides greater scalability and availability than Windows 2000 Server. It supports up to 8 GB of physical memory and can scale up to eight processors. Support for Cluster Service and NLB is integrated into the operating system and allows you to connect two servers to form a cluster.

Windows 2000 Datacenter Server

Windows 2000 Datacenter Server is the most powerful server operating system that Microsoft offers. It supports up to 32 processors and 64 GB of physical memory, and includes Cluster Service and NLB as standard features. Windows 2000 Datacenter Server supports clusters of up to four servers. It is thus designed to support large-scale enterprise environments such as

- E-commerce and online transaction processing (OLTP)
- Leading Internet service providers (ISPs) and Web hosting
- Large data warehouses and data centers
- Science and engineering simulations

Lesson Summary

Originally introduced as Microsoft Clustering Server and Windows Load Balancing in the Windows NT operating system, the two clustering technologies supported by the Windows 2000 family of servers are known in their updated form as Microsoft Cluster Service and Network Load Balancing.

Cluster Service increases the availability of servers hosting mission-critical applications. NLB is appropriate when multiple servers must manage a high number of network requests, such as when a large commercial Web site is hosted by many physical Web servers. Ultimately, your organization's requirements for clustering or load balancing will determine which Windows 2000 operating system you deploy. If you do not need to implement either clustering technology, Windows 2000 Server might suffice. If you need only two-node cluster support or basic NLB, you should deploy Windows 2000 Advanced Server. Organizations requiring two-node to four-node clustering, NLB, and maximum scalability should deploy Windows 2000 Datacenter Server.

Lesson 2: Overview of Microsoft Cluster Service

Although Windows 2000 Advanced Server and Windows 2000 Datacenter Server support both Cluster Service and NLB, the remainder of this chapter will focus on Cluster Service. For more information about NLB, see Chapter 10, "Introduction to Network Load Balancing" and Chapter 11, "Implementing Network Load Balancing." This lesson describes Cluster Service and the benefits of using a cluster.

After this lesson, you will be able to

- List the benefits of implementing Cluster Service
- Define the primary clustering terminology

Estimated lesson time: 45 minutes

What Is a Cluster?

A *cluster* is a group of two or more individual servers, called *nodes*, that work together and represent themselves to the network as a single server. This includes providing access to resources such as file shares, printers, and other network services. The servers in a cluster are both physically and programmatically connected, so they can coordinate communication in response to client requests. Each server in a cluster is able to provide redundant operations in the event of a hardware or application failure. As a result, the cluster provides a high degree of availability for applications and resources.

In addition, a cluster might also be used to implement static load balancing to share the workload among the individual servers in the cluster. If you need dynamic load balancing, you should consider using NLB.

Benefits of Using Cluster Service

Implementing Cluster Service provides a number of benefits. These include the following:

Increased Scalability

- Servers can be expanded to provide additional memory and processing resources without interrupting network services.

- Cluster Service allows integration of new server resources (both hardware and operating system software) with existing legacy resources. For example, using Cluster Service, you can combine Windows 2000 Advanced Server computers and Windows NT 4 Server computers in the same cluster.

High Availability

- Cluster Service can detect a hardware or software failure and quickly assign the application or service responsibility to another node in the cluster. This process is called *failover*.

- Cluster Service allows nodes that come back online after a failure to automatically resume their original responsibilities. This process is called *failback*.

- Cluster Service allows access to network resources and services during planned downtime. For example, if you need to upgrade a node in the cluster, you can manually move the network services that the node is providing to another node. Client requests will not be interrupted while the original node is offline.

- Cluster Service reduces single points of failure on your network. While Cluster Service alone cannot guarantee server uptime, it does provide a higher level of availability.

- Applications can be distributed over more than one server, which results in a faster response time.

Improved Manageability

- Cluster Service allows you to manage the devices and resources in a cluster as if they were all on a single server.

- Cluster Service provides a single point of control for administrators. Administration can also be accomplished remotely.

- Cluster Service allows applications and services, called *resources*, to be taken offline for upgrades or maintenance.

Clustering Terminology

The terminology used in Microsoft clusters includes the following:

- **Active/Active**   A type of cluster implementation in which each node is capable of managing the resource groups specified in the cluster. When one node fails, the other takes control of the resources. Each node is capable of dynamically assuming another's role.

- **Active/Passive**   A type of cluster implementation in which specific resource groups are assigned to a specified node as the resource's primary node. If the primary node fails, the resource will fail over. When the failed node returns online, it resumes control of the resource.

- **Cluster**   A group of individual servers working together as a single server.

- **Common resource**   A resource that is accessible by each node of cluster. These include the shared drive array and the private cluster network.

- **Dependencies**   A reliance between two resources that requires both to run within the same resource group.

- **Domainlet**   A substitute for a traditional domain with limited features. Because the nodes in a cluster must belong to the same domain, you can optionally configure the servers to be domain controllers. As a result, the amount of overhead on each server will increase. To minimize this, you can implement a domainlet, which provides limited capabilities regarding groups, policies, and authentication. Only the minimum requirements for service account authentication are included. This makes the use of domainlets for the cluster nodes preferable over a traditional domain.

- **Failback**   The process of returning control of a resource or group to the node where it was running before the failure occurred.

- **Failover**   The process of moving control of a resource or group from one node to another in the event of a failure.

- **Group, resource group**   A collection of resources used for the purpose of configuration and management. The terms *group* and *resource group* are used interchangeably; they are also sometimes referred to as *failover groups*. A group typically includes all of the resources required to support a given application, such as a disk drive, an IP address, a network name, appropriate application services, and so on. If resources are dependent, they must exist in the same group. All resources in a group must be online and on the same node in a cluster. A group is managed as a single logical unit.

- **IsAlive check**   Resource Monitors use the IsAlive check to do an exhaustive verification of the state of a resource. If the IsAlive check fails, the resource is moved offline and the failover process begins. You can specify the IsAlive polling interval to control how quickly Cluster Service is made aware of a failed resource.

- **LooksAlive check**   A simple check performed by the Resource Monitor to verify that the resource is running properly. If the LooksAlive check fails or cannot determine the state of the resource, the more thorough IsAlive check is used. You can specify the LooksAlive polling interval to control how quickly the Cluster Service is made aware of a failed resource.

- **Node**   A server in a cluster.

- **Offline**   In reference to a resource: unavailable and unable to provide service to the cluster.

- **Online**   In reference to a resource: available and providing service to the cluster.

- **Quorum resource**   A common resource that is located on a physical disk of the cluster's shared drive array. It stores a synchronized version of the cluster database. This database contains cluster management data. As a result, the quorum resource must be present in order for node operations to occur. The quorum resource also includes recovery logs that contain the transactions or changes that have been made against the cluster database.

- **Resources**   Physical or logical entities managed by Cluster Service, such as file shares, shared printers, and applications. Resources are the basic units managed by Cluster Service and can run on only a single node in the cluster at a time. Resources include both hardware and software components in the cluster. Resources can be brought online or offline and are controlled by only one node at a time.

- **Virtual server**   A mechanism by which applications and resources in a cluster can be exposed to clients. A cluster can support more than one virtual server based on how you group the resources and applications in the cluster. (See Figure 1.1.) This allows clients to access the resource regardless of which node is controlling the resource, through the same IP address or NetBIOS name. Each virtual server in a cluster has its own unique IP address and NetBIOS name.

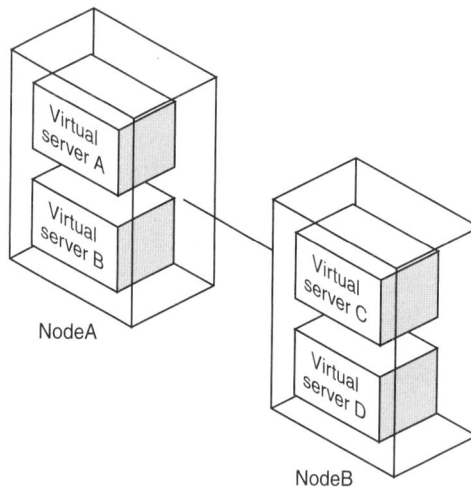

Figure 1.1   Virtual server

Lesson Summary

Cluster Service allows multiple individual servers to share resources and represent themselves to the network as a single server. As a result, a cluster provides hardware redundancy and high availability for network services such as file shares and mission-critical applications. The benefits of implementing a cluster include increased availability, improved scalability, and greater manageability.

Lesson 3: Cluster Service Architecture

This lesson describes the components in the Cluster Service architecture and how they interact.

After this lesson, you will be able to

- List and describe the components of the Cluster Service architecture
- Describe the differences between cluster-aware and cluster-unaware applications
- Describe how nodes in a cluster communicate

Estimated lesson time: 45 minutes

Cluster Service Components

In order to implement a cluster, you must have Cluster Service installed on each node. Each component of Cluster Service has specific responsibilities in maintaining the operation of the cluster, as described below. Figure 1.2 shows the components.

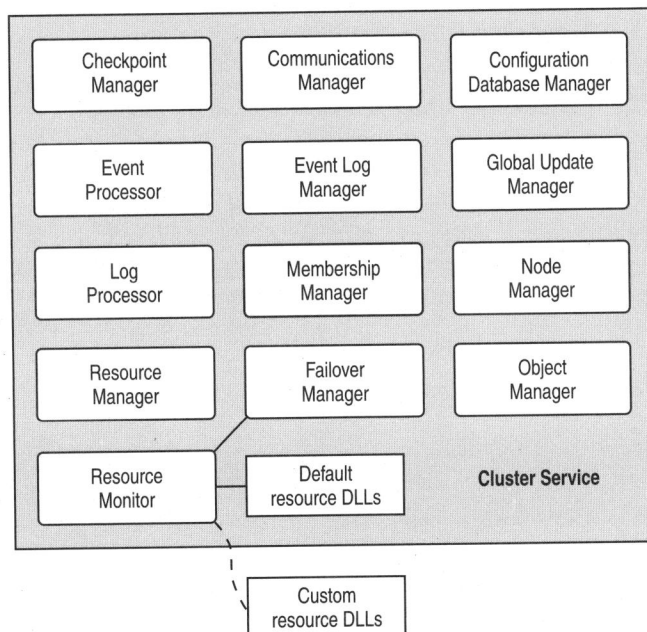

Figure 1.2   Cluster Service components

Checkpoint Manager

The Checkpoint Manager ensures that Cluster Service can successfully failover cluster-unaware applications by performing Registry checkpointing. The Checkpoint Manager monitors a resource's Registry data and saves any changes, called checkpoint data, to the quorum recovery log. The Checkpoint Manager also writes a checkpoint to the quorum disk when the resource is taken offline. When a node takes ownership of a new resource, the Checkpoint Manager updates the resource's Registry data before bringing the resource online.

Communications Manager

The Communications Manager (also known as the Cluster Network Driver) manages the communication between the nodes in the cluster. It maintains continual communication with the other nodes by using Remote Procedure Calls (RPCs). If a node fails, the Communications Manager notifies the other nodes in the cluster as part of the failover process.

In addition, the Communications Manager delivers cluster heartbeat messages (data packets sent between nodes to verify the health of the cluster), responds to cluster connection requests, and notifies the entire cluster when resources are brought online or taken offline.

Configuration Database Manager

The Configuration Database Manager, or Database Manager, manages and maintains information about the cluster configuration in the configuration database. The configuration database, which is stored in the Registry of each node in the cluster, contains information about all of the entities of the cluster, including the cluster itself, resources, and groups. The Database Managers on each node cooperate to ensure that updates to the database are consistent and accurate.

The quorum resource stores the most current version of the configuration database in the form of recovery logs and Registry checkpoint files. This allows nodes that join a cluster to receive the latest version of the configuration database for their local Registry.

Event Processor

The Event Processor initializes Cluster Service and passes messages to and from the nodes of the cluster. These messages, called *event signals*, are associated with activities, such as status changes and requests to open or close applications. Event signals include important information that must be disseminated to the other cluster components. In addition, the Event Processor supports the cluster API eventing mechanism, enabling developers to write cluster-aware applications that can send and receive cluster events.

Event Log Manager

The Event Log Manager ensures that each node of the cluster has the same event log entries. To accomplish this, it replicates the event log of one node to all other nodes in the cluster.

Failover Manager

The Failover Manager decides which node in a cluster takes control of a resource in the event of a failover. If the cluster consists of more than two nodes, the Failover Managers of each online node will negotiate control of the resources from the failed node.

If the nodes in a cluster cannot communicate with each other but are otherwise functioning properly, the Failover Manager will still initiate the failover process. Each node will assume that the other has failed and will attempt to communicate with the quorum resource. The quorum resource guarantees that only one node has a resource online at a time. The node that is in communication with the quorum resource will bring the other node's resources online. As a result, the node that cannot communicate with the quorum resource will take its resources offline.

Global Update Manager

The Global Update Manager provides an interface for other components in Cluster Service to initiate and mange updates. It also provides a single method for performing these functions. It allows changes in state to be propagated to other nodes in the cluster. All state changes are sent to active nodes in the cluster. The Global Update Manager provides an *atomic* (all or none) update service to cluster members. It also provides a global update service to cluster components.

Log Manager

The Log Manager writes changes to recovery logs stored on the quorum resource. The recovery logs—also known as quorum logs—contain the transactions that have been made against the quorum.

Membership Manager

The Membership Manager tracks and manages cluster membership. When a node fails, the Membership Manager triggers a regroup event, causing all remaining nodes to update their membership lists. When a failed node comes back online, the membership lists get updated, reflecting the availability of the node. Also, depending on your configuration, control of the resources originally managed on this node may be returned to the node.

Node Manager

The Node Manager assigns resource group control to nodes based on group preference lists and node availability. All node managers communicate to detect failure in the cluster using heartbeat messages that are delivered by the Communications Manager.

The Node Manager works closely with the Membership Manager. When a node fails, the Node Manager tells the Membership Manager to trigger a regroup event. This causes each node in the cluster to update its view of the current cluster membership. When a failed node comes back online, a regroup event is triggered to refresh the membership list.

Object Manager

The Object Manager maintains an in-memory database of all cluster objects, such as nodes, groups, and resources. It uses this database to manage Cluster Service objects by creating, searching, enumerating, and maintaining reference count objects of different types.

Resource Manager

The Resource Manager is responsible for all dependencies and resources. It oversees and initiates appropriate actions such as starting and stopping resources. It is also responsible for initiating resource group failover, and it receives resources and cluster state information from the resource monitor and node managers.

Resource Monitors

A Resource Monitor provides a communication mechanism between Cluster Service and a resource DLL. By default, a single Resource Monitor is enabled per node. However, you can optionally enable additional Resource Monitors. Resource Monitors each run in their own process and communicate with Cluster Service through RPCs. In addition, Resource Monitors enable resources to run separately from other Cluster Service resources. This design protects Cluster Service from individual failures among the cluster resources.

Resource Monitors verify that each resource of the cluster is operating properly, using callbacks to resource DLLs. They do this by monitoring the state of the resources and then notifying the cluster of any changes. The Resource Monitor uses the LooksAlive and IsAlive cluster APIs to verify the health and availability of resources.

Resource DLLs

A resource DLL provides an interface for Cluster Service to communicate with the various types of applications it supports, including cluster management applications, cluster-aware applications, and cluster-unaware applications. For example, Cluster Service uses resource DLLs to bring resources online and to monitor their health. It does this through Resource Monitors. All resource DLLs provided by

Microsoft for cluster-aware applications use a single Resource Monitor. Third-party resource DLLs are required to provide their own Resource Monitor.

- **Cluster management application**   These are applications that make calls to Cluster Service using the cluster APIs, such as Cluster Administrator.

- **Cluster-aware applications**   These are applications that run on a node in the cluster and take advantage of the features provided by Cluster Service. One important advantage they offer is the ability to fail over to other nodes in the cluster in the event of a failure. Because they can use their own application-specific resource DLLs, they are considered cluster-aware. They use the Cluster API to update and request cluster information.

  There are two types of cluster-aware applications: those that interact with the cluster (and not cluster resources) and those that are managed as cluster resources. The Cluster Administrator application is an example of a cluster-aware application that interacts with the cluster. Exchange 2000 is an example of a cluster-aware application that is managed as a cluster resource.

- **Cluster-unaware applications**   Like cluster-aware applications, cluster-unaware applications run on a node in the cluster and use a resource DLL to communicate with Cluster Service. However, this DLL is the default resource DLL that comes with Cluster Service. These applications do not use the cluster API and are not aware of the cluster. Therefore, they do not take full advantage of the features of Cluster Service. Because cluster-unaware applications communicate with Cluster Service through a resource DLL, they can potentially be moved to another node in the event of a failover.

How the Nodes Communicate

The nodes in a cluster can communicate in three ways:

- **Remote Procedure Calls**   Cluster Service uses RPCs on IP sockets with UDP packets to communicate information between the nodes that are active and online. For example, changes to a resource on one node are communicated to the other nodes by using an RPC. If a message must be sent to a node that is offline, a different communication method must be used.

- **Cluster heartbeats**   The nodes of a cluster verify that the others are online and active by periodically transmitting datagrams to each other, as shown in Figure 1.3. These datagrams, called *heartbeats*, are single UDP packets sent periodically by the nodes' Node Managers. These packets are used to confirm that a node's network interface is still active. If a node fails to respond to a heartbeat, it is considered to have failed and is marked as unavailable.

  The first server in a cluster to come online is, by default, responsible for sending heartbeats to the other nodes. However, this process begins only when another node joins the cluster. The other nodes are responsible for replying to each heartbeat transmitted by the original node.

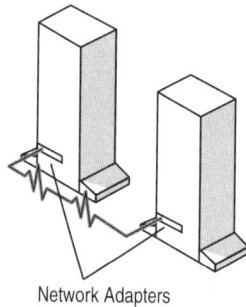

Network Adapters

Figure 1.3   Cluster node heartbeats

The first node sends heartbeats approximately every 0.5 seconds. The second node typically responds to each heartbeat within 0.2 seconds. Each heartbeat datagram is 48 bytes in size.

If a node fails to respond to a heartbeat, the original node begins a process of sending 18 heartbeats to the perceived failed node as follows:

- Four heartbeats at approximately 0.7-second intervals
- Three heartbeats within the next approximately 0.75 seconds
- Two heartbeats at approximately 0.3-second intervals
- Five heartbeats within the next approximately 0.9 seconds
- Two heartbeats at approximately 0.3-second intervals
- Two heartbeats approximately 0.3 seconds later

If the second node fails to respond to any of these heartbeats, it is marked as failed. The total time for the above process to complete is approximately 5.3 seconds.

If the first node to come online fails, the second node begins the process described above within 0.7 seconds of the last heartbeat received by the first node.

- **Quorum resource**   If a node is offline when a Cluster Service configuration change is made, the changes are stored in the quorum log on the quorum resource. These changes are then made available when the offline node is brought online. As a result, the quorum resource provides a third level of communication for nodes in a cluster.

Lesson Summary

In this lesson, you learned about each Cluster Service component and the function it performs in managing and maintaining a cluster. These components are

- Checkpoint Manager
- Communications Manager

- Configuration Database Manager
- Event Processor
- Event Log Manager
- Failover Manager
- Global Update Manager
- Log Manager
- Membership Manager
- Node Manager
- Object Manager
- Resource Manager
- Resource Monitors
- Resource DLLs

This lesson also explained the difference between cluster-aware and cluster-unaware applications and how each interacts with the cluster in the event of a failure. Finally, this lesson described the three methods of communication between the nodes in a cluster: RPCs, cluster heartbeats, and the quorum resource.

Lesson 4: Implementation Considerations

This lesson describes steps you must take before you deploy a cluster. These include

- Selecting an implementation model
- Selecting a configuration model
- Determining hardware and network requirements

After this lesson, you will be able to

- Describe what a virtual server is used for in a cluster
- List and describe the available cluster implementation models
- Select an appropriate model based on network requirements
- List the hardware requirements for a cluster
- Select appropriate hardware, including network components
- Compare and contrast the SCSI and Fibre Channel drive technologies

Estimated lesson time: 45 minutes

Virtual Servers

Each resource group in a cluster is associated with a unique IP address and a unique network name. These are considered virtual servers that clients can use to access the resources within the group. As a result, if a resource group fails over to another node in the cluster, the client access to the resource does not change. For example, if the client is accessing a virtual server using a UNC of \\MyServer\TheShare, the client will use the same UNC even if the resource has failed over to another node. This also means that the client does not know which physical node is responding to its request.

Implementation Models

The two models for implementing Cluster Service are Shared Device and Shared Nothing. These models are based on industry standards that define how the applications deployed on the cluster access the available hardware.

Shared Device

In this model, the software applications running on any node in the cluster can gain access to any hardware in the cluster. If two of the applications require the same processor, the data must be synchronized. In order to accomplish this, each application must include a component called a Distributed Lock Manager (DLM) that manages the synchronization.

DLMs keep track of references to hardware resources in the cluster and recognize and resolve conflicts. However, they introduce overhead into the system because of additional message traffic. In addition, there is a potential performance loss because multiple nodes will have access to all hardware resources in the cluster.

Shared Nothing

In this model, each node owns and manages its local disks. Common devices in the cluster are selectively owned and managed by a single node at any time. This makes it easier to manage disk devices and standard applications. In addition, the Shared Nothing model does not require special cabling and is designed to avoid overhead from DLMs. However, under this model, only one node can access a hardware resource at a time. During a failure, another node must assume ownership of the hardware resource to allow it to be accessed. When an application needs to access a resource, its request is sent to the node that currently owns the resource. This allows the creation of applications that are distributed across nodes in the cluster.

Cluster Service implements the Shared Nothing model by default. Because Cluster Service does not include a DLM, it relies on any application that needs access to shared hardware to provide its own DLM. As a result, if you deploy an application that comes with its own DLM, Cluster Service will automatically use the Shared Device model for this application.

Configuration Models

When you implement a cluster, you can select from among five configuration models, depending on your needs for the cluster. The configuration model you select will affect the overall performance of the cluster, the level of availability provided in the event of a failure, and the cost of implementing the solution.

Model A: High Availability with Static Load Balancing

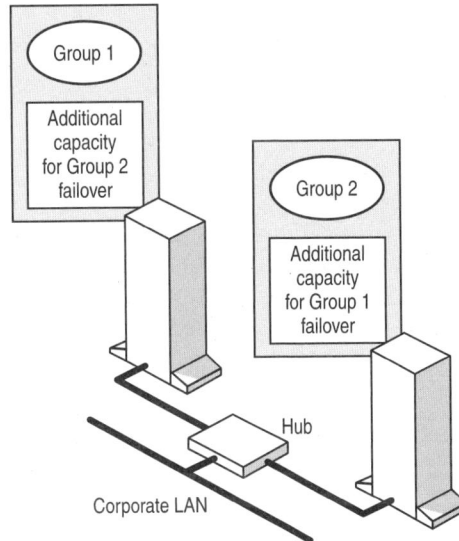

Figure 1.4   Model A

In Model A (shown in Figure 1.4), each node in the cluster is responsible for specific resources. Further, each node must have the capacity to support the other node's resources in the event of a failover. Therefore, each node is typically configured to run at 50 percent of full load. This model provides optimum performance balance because both nodes support cluster resources. However, performance can be reduced in the event of a failover because one node will support all of the cluster's resources until the failed node becomes available.

Model B: Hot Spare with Maximum Availability

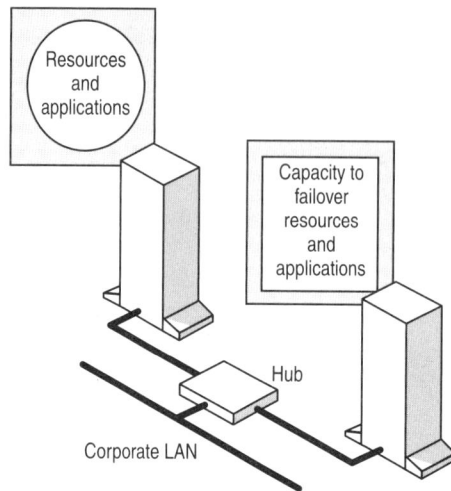

Figure 1.5 Model B

In Model B (shown in Figure 1.5), one node is completely responsible for managing the cluster's resources. The second node acts as a live backup that remains idle when both nodes are available. In the event of a failure, the idle node takes control of all the cluster's resources until the failed node becomes available. Unlike in Model A, the nodes are never fully utilized at the same time. Further, because one node remains idle during normal operations, the overall cost of this solution is higher than the other models. Performance is affected only if the nodes do not have the same hardware configurations. For example, if the "hot spare" node has less memory or CPU speed, the cluster's performance is reduced in the event of a failover.

Model C: Partial Cluster Service

In Model C (shown in Figure 1.6), the configuration is based on the Model B configuration in that one node provides complete support for all cluster resources at a time. However, unlike in Model B, the applications supported on the node include cluster-unaware applications that have some of their data stored on the local disks of one of the nodes. As a result, in the event of a failure, these applications are not failed over and remain offline until the original node is made available.

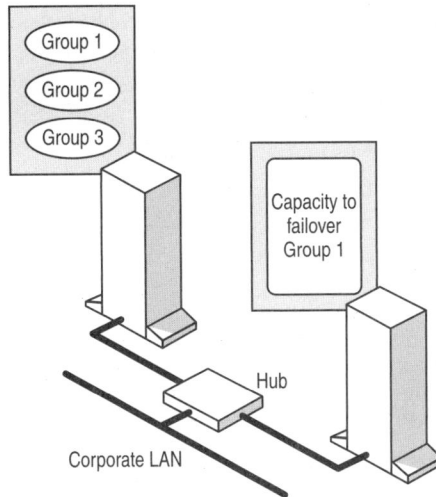

Figure 1.6   Model C

Model D: Virtual Server–Only (No Failover)

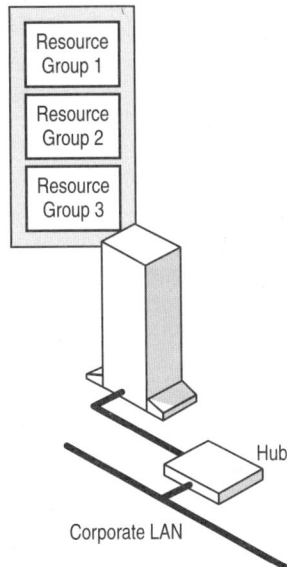

Figure 1.7   Model D

In Model D (shown in Figure 1.7), only one node is implemented in the cluster. As a result, there is no support for failover. Instead, the node is configured to support Cluster Service and allows for implementation of virtual servers to respond to client requests. Therefore, this configuration is not considered a cluster because only one node exists. This configuration is ideal if nodes will be added to the cluster in the future. It also allows resources to be grouped into virtual servers. When the cluster is fully implemented, clients do not have to be reconfigured based on any changes because the virtual servers used initially will still be valid.

Model E: Hybrid

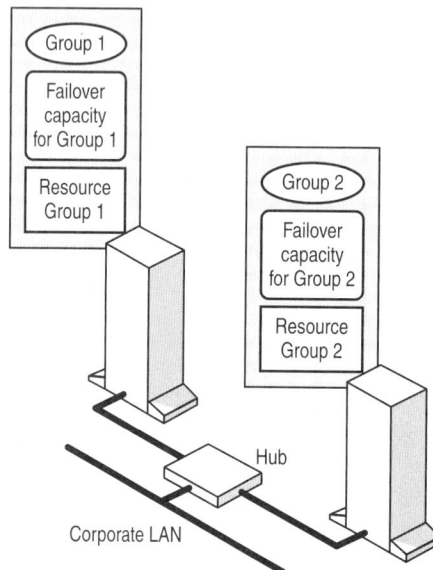

Figure 1.8   Model E

The Model E configuration (shown in Figure 1.8) is a combination of any of the other configurations. Under this model, each node manages its own resources and provides support for failover. However, some nodes might support cluster-unaware applications while other nodes might not have the physical capacity to allow specific resources or applications to be failed over. In addition, some nodes might support resources that are not configured for failover and might remain offline until the node is made available.

Configuration Model Comparison

Table 1.1 compares the configuration models based on performance, level of availability, and cost for a cluster with two nodes.

Table 1.1   Configuration Model Comparison

Model	Availability	Performance	Cost
A	High—availability is maintained during failover.	High—performance is reduced during failover.	High—both nodes must be able to support all resources.
B	Very High—availability is maintained during failover.	Very High—performance is maintained during failover.	Very High—half of the hardware investment sits idle until a failover occurs.
C	High—for resources that can be failed over. Unchanged—for other resources.	Normal—performance can be dramatically reduced.	Average—depends on the number of applications during failover.
D	Unchanged—failover is not supported.	Unchanged—performance is not enhanced by Cluster Service.	Low—requires only one node.
E	High—availability is maintained as needed during failover.	High—performance is reduced during failover.	High—depends on number of resources supported by the cluster.

Hardware and Networking Considerations

Before you implement a cluster, you must consider what hardware will be required based on your needs. This includes the appropriate network configuration, such as network interface cards and cabling, to provide for the communication requirements between nodes.

Drive Technology Overview

You can use two categories of drive technology for the shared devices in a cluster: Small Computer System Interface (SCSI) and Fibre Channel. You cannot implement an IDE hard drive as a shared device in a cluster because IDE does not support sharing of its drives among multiple servers.

SCSI

SCSI is a popular drive technology among enterprises. It supports up to 15 devices per adapter and multiple adapters per server. When you use SCSI, you can connect devices internally to a server or connect them externally, creating a chain of devices. The devices can thus be potentially shared among servers, allowing Cluster Service to use SCSI. The primary benefits of SCSI include increased performance (compared to IDE) and lower cost (compared to Fibre Channel). A limitation of SCSI, when used in a cluster, is that it can support only a two-node cluster. If your cluster will include four nodes (using Windows 2000 Datacenter Server), you must use Fibre Channel.

SCSI will be the primary drive technology discussed and used in this training kit.

Fibre Channel

Fibre Channel is an industry standard that was developed in 1988 to provide support for high-speed standardized connections to storage devices. It is supported on all of the Windows 2000 operating systems. However, only Windows 2000 Datacenter Server supports a four-node cluster using Fibre Channel.

Fibre Channel was designed to be superior to SCSI technology in three areas:

- A better connection for serial hard disk interfaces
- A faster connection for communication between servers
- A alternative networking medium to high-speed Ethernet

Disadvantages of Fibre Channel include higher cost, complex implementation, and increased maintenance compared to other drive technologies. Although Fibre Channel is not suitable for all storage solutions, it is rapidly gaining acceptance in large enterprise environments. Unlike Fiber Distributed Data Interface (FDDI), Fibre Channel was developed to support a greater number of protocols, including SCSI, IEEE 802.2, Internet Protocol (IP), and Asynchronous Transfer Mode (ATM), over a faster physical connection. Thus, Fibre Channel provides a single standard interface where other technologies require multiple interfaces.

Advantages of Fibre Channel include

- A fast transmission rate of 100 MBps in both directions.
- Increased transmission distance over other technologies, such as SCSI. Transmission distance is limited to about 20 meters for SCSI or up to10 kilometers for Fibre Channel.
- Support for real-time hot swapping between drives. You can add or remove several drives from an active channel without interfering with data communication.
- Support for arrays of up to 256 disk drives and drive sizes of up to 9 terabytes.
- Compatibility with the standard SCSI commands, which Cluster Service relies on.

Cluster Service Hardware Requirements

As mentioned earlier, both Windows 2000 Advanced Server and Windows 2000 Datacenter Server support Cluster Service. You should verify that the hardware you're using is on the hardware compatibility lists (HCLs) for both the operating system and Cluster Service.

The Windows 2000 HCL and the Cluster Service HCL are at *www.microsoft.com/ hcl/default.asp.*

Note The online HCL allows you to search on specific hardware components. However, clusters are certified only as a complete system, so you must use the Cluster HCL category to determine whether your hardware is supported.

General Hardware Requirements

Here is a general overview of the hardware required to implement Cluster Service:

- Windows 2000 Advanced Server or Windows 2000 Datacenter Server installed on the boot partition of each server. The boot partitions cannot be shared between the servers.
- A separate storage host adapter (PCI card) that supports SCSI or Fibre Channel. This must be separate from the adapter used for the boot device.
- Two PCI network interface cards (NICs) in each server.
- One or more external drives that can be connected to all the servers. Each of these external drives will be shared between the nodes in the cluster and is typically a SCSI drive. Ideally, each external drive should include multiple drives implemented in one or more RAID configurations.
- The appropriate cabling to connect each external drive to the servers. If you're using a SCSI drive and the host adapters self-terminate, you do not need to use a Y-cable. Otherwise, you need the required terminators for the Y-cables when you use a SCSI solution.
- You should also consider implementing the same RAM, processor, and local drive configurations in each server. If a node does not have the necessary hardware to support an application, it will not fail over. For example, an application might require a certain amount of RAM or hard drive space. Each node in the cluster should meet the minimum configuration requirements to support all the resources in the cluster.

Note All hardware between the servers should be identical. This includes the slot placement of the adapter cards, the brand of the cards (including the network interface cards, or NICs), and the cabling between the nodes and the external drives.

Cluster Service Shared Disk Requirements

In addition to the general hardware requirements, you should consider the following requirements when selecting a shared drive for your cluster:

- All the shared drives that will be used by the cluster, including the drive used for the quorum resource, must be physically attached to all nodes in the cluster.
- Be sure to first verify that the shared drives can be accessed from each node before you put the cluster into production.
- When you use SCSI drives, each drive and each SCSI adapter must have a unique SCSI ID.
- Each disk that is shared must be configured as a Basic disk, not a Dynamic disk.
- Every partition on the shared disks must be formatted using the NTFS file system.

Cluster Service Network Requirements

You also need to consider the following network requirements for your cluster:

- You must select a unique NetBIOS name for the cluster. This name will be used by clients for accessing resources in the cluster.
- When you implement a two-node solution, the cluster will require at least five unique IP addresses. Two of these addresses can be private and will be used for cluster communication between the nodes. Two must be public addresses from your network and will be used by the NICs that are connected to your LAN. The fifth address must also be from your public network and will be used by the cluster itself.
- Each node in the cluster must be configured as part of the same domain. One node can be a domain controller, while the other can be a member of the domain. If you decide to implement a domain controller, you can optionally make this the domain controller of a domainlet to reduce the amount of overhead.
- A domain user account must be created in the same domain as the nodes. However, if a trust relationship exists, the account can reside in another domain. This account is used by the Cluster Service running on each node.
- Although each node should have two NICs, one for the public network and one for the private network, you can configure one card per node. Note, however, that Microsoft does not support this configuration.

Cluster Planning Checklist

The following checklist can further help you plan your cluster implementation.

1. **Assemble the planning team.** The team should include members from various technical and business groups in the organization. Remember to include team members that can contribute information regarding third-party applications in addition to standard Microsoft technologies.

2. **Identify which applications and services require high availability.** These might include applications that have special hardware requirements, high volume of data, or unusual hours of operation in your organization. For example, an application might be needed 24 hours a day, seven days a week for multinational corporations with sales offices in many countries.

3. **Decide which cluster technology to implement.** Once you determine the applications and services to be supported by a cluster technology, you must decide between Cluster Service and NLB. This involves determining which applications should be used with NLB and which should be used with Cluster Service.

4. **Identify network risks, including points of failure and connectivity problems.** Be sure to consider external points of failure, such as the local telephone company or power utility.

5. **Determine server capacity requirements based on the clustering technology you've selected and the requirements of the applications and services.** Also consider the client demand and load that will need to be managed.

6. **Plan how each resource group will fail over and fail back.** You can specify the following properties on a per–resource group basis:

   - **Failover Timing**   This property affects when the resource group will fail over. You can also instruct Cluster Service to attempt to restart the resource a specified number of times. If it is possible to restart all the applications and services in the resource group, Cluster Service will not implement a failover.

   - **Preferred Node**   You can specify a particular node that should run a resource group when the node is available. Consider setting this property when a certain node is better suited to supporting the resource.

   - **Failback Timing**   You can specify that a resource that has failed over should fail back to its preferred node immediately or at a certain time of day. For example, you might want a resource to fail back only after normal business hours to ensure that service to your clients is not interrupted.

7. **Choose the role of each server.** You must consider whether the server should be configured as a domain controller or as a member server of a domain based on the applications and services it will support. For example, a domain controller typically requires additional overhead, so it might not be the best choice for installing a SQL Server database that will have heavy use.

8. **Select a cluster model based on your organization's requirements.**

9. **Consider the hardware requirements of each server based on the applications and services you intend to include in your cluster and the cluster model.** This includes the disk capacity required for the cluster, available RAM in each server, and CPU speeds.

10. **Plan a strategy for backing up the data in the cluster and recovering from a catastrophic failure.** This plan should include the following general considerations:

   - Synchronizing backups
   - Creating backup storage space
   - Storing backup media
   - Maintaining a backup catalog

Lesson Summary

This lesson introduced implementation considerations for Cluster Service and explained the implementation models, Shared Device and Shared Nothing. By default, Cluster Service uses the Shared Nothing model, but it can use the Shared Device model if an application provides its own DLM. This lesson also explained the five configuration models:

   - Model A: High Availability with Static Load Balancing
   - Model B: Hot Spare with Maximum Availability
   - Model C: Partial Cluster Service
   - Model D: Virtual Server–Only (No Failover)
   - Model E: Hybrid

This lesson also provided an overview of the hardware and networking requirements of Cluster Service. This included an overview of the SCSI and Fibre Channel drive technologies. Some of the key requirements include:

   - Windows 2000 Advanced Server or Windows 2000 Datacenter Server installed on the boot partition of each server
   - Two PCI NICs in each server
   - One or more external drives that can be connected to all of the servers
   - Formatting of every partition on the shared disks using the NTFS file system
   - Selecting unique IP addresses and NetBIOS names for each node, each virtual server in the cluster, and the cluster itself

This lesson also provided a cluster-planning checklist that included 10 considerations for planning the deployment of Cluster Service.

Review

?

The following questions are intended to reinforce key information presented in this chapter. The answers can be found in Appendix A.

1. You are the administrator for a new Internet startup. Management has asked you to recommend the best technology for the internal e-mail system. Because the e-mail system will be used 24 hours a day by internal staff members and remote sales personnel—a total of 567 users—the server must be available as much as possible. Which clustering technology should you implement, and why?

2. What is a cluster? (Choose all appropriate answers.)

   a. A group of individual servers that act as a backup for one another

   b. A group of individual servers that work together as a single computer

   c. A group of individual servers with the same name and IP address

   d. A group of individual servers that have the same components and resources

3. You have recently been hired as a network administrator for an insurance company. The company is currently running Windows NT 4 servers for its database and e-mail needs. Management has decided to implement a secure Web site that will provide claim information to the adjustors in the field. This Web site will also be used to process client applications submitted by agents in real-time. The company has more than 500 offices across the United States. Each office has at least four agents, who each process an average of 35 applications a day. If the Web site meets expectations, management might open the site to clients for instant access to their records, new application submission, finding a local agent, and so on. You have decided to use Windows 2000 Advanced Server for the Web site. Further, you have decided to use Cluster Service for increased availability. Should you also use NLB in this scenario?

4. What is a node?

   a. The name of a cluster

   b. The SCSI hard drive where the cluster information is stored

   c. A server in a cluster

   d. The component of Cluster Service that manages Cluster Service resources

5. You have been asked to implement a cluster for your organization's e-mail server. Which operating systems support Cluster Service?

6. How do cluster-unaware applications communicate with Cluster Service?

   a. Resource DLLs

   b. Cluster APIs

   c. Communications Manager

   d. Heartbeats

7. You have been asked to evaluate your company's network. A previous administrator implemented a cluster to host your company's Web server. However, management is worried that the upcoming marketing campaign will result in a dramatic increase in visitors to the Web site. NLB has not been implemented. Should you consider NLB?

8. What implementation models are supported by Cluster Service?

    a. Shared Device

    b. Shared Nothing

    c. Shared Everything

    d. Mixed

9. Describe when failovers and failbacks occur.

10. Your organization has asked you to implement a cluster using Cluster Service for its e-commerce Web site. You have decided to implement a solution that uses two nodes, one that hosts all the resources in the cluster and one that acts as a live backup in the event of a failure. Which configuration model does this represent?

    a. Model A

    b. Model B

    c. Model C

    d. Model D

    e. Model E

C H A P T E R   2

Preparing Windows 2000 Server for Cluster Service

About This Chapter

This chapter introduces key issues you should take into account before implementing a cluster in your organization. These include organizing resource groups, developing a failover policy, and identifying network risks. This chapter also discusses integrating Microsoft Cluster Service with specific network services that might exist in your organization's infrastructure, such as Dynamic Host Configuration Protocol (DHCP) and Domain Name Service (DNS). For example, you should understand the impact on the cluster nodes if your network is using DHCP rather than static IP addresses.

This chapter also describes how to set up and configure your hardware—such as shared storage devices and network interface cards (NICs)—before installing Cluster Service.

Before You Begin

To complete this chapter, you must have

- Completed Chapter 1
- The necessary hardware as outlined in the "About This Book" section in the Introduction
- The Microsoft Windows 2000 Advanced Server installation CD-ROM

Lesson 1: Planning Your Cluster

Before configuring the hardware and installing Cluster Service, you should take time to plan your cluster. This lesson describes the key preliminary requirements, which include planning the network protocols that will be used by the cluster, planning how you'll organize resource groups within the cluster, and deciding what policy you'll follow for planned as well as unplanned failovers. This lesson also discusses server capacity requirements based on the plans for your resource groups and failover policy. For example, you might want a second node in the cluster to support a certain resource in the event of a failover, but if the node does not include the necessary hardware, such as memory or hard drive space, the failover process will not be successful.

After this lesson, you will be able to

- Plan your Cluster Service implementation

Estimated lesson time: 30 minutes

Planning Resource Groups

A resource group consists of components that make up individual network services that have been installed on a cluster. For example, if your cluster is being used as a file share, you can organize the shares into resource groups. Typically, however, each application or primary service installed on the cluster is placed in a resource group. Cluster Service manages each resource group separately. As a result, if a service in the resource group fails, Cluster Service will attempt to fail over the entire group to another node. Therefore, you should carefully group your resources by function or dependency.

Clients access the network services support by a resource group through a virtual server. The virtual server has its own unique NetBIOS name and IP address on the public, or external, network. If a resource group needs to be failed over to another node, Cluster Service assigns the virtual server's computer name and IP address to the new node. Therefore, clients that access the services of a resource group never know which physical node they are connecting to. This lowers overall management overhead on the network because nodes can come online or be taken offline, and resource groups can move between the nodes, all without requiring updates to each network client.

The following types of resources are generally included in a resource group:

- IP Address
- Network Name
- Physical Disk
- The application or service being hosted

Consider the following steps when planning your resource groups:

1. List all the applications you intend to cluster. Remember that each group you create from this list will be its own virtual server.

2. Determine which resource groups can fail over based on whether the applications are cluster-aware or cluster-unaware.

3. List the nonapplication resources that will be included in the cluster. These include print spoolers and file shares that can be failed over in the event a node becomes unavailable.

4. List all the dependencies for each application to be hosted. Cluster Service ensures that all the dependent services will be successfully started before the application or service runs. This helps ensure that the application will either start correctly or be failed over, along with its dependencies, to another node.

5. Make initial grouping decisions based on the data you've collected. You should consider keeping a record of each application and its associated dependencies based on the previous steps. Then organize these based on what resource groups you think are appropriate. Keep in mind that organizing resources into groups might also make managing them easier. For example, if you're hosting file shares and print spoolers for various departments in your organization, you might consider creating groups and naming them appropriately for each department. This will make managing the specific department's resource easier at a later date.

6. Make final grouping decisions. To finalize your resource group plan, you might consider drawing arrows between the resources in the groups to establish a dependency tree. This can help you visualize the dependencies. An example of a simple dependency tree for a File Share resource is shown in Figure 2.1.

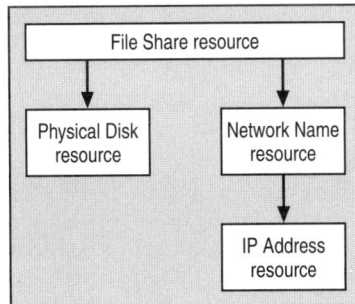

Figure 2.1   Resource dependency tree

Planning the Failover Policy

Independent resources within a group cannot fail over, so you should carefully consider the failover policy you implement and how it will affect the entire resource group. Because each group has its own failover policy, you can customize each according to your needs. The failover policy for a group specifies how the group reacts when a failover begins. The following options are specified by a resource group's failover policy:

- **Failover Timing**   By default, when a group fails, Cluster Service immediately starts the failover process in an attempt to move the resource group to another node. However, you can optionally have Cluster Service attempt to restart all the resources in the group a certain number of times before failing the group over to another node.

- **Preferred Node**   In some cases, a particular node might be better suited to hosting a certain resource group. The number of other groups, for example, might affect the overall performance of a certain node, and in order to better balance the load across the nodes, you might decide that a given resource group should always be hosted on a certain node when it is available. If you set the Preferred Node property, you can ensure that the group will always run on the node you specify.

  This property is used only when a resource group fails over to another node in the cluster. If you do not specify a preferred node, you must manually move the group back to the desired node.

- **Failback Timing**   This property specifies when a group that has failed over to another node in the cluster should fail back to the original, or preferred, node. By default, the group will fail back as soon as Cluster Service detects that the preferred node has come back online. However, this might negatively affect your clients if the failback occurs during peak business hours. Instead, you can set the Failback Timing property so that failback will occur after hours.

Planning Capacity Requirements for the Cluster

Once you chose a cluster model (see Chapter 1, Lesson 4), determine your resource group allocations, and plan each group's failover policy, you should determine the cluster's hardware capacity requirements—including hard drive storage requirements, CPU requirements, and memory requirements for the applications being included in the cluster. You should pay particular attention to the failover policies and whether the other nodes in the cluster can support running any, and possibly all, of the applications in each resource group. This is especially critical in a two-node cluster because only a single node will be available in the event of a failover.

Note that the shared device in a cluster must be configured as a Basic disk because Dynamic configuration is not supported; each partition must be formatted using NTFS. In addition, this drive cannot be extended later. Therefore, you must plan for future growth of the cluster.

Identifying Network Risks

Because the key reason for implementing Cluster Service is to increase the availability of network services, you must carefully consider potential points of failure in your network. These include items generally internal to an organization, such as hardware and software. However, some points of failure might be external, such as power supplied by the local utility company or WAN lines. You can significantly increase the level of availability for your cluster by

- Eliminating points of failure, if possible
- Developing backup plans to be used in the event of a failure (such as implementing Cluster Service, using uninterruptible power supplies, and having redundant access to the WAN)

Evaluating the Network Services Infrastructure

Depending on the network environment into which you intend to deploy a cluster, existing network services might affect the implementation plan. For example, although your network might not use the TCP/IP protocol, the private cluster network requires this protocol for its communication.

In order to install Cluster Service, you must ensure that each network adapter installed in each node is running the TCP/IP protocol. Depending on which set of adapters you are configuring—private or public—TCP/IP might be the only protocol supported. In addition, the private adapters should have NetBIOS over TCP/IP disabled. The public network adapters must have TCP/IP implemented and NetBIOS turned on as the networking protocol. NetBIOS is required for clients to browse to a virtual server by name or for administrators to use the Cluster Administrator utility from a remote computer. For more information about the Cluster Administrator, see Chapter 3, "Installing and Configuring Cluster Service." All other network protocols, including IPX/SPX, AppleTalk, and NetBEUI, are not supported by Cluster Service. Therefore, you should not configure these protocols for use on the private network adapters.

You must also base your decisions on the domain model used by your network. All nodes in a cluster should be, at the very least, member servers in the same domain with access to a domain controller. If you decide to make one of the nodes a domain controller, you should configure both nodes as domain controllers. If you want the nodes to be domain controllers of their own domain, consider implementing a domainlet in order to reduce overhead. Note, however, that the nodes cannot be part of a workgroup. Regardless of the domain model you implement, all nodes must have access to a DNS server (and possibly a WINS server) for name resolution.

In addition, you must consider using a domain user account to run Cluster Service. This account must be the same across all nodes in the cluster. Therefore, the nodes must be in the same domain or in domains that have the appropriate trust relationships. For example, you might want to create and use a Cluster Service account from an existing domain in your organization, in which case the nodes should be member servers in this domain.

You must also verify the IP configuration used by your network. For example, although it is possible to use a DHCP server to obtain the TCP/IP settings for the public adapters in a cluster, it is not recommended. Further, DHCP cannot be used for the private adapters; these must be configured with static address information. In addition, all virtual servers in your cluster must have static addresses. If you choose to use DHCP for the public adapters, you should implement permanent leases to ensure that the address information remains valid even if the DHCP service is temporarily unavailable. If the leases expire and the DHCP server is still down, your cluster will no longer be accessible to the network. Of course, if you implement permanent leases, it might be more efficient to use static addresses for the public adapters.

Additional Planning Considerations

The following sections cover some additional issues for you to consider before you implement a cluster server.

Selecting the Appropriate Hardware Resources

Although one of the primary goals of a Cluster Service implementation is high availability, you should carefully consider each node's hardware requirements based on the applications and services it will host. For example, if your cluster will be used primarily as a file server, you should consider using hardware configurations that provide fast disk access. This might involve buying a new server or selecting an appropriate server based on current hardware configurations. In this example, you should also review the network adapters being used. They should be able to provide high levels of throughput. Since a file share cluster will probably experience heavy amounts of data transfer, the network adapters could present a bottleneck to overall performance. However, since a file server typically doesn't require much memory or processing power, you can consider trading drive and network access for memory and processor speed. On the other hand, if the cluster is hosting an application that is processor and memory intensive, the drive and network speeds might not be as critical.

Another hardware consideration is the level of support provided by the original equipment manufacturer (OEM). Even though a particular hardware component, such as a SCSI adapter, might work with Cluster Service, the OEM and Microsoft might not support the device. Currently, Microsoft provides support only for complete cluster server configurations that have been validated. These are listed on the

Cluster Service Hardware Compatibility List (HCL) at http://www.microsoft.com/hcl/default.asp. Select Cluster from the In The Following Types list to retrieve a list of these validated configurations. Although individual components that qualify for the Windows 2000 logo are also included on the HCL, they are not supported by Microsoft when used with Cluster Service.

Planning for Disk Optimization

Windows 2000 uses a paging file, sometimes called a swap file, to allow programs to use more memory than is available on the physical RAM in a server by treating the disk as volatile memory. As a result, data is swapped in and out of physical memory to the paging file on the disk. Together, the paging file and the physical RAM constitute the server's virtual memory. You should consider installing a separate local drive in each node for the paging file in order to increase the performance of the nodes virtual memory. Never put the paging file on the shared disk. In addition, Microsoft recommends that for some memory-intensive applications, such as Microsoft SQL Server 2000, the paging file should be set to at least two and a half times the amount of physical RAM in the server.

Tuning Windows 2000 Services

By default, Windows 2000 Advanced Server supports specific services that are not required by Cluster Service. You might consider disabling these services or setting specific properties in the registry in order to optimize or even free the additional overhead that they require. Some services that you might consider optimizing are the Windows 2000 NetLogon Service, the Microsoft Computer Browser Service, and the Server service. Services that can be disabled, depending on your needs, include the Print Spooler and the Task Scheduler.

For example, the Computer Browser Service included with Windows 2000 is used to track servers and resources that are active on the network. At the very least, you should optimize this service for the best use of overhead. However, unless your cluster nodes are domain controllers, you should disable the Computer Browser service.

See Microsoft TechNet for the specific properties that you can set by using the Windows 2000 registry to optimize these services (if you decide not to disable them entirely).

Final Planning Considerations

Once you select your hardware and configure it properly for use with Cluster Service, you should consider the following guidelines when finalizing your plans.

Note All replacement hardware should be of the same brand and model as that used in your servers.

- Have replacement disks available on site.
- Have replacement SCSI controllers and cables available.
- Have replacement network adapters and extra cabling available.
- Implement uninterruptible power supplies (UPSs) on each server in the cluster. Be sure to also implement UPSs for the hubs, bridges, and routers used to connect the cluster to the network and for the shared device.
- Verify (and test) your backup procedures and backup hardware configuration. For example, you should be familiar with the recovery procedures required by the backup software and hardware you have selected.

Lesson Summary

This lesson described many of the decisions you must make before implementing Cluster Service. It discussed how to organize your applications into resource groups and set the failover policies for these groups. This lesson also covered capacity requirements of each node. You must make sure that, depending on your failover policies, each node in the cluster has the appropriate capacity in terms of hard drive space, CPU performance, and memory to support the applications being hosted by the cluster.

Specific points of failure as well as network infrastructure considerations were also presented in this lesson. You must carefully plan the network requirements of the cluster, such as TCP/IP settings, in relationship to your existing network infrastructure. For example, if your network uses DHCP, you must implement permanent leases, or static addresses, for the IP information on the public adapters. Additional planning considerations include using the Cluster Service HCL to select hardware and tuning Windows 2000 for Cluster Service.

Lesson 2: Installing and Configuring the Network Adapters

Cluster Service requires the use of PCI network adapters for communication between the nodes and with clients. Each node in the cluster requires at least two network adapters. One adapter, called the private network adapter, is used for private communication between the nodes. The other adapter, called the public network adapter, is used for communication with clients and remote administrators.

Before installing Cluster Service, you must configure these adapters based on their roles in the cluster. You can do this during the Windows 2000 Setup process or manually if the adapters are installed in an existing Windows 2000 server. This lesson describes the installation requirements and network cabling configuration required for Cluster Service. It is assumed that you'll use standard 10BaseT or 100BaseT adapters and associated cabling. This lesson also discusses how to configure TCP/IP on both the private and public adapters in each node of a cluster.

After this lesson, you will be able to

- Configure the private adapters before installing Cluster Service
- Configure the public adapters before installing Cluster Service

Estimated lesson time: 45 minutes

Installing the Network Adapters

The first step in configuring the network connections for each node is to properly install the network adapters for use by both the private and public networks. It is recommended that you use the same model adapter for both networks. Further, you should install the adapters in the same slots in each node. This will simplify the troubleshooting process if problems occur.

Although you can use a single set of adapters for both the private and public networks, this configuration is not recommended because a single point of failure will be introduced. Using two sets of network adapters, and configuring them appropriately, will introduce a higher level of redundancy.

Once the network adapters have been installed and the appropriate drivers have been loaded, you must plan how you'll connect the adapters to their appropriate network. You should consider using a crossover cable to connect the private network adapters. Although you can use a standard network hub to connect the private adapters, this introduces an unnecessary single point of failure.

Configuring the Network Adapters

In addition to using the same network adapters in both nodes, you should also install and configure the cards the same way in each node.

Setting the Adapter Properties

In general, all properties of each adapter in each node should be set to the same values. For example, the network adapters should be set to use the actual speed of the network, rather than allowing the adapters to auto-detect the network speed. If the adapters are allowed to detect the speed, some adapters might drop network packets while trying to determine the speed. All other network properties, such as Duplex Mode, Flow Control, and Media Type, should also be set to the same values on each adapter. See your network adapter's documentation if you're unsure how to verify these settings.

Selecting TCP/IP Settings

Configuring the private and public TCP/IP settings correctly is not only critical for supporting client requests, but Cluster Service also uses them to communicate the health of the cluster between nodes. The public adapters respond to client requests to applications on the cluster and, therefore, they use IP addresses associated with your corporate LAN. The private adapters are used only for communication between nodes. Therefore, they use private IP addresses.

Note You must install and configure TCP/IP before you start the Cluster Service installation process.

Because the private network does not have access to the LAN, you can use one of the reserved IP network classes. These include

- 10.0.0.0 to 10.255.255.255 (Class A)
- 172.16.0.0 to 172.31.255.255 (Class B)
- 192.168.0.0 to 192.168.255.255 (Class C)

When you assign IP addresses to the private network adapters, you must select one unique IP address for each adapter. You must also unselect the NetBIOS over TCP/IP option for each adapter.

Note You should configure the protocols supported on the private network adapters so that TCP/IP is the only protocol supported on those adapters.

As described in Lesson 1, DHCP should not be used to assign IP addresses to any of the adapters. Therefore, you should plan to configure all network adapters with static IP addresses. The IP addresses you select for your public adapters and virtual servers must fall within an address range used on your corporate network and must be reachable by clients.

Practice: Configuring the Network Adapters

In this practice, you will configure four network adapters, two in each server. Before starting, you should have Windows 2000 Advanced Server installed on each node. The network adapters should also have been installed in matching slots in each node. You will need to have connected the private adapters with a crossover cable. The public adapters should be connected to your corporate network. Figure 2.2 illustrates the cabling configuration for the cluster.

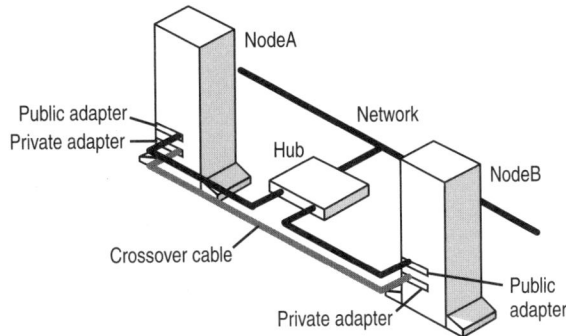

Figure 2.2   Network cable configuration

To determine which network adapter is public and which is private, you must check your wiring. This practice will assume that the Local Area Connection is connected to the public network and that the Local Area Connection(2) is connected to the private cluster network.

Changing the names of the network connections on the first node in the cluster will help you identify the network correctly. The new connection names will be replicated to the other nodes as they are brought online.

Renaming the Network Connections

1. From the Windows 2000 Server desktop, right-click My Network Places and click Properties. The Network And Dial-Up Connections window will open.
2. Right-click Local Area Connection and click Rename.
3. This exercise assumes the Local Area Connection is associated with your public network.
4. Type the name *Public Cluster Connection* and press Enter.
5. Repeat steps 2 and 3 for Local Area Connection(2) using the name Private Cluster Connection.
6. The Network And Dial-Up Connections window should now look like Figure 2.3.
7. Close the window.

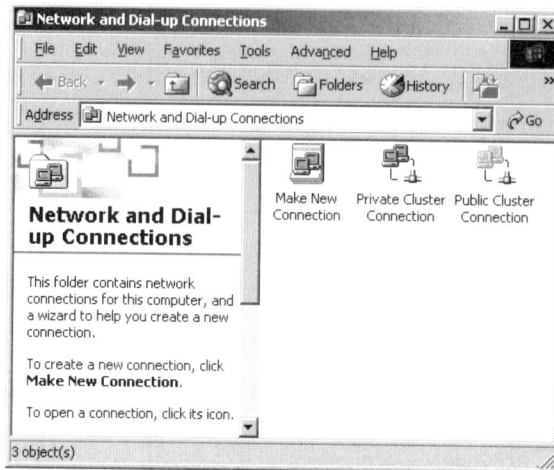

Figure 2.3   The Network And Dial-Up Connections window, showing a renamed network connection

Configuring the Public Network TCP/IP Settings

1. On the first server in the cluster, from the Windows 2000 Server desktop, right-click My Network Places and click Properties. The Network And Dial-Up Connections window will open.

2. Right-click Public Cluster Connection and click Properties.

3. Select Internet Protocol(TCP/IP) and then click Properties.

4. Verify that the Use The Following IP Address option is selected.

5. Verify that a valid public IP address has been entered. If no address exists, use the following information:

   IP address: 192.168.0.1

   Subnet mask: 255.255.255.0

6. Click OK, and then click OK again.

7. Repeat steps 1 through 6 on the second server using an IP address of 192.168.0.2 if one is not already provided.

Configuring the Private Network TCP/IP Settings

1. On the first server in the cluster, from the Windows 2000 desktop, right-click My Network Places and click Properties. The Network And Dial-Up Connections window will open.

2. Right-click Private Cluster Connection and click Properties.

3. Select Internet Protocol(TCP/IP) and then click Properties.

4. Verify that the Use The Following IP Address option is selected.

5. Enter the following IP address and subnet mask information:

   IP address: 10.0.0.1

   Subnet mask: 255.0.0.0

6. Click Advanced.

7. Select the WINS tab.

8. Make sure that the Disable NetBIOS Over TCP/IP option is selected.

9. Click OK to close the Advanced Properties dialog box.

   If you are prompted that the connection has an empty WINS address, click Yes to continue.

10. Click OK, and then click OK again.

11. Repeat steps 1 through 10 on the second server using an IP address of 10.0.0.2.

Configuring the Private Network Adapter Properties

1. On the first server in the cluster, from the Windows 2000 desktop, right-click My Network Places and click Properties. The Network And Dial-Up Connections window will open.

2. Right-click Private Cluster Connection and click Properties.

3. Click Configure and then select the Advanced tab.

4. Verify that all the properties match both servers in the cluster. Specifically, set the network adapter speed to the actual speed of the network, such as 10BaseTx or 100BaseTx. If the Auto Select or Hardware Default options are provided you should not use them.

Note Some adapters that are not Plug and Play–compliant require that you configure the card using the setup software provided with the adapter. In this case, you cannot configure the settings on these adapters as described above.

---

5. Click OK to close the Advanced Adapter Configuration dialog box.

6. Click OK to close the network adapter's Properties dialog box.

Lesson Summary

This lesson described the network adapter requirements for a cluster. Two adapters should be installed in each node, one for private communication between the nodes and one for communication with clients and remote administrators. You should configure the adapters identically to ensure that Cluster Service operates successfully. This lesson also included a practice that showed you how to configure the network adapters in your servers in preparation for installing Cluster Service.

Lesson 3: Configuring the Shared Storage Device

This lesson describes how to implement and configure the shared storage device to be used in a cluster. Although Cluster Service also supports Fibre Channel, this training kit will use Small Computer System Interface (SCSI) adapters and hard drives. The lesson introduces basic SCSI concepts and terminology and describes the requirements of the shared device.

After this lesson, you will be able to

- Describe how to select the appropriate hardware for a cluster implementation
- List the requirements of the shared device to be used in a cluster
- Configure the SCSI bus for use by Cluster Service
- Describe the primary RAID options
- Format and configure the partitions on the shared device

Estimated lesson time: 60 minutes

Selecting SCSI Hardware

It is highly recommended that you select the same SCSI adapters for use in each node of the cluster. You can technically use different cards, but you might encounter compatibility problems that lead to inefficiency in the cluster and, in some cases, inoperability. Typically, organizations purchase identical systems from the Cluster Service HCL (described in Lesson 1), which will ensure identical hardware between nodes.

You need the following hardware for your shared device:

- SCSI adapter cards (one for internal disks and one for the shared storage)
- SCSI hard drives (including external enclosure with an independent power supply)
- SCSI cabling (Y-cables when you use terminators)
- SCSI terminators (if the adapters do not provide onboard termination)

Note You should not configure removable storage devices, such as CD-ROM drives or tape drives, on the shared SCSI bus used by the cluster.

Although some SCSI adapters provide onboard termination, not all adapters provide this requirement when the host computer is powered down. In these cases, the SCSI chain will no longer be terminated and the shared device will no longer be accessible. However, some SCSI adapter cards can provide termination services even after a power failure. You can use these cards as an alternative to SCSI Y-cables and terminators.

Shared Device Requirements

A cluster's shared device can and often does include more than one physical disk drive. When more than one drive is being used, you can implement RAID or use the drives independently. Note, however, that all drives included in the shared device must be accessible to all the nodes in the cluster.

In order for the shared device to be used in a cluster, it must be physically connected to each node. As a result, each node must have read and write capability to the drives included in the shared device. Further, each disk must be configured as a Basic disk (not a Dynamic disk) and be formatted using NTFS. If fault tolerance is required, you can implement RAID, but you must use a hardware solution.

The shared device does not support the following:

- Encrypted file system
- Remote storage
- Mounted volumes
- Reparse point

Configuring the SCSI Hardware

In order to implement a cluster using SCSI hardware, you must select and install SCSI adapters in each server. You then connect the adapters to an external storage device, which is one or more SCSI hard drives within an external enclosure. Typically, the SCSI chain is terminated after the shared device.

You can use a Y-cable, with terminators on each end, or adapter cards that self-terminate. Figure 2.4 shows a SCSI configuration using Y-cables.

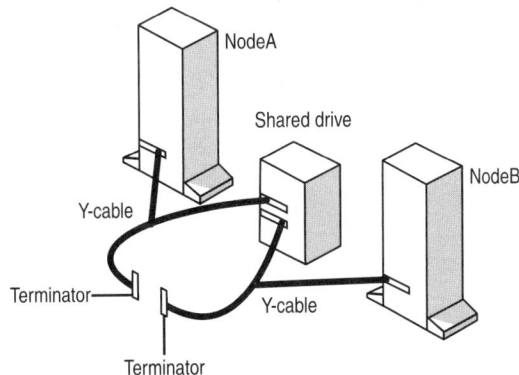

Figure 2.4   SCSI cabling configuration using Y-cables

Figure 2.5 shows a configuration using standard SCSI cables with adapters that provide termination.

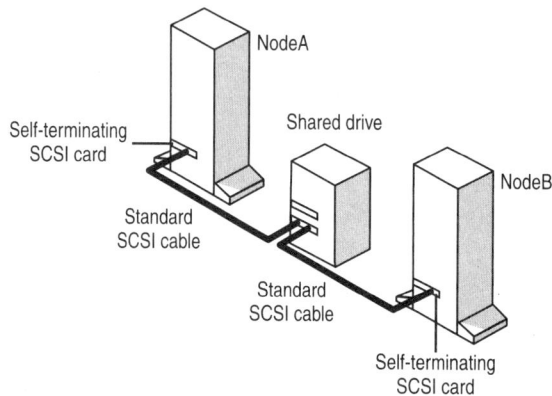

Figure 2.5 SCSI cabling configuration using self-terminating cards

In addition, each SCSI device, including each adapter, must be configured with unique SCSI IDs. Typically, the IDs are configured through the SCSI BIOS of each card. The SCSI drive's ID can be set by using jumpers on the drive or through the external enclosure. Some enclosures provide this functionality. Refer to your hardware's instruction manuals or check with your hardware manufacturer for information on how to configure SCSI IDs for your adapters and drives.

Implementing Fault Tolerance Using RAID

Redundant Array of Independent Disks (RAID) is a technique for implementing fault tolerance among hard drives. Eight levels of RAID are available, but many are proprietary and not supported by all RAID adapters.

The RAID model you select depends on the level of fault tolerance required. Windows 2000 provides support for software RAID; however, it is not supported in a cluster. You must implement a hardware-based RAID solution if fault tolerance is required.

Warning Cluster Service is not supported when you use the software implementation of RAID that is integrated into Windows 2000. If you want to use RAID for fault tolerance, you can do this at the hardware level or use a third-party software solution.

For information about implementing RAID at the hardware level, see the manufacturer's documentation.

The eight RAID levels are as follows:

- **RAID 0**   RAID 0, called *data striping without parity,* lets you take advantage of multiple hard drives to increase the overall performance of data access. While this provides the highest level of performance, it does not provide fault tolerance. If one of the drives fails, all the data stored across all the drives becomes unavailable to the server. If this happens, the data must be restored from tape backup.

- **RAID 1**   RAID 1, also known as *mirroring,* requires two hard drives. When data is saved, it is written automatically to both drives in the array. The result is a live backup that can be used immediately in the event one of the drives fails. The disadvantages of using RAID 1 include reduced write performance and higher cost.

- **RAID 2**   With RAID 2, data is stored on one drive and Hamming code error-correction data is stored on a second drive. RAID 2 is the most expensive RAID level because it requires each drive to have a dedicated second drive. Because SCSI drives almost always have onboard error correction and because RAID 2 requires multiple drives, RAID 2 is rarely used.

- **RAID 3**   RAID 3 involves both disk striping and parity. It provides fault tolerance by saving disk parity information to a dedicated drive and by striping the data across the other drives. RAID 3 provides the same read performance as RAID 0, but provides poorer write performance because of the overhead involved with parity calculations. However, if the drive storing the parity information fails, fault tolerance is lost. RAID 3 is also rarely used.

- **RAID 4**   RAID 4 is similar to RAID 3 in that disk parity information is saved to separate drives in the array. However, unlike RAID 3, which uses a single dedicated drive, RAID 4 synchronizes the data across multiple drives. This provides a higher level of fault tolerance than RAID 3.

- **RAID 5**   RAID 5, called *disk striping with parity,* provides the highest level of fault tolerance at the expense of the lowest performance. However, RAID 5 makes efficient use of the available hard drive space, unlike RAID 1, and allows you to quickly and easily "swap" a defective drive without restarting the server. The new replacement drive can be added to the array and the data rebuilt over time on the new drive. No data is lost in the event of a drive failure, which means that RAID 5 provides the highest level of redundancy. With this level of RAID, two drives must fail in the array to cause the entire array to fail. Because of the significant fault tolerance it provides, this level is often used.

- **RAID 6**   Similar to RAID 5, RAID 6 saves parity information across all disks in the array. However, additional parity information is stored, increasing the level of fault tolerance. With RAID 6, three drives must fail in order for the array to fail.

■ **RAID 10**   This level provides a combination of RAID 1 and RAID 0, which results in better overall performance with fault tolerance. Unlike RAID 0, RAID 10 provides fault tolerance by mirroring the striped disks. But unlike RAID 1 (disk mirroring), RAID 10 implements disk striping, which results in increased performance for disk reads.

Note   You cannot enable write caching on a RAID controller connected internally in a node. The data in the cache is lost if the node fails over. However, it is possible to use an external RAID controller with write caching enabled because the data in its cache is saved during a failover.

Partitioning the Shared Device

Once you connect your shared device, configure all cabling, and implement the appropriate level of RAID, you must partition the drive for use with Cluster Service. If your shared device does not include more than one drive, you must create at least two partitions, one for the quorum resource and one for the shared data to be used by all nodes in the cluster. However, in this configuration, if the shared device fails, the Quorum resource will also fail. Therefore, you should place the Quorum resource on its own dedicated shared drive.

The partition for Quorum resource should contain at least 50 MB of drive space; 500 MB of space is recommended. During installation of Cluster Service, you must specify a location for the Quorum resource.

Practice: Preparing the Shared Device for Cluster Service

In this practice, you will configure the shared drive for use with the cluster. This includes partitioning the drive and formatting it using the NTFS file system. This practice assumes that you're using a single drive for the shared device.

Configuring the Shared Device Partitions

1. From the Windows 2000 Start menu, point to Programs, point to Administrative Tools, and then click Computer Management.

2. Click Disk Management. If you don't see Unallocated Disk Space, right-click Disk 0, choose Write Signature, choose Disk 0, and click OK. This configures the disk as Basic.

3. Right-click Unallocated Disk Space.

4. Click Create Partition.

5. The Create Partition Wizard will start. In the Welcome dialog box, click Next.

6. In the Select Partition Type dialog box, click Next.

7. This partition will be used for the Quorum resource. Enter a partition size of at least 50 MB, preferably 500 MB, and then click Next.

8. In the Assign Drive Letter Or Path dialog box, select drive Q: for this partition, and then click Next.

9. In the Format Partition dialog box, verify that the file system type is NTFS, and then click Next. The partition will be created and then formatted as an NTFS drive.

10. When the Create Partition Wizard is done, repeat steps 3 through 9 for the remaining drive space. Use a drive letter of *W:* for the partition and format the drive as an NTFS file system. This second partition will be used for the shared hard drive.

Verifying Disk Access Between the Servers

1. On the first server, from the Windows 2000 Start menu, point to Programs, point to Accessories, and then click Notepad.

2. Type *Server One* and save the text file to the shared drive using the filename Test File.

3. On the second server, from the Windows 2000 Start menu, point to Programs, point to Accessories, and then click Notepad.

4. From the File menu, click Open, and then select the test file created in step 2.

5. Verify that the words *Server One* appear in the document.

6. Type *Server Two* and save the file.

7. Repeat steps 3 through 5 on the first server to verify that the changes made from the second server have been applied.

Lesson Summary

This lesson described how to select the appropriate SCSI hardware for a cluster server implementation. Although you can use Fibre Channel, this training kit assumes that you will be using SCSI adapters and hard drives. This lesson also described shared device requirements and limitations. For instance, the shared device must use the NTFS file system and cannot be encrypted. This lesson explained how to configure your SCSI shared device and discussed the various levels of RAID for implementing fault tolerance. Although Windows 2000 Advanced Server provides software support for RAID, Cluster Service does not. Therefore, if you require support for RAID, you must implement this at the hardware level.

The hands-on practice in this lesson showed how to configure the shared device to support installation of Cluster Service. The step-by-step instructions detailed how to configure partitions to support both the Quorum resource drive and shared data drive that will be used by the nodes in the cluster. You also verified that each server could access the shared device by editing a simple text file. The steps listed in this practice, just like those presented in the practice for Lesson 2, are required before you install Cluster Service.

Review

The following questions are intended to reinforce key information presented in this chapter. The answers can be found in Appendix A.

1. Which network protocols are supported by the private network used by Cluster Service?

2. When you decide to make a server in the cluster a domain controller, which of the following is *not* true?

   a. There will be added overhead when the server is configured as a domain controller.

   b. All servers in the cluster must be domain controllers.

   c. The server must have Active Directory installed.

   d. The server must have access to both a DHCP server and a DNS server.

3. Why is using DHCP to obtain the TCP/IP settings for the public adapters in a cluster not recommended?

4. Which of the following are true of the shared device when you use Windows 2000 Advanced Server?

   a. The shared device can be only one drive.

   b. The shared device can be more than one drive.

   c. The shared device must be a SCSI device.

   d. The shared device must be physically connected to all servers in the cluster.

5. You have four network adapters in your cluster configuration—two per node. How are the adapters configured?

6. When you use Windows 2000 Advanced Server and Cluster Service, which of the following drive types are supported for the shared device?

   a. SCSI

   b. EIDE

   c. ATA

   d. Fibre Channel

7. Cluster Service requires three IP addresses associated with your LAN. Where are these IP addresses assigned?

8. When you use a SCSI drive for the shared device, which of the following is *not* a requirement?

   a. A unique identification number.

   b. Each disk must be configured as Basic.

   c. Each disk must use a removable drive.

   d. Partitions must be in NTFS format.

9. What resides on the shared device?

10. Which of the following should you consider for a node in a cluster that will be used for file services?

   a. Large hard drives with fast access rates

   b. A large amount of virtual memory

   c. Multiple processors

   d. Network adapters that provide fast throughput

C H A P T E R   3

Installing and Configuring Cluster Service

About This Chapter

This chapter describes how to install and configure Microsoft Cluster Service. Once you configure your hardware correctly and develop an implementation plan, you can start the installation process. This chapter explains how to install Cluster Service as part of a new Microsoft Windows 2000 Advanced Server installation, how to install it on an existing server, and how to perform an unattended installation. It also explains how to perform a rolling upgrade of an existing cluster to the Windows 2000 Advanced Server platform.

Before You Begin

To complete this chapter, you must have

- Completed Chapter 1 and 2
- The necessary hardware as outlined in the section titled "About This Book" in the Introduction
- The Windows 2000 Advanced Server installation CD-ROM

Lesson 1: Installing Cluster Service

Although you typically install Cluster Service with a fresh installation of the Windows 2000 Advanced Server operating system, you can also install it manually on an existing operating system. You can also configure the Cluster Service setup program to run in unattended mode to automate the installation process. If you do this, you must include a standard Windows answer file to provide Setup with the information it needs to complete the Cluster Service installation. This lesson describes all the installation options and explains how to create and customize an answer file.

After this lesson, you will be able to

- Install Cluster Service on your operating system

Estimated lesson time: 90 minutes

Installation Options

Three options are available for installing Cluster Service:

- Installation with a fresh installation of Windows 2000 Advanced Server
- Installation on an existing installation of Windows 2000 Advanced Server
- Unattended Cluster Service installation

Regardless of the installation type you select, you will use the Cluscfg.exe application. Cluscfg.exe runs as a standard Windows 2000 wizard unless you automate the installation of Cluster Service. When you run Cluscfg.exe from the command line, it supports the command line options listed in Table 3.1.

Table 3.1   Cluscfg.exe Command-Line Options

Parameter	Description
ACC[OUNT] <accountname>	Specifies the domain service account used for Cluster Service.
ACT[ION] {FORM I JOIN}	Specifies whether to form a new cluster or join an existing cluster.
D[OMAIN] <domainname>	Specifies the domain used by Cluster Service.
EXC[LUDEDRIVE] <drive list>	Specifies which drives should not be used by Cluster Service as shared disks.
I[PADDR] <xxx.xxx.xxx.xxx>	Specifies the IP address for the cluster.
L[OCALQUORUM]	Specifies a disk on a nonshared SCSI bus that should be used as the quorum device.
NA[ME] <clustername>	Specifies the name of the cluster.
NE[TWORK] <connectionname> {INTERNAL I CLIENT I ALL} [priority]	Specifies how the network connection specified should be used by Cluster Service.
P[ASSWORD] <password>	Specifies the password for the domain service account used for Cluster Service.
Q[UORUM] <x:>	Specifies the drive letter to use for the quorum device.
S[UBNET] <xxx.xxx.xxx.xxx>	Specifies the subnet to use for the private network.
U[NATTEND] [<path to answer file>]	Suppresses the user interface in order to perform an unattended installation. Also specifies an optional external answer file.

Installation with Windows 2000 Advanced Server

The most common method for installing Cluster Service is to install it as an option during the operating system setup process. When you install Windows 2000 Advanced Server, you can select Cluster Service in the Windows Components Setup dialog box. This causes the Cluster Configuration Wizard to start at the end of the Windows setup process. When you install Cluster Service as part of a new setup, you must manually enter the appropriate information for Cluster Service. An alternative to this is the unattended installation option described later in this section. You must have administrative rights in order to install Cluster Service.

Installation on Existing Windows 2000 Advanced Server

You can also install Cluster Service on a computer that is already running Windows 2000 Advanced Server. When you do this, you can take some of the additional preparation steps outlined in Chapter 2, such as verifying that each server has read and write access to the shared device. Although this is not required, it will help ensure a successful installation of Cluster Service.

To install Cluster Service on an existing installation of Windows 2000 Advanced Server, you can use the Configure Your Server dialog box or Add/Remove Programs in Control Panel.

You must take the following steps before performing a manual Cluster Service installation:

- You must be logged on as an administrator.
- Because the installation steps vary slightly on the second node, you must decide which node will be installed first.
- During the installation, the second node must be powered off in order to ensure that the shared device does not become corrupt due to multiple computers accessing the drive.
- You should be prepared for a possible power outage during the installation. If both servers come online (when power is restored) before Cluster Service is fully installed, data on the shared device could be corrupted. One solution is to configure the second server, through Boot.ini, for a delayed start other than the default 30 seconds.

The complete setup steps for existing Windows 2000 Advanced Server installations will be presented later in this lesson.

Unattended Installation

If you are installing and configuring a number of clusters, you can elect to automate the setup process for Cluster Service—as part of a new Windows 2000 Advanced Server installation or as an installation on an existing server. In either case, you will use the Cluscfg.exe application with an associated answer file. When you use Cluscfg.exe to automate an installation, the answers it requires can come from the answer file used by Sysprep or from an external answer file that you create.

Note Sysprep is used to install only new instances of Windows 2000 Advanced Server. To automate the installation process of Cluster Service on an existing Windows 2000 Advanced Server, you must supply an external answer file.

Automating Cluster Service Setup on a New Server

You can automate the installation of Windows 2000 Advanced Server and Cluster Service using an answer file. This file is a script used by the setup program that provides answers to dialog boxes, resulting in an unattended installation. Since answer files are standard ASCII files, they can be created quickly using the Setup Manager utility or manually using any text editor. Even if you use Setup Manager to create an answer file, you can still edit the file with any text editor and create custom installations.

For even greater efficiency, you can use an image file in addition to an answer file. Image files are created with the Sysprep utility from an existing Windows 2000 configuration. Sysprep is used to install the same image onto multiple servers, resulting in identical installations. To further automate this process, you can use Setup Manager to create a Sysprep-specific answer file, called Sysprep.inf. The Sysprep.inf answer file can be customized as required.

To automate Cluster Service installation, you must specify the following settings to the standard answer file created by the Setup Manager or the Sysprep.inf answer file:

```
[Components]
Cluster = On
[GuiRunOnce]
%windir%\cluster\cluscfg.exe -u
[Cluster]
Name = MyCluster
Action = Form
Account = ClusterAdmin
Password = MyPassword
Domain = Reskit
IPAddr = 192.168.0.3
Subnet = 255.255.255.0
Network = Public,ALL
Network = Private,INTERNAL
```

The *[Components]* section contains requirements for installing components of Windows 2000. A value of *On* installs the component, and a value of *Off* prevents the component from being installed.

Cluster = On installs Windows Clustering and Administration components on Windows 2000 Advanced Server.

The *[GuiRunOnce]* section specifies applications that will run automatically after the setup program reboots the server. You must provide the path and filename information for Cluscfg.exe. You can optionally include the *–u* command line option to run Cluscfg.exe in unattended mode. The answers required for Cluscfg.exe will come from the *[Cluster]* section.

The *[Cluster]* section is described later in this lesson. Regardless of which technique you use to automate the installation process, you can add Cluster Service–specific information to the appropriate answer file to create an unattended installation of Cluster Service.

Note In order for Cluscfg.exe to run in an unattended manner, the setup process must first complete the installation of Windows 2000, reboot the server, and have you log in with administrative rights.

Automating Cluster Service Setup on an Existing Server

If you want to perform an unattended installation of Cluster Service on an existing installation of Windows 2000 Advanced Server, you can manually run the

Cluscfg.exe utility with its own answer file. The following command line can be used to run Cluscfg.exe with the CSAnswer.inf answer file:

```
Cluscfg.exe -u c:\CSAnswer.inf
```

The contents of the answer file you provide are similar to the contents of the answer file used when you install Cluster Service with a new installation of Windows 2000. This answer file needs to contain only a *[Cluster]* section. This section contains several keys, which are presented here with specific examples:

- Account

```
Account = <account name>
```

This key specifies the name of the account under which Cluster Service runs. This key is required only if Action = Form. (See below.)

Example:

```
Account = adminname
```

- Action

```
Action = <Form | Join>
```

This key specifies whether a cluster is to be formed or joined.

Form specifies that the cluster is to be created. If this is the first node in a cluster, you are creating a new cluster. When you specify *Form*, you must specify the Account and Domain keys.

Join specifies that your machine is to join an existing cluster. If at least one other node already exists, you are joining a cluster. When you specify *Join*, you should not specify the Account and Domain keys.

Example:

```
Action = Form
```

- Domain

```
Domain = <domain name>
```

This key specifies the domain to which the cluster belongs. It is required only if Action = Form.

Example:

```
Domain = domainname
```

- ExcludeDrive

```
ExcludeDrive = <drive letter>[, <drive letter> [, . . . ]]
```

This optional key specifies a drive to be excluded from the list of possible quorum devices.

Example:

```
ExcludeDrive = q, r
```

- IPAddr

```
IPAddr = <IP address>
```

This key specifies the IP address of the cluster.

Example:

```
IPAddr = 193.1.1.95
```

- LocalQuorum

```
LocalQuorum = Yes | No
```

This optional key specifies that a system drive should be used as the quorum device. (Normally, only a disk that is on a shared SCSI bus not used by the system disk can be selected as the quorum device.)

Example:

```
LocalQuorum = Yes
```

Note This parameter should be used only for demo, testing, and development purposes. The local quorum resource cannot fail over.

- Name

```
Name = <cluster name>
```

This key specifies the name of the cluster. The value can contain a maximum of 15 characters.

Example:

```
Name = MyCluster
```

- Network

```
Network = <connection name string>, <role>[, <priority>]
```

This key specifies the connection name associated with a network adapter and the role that adapter is to fulfill in the cluster. The first two parameters, <connection name string> and <role>, are required. The third parameter, <priority>, should be supplied only for network connections configured for internal communications.

The *<role>* parameter specifies the type of cluster communication for the network connection. Valid parameters are *All*, *Internal*, and *Client*. To use the network connections for communication with clients and between the nodes, specify *All*. To use the network connections only for internal communication between the nodes, specify *Internal*. To use the network connections only for communication with clients, specify *Client*.

The *<priority>* parameter specifies the order in which the network connections are used for internal communication.

Example:

```
Network="Local Area Connection 2", INTERNAL, 1
```

- Password

```
Password = <password>
```

This key specifies the password of the account under which Cluster Service runs.

Example:

```
Password = MyPassword
```

Note Some security risks are associated with using the Password key because the password is stored as plain text within the answer file. However, the Password key is deleted after the upgrade.

- Quorum

```
Quorum = <drive letter>
```

This key specifies the drive to be used as the quorum device.

Example:

```
Quorum = Q:
```

- Subnet

```
Subnet = <IP subnet mask>
```

This key specifies the IP subnet mask of the cluster.

Example:

```
Subnet = 255.255.0.0
```

The Cluster Service Configuration Wizard

To install Cluster Service, you use the Cluscfg.exe application, which is called the Cluster Service Configuration Wizard. When you run this wizard manually, you must respond to each dialog box; alternatively, you can run the wizard as an automated process using an answer file (as described earlier in this lesson). You can start the wizard manually through Add/Remove Programs in Control Panel. Complete steps for installing Cluster Service are included later in this lesson.

The following sections describe some important pages of the wizard and the configuration options available when you install Cluster Service.

Hardware Configuration

Although Cluster Service can be implemented on a variety of hardware configurations, Microsoft supports only Cluster Service installations performed on configurations listed on the Cluster Service Hardware Compatibility List (HCL). The wizard's Hardware Configuration page, shown in Figure 3.1, reviews this policy. For more information about these configurations, see Chapter 2, Lesson 1.

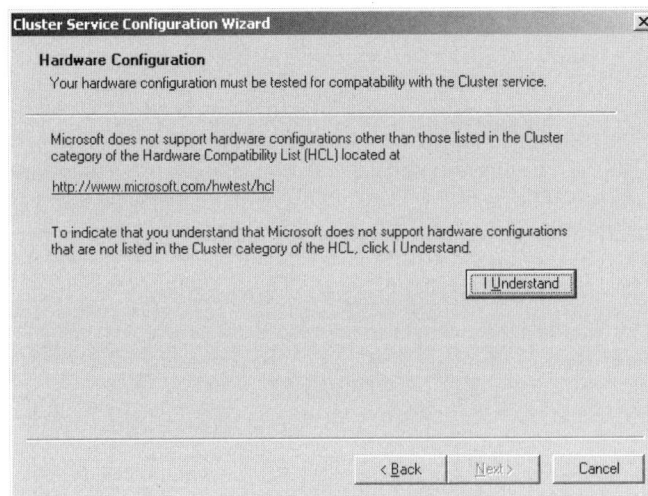

Figure 3.1   The Cluster Service Configuration Wizard's Hardware Configuration page

To continue with the installation of Cluster Service you must confirm that you understand Microsoft's support policy by clicking I Understand.

Create Or Join A Cluster

If a cluster does not already exist or if you do not want to join an existing cluster, you must create a new cluster. Otherwise, you will join an existing cluster. The Create Or Join A Cluster page, shown in Figure 3.2, provides these options. If you are joining an existing cluster, the cluster-specific information, such as the location of the quorum, will be provided for you automatically.

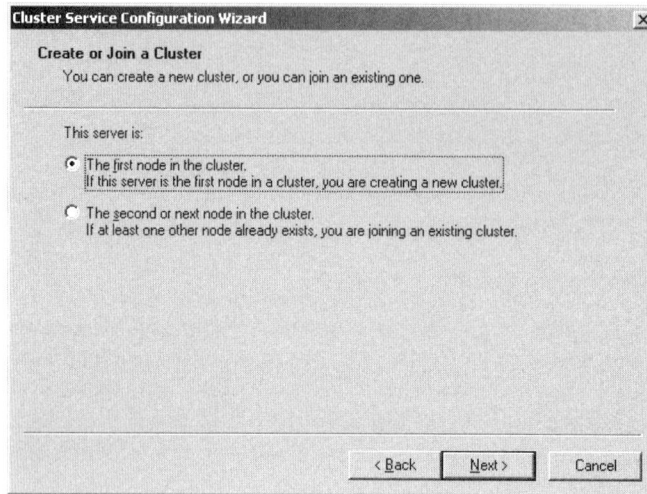

Figure 3.2   The Create Or Join A Cluster page

Select An Account

Before running the wizard, you must first create a domain user account for the cluster. This account must be a Domain Administrator or have local administrative rights on each node, plus the following permissions:

- Lock pages in memory
- Log on as a service
- Act as part of the operating system
- Back up files and directories
- Increase quotas
- Increase scheduling priority
- Load and unload device drivers
- Restore files and directories

The wizard requires you to enter this account information on the Select An Account page, shown in Figure 3.3.

After you enter the information for the Cluster Service account, the wizard validates the user account and password. If the node on which you are installing Cluster Service is a member server, you will be prompted to add this account to the local Administrators group.

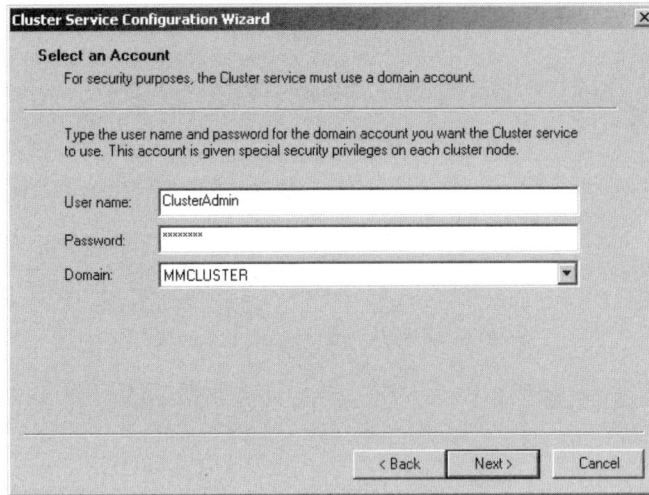

Figure 3.3   The Select An Account page

Add Or Remove Managed Disks

The Add Or Remove Managed Disks page, shown in Figure 3.4, provides a list of SCSI disks available to this server for use with Cluster Service. However, not all of the disks residing on the shared SCSI bus will necessarily appear in the list. Also, if the server has more than one SCSI bus, such as any for use by internal hard drives, these disks might appear but should not be made part of the cluster. You should remove these disks from the list.

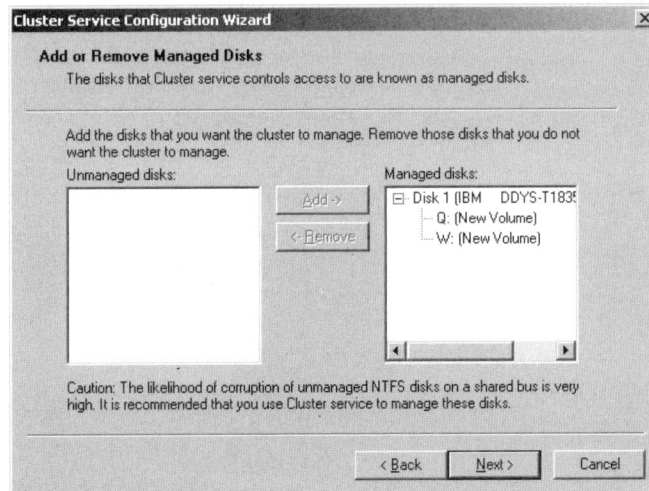

Figure 3.4   The Add Or Remove Managed Disks page

Cluster File Storage

The Cluster File Storage page, shown in Figure 3.5, lets you designate which shared partition or drive will store the cluster log files and checkpoint information. It is best to use a partition with at least 100 MB of free space to ensure that you do not run out of space even though the minimum size of a partition is only 50 MB of free space. For best results, this partition should have not have any user applications.

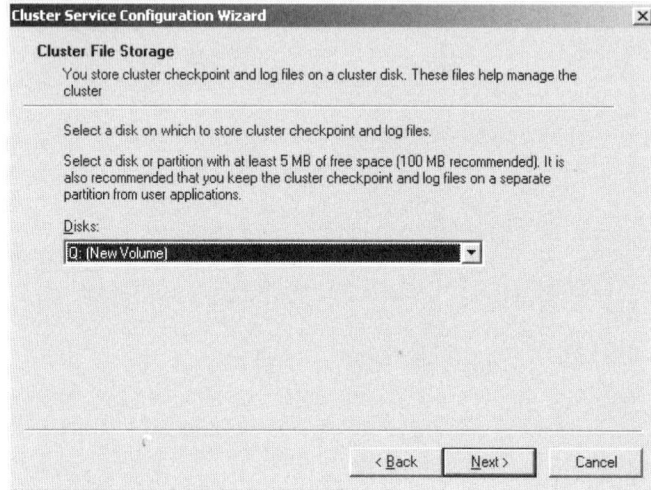

Figure 3.5   The Cluster File Storage page

Configure Cluster Networks

The Configure Cluster Networks page, shown in Figure 3.6, presents some basic recommendations that you should consider for your deployment of Cluster Service. An instance of this page is presented for each network adapter installed in your server. If you have only one adapter installed, the wizard will notify you that this configuration is not recommended because it introduces a single point of failure for communication between nodes.

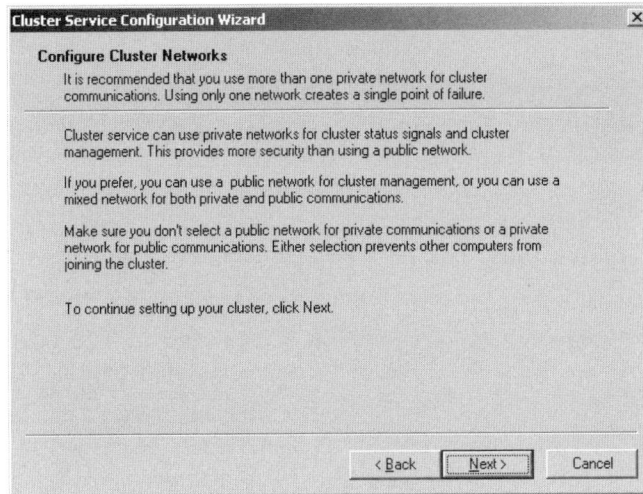

Figure 3.6   The Configure Cluster Networks page

Network Connections

The Network Connections page, shown in Figure 3.7, allows you to configure the cluster to allow it to communicate properly.

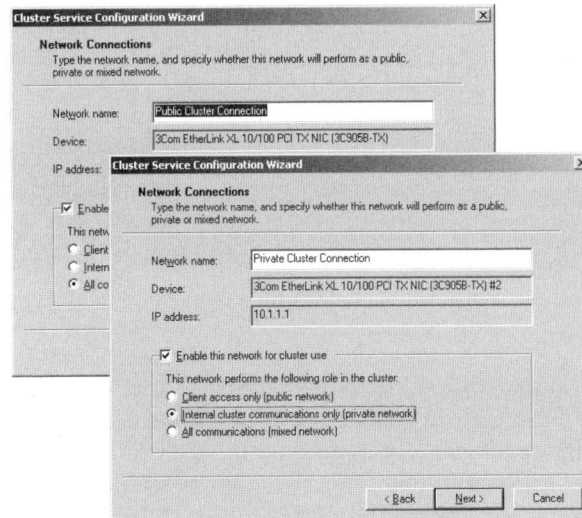

Figure 3.7   The Network Connections page

This page contains the following properties:

- **Network Name**   In the Network Name text box, enter the name of the connection. This should match the name used for the private network connection.

By naming your connections appropriately based on their use, it will be easier to manage and maintain the cluster. This is especially important when multiple administrators are managing the cluster.

- **Device**   The Device text box is populated automatically with the name of the network adapter currently being configured. Your server should have more than one adapter, so you should make sure to apply the private network settings and public network settings on the appropriate adapter.

- **IP Address**   In the IP Address text box, enter the IP address that the cluster will use to communicate with the other nodes in the cluster.

- **Enable This Network For Cluster Use**   If you select this option, Cluster Service will use this network adapter by default.

- **Client Access Only (Public Network)**   When this option is selected, the public network adapter will be used by the cluster only for communication with clients. No node-to-node communication will occur on this adapter. You should select this option only if you have another adapter that can act as a backup if the primary private adapter becomes unavailable.

- **Internal Cluster Communications Only (Private Network)**   If you select this option, Cluster Service will not use this adapter for any client communication. This adapter will be used only for internal node-to-node communication within the cluster. You should configure the second adapter in each node to act as a backup for this adapter in the event of a failure.

- **All Communications (Mixed Network)**   By default, this option is selected for the adapter card you are configuring. It specifies that Cluster Service can use this card for client communication as well as private, node-to-node communication. You should select this option if you have only two adapters and the other adapter is being used exclusively for node-to-node communication. If the other adapter fails, this adapter will assume responsibility for all cluster communication.

Internal Cluster Communication

The Internal Cluster Communication page, shown in Figure 3.8, allows you to change the order of the adapters for use by Cluster Service.

Cluster Service attempts to use the first adapter listed for node-to-node communication and will move to the next card if the first fails. Therefore, because Private Cluster Connection is used for private cluster communication between nodes, it should be placed at the top of the list. The second and all remaining adapters should be listed next, in order of their configuration for private communication. In the event of a failure, Cluster Service will automatically try the next adapter in the list.

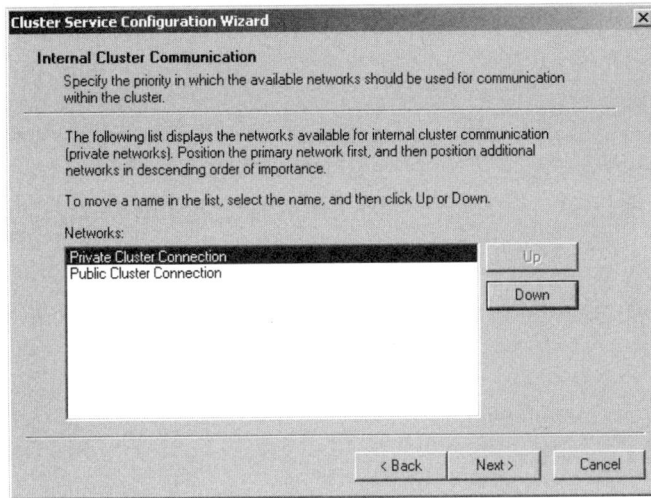

Figure 3.8 The Internal Cluster Communication page

Cluster IP Address

The Cluster IP Address page, shown in Figure 3.9, requires you to enter the public IP address assigned to the cluster.

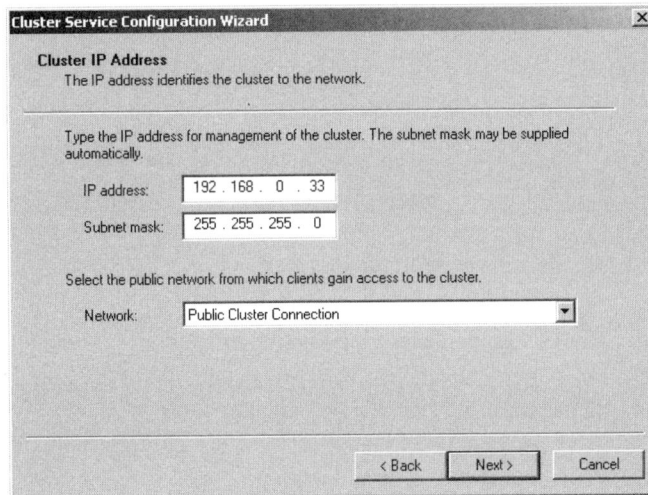

Figure 3.9 The Cluster IP Address page

This address is used for accessing the cluster for remote management by an administrator. You must use a unique static IP address that is available and accessible from your corporate network. You must also enter the appropriate subnet mask for this IP address. If you enter an invalid IP address or subnet mask, the wizard will not allow you to proceed.

Practice: Installing Cluster Service

In this practice, you will install Cluster Service on an existing Windows 2000 Advanced Server. You should already have Windows 2000 Advanced Server installed and configured on both nodes (and the shared device). (For information on how to do this, see the practices in Chapter 2.)

To see a demonstration of this practice, run the Cluster Install demonstration located in the Media folder on the companion CD.

Creating a Cluster User Account

1. On the first server, from the Windows 2000 Start menu, point to Programs, point to Administrative Tools, and then click Active Directory Users and Computers.

2. If reskit.com is not already expanded, click the plus sign to expand it.

3. Click Users.

4. Right-click Users, point to New, and click User.

5. In the First Name text box, type *ClusterAdmin*.

6. In the Last Name text box, type *Account*.

7. In the User Logon Name text box, type *clusteradmin*.

8. Click Next.

9. In the Password text box, type a password.

10. In the Confirm Password text box, type the same password.

11. Select the User Cannot Change Password and Password Never Expires check boxes.

12. Click Next.

13. Click Finish.

14. In the right pane of the Active Directory Users And Computers snap-in, right-click the Cluster ServiceAdmin Account and click Add Members To Group.

15. Click Administrators, and then click OK.

16. Close the Active Directory Users And Computers window.

Configuring the First Node

You must have the Windows 2000 Advanced Server CD-ROM in order to do this exercise. The second server to be included in this cluster must be turned off before you start.

1. On the first server, from the Windows 2000 Start menu, point to Settings, and click Control Panel.

2. Double-click Add/Remove Programs.

3. Double-click Add/Remove Windows Components.

4. Select Cluster Service.

5. Click Next.

6. The setup program will start copying files, and the Cluster Server Configuration Wizard will open. Click Next.

7. On the Hardware Configuration page, click I Understand and click Next.

8. You must now create the cluster. Select the This Is The First Node In The Cluster option, and then click Next.

9. On the Cluster Name page, enter the name *MyCluster* in the text box and click Next.

10. On the Select An Account page, enter the user name and password you created in the Creating A Cluster User Account exercise on the previous page. Click Next.

11. On the Add Or Remove Managed Disks page, which displays the SCSI disks that reside on the shared SCSI bus, add or remove disks as necessary. Click Next.

12. On the Cluster File Storage page, designate the disk drive on which to store the cluster's checkpoint and log files. Click Next.

13. On the Configure Cluster Networks page, click Next.

14. The Network Connections page will appear for each network adapter installed on your server. If this page is associated with the public adapter, skip to steps 19 through 23. Then return to this step to configure the private adapter.

15. Verify that the network name and IP address correctly identify the private network.

16. Verify that the Enable This Network For Cluster Use check box is selected.

17. Select the Internal Cluster Communications Only (Private Network) option.

18. Click Next.

19. The Network Connections page will appear again, this time for the public adapter.

20. Verify that the network name and IP address correctly identify the public network.

21. Verify that the Enable This Network For Cluster Use check box is selected.

22. Select the All Communications (Mixed Network) option.

23. Click Next.

24. The Internal Cluster Communication page, which appears next, lets you change the order of how the networks are used. Private Cluster Connection is a direct connection between nodes, so you should move it to the top of the list, if necessary, by selecting it and clicking on the Up button on the right.

This connection is used for normal communication between the nodes. However, in the case of a failure, Cluster Service will automatically attempt to use the next network in the list. Click Next.

Note Be sure that Private Cluster Connection is always first in the list.

25. On the Cluster IP Address page, enter the cluster's unique IP address (192.168.0.3) and the subnet mask (255.255.255.0). If you are connecting this cluster to your corporate LAN, be sure to enter an appropriate IP address and subnet mask.

26. Select Public Cluster Connection from the Network list. (Note: If you did not complete the practice in Chapter 2 or did not rename your network connection, Public Network Connection will not appear in this list.)

27. Click Next.

28. Click Finish to complete the Cluster Service installation.

29. The installation will complete and Cluster Service will start. Click OK when prompted.

30. Click Finish to close the wizard.

Verifying the Cluster Service Installation on the First Node

1. On the first server, from the Windows 2000 Start menu, point to Programs, point to Administrative Tools, and click Cluster Administrator.

2. Cluster Administrator should look like Figure 3.10. If you cannot open Cluster Administrator or if you see errors in it, the Cluster Service installation did not complete successfully or your node is incorrectly configured.

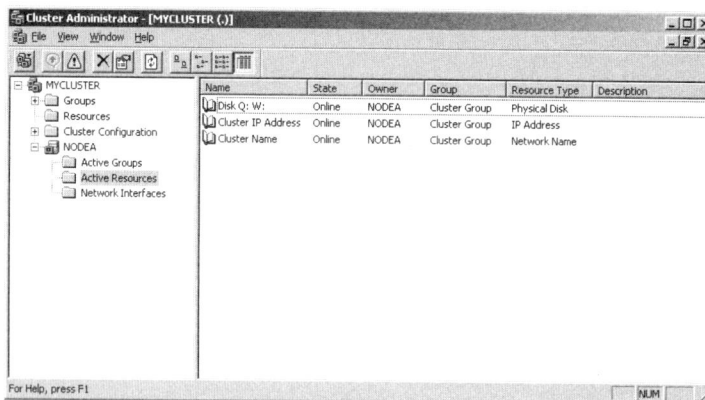

Figure 3.10   Cluster Administrator

3. Close Cluster Administrator.

Configuring the Second Node

For this exercise, the first node must be running with Cluster Service started.

1. Boot the second server and log in with an account that has administrative permissions.

2. From the Windows 2000 Start menu, point to Programs, point to Settings, and point to Control Panel.

3. Double-click Add/Remove Programs.

4. Double-click Add/Remove Windows Components.

5. Select Cluster Service.

6. Click Next.

7. The setup program will start copying files, and the Cluster Server Configuration Wizard will open. Click Next.

8. On the Hardware Configuration page, click I Understand, and then click Next.

9. You already created the cluster in the first exercise, so you want to join an existing cluster. Select the Second Or Next Node In The Cluster option. (If at least one other node already exists, you are joining a cluster.)

10. Click Next.

11. On the Cluster Name page, type the name of the cluster you created when you configured the first node (MyCluster).

12. Leave the Connect To Cluster As check box cleared. If the check box is selected, clear it.

13. Click Next.

14. On the Select An Account page, enter the password for the account listed and click Next.

15. Click Finish on the Completing The Cluster Service Configuration Wizard page.

16. The wizard will now copy the files needed for Cluster Service. Once the files are copied, the setup program will try to start Cluster Service. A message will appear stating that Cluster Service has been started. Click OK.

17. Click Finish on the Completing The Windows Components Wizard page.

Lesson Summary

This lesson introduced the installation modes supported by Cluster Service. Typically, you install Cluster Service when you install Windows 2000 Advanced Server. However, you can also manually install Cluster Service on an existing installation of Windows 2000 Advanced Server. In addition, through the use of an answer file, you can automate the setup process in order to perform an unattended installation. This lesson provided information about the creation and customization of answer files and provided a practice to demonstrate the installation of Cluster Service.

Lesson 2: Verifying the Cluster Service Installation

You can use a number of ways to verify that Cluster Service was installed and configured correctly. This lesson discusses each technique in terms of a cluster-related tool or a tool that's included in Windows 2000.

After this lesson, you will be able to
- List the techniques for verifying your cluster installation
- Use tools such as Cluster Administrator to verify your cluster

Estimated lesson time: 60 minutes

Cluster-Related Verification Techniques

After you install Cluster Service, you can verify the state of a cluster using various tools. In addition, if you have access to the Windows 2000 Server Resource Kit, you have an additional verification utility at your disposal.

Cluster Administrator

Cluster Administrator, which you can find among Administrative Tools, is installed automatically on each node when Cluster Service is installed. Cluster Administrator, or Cluadmin.exe, presents information about the groups and resources currently managed by this cluster. It also provides access to information about the cluster itself.

You can use Cluster Administrator from any node in the cluster to verify that your cluster is operating correctly. For example, as long as you can access the cluster, Cluster Administrator will visually present problems associated with Cluster Service and allow you to manually move resource groups from one node to another. The practice included later in this lesson will show you how to use Cluster Administrator to verify the installation of your cluster.

Cluster.exe

Included with Cluster Service is a second administrative application called Cluster.exe. You can use Cluster.exe to manage the cluster from the command line. You can also use it to execute cluster-related commands from scripts and to connect to the cluster to verify that it is operating correctly. See Microsoft TechNet for a complete list of the command line parameters supported by Cluster.exe.

Cluster Verification Utility

The Cluster Verification utility is a tool that ships with the Windows 2000 Server Resource Kit. It is also available at *www.microsoft.com/windows2000/library/ resources/reskit/tools/default.asp*. This tool allows you to verify that the two nodes in the cluster can communicate with each other and that they can both access the same shared drives.

Verification Tools in Windows 2000

You can also use tools included with Windows 2000 for verifying the state of the cluster. These include standard Windows utilities and general administrative tools for monitoring the overall health and state of a server running Windows 2000.

Service Failure or Shutdown

You can manually stop a required service, such as Cluster Service itself, to test your cluster configuration. This simulates a failure, so the failover process should begin. You can also manually shut down a node in order to start the failover process. Use Cluster Administrator on the working node to verify that all resource groups fail over as planned. Start the service, or reboot the second node, to verify that the failback process works correctly. Note that how you configure your resource groups will affect the results of these tests. For example, if you have specified that the failback process should happen after regular business hours, you might be constrained in your tests.

Services Snap-In

From the Administrative Tools menu, use the Services snap-in to verify that Cluster Service has started.

Ping Utility

Because the cluster has a unique network name and IP address, you should be able to open a command prompt and use the Ping utility to verify the name and address. If Cluster Service is running and the IP address and network name are valid, the Ping utility should be successful.

Cluster Service Registry Entries

You can verify that the Cluster Service installation process stored and updated the registry entries correctly by checking the HKEY_Local_Machine\Cluster key for the following entries:

- Groups
- Network interfaces
- Networks
- Nodes
- Quorum resources
- Resource types

Practice: Verifying the Cluster

Using Cluster Administrator

1. From the Windows 2000 Start menu on either node, point to Programs, point to Administrative Tools, and click Cluster Administrator.

2. In the left pane of Cluster Administrator, open each node to verify the resource being managed by both. If any errors exist, you will see groups, resources, or nodes marked as offline or unavailable.

Using the Cluster Verification Utility

As mentioned earlier, if you do not have the Windows 2000 Server Resource Kit, you can download this tool from *www.microsoft.com/windows2000/library/resources/reskit/tools/default.asp*.

1. Install the Cluster Verification utility on both nodes in the cluster. The installation asks you to specify where to install the utility. The default location is C:\Program Files\Resource Kit.

2. Insert a blank, preformatted floppy disk into drive A on the first node in the cluster.

3. Locate the file wpcvp.exe. (It should be at C:\Program Files\Resource Kit if you accepted the default installation path.)

4. Double-click wpcvp.exe. The Cluster Verification utility will open.

5. Click Verification.

6. In the Configuration Verification dialog box, enter the computer name, IP address, and shared drive letters of the cluster, as shown in Figure 3-11.

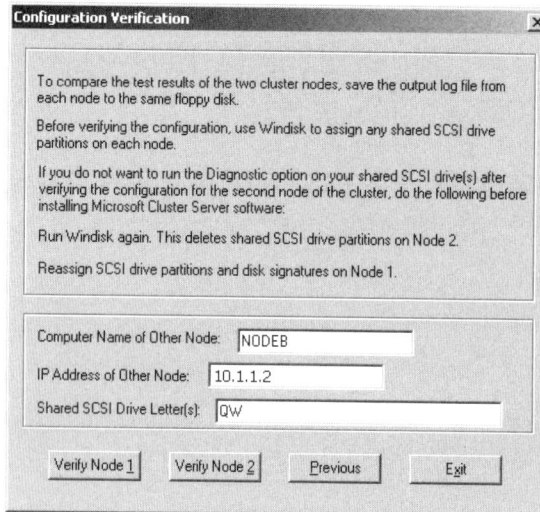

Figure 3.11   The Configuration Verification dialog box

7. Click Verify Node 1.

8. The Configuration dialog box will appear as shown in Figure 3-12, stating that the configuration (of the first node in the server) has passed the configuration test.

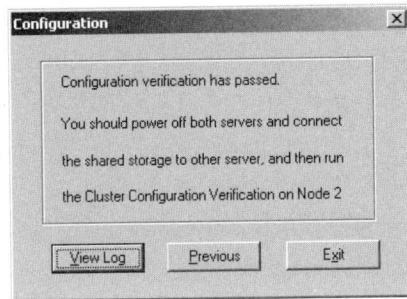

Figure 3.12   The Configuration dialog box

9. Power off both servers. Disconnect the SCSI cable from the first node in the cluster.

10. Remove the floppy disk from the A drive on the first node, and place it into the A drive of the second node.

11. Repeat steps 3 through 6. Then click Verify Node 2.

12. The Configuration dialog box will appear, stating that the configuration (of the second node in the server) has passed.

Lesson Summary

After you install Cluster Service on each node in the cluster, you can use the techniques described in this lesson to verify that the installation was successful. For example, you can use Cluster Administrator to check the settings on a Cluster Service installation. This assumes, of course, that you have successfully installed Cluster Administrator. This lesson also discussed other options, such as verifying registry settings and checking the service itself. A practice was also included for verifying the cluster installation that was described in Lesson 1 of this chapter.

Lesson 3: Upgrading a Cluster to Windows 2000

Microsoft Windows NT 4 Enterprise Edition introduced the ability to upgrade the operating systems of each node in a cluster without interrupting service. This process, called a *rolling upgrade*, also applies to Cluster Service included with Windows 2000 Advanced Server. This lesson explains the concept of performing a rolling upgrade and includes an optional practice for performing a rolling upgrade from a Windows NT 4 Enterprise Edition cluster to a Windows 2000 Advanced Server cluster.

After this lesson, you will be able to

- Explain the concept of a rolling upgrade
- Describe when to use a rolling upgrade
- List which operating systems support rolling upgrades
- Perform a rolling upgrade from Windows NT 4 Server Enterprise Edition

Estimated lesson time: 45 minutes

Overview of Rolling Upgrades

A rolling upgrade is a planned process that takes one node offline to be upgraded while a second node assumes full responsibility for the resources in the cluster. This process is typically used to upgrade an operating system, but it can also be used to apply service packs to the operating systems on each node. Rolling upgrades can also apply to non–operating system upgrades, such as installing the latest version of a mission-critical application across the nodes in the cluster or upgrading hardware on a node.

Note Windows 2000 Datacenter Server does not support rolling upgrades to the operating system. You can perform a rolling upgrade only from Windows NT 4 to Windows 2000 Advanced Server. However, after you install Windows 2000 Datacenter Server, you can perform rolling upgrades to the operating system, applications, or hardware.

Cluster Service also supports a mixed-mode cluster, which includes nodes that are running different operating systems, such as Windows NT 4 on a legacy server and Windows 2000 on a new server. Cluster Service will have the same level of availability as when both nodes are running the same operating system. This also means that a server running Windows NT 4 can join a Windows 2000 Server cluster running in mixed mode, and vice-versa.

Performing a Rolling Upgrade

A rolling upgrade must be performed in four steps:

Step 1: Preliminary Tasks

- Each node must be running Windows NT 4 Enterprise Edition, Service Pack 4 or later.
- Microsoft Cluster Server (MSCS) must be running on each node.
- If the cluster has Internet Information Services (IIS) as a resource, it should be IIS 4.
- The latest Windows NT 4 Enterprise Edition Service Pack must be applied to each node after MSCS and IIS have been installed, even if it was previously applied.

Step 2: Upgrade the First Node

- Pause the first node so that the second node handles all of the cluster resources.
- Upgrade the first node to Windows 2000 Advanced Server.

Step 3: Upgrade the Second Node

- Configure the first node to rejoin the cluster.
- Pause the second node so that the first node handles all of the cluster resources.
- Upgrade the second node to Windows 2000 Advanced Server.

Step 4: Final Tasks

- Configure the second node to rejoin the cluster.
- Distribute resource groups to their appropriate nodes if needed.

Advantages of Rolling Upgrades

There are several advantages to performing a rolling upgrade.

- Performing a rolling upgrade allows for minimal interruption of service to clients. The only impact is on the performance of the cluster when one of the nodes is being upgraded.
- Your cluster configuration remains intact while you perform a rolling upgrade. You do not need to reconfigure any of the applications, services, resource groups, or virtual servers that existed before the upgrade. Furthermore, the setup and configuration of your SCSI and network adapters is already in place and does not need to be reconfigured.

- A rolling upgrade reduces risk in the event of an upgrade failure. Because service to clients has not been interrupted, the server being upgraded can be repaired or replaced at your discretion without the added pressure of downtime for clients.

- A rolling upgrade allows for flexibility in scheduling the upgrade. Typically, server downtime for planned upgrades would need to be scheduled after normal business hours. When you use a rolling upgrade, you can perform a planned upgrade during the normal workday.

Limitations on Rolling Upgrades

The limitations on performing a rolling upgrade are in effect when you run both Windows NT 4 Enterprise and Windows 2000 Advanced Server in the same cluster. This mixed-version cluster requires that the different versions of the operating system running on each node be able to communicate with one another. This requirement results in the following restrictions:

- You can perform a rolling upgrade only if you have at least Service Pack 4 or later installed on Windows NT 4 Enterprise Edition. Having the latest Service Pack is recommended.

- Every resource managed by the cluster must be capable of being upgraded along with the operating system.

- When a resource is moved to another node, it must be temporarily stopped. Open client connections will be interrupted. Therefore, while a rolling upgrade can occur during a regular business day, it still requires careful planning.

- With a two-node cluster, the second node managing all cluster resources could potentially fail during the upgrade of the first server.

- Not all applications support a rolling upgrade. Be sure you know which applications supported by the cluster are not capable of supporting a rolling upgrade and what steps you must take to bring them back online after the upgrade.

In general, applications can support a rolling upgrade if they do not

- Store any program files on a shared disk
- Change the resource DLL's name or location
- Delete application registry keys in the system registry or in the cluster database
- Change application on-disk data structures

If these limitations cannot be overcome, you should find an alternative to performing a rolling upgrade.

Rolling Upgrade Considerations

When you perform a rolling upgrade to a Windows NT 4 Server Enterprise Edition node, you must take steps to ensure that the process is successful.

Location of Temporary Files

When you begin the Windows 2000 setup process, Winnt32 requires a drive location to store temporary files. You must ensure that this drive is not a clustered drive since the current node may not have control of the drive. Therefore, you should use the */tempdrive* command line parameter to specify a nonclustered drive for the temporary files. The following code is an example of the use of this parameter that specifies the F: drive for setup's temporary files:

```
Winnt32 /tempdrive:F
```

Print Spooler Resource

The Print Spooler resource does not support rolling upgrades for port types other than LPR and standard TCP/IP ports. You should not try to modify the print spooler or printer configuration while you're running a cluster in mixed mode. The Windows 2000 print processor is not compatible with Windows NT 4. If you're using the Enhanced Metafile (EMF) port processor, you should change it to raw data format before you begin the upgrade.

Time Service Resource

The Windows NT 4 version of MSCS uses the Time Service utility to synchronize time between the nodes in the cluster. With Windows 2000, the nodes use the domain controller for time management. Therefore, the Time Service resource that is associated with the original MSCS cluster must be taken offline and removed once the cluster has been updated to Windows 2000.

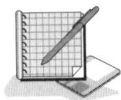

Optional Practice: Performing a Rolling Upgrade

In this optional practice, you'll perform a rolling upgrade from Windows NT 4 Server Enterprise Edition to Windows 2000 Advanced Server on a two-node cluster. Before starting, you should have installed a two-node cluster using Windows NT 4 Server Enterprise Edition. You must have compatible hardware and all of the required software for a MSCS cluster, plus your hardware should conform to the Windows 2000 Advanced Server Cluster Service HCL. You must also verify that the latest Service Pack has been applied to the Windows NT 4 servers.

For the purposes of this practice, the two nodes of the MSCS cluster will be NodeA and NodeB, and the domain name will be reskit.com.

Prepare for a Rolling Upgrade

1. Synchronize the time on all cluster nodes using the following command line:

   ```
   Net time /domain:reskit.com /set
   ```

2. From the Windows NT Start menu on NodeA, point to Programs, point to Administrative Tools, and then click Cluster Administrator.

3. If NodeA is not visible, click the plus sign in the left pane of Cluster Administrator to expand the cluster tree. Select NodeA.

4. From the File menu, click Pause Node. The status of NodeA will change to Paused.

5. In the right pane, double-click Active Groups.

6. In the right pane, select the first group.

7. From the File menu, click Move Group.

8. Repeat steps 6 and 7 for each group listed.

While you move each group, service to that group will be interrupted. Once all of the groups are moved, NodeB will manage all client requests and NodeA will be idle.

Upgrade NodeA

1. Start the Windows 2000 Advanced Server setup process to upgrade NodeA from Windows NT 4 Enterprise Edition. Setup will detect the earlier version of clustering on NodeA and automatically install Cluster Service for Windows 2000 Advanced Server. At the end of the upgrade, NodeA will automatically rejoin the cluster. However, it will still be paused and will be unavailable for managing any client requests to the cluster.

Note Be sure that the Windows 2000 Advanced Server setup process does not place its temporary files on a clustered disk. You can assign the drive for the temporary files by using the *tempdrive:X* command line parameter.

2. Perform tests on NodeA to verify that the node is functioning properly. For information on performing verification, see Lesson 2 earlier in this chapter.

Complete the Rolling Upgrade

1. From the Windows 2000 Start menu on NodeA, point to Programs, point to Administrative Tools, and then point to Cluster Administrator. You should see both nodes in the cluster. NodeA's state will be Paused and NodeB's state will be Up.

2. Click Resource Types to review the new resource types installed with the newer version of Cluster Service.

3. In Cluster Administrator, click NodeA.

4. From the File menu, click Resume Node.

5. Repeat these steps to perform the rolling upgrade on NodeB.

Once both nodes have been upgraded to Windows 2000 Advanced Server, you should take the Time Service resource offline and then delete it.

Remove the Time Service Resource

1. Open Cluster Administrator.

2. Click Cluster Group.

3. In the right pane, select the Time Service resource.

4. From the File menu, click Take Offline.

5. From the File menu, click Delete and then click Yes to confirm.

Lesson Summary

This lesson explained how to perform rolling upgrades of a cluster from Windows NT 4 Enterprise Edition to Windows 2000 Advanced Server or Windows 2000 Datacenter Server. A rolling upgrade is performed anytime you want to upgrade the operating system on a cluster node while maintaining the availability of the cluster to clients. However, you can also perform a rolling upgrade when you upgrade an application hosted on the cluster or upgrade a node's hardware. The optional practice described how to perform a rolling upgrade from Windows NT 4 Enterprise Edition to Windows 2000 Advanced Server. This lesson also discussed the advantages of rolling upgrades over other methods of upgrading a cluster and the limitations on performing rolling upgrades.

Review

The following questions are intended to reinforce key information presented in this chapter. The answers can be found in Appendix A.

1. When the Internal Communications Only (Private Network) option is selected for a network adapter, what is the result?

2. Which command-line option does the Cluster Service setup program use for an unattended installation?

   a. *-u*

   b. *-s*

   c. *-a*

   d. *-i*

3. Why should the private connection be listed first?

4. Which of the following applications is used to install Cluster Service?

   a. Sysprep.exe

   b. Cluscfg.exe

   c. Setup Manager

   d. Winnt.exe

5. Where can you find the Cluster Verification utility?

6. Which of the following must exist before you install Cluster Service?

   a. Three network adapters per node

   b. An IP address for the cluster

   c. A unique domain name for the cluster

   d. A domain account with administrative permission for Cluster Service

7. Which wizard page is displayed during the installation of the first node but not during the installation of the second node?

8. When you configure the Cluster Service account, which of the following user rights are required in addition to administrative permission?

   a. Log on as a service

   b. Act as part of the operating system

   c. Back up files and directories

   d. All of the above

9. In order to perform a rolling upgrade to Windows 2000 Advanced Server, which Windows NT operating system and service pack must you have installed on the existing cluster nodes?

10. Which of the following operating systems that uses MSCS supports a rolling upgrade to Windows 2000 Datacenter Server?

    a. Windows 2000 Advanced Server

    b. Windows NT 4 Enterprise Edition, Service Pack 5

    c. Windows NT 4 Enterprise Edition, Service Pack 6

    d. None of the above

C H A P T E R   4

Administering and Managing a Cluster

About This Chapter

This chapter describes how to administer and manage a cluster. The first lesson shows you how to administer a cluster using Cluster Administrator and the Cluster.exe command-line utility. Cluster Administrator can be run from any node in the cluster or, for remote administration purposes, on a computer that is not part of the cluster. This chapter also discusses how to implement resource groups on a cluster and how to configure resource dependencies. The practice provides steps for implementing file share resource groups. The chapter concludes with a lesson on how to manage nodes within a cluster.

Before You Begin

To complete the lessons in this chapter, you must have

- The necessary hardware as outlined in the section "About This Book" in the Introduction
- A two-node cluster installed

Lesson 1: Using the Cluster Administration Utilities

When you have Cluster Service installed on each node, you can use two utilities included with Cluster Service to administer the cluster: Cluster Administrator, which provides a graphical user interface (GUI), and Cluster.exe, which is a command-line utility. Cluster Administrator can be run from any node to manage the entire cluster. Cluster.exe is run from the command line, allowing you to execute administrative tasks on multiple nodes or from a script. This lesson describes how to use both utilities.

After this lesson, you will be able to

- Describe the administrative utilities included with Cluster Service
- List common cluster administration tasks
- Describe when to use Cluster Administrator and when to use Cluster.exe
- Perform common administrative tasks using both Cluster Administrator and Cluster.exe

Estimated lesson time: 45 minutes

Using Cluster Administrator

Cluster Administrator (Cluadmin.exe) is the primary tool for cluster management, maintenance, and troubleshooting. On each node in the cluster, Cluster Administrator (shown in Figure 4.1) is installed automatically and placed on the Administrative Tools menu.

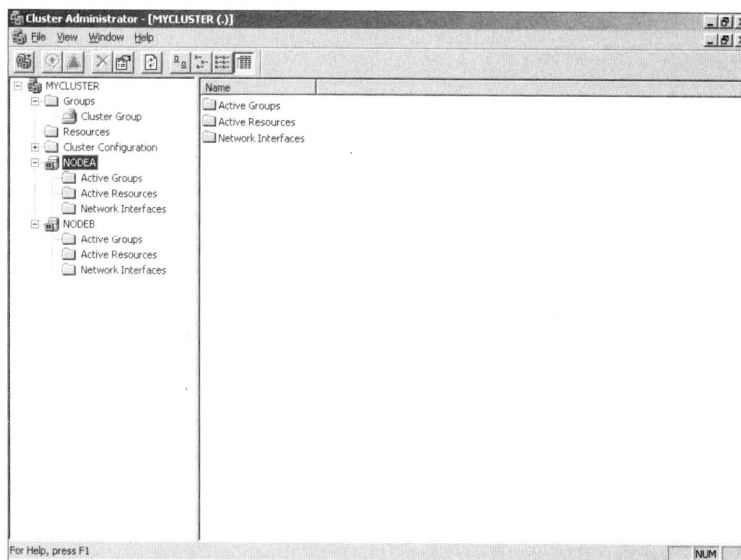

Figure 4.1   Cluster Administrator

In addition to using Cluster Administrator from any node in order to manage the cluster, you can install it on nonclustered computers for remote administration. The cluster domain must be able to authenticate the account you use on the remote system. To install it on a computer that is not part of the cluster, you can use the Adminpak.msi installer file included with Windows 2000.

Cluster Administrator supports the following operating systems:

- Windows NT 4 Server Enterprise Edition, Service Pack 3
- Windows 2000 Server
- Windows 2000 Advanced Server
- Windows 2000 Datacenter Server

To install Cluster Administrator manually on a computer that isn't a node of a cluster, follow these steps:

1. From the Windows 2000 Start menu, click Run.
2. Type *Adminpak.msi* and press Enter.
3. Follow the instructions on the screen.

After the installation is complete, Cluster Administrator will be listed on the Windows 2000 Administrative Tools menu.

Starting Cluster Administrator

When you open Cluster Administrator for the first time, you will be prompted to enter the cluster name, or individual node, that you want to connect to. Once Cluster Administrator is connected to a cluster, you can manage any node within that cluster.

If you are not sure of the cluster name, you can use the Browse command, as shown in Figure 4.2, to obtain a list of all the clusters in your current domain. If you are opening Cluster Administrator on a node within a cluster, you can enter a single period (.) to specify that it should connect to the current cluster. You can also connect to more than one cluster simultaneously, although this might slow the performance of Cluster Administrator.

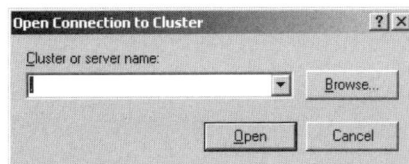

Figure 4.2   Cluster Administrator's Open Connection To Cluster dialog box

You should use only a given node's name if you cannot connect to the cluster directly. (This might be the case if the cluster is configured incorrectly or there is a problem with Cluster Service.)

When you start Cluster Administrator, any previously opened connections will be restored automatically. You will be asked only to specify a cluster name or node name if there are no previous connections to restore.

Common Cluster Administrator Tasks

The following list describes some of the most common tasks that Cluster Administrator is used for.

- **Creating new resources and resource groups**   Cluster Administrator includes wizards to help you add a new resource or create a new resource group in the cluster. This includes assigning resource dependencies. You cannot configure all resource and group properties using the wizard. Once a resource or group has been created, you must use the object's property sheet to configure a group's failover and failback policy settings or a resource's Restart, LooksAlive, and Pending Timeout settings.

- **Renaming resources and resource groups**   You can use Cluster Administrator to rename groups and edit their properties.

- **Removing resources and resource groups**   Using Cluster Administrator, you can delete resources and groups. When a group is deleted, all the resources that were members of the group are also deleted. A resource cannot be deleted until all resources that depend on it are deleted.

- **Viewing default groups**   Every new cluster includes two default groups: the Cluster Group and the Disk Group. These groups contain default cluster settings and general information about failover policies for the cluster.

  The default Cluster Group includes the IP Address and Network Name resources for the cluster. The resource information presented in this group was entered when you configured the new cluster using the Cluster Service Configuration Wizard. This group is required for administration of the cluster and should not be renamed.

  The Disk Group is also created when you initially install Cluster Service. Each disk on the shared storage device will receive its own disk group that includes a Physical Disk resource.

  When you create new groups, you should implement them as modifications to the disk groups. You can then rename each group to something meaningful. For example, you might add resources to Disk Group 1 that will be used by your Web server. Once the resources have been added, you can rename Disk Group 1 to Web Group. The Cluster Group name does not change.

- **Modifying the state of groups and resources**   You can use Cluster Administrator to bring resources and groups online or take them offline. If you change the state of a group, all the resources within that group will be updated automatically. These resources have their state changed in the order of their dependencies.

- **Changing ownership**   Using Cluster Administrator, you can specify the ownership of a resource or an entire group. Resources are owned by groups, and groups, in turn, are owned by a node. You can transfer resources between groups to satisfy dependencies and application requirements. You can also transfer group ownership, using the Move Group command, to assign groups to other nodes in the cluster.

  You typically transfer group ownership when you need to bring down a node for maintenance or upgrades. When a group's ownership is moved to another node, all resources in that group are taken offline, the group is then transferred, and the resources are brought back online. As a result, you must carefully plan when to move groups because clients might be affected temporarily as the resources are shut down and then restarted.

  Once the resource ownership has changed, the resource will be automatically brought online. However, when a resource is moved between groups on the same node, it will not be taken offline.

- **Changing the maximum Quorum log size**   By default, the Quorum log file size is set to 64 KB. Depending on the number of shares supported on the cluster and the number of transactions managed by the cluster, this might be too small. In this case, you will receive a notification in the Event Viewer. When the Quorum log reaches the specified size, Cluster Service will save the database and reset the log file. If you change the Quorum size on one node, it will automatically take affect on the other.

- **Initiating a failure**   In order to help you test your failover policies, Cluster Administrator can initiate a failure. This feature also allows you to test the restart settings on individual resources.

- **Identifying failovers**   In addition to configuring and managing a cluster, Cluster Administrator can also quickly provide information on the health of the cluster. This is accomplished with indicators such as the Node Offline icon shown in Figure 4.3.

NODE2

Figure 4.3   The Node Offline icon

In this case, the node has been taken down and all resources that can be failed over have been failed over to the other node in the cluster. You should check the status of the nodes frequently to make sure the cluster is up and healthy. You can also use third-party software to help monitor your cluster. The overall performance of the cluster can be hurt if all the resources are running on a single node due to a failure. And if the second node fails, the cluster will be completely offline. You should periodically check the ownership of the various resource groups to verify that failover and failback policies are meeting expectations.

- **Renaming the cluster**   In some cases, you might need to rename the cluster. Because the name must be unique on the network, a conflict might occur that requires you to rename the cluster. Using Cluster Administrator, you can change the cluster's name, but the change will not take affect until you take the Cluster Name resource offline and bring it back online.

- **Deploying clustered applications**   Cluster Administrator includes a wizard to lead you through the process of adding an application to the cluster. Before starting the Cluster Application Wizard, you should have all the required information ready, such as a virtual server name, an IP address for the server, and your failover policy for the application. Table 4.1 describes the Cluster Application Wizard's required information.

Table 4.1   Required Cluster Application Wizard Information

Information	Description
IP address	If the application will run on a new virtual server, you need a unique IP address. You do not need an IP address if your application will run on an existing virtual server.
Virtual server	Even though the application resides on the cluster, clients access the application using a standard computer name. If you do not want to run the application on an existing virtual server, the wizard will prompt you for the new virtual server's name and a unique IP address. The wizard will then create the appropriate resource group and implement the virtual server.
Resource type for your application	The wizard lets you create a resource to manage your application. You must select the appropriate resource type for your needs.
Application resource name	If you use the wizard to create a resource for your application, you must name the resource.
Application resource dependencies	If the application requires other resources in order to run, you can create resource dependencies using the wizard.

- **Changing the Quorum resource location**   You can use Cluster Administrator to configure the location of the Quorum resource after you install Cluster Service. The cluster's Property page includes a Quorum tab with a number of settings, including the location of the Quorum resource. You can edit and reconfigure the Quorum resource settings as needed.

Using Cluster.exe

In addition to managing your cluster using the GUI-based Cluster Administrator, you can also execute administrative tasks from the command line. For example, you might need to configure a property on more than one cluster. Using Cluster.exe, you can set properties through a single command execution. You can also execute command line tasks from within a script to automate the configuration of many clusters, nodes, resources, and resource groups.

Cluster.exe is automatically installed with Cluster Service on each node. You can also run Cluster.exe in Windows NT 4 Server Enterprise Edition with Service Pack 3 or later.

Note Unlike Cluster Administrator, Cluster.exe does not automatically restore previous connections when you use it to administer a cluster.

Table 4.2 describes the primary arguments supported by Cluster.exe. For a complete listing of the properties and options supported by each command, see Appendix B.

All but the first two options listed in Table 4.2 apply to the /CLUSTER options. If these options are used alone, Cluster.exe will attempt to connect to the cluster on the node that is running Cluster.exe and apply the command-line option to this cluster.

Table 4.2   Cluster.exe Command-Line Arguments

Argument	Description
/LIST[:domain-name]	Displays a list of clusters in the specified domain. If no domain is specified, the domain that the computer belongs to is used. Do not use the cluster name with this option.
[[/CLUSTER:]cluster-name] <options>	If you do not specify the cluster name, Cluster.exe will attempt to connect to the cluster running on the node that is running Cluster.exe. If the name of your cluster is also a cluster command or its abbreviation, such as *cluster* or *c*, use */cluster:* to explicitly specify the cluster name.
/PROP[ERTIES] [<prop-list>]	Displays or sets the cluster's common properties. See Appendix B for more information on common properties.
/PRIV[PROPERTIES] [<prop-list>]	Displays or sets the cluster's private properties. See Appendix B for more information on private properties.
/REN[AME]:cluster-name	Renames the cluster to the specified name.
/VER[SION]	Displays the Cluster Service version number.
/QUORUM[RESOURCE][:resource-name] [/PATH:path] [/MAXLOGSIZE:max-size-kbytes]	Changes the name or location of the Quorum resource or the size of the Quorum log.

Table 4.2   Cluster.exe Command-Line Arguments   *(continued)*

Argument	Description
/REG[ADMIN]EXT:admin-extension-dll[,admin-extension-dll...]	Registers a Cluster Administrator extension DLL with the cluster.
/UNREG[ADMIN]EXT:admin-extension-dll[,admin-extension-dll...]	Unregisters a Cluster Administrator extension DLL from the cluster.
NODE [node-name] node-command	A node-specific cluster command. See Appendix B for a list of available commands.
GROUP [group-name] group-command	A group-specific cluster command. See Appendix B for a list of available commands.
RES[OURCE] [resource-name] resource-command	A resource-specific cluster command. See Appendix B for a list of available commands.
{RESOURCETYPE|RESTYPE} [resourcetype-name] resourcetype-command	A resource type–specific cluster command. See Appendix B for a list of available commands.
NET[WORK] [network-name] network-command	A network-specific cluster command. See Appendix B for a list of available commands.
NETINT[ERFACE] [interface-name] interface-command	A network interface–specific cluster command. See Appendix B for a list of available commands.
/? Or /help	Displays cluster command line options and syntax.

Practice: Administering a Cluster Using Cluster Administrator

Opening Cluster Administrator

1. From either node in a cluster, open the Windows 2000 Start menu, point to Programs, point to Administrative Tools, and click Cluster Administrator.

2. Type the cluster's name, *Mycluster*, or a single period (.) to specify the current cluster, and then click OK. (Using the period notation for the cluster name is supported only when Cluster Administrator is running on a node in the cluster.) Cluster Administrator will open and connect to the current cluster.

Moving a Group to Another Node

1. From the Windows 2000 Start menu, point to Programs, point to Administrative Tools, and click Cluster Administrator.

2. If NodeA is not already expanded, click + to expand it.

3. Click Active Groups. Verify that the default Cluster Group is listed.

4. In the left pane, double-click Groups.

5. In the left pane, right-click Cluster Group and click Move Group. The group will be moved from NodeA to NodeB. Verify that the Owner column has been updated in the Cluster Administrator and now appears under NodeB's Active Groups.

6. Repeat the process to return the Cluster Group to NodeA.

Changing the Size of the Quorum Resource

1. In the left pane, right-click the cluster's name, MYCLUSTER, and click Properties.

2. Click the Quorum tab.

3. In the Reset Quorum Log field, type *128* and click OK.

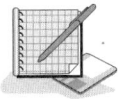

Practice: Administering a Cluster Using Cluster.exe

In this practice, you will use Cluster.exe to perform simple administrative tasks such as renaming the cluster, moving a resource group to another node, setting the maximum size of the Quorum log, pausing a node, and resuming a node.

Verifying That All Groups and Resources Are on NodeA

1. From the Windows 2000 Start menu, point to Programs, point to Administrative Tools, and click Cluster Administrator.

2. Click on the Groups folder in the tree. You will see a list of all the cluster groups in the right pane. Verify that the owner for each group is NodeA. At this point, the only group present is the Cluster Group.

3. If any group is owned by NodeB, right-click on the group and click Move Group to move the group to NodeA. Repeat this process until all groups are on NodeA.

4. Leave Cluster Administrator open for the remainder of this practice.

Moving a Resource Group to Another Node

1. Switch to the Windows 2000 command prompt window, type *cluster GROUP "Cluster Group" /MOVE:NODEB* at the command prompt, and press Enter. You should see the following message displayed:

```
Moving resource group 'Cluster Group'...
Group          Node    Status
-------------  ------  ------
Cluster Group  NODEB   Pending
```

2. Switch to Cluster Administrator and click on the plus sign to expand the Groups folder. Notice that the owner of Cluster Group is now NodeB.

Modifying the Maximum Quorum Log Size

1. Switch to the Windows 2000 command prompt window, type *cluster /QUORUM /MAXLOGSIZE:256* at the command prompt, and press Enter. This command will change the maximum allowed size of the Quorum log from the current value of 128 KB to 256 KB.

2. Switch to Cluster Administrator, right-click on MYCLUSTER, and click Properties.

3. In the MYCLUSTER Properties dialog box, click the Quorum tab. The Reset Quorum Log At field should show 256 KB.

4. Type *128* in the Reset Quorum Log At field and click OK. This will return the maximum Quorum log size to its original value.

Pausing and Resuming a Node

1. Switch to the Windows 2000 command prompt window, type *cluster NODE NODEA /PAUSE* at the command prompt, and press Enter. A message will indicate that NodeA has been paused.

2. Switch to Cluster Administrator. You should see an icon with a exclamation point in a yellow triangle on NodeA, indicating that it has been paused.

3. Switch to the Windows 2000 command prompt window, type *cluster NODE NODEA /RESUME* at the command prompt, and press Enter. A message will indicate that NodeA has resumed.

4. Switch to Cluster Administrator.

5. The icon indicating that NodeA was paused should no longer be present.

Lesson Summary

This lesson described techniques for administering a cluster using the two utilities provided with Cluster Service. Cluster Administrator provides a GUI for completing common tasks, while the Cluster.exe command line utility lets you administer a cluster from the command line or from a script. This lesson also described how to use Cluster Administrator from a computer that is not part of the cluster. Using the Adminpak.msi installer file, you can configure Cluster Administrator to run remotely across your network. The lesson concluded with a practice that described tasks that you might need to perform when administering a cluster.

Lesson 2: Configuring Resources, Resource Groups, and Virtual Servers

This lesson describes how to implement resources and resource groups in a cluster. It describes the default resource types and their common dependencies. Using the Generic Application and Generic Service resource types, you can increase the availability of cluster-unaware applications and services. The lesson also discusses failover and failback policies for resource groups. A practice details the steps for creating resources and implementing resource groups. Finally, this lesson shows you how to create and use virtual servers on a cluster.

After this lesson, you will be able to

- List the default resource types included with Cluster Service
- Describe common dependencies for applications and services
- Create a new resource and configure a resource group

Estimated lesson time: 45 minutes

Cluster Resource Types

Resources are categorized by type. Several default types are provided with Cluster Service. These are associated with resource DLLs. If you want to deploy a cluster-unaware application, the two generic resource types might meet the needs of your application. However, if your application cannot interact with the cluster using these resource types, you must create a custom resource DLL for the application. This will effectively make a cluster-unaware application cluster-aware. Not all applications can support a custom resource DLL. But if you can develop a resource DLL for an application, you will have a new resource type specific to that application. (The procedure for creating custom resource DLLs is outside the scope of this training kit.)

Standard Resource Types

A number of standard resource types are available for implementing applications and services. In addition, you can use specific types when you deploy certain applications and services such as Dynamic Host Configuration Protocol (DHCP) and Windows Internet Name Service (WINS).

The following are standard resource types that you can use when you configure applications on a cluster:

- **Physical Disk**   This resource type is for managing shared drives on your cluster. Because data corruption can occur if more than one node has control of the drive, the Physical Disk type allows you to configure which node has control of the resource at a given time.

- **DHCP and WINS**   Cluster Service provides direct support for both the DHCP and WINS services. Using the DHCP resource type, you can implement the DHCP service on your cluster. Likewise, using the WINS resource type, you can install WINS for client use. In both cases, you can install the databases associated with these services on a shared drive to support failover from one node to another. For complete information about implementing these services, see Chapter 6.

- **Print Spooler**   Using this resource type, you can configure your cluster to support network printers. Only network printers are supported on the cluster because a locally connected printer will not fail over. You can implement multiple print spoolers on a cluster, but no more than one can appear in a given resource group. Clients can access the clustered network printer using standard network names or IP addresses.

  If a Print Spooler resource fails over, the document that was being printed at the time will start over on the other node. If a Print Spooler resource is taken offline or is manually moved, Cluster Service will attempt to first finish any queued print jobs. Any documents that are currently spooling will be discarded. They must be resubmitted once the resource group finishes failing over to the other node.

  In addition to creating a Print Spooler resource, you must ensure that each node in the cluster has the appropriate ports and drivers configured for the printer. A complete practice illustrating how to implement clustered print spoolers is provided later in this chapter.

- **File Share**   Using this resource type, you can cluster drive access points if the cluster is acting as a file server. There are three File Share resource types:

  - **Basic**   A basic File Share resource provides high availability to a single folder using a standard network share name

  - **Share subdirectories**   The File Share resource can be used to cluster a number of folders and their subfolders in subdirectories. This provides an easy way to increase availability for large numbers of folders on a clustered file server.

  - **DFS root**   The File Share resource can also be used to cluster a distributed file system root folder (DFS root). Like the other File Share resource types, a DFS root can be accessed by using a network name and the associated IP address. Therefore, dependent Network Name and IP Address resources must be associated with the clustered DFS root. Note, however, that you cannot implement fault tolerant DFS roots on a cluster.

- **IP Address**   A number of cluster implementations require IP addresses. The IP Address resource type is used for this purpose. Typically, the IP Address resource is used with a Network Name resource in order to create a virtual server.

- **Network Name**   This resource type is used to assign a name to a resource on the cluster. This is typically associated with an IP Address resource type in order to create a virtual server. Many applications and services that you might want to cluster require a virtual server.

- **Generic Application**   When you implement an application that is not cluster-aware, you can use this resource type to provide basic clustering capabilities. If the application qualifies to be clustered and can support being terminated and restarted as the result of a failover, the Generic Application type might be all that is required to increase the the the application's availability. If the application is not compatible with the generic type, you might need to implement a cluster resource DLL in order for the application to support Cluster Service.

  When you implement a cluster-unaware application using the Generic Application resource type, you must verify that the application can run from both nodes in the cluster. This includes installing copies of the application on each node. If you want the application to support failing over, you must configure it to use a shared disk for data storage. In this way, if the application fails over to the other node, it can still access the required data.

  An alternative to installing the application on each node is to install the application to a shared disk. While this implementation offers the benefit of using less drive space (because it does not have to be installed twice), it does not support rolling upgrades. If you intend to perform rolling upgrades to the application, the application will need to be installed locally on each node.

- **Generic Service**   This is similar to the Generic Application resource type. If you intend to support a cluster-unaware service, you can use the Generic Service resource type for basic cluster functionality. This resource type will provide only the most fundamental level of clustering services. If your service requires advanced clustering support, you must develop and use a custom resource DLL for the service.

Cluster Resource Dependencies

When you configure a cluster resource, you often need to implement dependencies for the resource. A resource with dependencies requires additional resources in order to operate correctly. All the resources associated with the application or service must be configured in the same resource group. Cluster Service brings resources online, or takes them offline, based on the dependencies you specify. For example, if an application is dependent on Network Name and IP Address resources, Cluster Service ensures that these resources are available before the application starts. Table 4.3 lists common resources and their dependencies.

Table 4.3   Common Resource Dependencies

Resource	Dependencies (Required or Recommended)
DHCP Service	▪ Physical Disk or other storage class device (on which the files are located) ▪ IP Address (for client access to the DHCP server) ▪ Network Name
Distributed Transaction Coordinator	▪ Physical Disk or other storage class device ▪ Network Name
File Share	▪ Network Name (for a file share that is configured as a DFS root). A file share that is not DFS has no required dependencies.
Generic Application	None
Generic Service	None
IIS Server Instance	▪ IP Address (that corresponds to the virtual root) ▪ Physical Disk or other storage class device ▪ Network Name (so that remote clients can access it)
IP Address	None
Message Queuing	▪ Physical Disk or other storage class device ▪ Network Name (so that remote clients can access it)
Network Name	▪ IP Address (that corresponds to the name)
Physical Disk	None
Print Spooler	▪ Physical Disk or other storage class device ▪ Network Name (so that remote clients can access it)
WINS Service	▪ Physical Disk or other storage class device ▪ IP Address (for client access to the WINS server) ▪ Network Name

Resource-Specific Properties

In addition to the standard properties that each resource type includes, such as name and description, specific properties might need to be configured. Table 4.4 lists resource-specific properties.

Table 4.4   Resource-Specific Properties

Resource	Property
DHCP Service	▪ DHCP database file path ▪ DHCP database files backup path ▪ Audit log file location
Distributed Transaction Coordinator	None
File Share	▪ Access permissions ▪ Simultaneous user limit ▪ Share name and comment ▪ Path
Generic Application	▪ Command line ▪ Current directory ▪ Use network name for computer name ▪ Whether the application can interact with the desktop
Generic Service	▪ Service name ▪ Startup parameters ▪ Use network name for computer name
IIS Server Instance	▪ Service for this instance (FTP or WWW) ▪ Alias used by the virtual root
IP Address	▪ IP address ▪ Subnet mask ▪ Network parameters ▪ NetBIOS option
MSMQ Server	None
Network Name	▪ Computer name
Physical Disk	▪ Drive to be managed (cannot change once the resource has been configured)
Print Spooler	▪ Path for the print spooler folder ▪ Job completion time-out
WINS Service	▪ Path to WINS database ▪ Path to WINS backup database

Cluster Resource Groups

Resources must be organized into groups, called *resource groups*, which are managed by Cluster Service. In addition to the general properties such as name, description, and preferred owner, groups also have failover and failback properties. Together, these properties control how the resource group and the associated application or service responds when a node is taken offline.

Failover Policy

The failover policy for a group is set using the Failover tab of the group's property sheet. You can set the Failover Threshold and Failover Period properties based on your needs. The Failover Threshold specifies the number of times the group can fail within the number of hours specified by the Failover Period property. If the group fails more than the threshold value, Cluster Service will leave the affected resource within the group offline. For example, if a group Failover Threshold is set to 3 and its Failover Period is set to 8, Cluster Service will fail over the group up to three times within an eight-hour period. The fourth time a resource in the group fails, Cluster Service will leave the resource in the offline state instead of failing over the group. All other resources in the group will be unaffected.

Failback Policy

By default, resource groups are not configured to fail back to the original node. Instead, after a failover, the group remains on the second node until you manually move the group to the appropriate node. If you want a group to run on a preferred node and return to that node after a failover, you must implement a failback policy for the group. You can specify whether the group should fail back immediately after the original node comes back online or at a specified time during the day. For example, you might want to fail back a group only during non-business hours to minimize the impact on clients. In order for a group to fail back to a specific node, you must set the Preferred Owners property of the group.

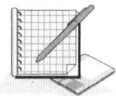

Practice: Creating a File Share Resource

In this practice, you will configure a File Share resource and associated group and then manually bring the group online.

Creating a Group

1. Open Cluster Administrator. The Open Connection To Cluster dialog box appears.

2. Type the name of the cluster (in this case, MYCLUSTER) and click Open.

3. Right-click Groups, point to New, and click Group. The New Group Wizard will start.

4. Type *Cluster Printer* in the Name box.

5. Type *Group For Printer Resources* in the Description box.

6. Click Next.

7. In the Preferred Owners dialog box, add both nodes to the Preferred Owners list.

8. Click Finish. A message box will appear stating that the group was created successfully.

9. Click OK.

Transferring a Resource

1. Open the Resources folder.

2. Right-click Disk W:, and from the popup menu that appears, click Change Group. A listing with all of the available groups in the cluster will appear.

3. Click the Cluster Printer group. A message box will appear asking if you are sure you want to change the group.

4. Click Yes. The Disk W: resource will be displayed as part of the Cluster Printer group. Having the disk resource as part of the group will allow you to add resources to the Cluster Printer group that have a dependency on a disk resource.

Creating a File Share Resource

Before you begin this practice, create a Test folder on drive W.

1. Click the Groups folder.

2. Right-click Cluster Printer, point to New, and click Resource.

3. In the New Resource dialog box, type in the information below:

Name	*Test Share A*
Description	*Test file share*
Resource Type	*Choose File Share*
Group	*Choose Cluster Printer*

4. Click Next.

5. Both nodes should appear in the Possible Owners list. If they do not, add them to the list.

6. Click Next.

7. In the Dependencies dialog box, add the Disk W: resource to the Resource Dependencies list and click Next.

8. In the File Share Parameters dialog box, type in the following information:

Share Name   *TestShareA*

Path   *W:\Test*

Comment   *Test share for the cluster*

Specifying the path will not automatically create the folder, so the test folder must already exist on the W: drive before this step can be successful.

9. Click Finish. A message box will appear stating that the file share was created successfully.

10. Click OK.

Bringing the Resources Online

1. Right-click Cluster Printer, and click Bring Online.

2. Close Cluster Administrator.

Virtual Server Overview

When an application is installed on a cluster, clients access the application as they would any normal server on the network. However, because the physical server itself can potentially change as the result of a failover, Cluster Service implements virtual servers for client access. A virtual server consists of a resource group that includes a dedicated, and unique, network name and IP address. Each virtual server therefore has its own failover and failback policy (as described earlier in this lesson). The virtual server also consists of one or more resources associated with the application being hosted. As a result, in the event of a failover, all the resources associated with the virtual server are moved to the other node in the cluster. Cluster Service reassigns the network name and IP address to the surviving node, and client requests continue to be sent to this virtual server. The client itself never needs to know which node is currently hosting the application.

A virtual server has the same basic characteristics as a physical server on the network, including the following:

- It allows clients access to network resources, such as file and print shares.

- It appears on the network as a normal, physical server.

- It has both a network name and IP address for client access.

Practice: Creating a Virtual Server

Creating a Group

1. Open Cluster Administrator.

2. In the Open Connection To Cluster dialog box, type the name of the cluster (in this case, MYCLUSTER) and click Open.

3. Right-click Groups, point to New, and click Group.

4. Type *Virtual Server* in the Name box.

5. Type *Group for virtual server* in the Description box.

6. Click Next.

7. In the Preferred Owners dialog box, add NodeA to the Preferred Owners list.

8. Click Finish. A message box will appear stating that the group was created successfully.

9. Click OK.

Creating an IP Address Resource

1. In Cluster Administrator, click the Groups folder.

2. Right-click Virtual Server, point to New, and click Resource.

3. In the New Resource dialog box, type in the information below:

Name	*Server IP Address*
Description	*IP address of virtual server*
Resource Type	*Choose IP Address*
Group	*Choose Virtual Server*

4. Click Next.

5. Both nodes should appear in the Possible Owners list. If they do not, add them to the list.

6. Click Next.

7. In the Dependencies dialog box, the Resource Dependencies list should be blank. Click Next.

8. In the TCP/IP Address Parameters dialog box, type in the following information:

Address	*192.168.0.2*
Subnet Mask	*255.255.255.0*
Network	*Public Cluster Connection*

   Do not select the Run This Resource In A Separate Resource Monitor check box. You can leave Enable NetBIOS For This Address selected. By default, NetBIOS calls can be made over the TCP/IP connection.

9. Click Finish. A message box will appear stating that the IP Address resource was created successfully.

10. Click OK.

Creating a Network Name Resource

1. Click the Groups folder.

2. Right-click Virtual Server, point to New, and click Resource.

3. In the New Resource dialog box, type in the information below:

Name	*Test Share A*
Name	*Network Name*
Description	*Network name for virtual server*
Resource Type	*Choose Network Name*
Group	*Choose Virtual Server*

   Do not select the Run This Resource In A Separate Resource Monitor check box.

4. Click Next.

5. NodeA should appear in the list of Possible Owners. If it does not, add it to the list.

6. Click Next.

7. In the Dependencies dialog box, add the server IP Address resource to the Resource Dependencies list and click Next.

8. In the Network Name Parameters dialog box, type *CLUSTERSVR*.

9. Click Finish. A message box will appear stating that the Network Name resource was created successfully.

10. Click OK.

Practice: Cluster Service Properties

Several properties for resources and groups determine the actions that occur during a failover or failback. To set these properties, you can use Cluster Administrator or the Cluster.exe command-line utility. This practice will introduce several of the properties that are important in configuring and monitoring the failover and failback processes.

Viewing Properties for a Cluster Service Group

1. From the Windows 2000 Start menu, point to Programs, point to Administrative Tools, and then click Cluster Administrator.

2. If needed, expand the My Cluster tree in the left pane.

3. Expand the Groups folder and then click on the Cluster Group in that folder.

4. Verify that the Cluster Group and all of its resources are online on the node you are using for this practice.

5. Right-click on Cluster Group and click Properties. View the settings on the Failover and Failback tabs.

6. From the Windows 2000 Start menu, click Run, and then type *command* in the Open field. Click OK to open a command window.

7. At the command prompt, type *cd\winnt\cluster*, and then press Enter.

8. At the command prompt, type *cluster group "Cluster Group" /prop*, and then press Enter. You should see a result similar to the following:

```
Listing properties for 'cluster group':
T     Resource Group      Name                 Value
--    --------------      -----------------    ---------------------
SR    Cluster Group       Name                 Cluster Group
S     Cluster Group       Description
D     Cluster Group       PersistentState      1 (0x1)
D     Cluster Group       FailoverThreshold    10 (0xa)
D     Cluster Group       FailoverPeriod       6 (0x6)
D     Cluster Group       AutoFailbackType     0 (0x0)
D     Cluster Group       FailbackWindowStart  4294967295 (0xffffffff)
D     Cluster Group       FailbackWindowEnd    4294967295 (0xffffffff)
D     Cluster Group       LoadBalState         1 (0x1)
```

The following are definitions for some of these group properties. (See Appendix B for more information on resource group properties and settings.)

- **PersistentState**   This property holds the last known state of a group or resource. When it is set to True, the group or resource is online. When it is set to False, the group or resource is offline.

- **FailoverThreshold**   This property specifies the number of times that Cluster Service will attempt to fail over a group before it decides that the group cannot be brought online anywhere in the cluster.

- **FailoverPeriod**   This property specifies the interval, in hours, during which Cluster Service will attempt to fail over a group.

- **AutoFailbackType**   This property specifies whether a Cluster Group is allowed to fail back. The ClusterGroupPreventFailback (0) setting prevents failback, and the ClusterGroupAllowFailback (1) setting allows failback.

- **FailbackWindowStart**   This property specifies the start time, on a 24-hour clock, for a group to fail back to its preferred node. You can set values from *0* (midnight) to *23* (11:00 P.M.) in local time for the cluster. For immediate failback, you must set both FailbackWindowStart and FailbackWindowEnd to −1.

- **FailbackWindowEnd**   This property specifies the end time, on a 24-hour clock, for a group to fail back to its preferred node. You can set values from *0* (midnight) to *23* (11:00 P.M.) in local time for the cluster. For immediate failback, you must set both FailbackWindowStart and FailbackWindowEnd to −1.

Setting Resource Group Failback Properties

1. At the command prompt, type *cluster group "Cluster Group" /prop AutoFailbackType = 1*, and then press Enter. This will set the Cluster Group to allow failback after a failover occurs.

2. At the command prompt, enter the following commands to set the Cluster Group to fail back only between 8 A.M. and 6 P.M.:

```
cluster group "Cluster Group" /Prop FailbackWindowStart = "8"
cluster group "Cluster Group" /Prop FailbackWindowEnd = "18"
```

3. In Cluster Administrator, right-click on Cluster Group, and then click Properties. On the Failback tab, you should see that failback is allowed between the 8th and 18th hours, as seen in Figure 4.4. Click OK to close the Cluster Group Properties dialog box.

4. At the command prompt, enter the following commands to set the Cluster Group to fail back immediately:

```
cluster group "Cluster Group" /Prop FailbackWindowStart = "-1"
cluster group "Cluster Group" /Prop FailbackWindowEnd = "-1"
```

5. In Cluster Administrator, right-click on Cluster Group, and then click Properties. On the Failback tab, you should see that failback is set to occur immediately.

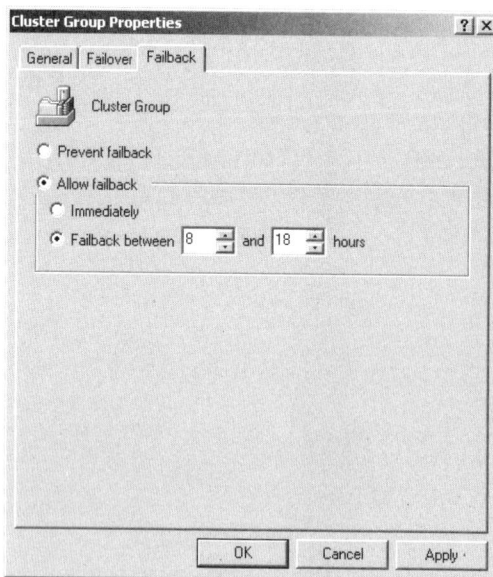

Figure 4.4. The Failback tab of the Cluster Group Properties window.

6. Click the option to prevent failback and then click OK to close the Cluster Group Properties dialog box.

Viewing Properties for a Cluster Service Resource

At the command prompt, type *cluster resource "Cluster IP Address" /prop*, and then press Enter. You should see a result similar to the following:

```
Listing properties for 'Cluster IP Address':

T     Resource               Name                    Value
--    -----------------      ----------------------  -----------------------
SR    Cluster IP Address     Name                    Cluster IP Address
S     Cluster IP Address     Type                    IP Address
S     Cluster IP Address     Description
S     Cluster IP Address     DebugPrefix
D     Cluster IP Address     SeparateMonitor         0 (0x0)
D     Cluster IP Address     PersistentState         0 (0x0)
D     Cluster IP Address     LooksAlivePollInterval  5000 (0x1388)
D     Cluster IP Address     IsAlivePollInterval     60000 (0xea60)
D     Cluster IP Address     RestartAction           2 (0x2)
D     Cluster IP Address     RestartThreshold        3 (0x3)
D     Cluster IP Address     RestartPeriod           900000 (0xdbba0)
D     Cluster IP Address     RetryPeriodOnFailure    4294967295 (0xffffffff)
D     Cluster IP Address     PendingTimeout          180000 (0x2bf20)
D     Cluster IP Address     LoadBalStartupInterval  300000 (0x493e0)
D     Cluster IP Address     LoadBalSampleInterval   10000 (0x2710)
D     Cluster IP Address·    LoadBalAnalysisInterval 300000 (0x493e0)
D     Cluster IP Address     LoadBalMinProcessorUnits 0 (0x0)
D     Cluster IP Address     LoadBalMinMemoryUnits   0 (0x0)
```

The following are definitions for some of these resource properties. (See Appendix B for more information on resource properties and settings.)

- **LooksAlivePollInterval**   This property specifies how often, in milliseconds, Cluster Service should poll a resource to determine whether it appears operational. If this property is not set or is set to –1 for a resource, the default LooksAlivePollInterval property for the resource type associated with the resource is used. If the property set to 0, the resource will not be polled to see whether it is operational.

- **IsAlivePollInterval**   This property specifies the amount of time, in milliseconds, that Cluster Service will poll a resource to determine whether it is operational. If this property is not set or is set to –1 for a resource, the default IsAlivePollInterval property for the resource type associated with the resource is used. This property cannot be set to 0.

- **RestartAction**   This property specifies the action to perform if a resource fails. You can use one of the following settings:

- **ClusterResourceDontRestart (0)**   Do not restart after a failure.

- **ClusterResourceRestartNoNotify (1)**   Attempt to restart the resource after a failure. If the restart threshold is exceeded by the resource within its restart period, Cluster Service will not attempt to fail over the group to another node in the cluster.

- **ClusterResourceRestartNotify (2)**   Attempt to restart the resource after a failure. If the restart threshold is exceeded by the resource within its restart period, Cluster Service will attempt to fail over the group to another node in the cluster. This is the default setting.

  Unless the RestartAction property is set to ClusterResourceDontRestart, Cluster Service will attempt to restart a failed resource.

- **RestartThreshold**   This property specifies the number of restart attempts that will be made on a resource before Cluster Service initiates the action specified by the RestartAction property. These restart attempts must also be made within the time interval specified by the RestartPeriod property. Both the RestartPeriod and the RestartThreshold properties are used to limit restart attempts.

- **RestartPeriod**   This property specifies the amount of time, in milliseconds, during which restart attempts will be made on a resource. The number of attempts allowed within a RestartPeriod is determined by the RestartThreshold setting. Both the RestartPeriod and the RestartThreshold properties are used to limit restart attempts. The RestartPeriod property is reset to 0 once the interval setting is exceeded. If no value is specified for RestartPeriod, the default value of 90000 is used.

- **PendingTimeout**   This property specifies the amount of time, in seconds, that a resource in a Pending Online or Pending Offline state must resolve its status before Cluster Service fails the resource or puts it offline. The default value is three minutes.

  PendingTimeout has the following relationship with RestartPeriod and RestartThreshold:

  RestartPeriod >= RestartThreshold x PendingTimeout

- **RetryPeriodOnFailure**   This property specifies the amount of time, in milliseconds, that a resource will remain in a failed state before Cluster Service attempts to restart it. Until an attempt is made to locate and restart a failed resource, the resource will remain in a failed state by default. Setting the RetryPeriodOnFailure property allows a resource to automatically recover from a failure.

Setting Resource Failover Properties

1. Enter the following commands at the command prompt to change the restart properties for the IP Address resource:

```
cluster resource "Cluster IP Address" /Prop RestartThreshold = 5
cluster resource "Cluster IP Address" /Prop RestartPeriod = 1000
cluster resource "Cluster IP Address" /Prop PendingTimeout = 50
```

2. In Cluster Administrator, right-click on the Cluster IP Address resource located in the Cluster Group, and then click Properties. On the Advanced tab, you should see the RestartThreshold, RestartPeriod, and PendingTimeout properties set to the new values you entered, as shown in Figure 4.5.

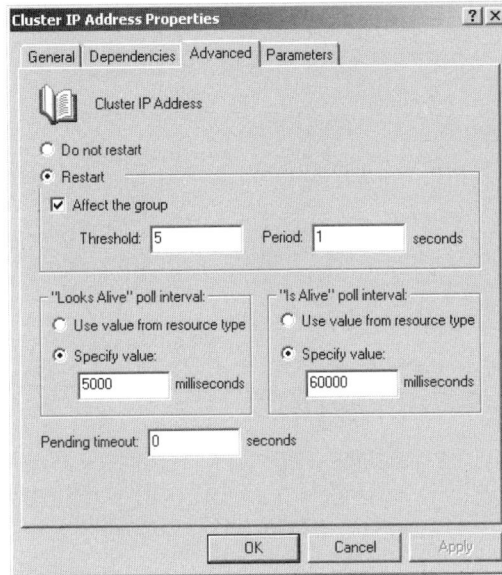

Figure 4.5.   The Advanced tab of the Cluster IP Address Properties window.

3. Make sure that the resource is set to restart after a failure, and set the Restart Threshold back to its original value of 3.

4. Set the Restart Period back to its original value of 900000 seconds.

5. Set the Pending Timeout field back to its original value of 180000 seconds.

6. Close the Cluster IP Address Properties dialog box to save the new settings.

Lesson Summary

This lesson described the default resource types included with Cluster Service. General resource types, such as IP Address and Network Name, are commonly used for virtual servers when an application is configured on a cluster. Using the two generic resource types, Generic Application and Generic Service, you can install cluster-unaware applications for increased availability. This lesson also described common dependencies that certain applications and network services require when they are implemented on a cluster. The lesson included a practice illustrating how to create a new resource and implement a resource group. It also described virtual servers and included two practices, one showing how to create a virtual server and another on how to set properties from the command line.

Lesson 3: Administering and Managing Nodes

Another important task when you administer a cluster is managing the nodes within the cluster. This includes adding and removing servers as nodes in the cluster and taking nodes down for maintenance. In addition to these topics, this lesson discusses implementing security on a cluster and controlling administrative access to the cluster and client access to resources on the cluster.

After this lesson, you will be able to

- Describe how to control administrative access to the cluster
- Configure client access permission to resources on a cluster
- Describe the techniques for maintaining nodes in a cluster

Estimated lesson time: 30 minutes

Managing Security in a Cluster

Cluster Service uses Windows 2000 for its security requirements. This includes communication between nodes, joining nodes to the cluster, and controlling client authentication and access to resource in the cluster. You can use Cluster Administrator to specify which users or groups can

- Administer the cluster
- Access files or folders on File Share resources
- Change the Cluster Service account or password

Administrative Access

Windows 2000 users and groups can be granted permission to administer the cluster. Using Cluster Administrator, you can configure the security settings to suit your organization's requirements. By default, the Domain Admins group and the local Administrators group on each node have administrative permission.

In order to fully administer the cluster, your account must have administrative permissions on each node. If the account you are using has only administrative permission on one node, certain configuration settings will not be available. You will not be able to

- Change the cluster description
- Change the cluster security
- Register extensions

If you will administer the cluster from a remote computer, your account must have administrative permission on each node in the cluster or have specific permission to administer the cluster. This permission can be granted from within Cluster Administrator.

The local Administrator account and local system account always have access to the cluster.

Practice: Granting Administrative Permission to Users

In this practice, you will create a test user and grant that user Administrative access to the cluster. You will also grant the user permission to log on locally so that you can verify the user's administrative permissions. In addition, you will remove the user's administrative permissions for the cluster and verify that the user can no longer access the cluster.

Creating a User Account for Administering the Cluster

1. On NodeA, from the Windows 2000 Start menu, point to Programs, point to Administrative Tools, and click Active Directory Users And Computers.
2. If reskit.com is not already expanded, click the plus sign to expand it.
3. Click Users.
4. Right-click Users, point to New, and click User.
5. In the First Name text box, type *Test*.
6. In the Last Name text box, type *User*.
7. In the User Logon Name text box, type *test*.
8. Click Next.
9. In the Password text box, enter a password.
10. In the Confirm Password text box, enter the same password.
11. Select the User Cannot Change Password and Password Never expires check boxes.
12. Click Next.
13. Click Finish.
14. Close the Active Directory Users And Computers snap-in.

Granting the User Permission to Log On Locally

1. From the Windows 2000 Start menu, point to Programs, point to Administrative Tools, and click Active Directory Users And Computers.
2. Right-click Domain Controllers, and click Properties.

3. Click the Group Policy tab.

4. Click Default Domain Controllers Policy, and click Edit.

5. Expand Computer Configuration, expand Windows Settings, expand Security Settings, expand Local Policies, and click User Rights Assignment.

6. Double-click the Log On Locally policy.

7. Click Add and type *reskit\test* in the Add User Or Group box.

8. Click OK twice. Close the Group Policy Editor dialog box.

9. Click OK to close the Domain Controller Properties dialog box.

10. Close the Active Users and Computers snap-in.

Giving a User Global Administrative Access to the Cluster

1. On NodeA, from the Windows 2000 Start menu, point to Programs, point to Administrative Tools, and click Cluster Administrator.

2. Right-click MYCLUSTER at the root of the tree.

3. Click Properties and then click the Security tab.

4. Click Add.

5. In the Select Groups dialog box, click on the Look In drop-down list and change the value to *reskit.com*.

6. In the list of users and groups, click on Test User, click Add, and then click OK. This will add the user to the list of users with access to the cluster.

7. Click OK to close the MYCLUSTER Properties dialog box.

Verifying the User's Access to the Cluster

1. On NodeA, from the Windows 2000 Start menu, point to Shut Down.

2. In the Shut Down Windows dialog box, select Log Off Administrator as the action for the computer to take, and then click OK.

3. Press Ctrl+Alt+Del and log on to Windows using the Test User account.

4. From the Windows 2000 Start menu, point to Programs, point to Administrative Tools, and click Cluster Administrator.

5. In the Open Connection dialog box, select MYCLUSTER in the Cluster Or Server Name field, and then click OK. This will open a connection to the cluster.

6. Expand MYCLUSTER if necessary and expand the Groups folder in the tree.

7. Right-click on the Cluster Group and click Move Group. Because Test User has administrative access to the cluster, the group should be moved to the other node from whichever node it is currently located. Verify that the resource comes back online on the node to which it was moved.

8. Close Cluster Administrator, and from the Windows 2000 Start menu, point to Shut Down.

9. In the Shut Down Windows dialog box, select Log Off Test as the action for the computer to take, and then click OK.

Preventing a User from Accessing the Cluster

1. Log on to Windows using the Administrator account.

2. From the Windows 2000 Start menu, point to Programs, point to Administrative Tools, and click Cluster Administrator.

3. Right-click MYCLUSTER at the root of the tree.

4. Click Properties, click the Security tab, and then click on Test User in the list of users and groups.

5. For the Full Control permission, clear the Allow check box and click Apply. The Test User will be prevented from administering the cluster.

6. Click OK to save your changes.

7. Close Cluster Administrator. From the Windows 2000 Start menu, point to Shut Down.

8. In the Shut Down Windows dialog box, select Log Off Administrator as the action for the computer to take, and then click OK.

Verifying That Access Has Been Prevented

1. Log on to Windows using the Test User account.

2. From the Windows 2000 Start menu, point to Programs, point to Administrative Tools, and click Cluster Administrator.

3. In the Open Connection dialog box, select MYCLUSTER in the Cluster Or Server Name field, and then click OK. You should get an error message stating that access is denied to Cluster Administrator.

Limiting Client Access to Cluster Resources

In addition to controlling administrative access to the cluster, you can also control client access to resources on the cluster. Typically, you set permissions on the individual applications and services as you would normally. However, you should always set File Share resource security policies using Cluster Administrator because File Share security policies that are configured using Windows Explorer will be lost if the File Share resource fails over.

Table 4.5 lists the security implementations you can use to control client access to cluster resources.

Table 4.5   Client Access Security Implementations

Resource Type	Security Implementation
DHCP Service	Controlled by DHCP
File Share	NTFS share-level security configured with a cluster management application
Generic Application	Windows 2000 network authentication and NTFS security applied to the shared file system
Generic Service	Determined by Windows 2000 service configuration
IIS Server	Windows 2000 network, IIS, and NTFS file-level security
IP Address	N/A
Distributed Transaction Coordinator	Controlled by MS DTC
Message Queue Service	Controlled by Message Queue Service
Network Name	N/A
Physical Disk	NTFS file-level security
Print Spooler	Windows 2000 Network and print-level permissions
WINS	Standard WINS security

Securing Shared Data in a Cluster

Another common security consideration for a cluster is access to shared data. You should use Cluster Administrator to specify the required security settings. If you use Windows Explorer to set permissions on the shared drive, these settings will be lost if the resource is taken offline.

Auditing Access

To audit access to the files and folders on a shared drive, you can use the standard Windows 2000 security features. You can use Windows Explorer, for example, to enable auditing. Cluster Administrator does not provide auditing capabilities. Therefore, you should be familiar with standard Windows 2000 auditing techniques.

The events generated as the result of an audit appear only in the Security log on the node that controls the shared drive. Therefore, in order to ensure full auditing is enabled, you must configure auditing on each node in the cluster.

Managing and Maintaining Nodes

The same general rules apply to managing a node in the cluster that apply to a standard computer running Windows 2000, with the following exceptions:

- You cannot change the computer name of a node in the cluster.
- You must first remove a drive's resources, using Cluster Administrator, before you reformat the drive.
- You must restart both nodes in the cluster after you reformat any disk on the shared bus.
- If a network name has an IP address dependency, you cannot change the IP address unless both resources are first taken offline.
- You should not change the drive letter of any system disks on any of the nodes.

If a node must undergo maintenance, you have two options for the node. A node can remain a member of the cluster or you can remove, or evict, the node before you perform the required maintenance.

Maintenance Without Eviction

If you decide to leave the node in the cluster and the cluster is using a SCSI bus for any shared devices, you should verify that the SCSI termination will remain intact if the node is taken offline. Some SCSI adapters provide this level of termination.

To maintain a node without evicting it from the cluster

1. Open Cluster Administrator.
2. In the left pane, select the node requiring maintenance.
3. From the File menu, click Pause Node.
4. In the Details pane, double-click Active Groups.
5. In the Details pane, select each group, and from the File menu, click Move Group. All the groups on the paused node move to the other node.
6. Perform the required maintenance on the paused node.
7. In Cluster Administrator, select the node.
8. From the File menu, click Resume Node.

Maintenance with Eviction

You use the Evict Node option to permanently remove a node from a cluster. Cluster Service will not be uninstalled on the node, but the node will be removed from the cluster's database. To reinstall or reconfigure Cluster Service on the evicted node, you must first uninstall and then reinstall Cluster Service.

To evict a node from the cluster

1. On the node to be evicted, open Cluster Administrator.
2. Stop Cluster Service.
3. From the File menu, click Evict Node.
4. You can now remove the node from the shared bus.
5. Uninstall Cluster Service.
6. Perform the required maintenance on the server.
7. Reconnect the node to the shared bus and turn on the computer.
8. Reinstall Cluster Service and join the cluster.
9. Reconfigure the preferred owners for groups in the cluster, if necessary.

Pausing and Resuming a Node

Sometimes it might be useful to simply pause a node in a cluster. A node that has been paused will not allow any new resource groups to come online, but any currently online groups will remain online. You might consider pausing a node in order to perform live maintenance or to conduct a test. A node can be in one of the following states:

- **Up**   A node in this state appears healthy to Cluster Service and is running normally.
- **Down**   A node in this state cannot communicate with the cluster, and any resource groups owned by that node will be failed over to the remaining node.
- **Joining**   A node that is in the process of joining a cluster is shown in the Joining state. Once the node has joined the cluster, its state changes to Up.
- **Paused**   A node can be paused to perform maintenance or testing. Resource groups on a paused node will remain active, but new resources will not be brought online until the node's state is changed to Up.
- **Unknown**   If Cluster Service cannot determine the state of a node, it is set to Unknown.

Often, the state of a node is controlled automatically as the result of a system operation on the cluster, such as a node rebooting. However, you can manually control the state of a node depending on your needs. For example, if you need to maintain a node and do not want to evict it from the cluster, you can pause the node and resume its operations later.

To pause a node

1. Open Cluster Administrator.
2. In the left pane, select the node to be paused.
3. From the File menu, click Pause Node.

To resume a node

1. Open Cluster Administrator.
2. In the left pane, select the paused node to be resumed.
3. From the File menu, click Resume Node.

Lesson Summary

In addition to managing resources and resource groups in a cluster, common administrative tasks include configuring security on the cluster and managing the cluster's nodes. This lesson described configuring administrative access as well as client access to the cluster. A practice was provided detailing how to allow a specific user administrative access to the cluster using Cluster Administrator. This lesson also discussed managing cluster nodes. You can remove (evict) a node from the cluster or take it offline for maintenance. If you evict a node before performing scheduled maintenance, you must remove and reinstall Cluster Service before the node can rejoin the cluster.

Review

?

The following questions will help you review key information presented in this chapter. You'll find the answers in Appendix A, "Questions and Answers."

1. You have been asked to port a legacy application that was developed in-house to reside on a new cluster. The application was not developed to be cluster-aware. Which resource type can you use to provide basic failover capability to increase the availability of this application?

2. Which of the following can be performed in Cluster Administrator?

    a. Connecting to a cluster

    b. Identifying a failover

    c. Initiating resource failure

    d. Transferring ownership of a group or resource

3. Every new cluster includes the default resource group, Cluster Group. Which two resources are automatically included in this group?

4. Which of the following statements about dependencies are true?

    a. A dependent resource and all of its dependencies must be in the same group.

    b. All resources, regardless of dependencies, are brought online and offline together.

    c. A dependent resource is taken offline before its dependencies.

    d. A dependent resource is brought online after its dependencies.

5. Which two resources are required to create a virtual server?

6. Which of the following property types is not associated with resources?

    a. General

    b. Advanced

    c. Dependency

    d. Failback

7. Beside global groups, which two groups, when installed on a domain, can be given access to administer the cluster?

8. Which of the following cannot be set using the New Resource Wizard?

    a. Pending timeout settings

    b. Resource name

    c. The node the resource will run on

    d. Resource type

9. What state is a node in if it is currently supporting resources but not allowing new resources to come online?

10. Which of the following are valid resource types?

    a. Physical Disk

    b. IP Address

    c. Print Share

    d. File Share

C H A P T E R   5

Managing and Supporting a Cluster

About This Chapter

This chapter discusses file shares, print services, and storage management for a cluster. It describes how to create and manage the File Share, Print Spooler, and Physical Disk resources on a cluster and explains how these resources integrate with their physical counterparts in the cluster, such as the file system, print queues, and disk storage.

The chapter also discusses other cluster file management topics such as shared file and folder security and Distributed File System installation, configuration, and management. It covers configuration and management of print servers and queues, adding and replacing shared SCSI buses and disks, and monitoring these resources in a cluster environment.

Before You Begin

To complete this chapter, you must have

- The necessary hardware as outlined in the section titled "About This Book" in the Introduction
- The Windows 2000 Advanced Server installation CD-ROM
- Cluster Service installed in a two-node Windows 2000 Advanced Server cluster

Lesson 1: Implementing Clustered File Shares

This lesson describes network file shares on a cluster and explains how to set security and implement Distributed File System (Dfs) shares. Most network servers offer centralized file storage that allows users to easily share files. Windows 2000 provides secured file sharing and uses Dfs to provide a single point of access to multiple physical file storage locations. You can apply security permissions for file shares to files, subdirectories, or a Dfs root. This lesson also discusses Dfs installation and configuration and how to create a Dfs root in a cluster.

After this lesson, you will be able to

- Describe security considerations related to implementing clustered file shares
- Implement a clustered file share that includes a large number of folders, such as your users' home directories
- Implement a Dfs clustered share
- Troubleshoot a clustered file share

Estimated lesson time: 45 minutes

Centralized file storage is an essential service provided by network servers that allows users to easily share and organize files. Many network servers also allow you to store private, secure, or encrypted files and can provide a single point of backup for many users. In many organizations, it is crucial that network file shares be available to users when they need them. Microsoft Cluster Service can provide high availability for these network file shares.

Security Considerations

You should try to keep your file and folder security as simple as possible. The type of security to implement should be planned in advance by a standards team or the appropriate IT division in your organization. Remember that administrative complexity will increase greatly if you mix share-level and file system–level permissions. File system permissions should be your first choice in most situations. The following sections outline the important security considerations.

General Considerations

You should never grant rights to a local group for a directory hosted on a cluster shared drive. If the storage resource and file share fail over to another node, local permissions will no longer apply because each server has its own unique user database with Access Control Entries that reference a local SID. This SID has no meaning to other nodes in the cluster. Therefore, you should use global groups when you set permissions to File Share resources on a cluster shared drive. Also, the Cluster Service account requires a minimum of NTFS read permissions to the directory in order to properly create a share.

Types of File Shares

You must decide where in your file system access will be controlled. Here are the considerations for each type of file share:

- **Normal shares**   This type of share involves a folder and its content. In terms of file security, normal shares are easy to understand and very flexible. Normally, you administer NTFS-level security using Microsoft Windows Explorer, but you administer share-level security for normal shares on a cluster using Cluster Administrator.

- **Shared subdirectories**   This type of share has a root directory, with all subdirectories one level below the root created as normal shares, which automatically inherit the same share-level permissions as the root share. In most cases, share-level permissions are kept at the default setting of Everyone and file system–level security is implemented for all additional security. With this type of share, administrators can rapidly create directories to host large numbers of file shares. Subdirectory shares are available only in Microsoft Windows NT 4 with Service Pack 5 or later.

- **Distributed File System roots**   Dfs roots allow you to combine multiple shared folders into a single hierarchy. The Dfs file system is automatically installed with Windows 2000. There are two types of Dfs roots: stand-alone Dfs roots and domain Dfs roots. Stand-alone Dfs roots can be administered from within a cluster. You can use Cluster Administrator to administer share-level permissions for a Dfs root, and you can administer each link using file share permissions on the appropriate server. However, for Dfs trees spanning a large number of servers and links, this method of controlling access becomes complex and difficult to administer. A better approach is to administer these Dfs trees by using NTFS permissions rather than file share–level permissions to restrict access.

Managing Clusters with Many File Shares

Your cluster's performance is affected by every cluster resource you create. Also, Cluster Service periodically polls every resource to determine whether it has failed. Therefore, as the number of cluster resources increases, the overall performance of your cluster decreases.

If possible, you should use a single File Share resource to manage file shares on your cluster. This requires that the folders you need to share on your network all be subfolders of the same folder. For example, if each user on your file server has a private folder that is a subfolder of the Users folder, you can use a single File Share resource to support hundreds of users. Another option is to hide folders that are not necessary to a group of users. This allows users to view only the part of a directory tree that they need access to.

Managing Home Folders

In large enterprise environments with thousands of users, it is not efficient to create a cluster File Share resource for each user's home folder on your server. As with large numbers of file shares of any type, this configuration will consume more memory and CPU resources than required and will require extra administrative work for no purpose.

The best method for housing home folders on a server cluster is to use the shared subdirectories feature or the dynamic shares feature in Windows 2000. The dynamic shares feature allows you to create an independent file share for every folder under a single cluster File Share resource. The following example shows how you can implement dynamic shares.

Consider the following directory structure:

W:\

W:\Users

W:\Users\MikeR

W:\Users\EltonJ

W:\Users\CherylC

W:\Users\SarahM

Drive W: represents a cluster shared disk. The root share that contains all of the users' home folders is W:\Users. To manage these folders, you first create a single File Share resource on the cluster with W:\Users as the root folder, give the Everyone group Full Control share-level permissions to the file share, and select the option to share all subdirectories. Then you set appropriate NTFS permissions on each user folder. Remember that the Cluster Service account also needs a minimum of Read permissions for each folder.

All folders under W:\Users should now be shared with the same network permissions as the root share. When you use dynamic shares to add a new user, you simply create a new home folder under W:\Users and assign the appropriate NTFS permissions. The new folder will be automatically shared.

You use the Hide Subdirectory Shares check box on the Parameters tab of the cluster File Share resource to activate hidden folders. This will append a $ to the name of each folder under the file share root W:\Users.

Implementing Dfs

Dfs makes organizing and managing network data simpler by giving users a logical view of distributed physical storage. Despite what its name implies, Dfs is software, not a new file system. With Dfs, physical data in different locations on one or more servers appears as one unified hierarchical file system. Thus, you can use Dfs to make files stored on multiple servers in a domain appear to reside on a single server. Network users can thus find needed information in one location instead of having to connect to multiple servers. Thousands of file shares can be connected in one logical system using Dfs.

Dfs Considerations

Both Windows and non-Windows servers can be included in the Dfs namespace because Dfs is protocol independent. Dfs uses Common Internet File System (CIFS) to determine which file server will be accessed by a client. The client then uses its native protocol to access the target file server once it is located. Therefore, NetWare Core Protocol (NCP) is used by servers with a NetWare-based operating system, Network File System (NFS) is used by servers with a UNIX-based operating system, and all servers still support Dfs shares.

File operations such as indexing, virus scanning, and backup are not part of the design capabilities of Dfs. Network traffic would increase substantially if Dfs were able to access very large numbers of files in a sequential or repetitive manner. Also, backup and restore operations are not suitable when you use Dfs replicas because there is no way to determine which file server in a replica set is being accessed. The sole purpose of Dfs is to provide access to files for users and applications.

As a network administrator, you might want to implement Dfs if you have Windows 2000 servers in your organization. However, it is not required. The following are some situations in which you should consider Dfs:

- Users need to access data from multiple locations.
- Users are sharing data between multiple sites.
- Redistribution of shared resources could improve network load balancing.
- Internal or external Web sites are implemented within the organization.

Installing Dfs

Dfs shares are administered using the Dfs Administrator snap-in. Both Dfs and the Dfs Administrator snap-in are automatically installed with Windows 2000 Server. However, Dfs must be configured before it can be used.

Configuring Dfs

In a Windows 2000 domain, a Dfs root can be integrated with Active Directory to create fault-tolerant Dfs roots, called *domain Dfs roots*. Any server in your Windows 2000 domain can host and provide fault tolerance for a domain Dfs root. Active Directory provides fault tolerance and redundancy for domain Dfs roots by ensuring that the domain controllers in your domain all share a common Dfs topology.

Stand-alone Dfs roots can also be created. Stand-alone Dfs roots do not provide fault tolerance because information is stored in the local registry rather than in Active Directory. Each domain can have an unlimited number of Dfs roots, but each domain controller can host only a single Dfs root. One Dfs root can be hosted by up to 32 domain controllers. Load balancing, fault tolerance, and site preference for directory service–aware network clients are improved when multiple computers host a Dfs root or child nodes to the root. Dfs links to child nodes below the root can also reside on any UNC path that is accessible to the Dfs server.

Creating a Cluster Dfs Root

Before you create a Dfs root on your cluster, make sure that none of the nodes in the cluster already has a Dfs root configured. You should also make sure that the folder on the cluster shared disk that you're specifying as the Dfs root already exists. Cluster Administrator can only create the share. The directory must be created first.

You can then use Cluster Administrator to create a new file share as a Dfs root or use the following Cluster.exe command at a command prompt:

```
Cluster RESOURCE "<resname>" /priv isdfsroot=1
```

Until a Dfs-type File Share resource has been brought online on a node, the Distributed File System snap-in cannot see a new Dfs root configuration because the replication of local registry configuration information is not shared in real time between the nodes of a cluster.

Any changes you make in the Distributed File System snap-in, such as deleting or creating a Dfs root, will not be reflected in the Cluster Administrator configuration. For example, if you delete the Dfs root in the snap-in, Cluster Administrator will still see the file share as a Dfs root and the file share will fail. If the File Share resource was set to restart on failure, it will re-create the Dfs root configuration when it comes back online. However, any link information for child nodes will not return because links are managed by the snap-in and are not part of the cluster replication that is affected by Dfs management.

Practice (Optional): Configuring a Dfs Root on a Cluster Service Cluster

In this practice, you'll create and configure a Dfs root on the cluster shared disk. First, you'll create a folder on the cluster shared disk to use for the Dfs root. Then you'll configure a new application with a file share resource. This file share resource will be set to a Dfs root type of file share. Finally, you'll verify the Dfs root in the Distributed File System snap-in.

Creating a Folder on the Cluster Shared Disk

1. From the Start menu on NodeA, point to Programs, point to Administrative Tools, and click Cluster Administrator.

2. If needed, expand the My Cluster tree and locate the resource group that contains the Physical Disk resource for the drive on which you'll create the Dfs root. For this practice, we'll use W: for the drive.

3. Verify that NodeA owns the Physical Disk resource.

4. From the Windows 2000 desktop, double-click My Computer.

5. In the My Computer window, double-click the W: drive.

6. In the W: drive window, click File, point to New, and click Folder to create a new folder.

7. Change the name of the new folder to *DfsRoot*.

8. Close the W: drive and the My Computer window.

Creating a Dfs Root File Share Resource

1. In Cluster Administrator, click File, and then click Configure Application to start the Application Configuration Wizard. Click Next.

2. Select the option to use an existing virtual server, and select the cluster group containing the Physical Disk resource for drive W: as the virtual server. Click Next.

3. If the group containing the Physical Disk resource does not contain an IP Address and Network Name resource, you must either move these resources from another group or create them. For this practice, Cluster Group is used.

4. Make sure the option Create A Cluster Resource For My Application is selected, and click Next.

5. From the Resource Type drop-down list, select File Share. Click Next.

6. Type *Dfs Root File Share* for the name of the resource and *File share for Dfs root* for the description. Click the Advanced Properties button.

7. In the Advanced Resource Properties dialog box, click the Dependencies tab.

8. Click the Modify button, and add the Physical Disk, IP Address, and Network Name resources as dependencies.

9. Click OK to close the Modify Dependencies dialog box, click OK to close the Advanced Resource Properties dialog box, and then click Next.

10. Type in *DfsShare* as the share name and *W:\DfsRoot* as the path. Click the Advanced button.

11. In the Advanced File Share Properties dialog box, select the Dfs Root option. Click OK to close the dialog box, and then click Next.

12. Click Finish to close the Application Configuration Wizard.

Verifying the Dfs Root File Share

1. If needed, expand the Groups folder and click on Cluster Group in the left pane.

2. Right-click on Dfs Root File Share in the right pane, and click Bring Online to bring the resource online. If any of the other resources in the group are offline, you must bring them online as well.

3. From the Start menu, point to Programs, point to Administrative Tools, and then click Distributed File System.

4. Expand the Distributed File System tree to display the newly created Dfs Root, which should have a name similar to *MYCLUSTER\DfsShare*.

5. Right-click on the Dfs root, and click Check Status to check the status of the Dfs root. A green check mark will appear next to the item in the tree if the status is OK.

Troubleshooting Clustered File Shares

The following are some common problems with clustered file shares and Dfs roots and some suggestions for solving them.

Error Occurs While Trying to Create a Dfs Root File Share Resource

If you get the following error message when you use Cluster Administrator to configure a File Share resource as a Dfs root, a Dfs root is already configured on one of the cluster nodes and has not been deleted. You can create only one Dfs root per server cluster.

Cluster Administrator Standard Extension: An error occurred attempting to set properties: A Dfs root already exists in this cluster node. Error ID: 5088 (000013e0).

Dfs Root Is Not a Cluster Resource

This problem occurs if the Dfs root in the Distributed File System snap-in does not match the associated clustered resource in Cluster Administrator. Use the snap-in to fix the problem by selecting the Root Configured option for the Dfs root and then deleting the Dfs root.

Dfs Root Is a Cluster Resource

If a Dfs root that is a cluster resource is no longer needed, take the resource offline, configure it as a normal file share, or delete it. To update the changes to the Dfs root on the other nodes in the cluster, move the group that contains the old Dfs root to the other node.

Incorrect or Missing File Share Directory

If the directory specified for a File Share resource does not exist, an attempt to bring the resource online will result in the following errors in the Windows Event Log:

Event ID: 1053

Source: ClusSvc

Description: Cluster File Share *<sharename>* cannot be brought online because the share could not be created.

Event ID: 1069

Source: ClusSvc

Description: Cluster resource *<sharename>* failed.

You can solve this problem by specifying a valid directory for the File Share resource and then attempting to bring the resource online again.

Dfs Service Has Stopped

You might get the following error messages in the Windows Event Log related to clustered file shares even though no resource problems are reported in Cluster Administrator:

Event ID: 1055

Source: ClusSvc

Type: Error

Description: Cluster File Share resource *<sharename>* has failed a status check. The error code is 1355.

Event ID: 1069

Source: ClusSvc

Type: Error

Description: Cluster resource *<sharename>* failed.

These error messages likely indicate that the Dfs service was stopped on a node in the server cluster while the File Share resource was still online on this node. The Dfs service could have been stopped by a problem with the service or by manual intervention.

If the Dfs root File Share resource is configured to not restart after a failure or if the restart threshold for the resource was exceeded, the resource will be shown in a failed state in Cluster Administrator. However, if the Dfs root File Share resource is configured to restart and the restart threshold of the resource was not exceeded, these errors are logged to the system event log and Cluster Service will try to bring the resource back online. If the Dfs service is not started, Cluster Service will attempt to start it when it tries to bring the File Share resource online.

If Cluster Administrator shows the File Share resource to be online, no immediate recovery action is required. There should be events in the log with the source Dfs that contain more information about why the Dfs service has stopped unless the service was stopped manually. These events can help you troubleshoot the service.

If Cluster Administrator shows the File Share resource to be failed or offline, try to bring the resource online. The Dfs service will also attempt to start. More detailed events should be logged in the system event log from Dfs or ClusSvc if the Dfs service continues to fail. For a complete course of action, view these errors.

Lesson Summary

This lesson discussed network file sharing in a cluster, including setting and managing permissions for file shares and implementing Distributed File System shares. Files and folders that are provided by cluster storage can be shared across your network with permissions to control access. You can also use Dfs to consolidate different file shares to a single namespace. This lesson also explained how to install and configure Dfs in a cluster to support this enhanced form of file sharing.

Lesson 2: Implementing Clustered Print Services

This lesson discusses configuration and management considerations for clustering network printers, including implementing print servers and managing print queues on your cluster. Although a print server can be set up on any Windows 2000 computer with a printer attached, only network printers can be set up as print servers in a cluster. This lesson describes how to create and manage a cluster Print Spooler resource and associate it with a network, printer, and it also discusses how to use Windows System Monitor to monitor and manage a clustered print queue.

After this lesson, you will be able to

- Describe how Cluster Service supports network printers
- Create and configure a clustered print spool

Estimated lesson time: 30 minutes

Configuring Network Printing

Any computer running Windows 2000 can be a print server if it manages printers. A Windows 2000 computer can also be a specialized print server unit. Physical printers can be connected to a server, to a client computer, or directly to the network. However, software on a print server actually makes the physical printer visible to the network and able to accept print jobs from clients.

Print servers are usually installed as member servers on a network rather than as domain controllers to avoid the additional overhead associated with tasks performed by a domain controller. However, in many cases, a server is configured as both a file server and a print server to save on hardware resources.

Printing resources can be shared across an entire network with Windows 2000 Server. Print jobs can be sent from clients on a variety of platforms. Printers can be attached locally to a Windows 2000 print server or be available remotely across an Internet or intranet connection. Printers can also be connected directly to the network using internal network interface cards, external network adapters, or another server.

Print Server Clustering

You can achieve a high level of availability by clustering a Windows 2000 print server. If you take down one node of a clustered print server for maintenance, its print jobs will be processed by the other node in the cluster. Windows 2000 Advanced Server also uses new port monitors to automatically copy the print server ports and settings to the other node. However, clustering does not support all of the features of a stand-alone print server because of the requirement that the clustered print server manage a network printer.

Configuring Print Services

To get the port configuration for each node, you no longer need to create locally defined printers on each node. The port configuration is now shared between the cluster nodes using the Cluster Registry. However, the printer drivers cannot be shared between nodes because unique share names must be used in the cluster. This is actually a restriction in Windows 2000 Server. The node that owns the Print Spooler resource also owns the print share because it is mapped to the local Winnt\System32\Spool folder. When you install a printer driver on a cluster, it connects to this local share. Thus, the print drivers for a clustered printer must be installed on each node in the cluster.

Monitoring Print Queues

In Windows 2000, you can monitor print queues using Windows System Monitor. You use the Print Queue object in System Monitor to monitor the performance of a clustered print server. You can measure a variety of performance criteria for your print queue by setting up counters for the Print Queue object. These counters can measure items such as bytes printed per second, job errors, or total pages printed. Table 5.1 shows the performance counters available with the Print Queue object.

Table 5.1   Print Queue Performance Monitors

Counter	Description
Add Network Printer Calls	Number of calls to add shared network printers made by other print servers since the last restart.
Bytes Printed/sec	Rate of printing in a print queue in bytes per second. Roughly represents the workload of a printer and can be used for bottleneck detection.
Enumerate Network Printer Calls	Number of calls to request network browse lists made to this print server from browse clients since the last reboot of the server.
Job Errors	Number of job errors that occurred in a print queue since the last restart. Job errors occur when the connection to the printer has errors due to network problems.
Jobs	Number of current jobs in a print queue. You can use this counter to detect excessive use of a print queue by one or more users.
Jobs Spooling	Number of jobs currently spooling in a print queue.
Max Jobs Spooling	Maximum number of jobs recorded at one time in a print queue since the last restart.
Max References	Peak number of open handles to a printer.
Not Ready Errors	Number of not-ready errors received in a print queue since the last restart.
Out of Paper Errors	Number of out-of-paper errors received in the print queue since the last restart.
References	Current number of references to a print queue from a user or a program that is connecting to a printer and opening a print queue.
Total Jobs Printed	Number of jobs printed on a print queue since the last restart.
Total Pages Printed	Number of pages printed through the Graphics Device Interface (GDI) on a print queue since the last restart.

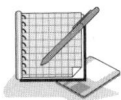

Practice: Creating a Print Spooler Resource

In this practice, you'll create a Print Spooler resource for the cluster and then attach a network printer to the cluster to use the resource. Once the network printer is set up and the Print Spooler resource is brought online, you'll verify the setup by sending a test job to the printer. You must have created the group already (in the previous practice).

Note This practice assumes that you're configuring a cluster server that has no preexisting resources or groups.

Creating an IP Address Resource

1. Open Cluster Administrator.
2. Click the Groups folder.
3. Right-click Cluster Printer, point to New, and click Resource.
4. In the New Resource dialog box, type *Printer IP Address* in the Name box, type *IP Address of printer* in the Description box, select IP Address as the resource type, and select Cluster Printer as the group. Click Next.
5. Both nodes should appear in the list of Possible Owners. If they do not, add them to the list. Click Next.
6. In the Dependencies dialog box, the Resource Dependencies list should be blank. Click Next.
7. In the TCP/IP Address Parameters dialog box, type the following information:

   Address   *192.168.0.3*

   Subnet Mask   *255.255.255.0*

   Network   *Public Cluster Connection*

8. Click Finish. A message box will appear stating that the IP Address resource was created successfully.
9. Click OK.

Creating a Network Name Resource

1. Click the Groups folder.
2. Right-click Cluster Printer, point to New, and click Resource.
3. In the New Resource dialog box, type *Network Printer Name* in the Name box, type *Network name for printer* in the Description box, select Network Name as the resource type, and select Cluster Printer as the group. Click Next.
4. Both nodes should appear in the list of Possible Owners. If they do not, add them to the list. Click Next.

5. In the Dependencies dialog box, add the Printer IP Address resource to the Resource Dependencies list and click Next.

6. In the Network Name Parameters dialog box, type *CLUSTERPRN*.

7. Click Finish. A message box will appear stating that the Network Name resource was created successfully.

8. Click OK.

Creating a Print Spooler Resource

Before you begin this practice, create a folder named Spooler on the W: drive.

1. Click the Groups folder.

2. Right-click Cluster Printer, point to New, and click Resource.

3. In the New Resource dialog box, enter *Print Spooler* in the Name box, type in *Print spooler resource for printer* in the Description box, select Print Spooler as the resource type, and select Cluster Printer as the group. Click Next.

4. Both nodes should appear in the Possible Owners list. If they do not, add them to the list. Click Next.

5. In the Dependencies dialog box, add the Disk W: and Network Name resources to the Resource Dependencies list and click Next.

6. In the Print Spooler Parameters dialog box, type *W:\Spool* for the spool folder:

   Specifying the path will not automatically create the folder. Therefore, the Spool folder must already exist on the W: drive before the spooler can be used.

7. Click Finish. A message box will appear stating that the Print Spooler resource was created successfully.

8. Click OK.

9. Right-click Cluster Printer, and click Bring Online.

Creating a Printer on the Cluster

This practice assumes that you have the following:

- HP Jet Direct 170x network card
- Okidata OL 600E printer
- IP address of the network printer

You might need to configure the printer differently, depending on your hardware.

1. Click Start, and click Run.

2. Type *\\CLUSTERPRN* and click OK.

3. Double-click the Printers folder.

4. Double-click the Add Printer icon.

5. Click Next on the Add Printer Wizard welcome page.

6. Notice on the Local Or Network Printer page of the wizard that the only option available is the Remote Print Server \\CLUSTERPRN option. Click Next.

7. On the Select The Printer Port page, select the Create A New Port option. Click Next. The Add Standard TCP/IP Port Wizard will open.

8. Click Next on the Add Standard TCP/IP Port Wizard welcome page.

9. In the Printer Name Or IP Address box, enter the IP address of the network printer.

10. The Port Name box will automatically be populated with the IP address from the above step. Click Next.

11. Select Parallel 1 from the drop-down list, and click Next.

12. Click Finish on the Completion page of the Add Standard TCP/IP Port Wizard. The Add Printer Wizard page will reappear.

13. On the Add Printer Wizard page, if the correct printer has not been selected, select the correct manufacturer and printer. Click Next.

14. On the Use Existing Driver page, select the Keep Existing Driver (Recommended) option and then click Next.

15. Accept the default printer name in the Printer Name box, and click Next.

16. Select the Shared option, accept the default share name, and then click Next.

17. On the Location And Comment page, type a location and a comment and click Next.

18. Select the Yes option to print a test page, and click Next.

19. On the Completing The Add Printer Wizard page, click Finish. A message will appear saying that your test page has been sent to the printer.

20. Click OK.

Verifying the Printer from NodeB

1. Click Start, and click Run.

2. Type *CLUSTERPRN* and click OK.

3. Double-click the Printers folder.

4. Double-click the Okidata OL-600E icon. A message will appear saying that before you use the \\CLUSTERPRN computer you must configure it on the local computer. The message will also ask whether you want to configure the printer now. Click Yes.

5. Right-click the Okidata OL-600E icon, and click Properties.

6. On the General tab, click Print Test Page.

Lesson Summary

This lesson discussed how to cluster Windows 2000 print services and how to set up network printers, configure print servers, and manage print queues. It also described the relationship between a Print Spooler resource and a print server. Some of the enhanced features of clustered print servers, such as port monitors, were introduced. The lesson also discussed monitoring and managing clustered print servers using Windows System Monitor.

Lesson 3: Managing Clustered Storage

A Physical Disk resource provides the basis for managing storage in a cluster. Any application or service that stores information on the cluster or uses the Quorum disk requires a Physical Disk resource. This lesson explains how to create and manage this resource type using Cluster Administrator and Cluster.exe. It also introduces private properties of the Physical Disk resource and explains how you can use them to monitor the health and maintenance of clustered disk drives. You use Cluster.exe to display this information about the Physical Disk resource. Finally, the lesson discusses storage management tasks such as replacing failed disk drives, expanding physical disk storage, extending cluster disk space, installing additional SCSI buses or devices, and replacing failed cluster disks.

After this lesson, you will be able to

- Describe the use of the Physical Disk resource
- List the steps for supporting a clustered storage array, including adding and removing hard drive storage devices

Estimated lesson time: 45 minutes

Creating a Physical Disk Resource

A Physical Disk resource is required for applications to access a shared cluster disk. You must create a Physical Disk resource before a shared disk will be usable in the cluster. At least one Physical Disk resource is created when you first install and configure the cluster using the Cluster Service Configuration Wizard. This disk resource, called the Quorum resource, includes the Quorum disk. You should create additional Physical Disk resources only for disks that are accessible by all cluster nodes and not associated with existing Physical Disk resources.

Physical Disk resources can be created only for entire physical drives, not for partitions or logical drives. Only an entire physical drive can be failed over because you cannot independently fail over drive partitions on the same disk. Thus, a Physical Disk resource created on a partitioned drive will be associated with the entire disk, regardless of how many partitions and drive letters are formed on it. You can use Cluster Administrator or Cluster.exe to create a new Physical Disk resource.

Creating a Physical Disk Resource Using Cluster Administrator

You can create a new Physical Disk resource using Cluster Administrator if you have added or replaced one or more disks in your cluster. Since only one Physical Disk resource can be created for each physical disk in your cluster, the resource can designate multiple logical drives if they are partitions of the same physical disk. Also, because the Physical Disk resource is the only default resource type that can operate as a Quorum resource for the cluster, many other resource types require a Physical Disk resource as a dependency.

Table 5.2 describes the properties of the Physical Disk resource in Cluster Administrator.

Table 5.2   Physical Disk Resource Properties

Property	Description
Name	Required. Specifies the name of the resource.
Description	Optional. Describes the resource.
Possible Owners	Required. Specifies which nodes own the resource. If the Quorum resource resides on the disk, all nodes must be owners.
Required Dependencies	None
Disk	Required. Specifies the drive letter or letters for the Physical Disk resource.

Once created, the Physical Disk resource can be brought online, used as a dependency, or otherwise controlled using the Resource Management functions. It will appear as a Cluster resource in Cluster Administrator and in Cluster.exe. You can view and set the Physical Disk resource properties by using the Properties page, shown in Figure 5.1.

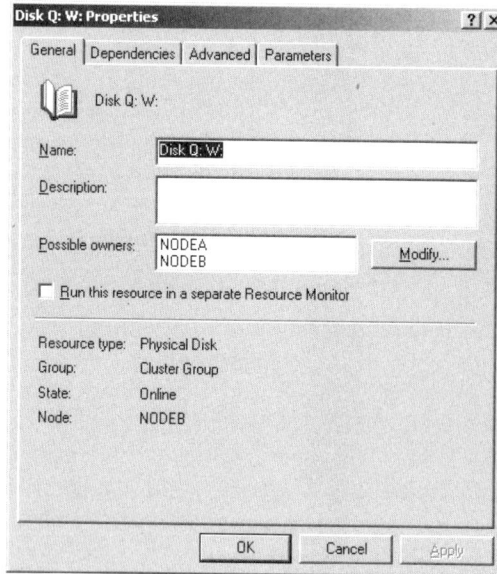

Figure 5.1 Physical Disk resource properties page

Creating a Physical Disk Resource Using Cluster.exe

Creating a new Physical Disk resource using Cluster.exe is more tedious than doing so using Cluster Administrator. The only situation in which you might want to do this is for a script that will automatically create the resource at a remote site.

To create a new disk resource using Cluster.exe, you use the /Create option. You must specify all required parameters for the resource before it can be brought online. The /Create option allows you to create resources that will be in an incomplete state. You must set additional disk resource properties as appropriate using subsequent commands.

For example, here's the command sequence for adding a Physical Disk resource. (Note that the log entry lines shown here have been wrapped because of space constraints in this book. The lines do not normally wrap.)

```
CLUSTER mycluster RESOURCE mydisk /Create /Group:mygroup /
Type:"Physical Disk"
CLUSTER mycluster RESOURCE myshare /PrivProp Drive="W:"
```

You must include the group name and resource type when you create the resource. Once the resource is created with valid parameters, it can be brought online.

Physical Disk Resource Private Properties

Physical Disk resources have private properties that determine settings and status for the disk on which they're created. These private properties are useful for monitoring and troubleshooting the resource, and are described below.

Drive

The Drive property specifies the drive letter for the Physical Disk resource. If you're using the Drive property and multiple drive letters are associated with the disk, you must set the Drive property to include all of the drive letters. You must also make sure that the assigned drive letter does not conflict with existing drive letters anywhere in the cluster, including each node's local drives.

Signature

The Signature property specifies an identifier for the disk. It is a DWORD value with a range from 0 to 0xFFFFFFFF. When you create a new disk resource using Cluster.exe, you set the Drive or Signature private property to the drive or signature of the disk. You must set one of these two properties, but you cannot set both. Neither property can be changed once the assignment is made and the resource is created. When you create a new disk resource using Cluster Administrator, you're not required to provide one of these properties. Instead, a list of available disks is displayed for you to choose from.

SkipChkdsk

The SkipChkdsk property determines whether the operating system runs chkdsk on a physical disk before attempting to mount the disk. A TRUE setting causes the operating system to mount the disk without running chkdsk. A FALSE setting causes the operating system to run chkdsk first and, if errors are found, take action based on the ConditionalMount property. However, if both the SkpChkDsk and ConditionalMount values are *0* (FALSE), chkdsk will not run and the disk will be left offline. Table 5.3 summarizes the interaction between SkipChkdsk and ConditionalMount.

Table 5.3   SkipChkdsk and ConditionalMount Interaction

SkipChkdsk Setting	ConditionalMount Setting	Chkdsk Runs?	Disk Mounted?
FALSE	TRUE	Yes	If chkdsk reports errors, no. Otherwise, yes.
FALSE	FALSE	No	No
TRUE	TRUE	No	Yes
TRUE	FALSE	No	Yes

Because forcing a disk to mount when chkdsk reports errors can result in data loss, you should exercise caution when changing these properties.

ConditionalMount

The ConditionalMount property determines whether a physical disk is mounted, depending on the results of chkdsk. A TRUE setting prevents the operating system from mounting the disk if chkdsk reports errors. A FALSE setting causes the operating system to attempt to mount the disk regardless of chkdsk failures. The default is TRUE. Note that if chkdsk has not run, it will not produce errors, so the operating system will attempt to mount the disk regardless of the ConditionalMount setting.

MountVolumeInfo

The MountVolumeInfo property stores information used by the Windows 2000 Disk Manager. Cluster Service updates the property data stored in MountVolumeInfo whenever a disk resource is brought online. Cluster Service also updates MountVolumeInfo when the drive letter of a disk resource is changed using Disk Manager.

MountVolumeInfo data consists of a byte array organized as follows:

- A 16-byte "header" consisting of the disk signature (first 8 bytes) and the number of volumes (second 8 bytes).

- One or more 48-byte descriptive entries. (See Table 5.4.)

Table 5.4   MountVolumeInfo Data

Position	Data
First 16 bytes	Starting offset
Second 16 bytes	Partition length
Next 8 bytes	Volume number
Next 2 bytes	Disk type
Next 2 bytes	Drive letter
Last 4 bytes	Padding

Displaying Private Properties

You can display the Physical Disk resource private properties by using Cluster.exe. These properties can help administrators determine when to run chkdsk against a cluster disk. You can use the following command to display disk resource private properties:

```
cluster <clustername> resource "Disk Q:" /priv
```

Here's an example of the output for a disk resource named Disk Q:

```
Listing private properties for 'Disk Q:':
T Resource   Name            Value
D Disk Q:    Signature       1415371731 (0x545cdbd3)
D Disk Q:    SkipChkdsk      0 (0x0)
D Disk Q:    ConditionalMount  1 (0x1)
B Disk Q:    DiskInfo        03 00 00 00 ... (264 bytes)
B Disk Q:    MountVolumeInfo  D3 DB 5C 54 ... (104 bytes)
```

The values assigned to SkipChkdsk and ConditionalMount determine the behavior of chkdsk. If the MSCS folder on the Quorum drive is inaccessible or if the disk is found to be corrupt (via checking of the dirty bit), chkdsk will behave as follows:

- If SkipChkdsk = 1 (which means TRUE), Cluster Service will not run chkdsk against the dirty drive and will mount the disk for immediate use. (Note that SkipChkdsk = 1 overrides the ConditionalMount setting and that Cluster Service performs the same no matter what the ConditionalMount property is set to.)

- If SkipChkdsk = 0 (which means FALSE) and ConditionalMount = 0, Cluster Service fails the disk resource and leaves it offline.

- If SkipChkdsk = 0 and ConditionalMount = 1, Cluster Service runs chkdsk /f against the volume found to be dirty and then mounts it. This is the current default behavior for Windows 2000 clusters and is the only behavior for Windows NT 4 clusters.

You can use the following commands to modify these resource private properties:

```
cluster clustername res "Disk Q:" /priv Skipchkdsk=0[1]
cluster clustername res "Disk Q:" /priv ConditionalMount=0[1]
```

You can track disk management changes using the fixed-length values returned by the MountVolumeInfo property. MountVolumeInfo replaces DiskInfo in Windows 2000.

Here's a sample MountVolumeInfo entry:

```
D3DB5C5404000000000002000000000000000040060000000000100000007460000000024
0060000000000FE3F06000000000200000074B00000000800C000000000000400600
00000003000000074C00000040C0120000000000C03F06000000000400000007490000
```

The signature is D3DB5C54, and the number of volumes is 04000000. The table below describes how to interpret the rest of the information.

Offset	Partition Length	Volume Letter	Disk Type	Drive Number	Padding
00020000.00000000	00004006.00000000	01000000	07	46	0000
00024006.00000000	00FE3F06.00000000	02000000	07	4B	0000
0000800C.00000000	00004006.00000000	03000000	07	4C	0000
0040C012.00000000	00C03F06.00000000	04000000	07	49	0000

For compatibility in a mixed-node cluster where one node is running Windows 2000 and the other is running Windows NT 4, DiskInfo is retained in the properties of the disk resource.

Whenever a disk resource is brought online, Cluster Service checks the physical disk configuration and updates the information in MountVolumeInfo and DiskInfo. Corrections are made to the physical disk configuration registry entries as needed. When changes are made using Disk Manager, any values related to drive letters are updated dynamically.

Planning Cluster Storage

When you plan for cluster storage, you must consider the storage requirements of the shared disk and of each node in the cluster. Each cluster node requires enough hard-disk capacity to store permanent copies of all applications and other resources required to run all groups. For each node, you must calculate the storage requirements as if all resources in the cluster were running on that node. You must also plan for additional disk space so that any other node can effectively run all resources during failover, make allowances for any applications that are not clustered, and consider virtual memory requirements.

You might also want to use fault-tolerant disk sets for cluster storage devices to ensure higher availability of data on disk sets in your cluster in case a member of the disk set fails. Keep in mind that you can connect physical disk or hardware RAID devices only to the cluster shared bus. Other devices, such as tape drives, CD-ROM drives, or removable storage are not allowed on the shared bus. If necessary, you can use these devices for local storage on a cluster node. You should also plan to make frequent and accurate backups of your cluster storage.

Extending the Disk Space of an Existing Shared Disk

You can extend the disk space of an existing cluster server disk at the hardware level in two ways. You can either create a new partition on the current physical disk or delete the current partition and create a new partition. You must also perform additional steps to ensure that the additional disk space is recognized by the system. The process requires that you use the Windows Registry editor to edit Registry entries. You should use extreme caution when modifying the Registry. Incorrect Registry entries can cause problems that require you to reinstall your operating system.

Follow these steps to delete the existing partition and create a new partition that includes all available disk space:

1. Back up and verify all the information on the shared disk that you're extending.

2. Change the startup value to Manual for the following items on the second node: Clusdisk (in Device Manager) and Cluster Service (in the Services snap-in).

3. Restart the second node.

4. When the OS Loader Boot menu is displayed, press the Spacebar to prevent Windows from loading. (This step is necessary on some hardware configurations to maintain termination on the shared SCSI bus.)

5. Change the startup value to Manual for the following items on the first node: Clusdisk (in Device Manager) and Cluster Service (in the Services snap-in). Do not attempt to stop Clusdisk; doing so can result in errors.

6. Follow the directions provided by your hardware vendor to extend the existing disk space at the hardware level.

7. Restart the first node.

8. Delete any partitions on the shared disk that are to be extended.

9. Create a new partition that uses all of the free space on the shared disk.

10. Format the disk with the NTFS format, and then give the disk the same drive letter as the previous disk.

11. Restore the data on the shared disk from the backup, and verify that it restored correctly.

12. Run the Regedt32.exe program.

13. Locate HKey_Local_Machine.

14. From the Registry menu, click Load Hive.

15. Browse to \%System_root%\Cluster, and then click the Clusdb file.

16. Open the file, and when it prompts you for a name for the registry key, type *cluster*.

17. Expand the cluster hive, and locate and expand the Resources key. A list of resources and their GUIDs will be displayed.

18. Click the first GUID. The right pane will display information about it. Continue to click each GUID until you find the one for the disk that you just extended. The Type field will show the physical disk type, and the Name field will display the name of the physical disk. When you locate the disk that you extended, expand the GUID key for that disk to view the Parameters key located under the GUID key.

19. Click the Parameters key. The right pane will display two values: a Diskinfo key and a Signature key.

20. Click the Diskinfo key, and then delete it. Do not delete the Signature key.

21. Locate the root of the cluster hive, and from the Registry menu, click Unload Hive. If you get a message indicating that the key and all of its subkeys are to be removed, click OK. This message is expected behavior.

22. Close the Regedt32.exe file.

23. Open Windows Explorer, and browse to your quorum drive.

24. Locate the MSCS folder on your quorum drive.

25. Locate any files in the MSCS directory named Chk***.tmp, and rename them. Although you can delete these files, it's usually preferable to rename them in the event that Cluster Service fails to start and you must restore them.

26. In Device Manager, start the cluster disk device and reset its startup method to System.

27. In the Services snap-in, start Cluster service and reset its startup method to Automatic.

28. Open Cluster Administrator on the first node, and verify that all of the resources have come online successfully.

29. From the second node, fail the resource group with the newly extended disk over to the second node and back to the first node to verify that it comes online on either node.

In some cases, you can increase the drive space on a hardware-defined disk without losing the existing data and having to restore from backup. Once the space is extended, this type of disk will appear to Windows as a larger size disk partition. However, Windows will not give any indication that the disk has actually been extended.

Creating a software volume made up of existing disk space and newly added space is an additional method for extending partition size. However, since Cluster Service does not support dynamic disks, which are required for these types of software volumes, this is not a valid option for extending cluster shared disk space.

Installing an Additional Shared SCSI Bus

The drive letter assignments on a node should not be affected when you add another shared SCSI bus. Use the following steps to install an additional shared SCSI bus between two nodes:

1. Shut down the storage device and all cluster nodes.
2. Prepare and install each SCSI controller for the shared SCSI bus in a node, referring to your SCSI bus owner's manual for instructions. Make sure the SCSI controllers are using different SCSI IDs, and do not connect the shared SCSI bus to both servers while you configure the two systems.
3. Connect the shared SCSI devices to the shared bus, and then connect the shared SCSI bus to both nodes. After the shared SCSI bus is connected to both nodes, do not run Windows on both nodes simultaneously until you have completed this installation.
4. Start one node, and boot Windows. Start the second node, but do not allow Windows to start. Boot to the command prompt.
5. On the first node, run Disk Management and assign drive letters to the disks available on the new SCSI bus.
6. Shut down the first node, but do not turn off the computer.
7. On the second node, boot Windows.
8. On the second node, run Disk Management and assign drive letters to the disks on the shared SCSI bus using the same drive letters as those set on the first node.
9. Restart the first node.

Adding Devices to the Shared SCSI Bus

The procedure for adding disk devices to the shared SCSI bus is as follows:

1. Shut down the storage device and all cluster nodes. (Data loss can occur if you attempt to add devices to the shared SCSI bus while the cluster nodes and shared disk are in use.)
2. Add the new device or devices using the same method used for adding them to a standard SCSI bus. Make sure that the device configuration is correct for the bus, that you choose a unique SCSI ID for the new device, and that the bus is properly terminated after the new device is added.

3. Verify cables and termination before applying power. Use the SCSI host adapter utilities to determine whether the adapter can identify all disk devices on the bus. Perform this check on each node with the other node turned off. If the tests are successful, check the drive identification at the operating-system level by using Disk Manager. Do this procedure on each node with the other node turned off.

4. Bring one cluster node online, and use Disk Administrator, shown in Figure 5.2, to assign a drive letter and format each new device.

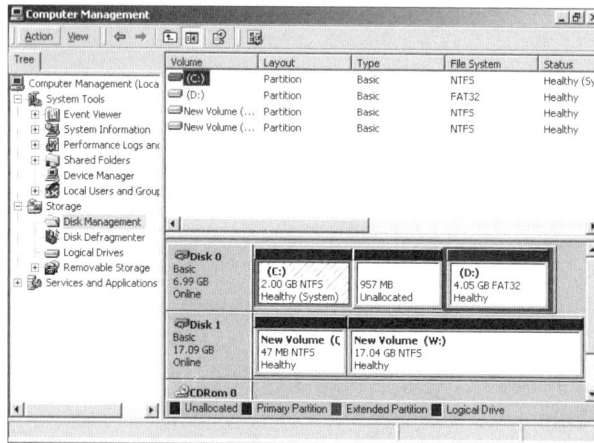

Figure 5.2   Disk Administrator

5. Use Cluster Administrator to create Physical Disk resources for the new drives.

6. Verify that the new resources come online successfully. For a shared drive to go online, Cluster Service must be started if it has been installed. If the device fails, recheck the device configuration, cables, and termination.

7. Bring the second cluster node online. File-system corruption can result if you bring both nodes online and you haven't first created Physical Disk resources for the new device.

Replacing Cluster Disks

If you make a mistake while replacing a cluster disk, you can lose all the data on the disk. If the Quorum disk is lost, the configuration data for the cluster is also at risk. These risks show the importance of successfully replacing a failed cluster disk as well as doing frequent backups.

The following sections outline the steps necessary to successfully replace a cluster disk. You must also have a backup of the cluster to complete these steps. In addition, the disk that requires replacement might still be online or might have failed completely. The steps for each of these conditions are covered in the following sections.

Replacing a Cluster Disk That Is Online

Before you replace a failed cluster disk that is currently online, you must take the following preliminary steps:

1. If possible, perform a full backup of the cluster. Be sure to verify during the backup process all data on the disks that will be replaced. It is critical that you fully back up the disk before replacing it to prevent any risks to data, especially if the disk that you replace is the Quorum disk.

2. Shut down all but one of the cluster nodes.

3. On the remaining active node, take any resources offline that are dependent on the disk you are replacing.

4. Change the drive letter of each disk you are replacing using Disk Manager. Use a drive letter that is not being used by any other volume.

5. Set the Physical Disk resource to not restart on failover, and then rename it. If the disk that you replace is the Quorum disk, you must designate a different disk as the Quorum resource before removing the old disk from the cluster.

6. Disable Cluster Service by using Services Manager.

7. Disable the cluster disk driver by using Device Manager.

To replace the cluster disk, take the following steps:

1. Physically replace the disk with a new one. Because of dependencies on the replaced disk, some cluster resources might no longer work. For each resource that fails to come online, modify any disk dependencies to map to the new Physical Disk resource.

Note You can avoid this type of failure if you modify the disk dependencies before changing the disk.

---

2. Format and partition the new disk using information from the DumpConfig output text file on your backup. This will ensure that the new disk is set up identically to the failed one. In the [Volumes] section of the DumpConfig output text file, the Number Of Members and Member [Number] fields will include the partition data (Starting Offset and Length) that you need to reproduce the volume configuration of the failed disk.

3. Using the Computer Management snap-in, double-click Storage, and then click Disk Management to open Disk Manager. The new disk will be displayed as "unallocated space" in the lower right pane of Disk Manager.

4. Right-click in the unallocated space, and click Create Partition to run the Create Partition Wizard, shown in Figure 5.3. The wizard will create the partitions needed to restore the disk to its original state.

5. When the wizard prompts you to assign a drive letter, assign the drive letter used by the disk you replaced.

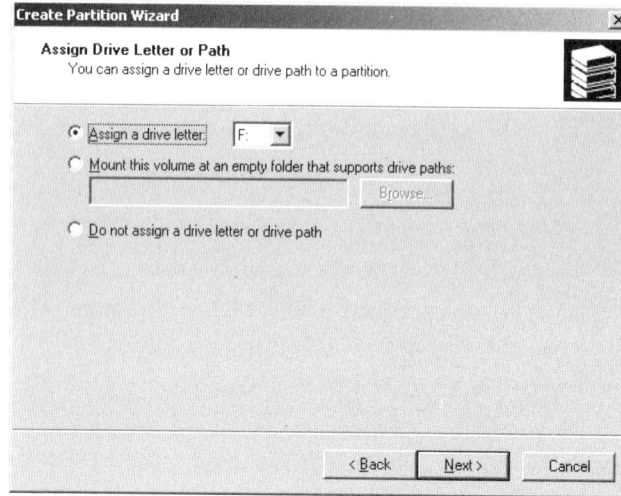

Figure 5.3   Assigning the drive letter in the Create Partition Wizard

6. Use the data from the DumpConfig file to format the partition. You must format cluster disks using the NTFS file system.

7. At the command prompt, run Dumpcfg.exe to obtain the current disk signatures.

8. Compare the current disk signatures to the disk signatures from the DumpConfig output text file. Write the old disk signature to the new disk. (The signature for the replaced disk should be missing from the current DumpConfig output file and present in the old DumpConfig output file. The signature of the new disk should be present in the current DumpConfig output file and missing from the old DumpConfig output file.)

9. To write the disk signature of the failed disk to the new disk, type the following at a command prompt:

```
dumpcfg.exe /s signature disknumber
```

In this command, *signature* is the disk signature and *disknumber* is the number of the disk that you replaced.

10. In the Computer Management window, double-click System Tools, and then click Device Manager.

11. In the Non–Plug And Play Drivers section, open the Cluster Disk Driver Properties dialog box. If the Non–Plug And Play Drivers section isn't showing, click Show Hidden Devices on the View menu.

12. Click the Driver tab, set the startup for the cluster disk to System, and then start the cluster disk driver.

13. In the Services And Applications section, click Services and change the properties for Cluster Service to Automatic.

14. Start Cluster Service.

To create and configure a Physical Disk resource for the new disk:

1. In Cluster Administrator, create a Physical Disk resource for the new disk in the same group as the old Physical Disk resource, giving it the same name as the old Physical Disk resource.

2. For each resource that was dependent on the old Physical Disk resource, specify the new Physical Disk resource as a dependency and remove the old Physical Disk resource as a dependency. Do not bring any resources online at this time.

To bring resources back online and restore the cluster configuration:

1. Bring the new Physical Disk resource online.

2. Restore data from backup onto the new disk.

3. Bring any resources that depend on the new Physical Disk resource online.

4. Restart the remaining cluster nodes.

5. Verify that all nodes show up in Cluster Administrator. You might need to press F5 to refresh the screen.

6. In Cluster Administrator, delete the Physical Disk resource associated with the old disk. Check resource properties to make sure that no resources still depend on the old Physical Disk resource. Change the dependency to the new Physical Disk resource for any that do.

7. Verify group failover for the group to which the new Physical Disk resource belongs.

Replacing a Failed Cluster Disk

Replacing a failed cluster disk requires less effort if the disk is offline. Use the following steps to replace an offline cluster disk that has failed:

To physically replace the disk:

1. Shut down all cluster nodes.

2. Remove the disk that needs replacing.

3. Follow the instructions from your hardware manufacturer to install a replacement disk in your cluster storage device.

4. Turn on only one of the cluster nodes. Because of dependencies on the failed disk, some cluster resources might have failed. Change the disk dependency for each failed resource to the new Physical Disk resource.

To disable Cluster Service and the cluster disk driver:

1. In the Computer Management snap-in, double-click Services And Applications, and then click Services.

2. Click Cluster Service.

3. In the Properties dialog box, change the Startup setting to Disabled, and then click OK.

4. In the Computer Management window, double-click System Tools, and then click Device Manager.

5. On the View menu, click Show Hidden Devices. Non–Plug And Play Drivers will appear in the list in the right pane.

6. Double-click Non–Plug And Play Drivers, right-click Cluster Disk, and then click Disable.

7. When you're asked whether you want to disable the cluster disk, click Yes.

8. When prompted to restart the computer, click Yes.

To configure, format, and partition the new disk:

1. Open the DumpConfig output text file from your backup for the cluster disks.

2. In the [Volumes] section of the file, the Number Of Members And Member [Number] fields will include the partition data (Starting Offset and Length) that you need to reproduce the volume configuration of the failed disk.

3. From the Computer Management snap-in, double-click Storage, and then click Disk Management to open Disk Manager. The new disk will be displayed as "unallocated space" in the lower right pane of Disk Manager.

4. Right-click in the unallocated space, and click Create Partition to run the Create Partition Wizard. The wizard will create the partitions needed to restore the disk to its original state.

5. When the wizard prompts you to assign a drive letter, assign the same drive letter as for the disk you replaced.

6. Use the data from the DumpConfig file to format the partition.

7. At the command prompt, run Dumpcfg.exe to obtain the current disk signatures.

8. Compare the current disk signatures to the disk signatures from the DumpConfig output text file. Write the old disk signature to the new disk.

9. Type the following command at a command prompt to write the disk signature of the failed disk to the new disk:

```
dumpcfg.exe /s signature disknumber
```

In this command, *signature* is the disk signature and *disknumber* is the number of the disk that you replaced.

10. In the Computer Management window, double-click System Tools, and then click Device Manager.

11. In the Non–Plug And Play Drivers section, open the Cluster Disk Properties dialog box.

12. Click the Driver tab, set the startup for the cluster disk to System, and then start the cluster disk driver.

13. In the Services And Applications section, click Services and change the properties for Cluster Service to Automatic.

14. Start Cluster Service.

15. Verify the configuration.

Lesson Summary

This lesson described cluster storage management issues. It explained how to create Physical Disk resources using Cluster Administrator or Cluster.exe and how to use Cluster.exe to display Disk Resource private properties that are used to monitor and manage cluster physical disks. Managing cluster storage also involves planning for disk failures and additional disk space. This lesson detailed how to extend disk space and add SCSI buses or devices. It also described the process of replacing a failed cluster disk.

Review

The following questions will help you review key information presented in this chapter. You'll find the answers in Appendix A, "Questions and Answers."

1. Describe what Dfs is and what it is used for.

2. Which of the following issues should you consider when you implement Dfs?

   a. Users accessing the shared resources will be distributed across multiple sites.

   b. Your organization uses internal and/or external Web sites.

   c. Redistributing shared resources can improve Network Load Balancing performance.

   d. All of the above.

3. Which of the following statements about file shares is true?

   a. Normal shares are the most flexible, and their security terms are easy to understand.

   b. Subdirectory shares are available in Windows NT 4 Service Pack 4.

   c. Dfs root shares are available in Windows NT 4 Service Pack 4.

   d. A normal share allows administrators to create directories that host a large number of shares.

4. Which disk management wizard is used to replace cluster disks?

5. In Windows 2000, printers do not need to be locally defined on each node in the cluster. Why? (Choose all that apply.)

   a. The port configuration is stored in the Cluster Registry.

   b. The cluster nodes share the port configuration.

   c. The printer driver files can be shared between the nodes.

   d. Cluster Service provides failover of the print server.

6. How do System Monitor and the Print Queue object help you?

7. Which of the following Physical Disk resource properties are not required?
   a. Name
   b. Description
   c. Possible Owners
   d. Required Dependencies
   e. Disk

8. What are the required dependencies for a Physical Disk resource?

9. From which of the following can a Physical Disk resource be created?
   a. A disk partition shared in the cluster
   b. A tape drive shared in the cluster
   c. A disk drive shared in the cluster
   d. The disk where the Quorum resource resides

10. In what situation must all nodes be possible owners of a Physical Disk resource?

C H A P T E R   6

Implementing Applications and Network Services on a Cluster

About This Chapter

This chapter discusses how you can implement applications and services in a cluster. This includes configuring cluster-aware applications and services that are capable of interacting with Cluster Service and responding to failure. The chapter also discusses cluster-unaware applications and services that use Cluster Service to provide failover ability. You'll also learn how to configure and manage the Dynamic Host Configuration Protocol (DHCP) and Windows Internet Naming Service (WINS) network services for Cluster Service. This chapter concludes with a lesson that describes implementing and deploying Web sites on a cluster using Microsoft Internet Information Services (IIS).

Before You Begin

To complete the lessons in this chapter, you must have

- The necessary hardware as outlined in the section titled "About This Book" in the Introduction

- The Windows 2000 Advanced Server installation CD-ROM

- Cluster Service installed in a two-node Windows 2000 Advanced Server cluster

Lesson 1: Implementing Clustered Applications

This lesson describes the two types of applications that you can install in a cluster—cluster-aware and cluster-unaware—and how to manage them. If you plan to implement or develop an application that will be deployed on a cluster, you must consider the requirements of the application and the application's ability to interact with a cluster.

After this lesson, you will be able to

- Compare and contrast cluster-aware and cluster-unaware applications
- List the functionality of a cluster-aware management application

Estimated lesson time: 20 minutes

Cluster-Aware Applications

When you implement applications on a cluster, they are either cluster-aware or cluster-unaware. An application with the following features is potentially cluster-aware:

- Supports TCP/IP
- Stores its data in a customizable location
- Supports transactions

If an application meets these fundamental requirements, it can typically be configured to run as a cluster-aware application. Examples of potentially cluster-aware applications include client/server database applications, file or print server applications, and various groupware applications. Cluster-aware applications can be categorized as follows:

- **Cluster management applications**   Applications that interact with the cluster but are not designed to run as a cluster resource. Examples include Cluster Administrator and the Cluster Verification tool included in the Windows 2000 Server Resource Kit.

- **Cluster resource applications**   Applications that configured such that they can take advantage of Cluster Service features such as failover. As a result, their availability increases and clients can access the application via a virtual server. In addition, the application can take advantage of any customized failure detection that you might have implemented. Although Cluster Service provides a number of general resource types, you must create a custom resource type for your application.

Developing Cluster-Aware Management Applications

If you intend to develop your own cluster-aware management application, you must decide what Cluster Service functionality is required. You determine this based on the tasks the application must perform. In general, this functionality includes

- The ability to receive cluster events
- The ability to access cluster-related information
- The ability to change the cluster configuration

Cluster-aware applications use the Cluster API to obtain the information required for these three types of functionality. Table 6.1 presents examples of different kinds of cluster-aware applications and the tasks that they must perform in relation to the cluster.

Table 6.1   Tasks and Events for Cluster-Aware Applications

Type of application	Cluster events	Cluster-related information needed	Cluster configuration tasks
Cluster-aware setup application	None	Detects cluster version, accesses the cluster's list of nodes, and lists available disks	Creates and configures test groups
Remote Failover Monitor and Performance Tracker	Responds to events associated with group or resource changes	Accesses the cluster's list of nodes and their groups and resources	None
Resource Configuration Wizard	None	Provides user feedback based on the proposed changes	Backs up the cluster database, creates groups, creates resources, changes properties, creates dependencies, changes which node owns a group, updates the Registry, and changes group and node states

Cluster-Unaware Applications

Cluster-unaware applications do not include their own resource DLLs that implement the Cluster API, so they cannot interact with Cluster Service. Therefore, these applications cannot take full advantage of the features of the cluster. However, you can configure cluster-unaware applications to interact with the cluster at very basic levels. One way to configure an application to take advantage of the cluster's failover capabilities is to use the Generic Application resource or the Generic Service resource. But keep in mind that cluster-unaware applications cannot interact with Cluster Service, so their ability to clean up in the event of a failover might be limited. For example, the application might not properly close its connections to a database and therefore would not write the latest changes when it terminates.

An alternative to using one of the generic resources, which might not fully support the given cluster-unaware application you need to deploy, is to develop a custom resource. The Cluster API lets you create application-specific resource DLLs. Because these DLLs are written for a specific application, they can provide increased functionality to ensure that the application initializes and terminates correctly in the event of a failure on the cluster. Of course, if you implement a custom resource DLL, the application is considered cluster-aware. If the application works properly using one of the generic resources and is able to shut down and restart as the result of a failover, you can leave it as cluster-unaware.

Lesson Summary

This lesson discussed the two types of applications that you can install on a cluster—cluster-aware and cluster-unaware. Cluster-aware applications use a cluster resource DLL and can benefit from Cluster Service functionality. You also learned about the differences between the two types of cluster-aware applications, cluster management and cluster resource applications. Cluster-unaware applications are unable to interact with the Cluster API and can therefore gain only limited cluster functionality through the Generic Application or Generic Service resources. The lesson explained some of these shortcomings and also discussed the development of cluster-aware management applications and the functionality they can employ.

Lesson 2: Implementing DHCP Server Clusters

You can also implement network services such as DHCP Server on a cluster. This lesson describes how to implement DHCP Server on a cluster, cluster-specific considerations such as DHCP resource settings, and DHCP Server-specific considerations such as IP addressing options for clients. You'll also learn how to configure DHCP scopes on a cluster and about the benefits and limitations of clustering DHCP. Finally, you'll learn about the hardware, software, and network considerations involved in planning a DHCP Server cluster.

After this lesson, you will be able to

- Describe the purpose of the DHCP Server service
- Compare and contrast methods of increasing the availability of a DHCP server
- Describe the implementation considerations and process for clustering a DHCP server

Estimated lesson time: 45 minutes

Overview of DHCP Server Clusters

The DHCP Server service provides dynamic TCP/IP configuration information to clients on a network. DHCP eliminates the need to implement and maintain static IP addresses on a network. Windows 2000 Advanced Server and Windows 2000 Datacenter Server provide integrated support for clustering DHCP Server. When a node that provides a DHCP virtual server instance fails, the DHCP server is automatically failed over to another node in the cluster. The failover process for a DHCP server usually takes less than a minute, so downtime for any clients is minimized. Since DHCP is widely used as a method of dynamically supplying TCP/IP information, it is an excellent choice for clustering.

For best performance, DHCP clusters should be in an active/passive configuration (shown in Figure 6.1). In this configuration, DHCP Server is installed on both nodes in the cluster. The DHCP Server service runs on the active node, while the passive node remains in a standby state. In this state, the passive node monitors the health of the active node. If the active node fails, the passive node assumes the task of running DHCP Server. Because the cluster nodes share a common DHCP database and configuration, either node can provide the DHCP Server service to clients. Using the active/passive configuration for clustering DHCP Server makes it easier to maintain and upgrade DHCP servers. Maintenance can be performed on the passive node without affecting DHCP Server performance. Once maintenance on the passive node is completed, the roles of the nodes can be reversed. This allows maintenance or upgrades to be performed on the normally active node while the normally passive node assumes responsibility for the DHCP Server service.

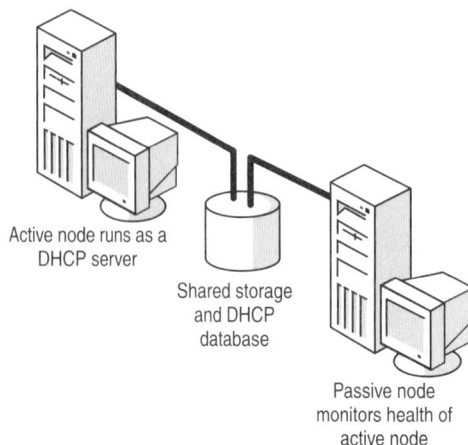

Figure 6.1   A two-node active/passive DHCP Server cluster

Benefits of Clustering DHCP Servers

While some network services, such as Dynamic Domain Name System (DDNS) and WINS, support server-to-server replication, this is not possible with DHCP. Therefore, the only method of increasing the availability of stand-alone DHCP servers is to divide DHCP scopes between multiple servers. If one server becomes unavailable, a percentage of the available IP addresses remains available through a second DHCP server. An 80/20 split of each scope is generally used between two DHCP servers. Unfortunately, this method of increasing availability might not be possible in cases where there are a limited number of IP addresses. Because the DHCP Server service in Windows 2000 is cluster-aware, there is no need to divide IP address scopes if DHCP servers are clustered. However, you can provide even greater fault tolerance by combining DHCP Server clustering with a split scope configuration.

An additional advantage of DHCP Server clustering is the possibility of integrating it with other Windows 2000 cluster-aware services, such as WINS. A cluster that supports multiple network infrastructure services has increased availability, redundancy, and manageability.

Limitations of Clustering DHCP Servers

The resource type that allows you to manage the DHCP Server service in a cluster is stored in a database. In order for a DHCP resource to fail over, the database must be stored on the cluster's shared disk. If this device fails or loses power, the entire cluster, including DHCP, will fail. The DHCP server should not be used to provide any of the TCP/IP configuration information for the network interfaces within the cluster. Further, when you use a mixed-node cluster, DHCP will not fail over from Windows 2000 to Windows NT 4.

Implementation Considerations for Clustering DHCP Servers

When you implement DHCP Server on a cluster, you must consider many of the same questions that you would when implementing a stand-alone DHCP server, plus additional ones. For example, you must exclude the IP addresses of any virtual servers in the cluster from the DHCP scope. This ensures that these IP addresses will not be circulated to clients by the DHCP server. You should also configure the database path, the audit log file path, and the database backup path using the Cluster Administrator tool rather than the DHCP Administrator tool. The following section details some of the basic deployment considerations for DHCP servers on a cluster.

Identifying Hardware and Storage Requirements

Installing the DHCP Server service on your cluster might require additional resources. The disk, memory, and CPU capacity of your hardware should be able to support the additional tasks performed by a Windows 2000 DHCP Server node. Because the DHCP Server service requires only negligible space on the nodes and shared disk, no special allowances need to be made for disk capacity. However, due to the overhead requirements of the DHCP Server service, you might need to increase CPU processing capacity and RAM.

New DHCP Server Service Features in Windows 2000

In addition to anticipating the growth of your network before you implement a DHCP cluster, you must also consider the impact of supporting additional features in DHCP. The following are some of the new DHCP features that you should take into account when you implement a DHCP cluster on Windows 2000:

- DDNS registration, updates, and removal of forward and reverse lookup records for DHCP-provided IP addresses.

- Enhanced monitoring and statistical reporting features. These provide notification when IP addresses run below a user-defined threshold.

- Allocation of IP addresses through Multicast Address Dynamic Client Allocation Protocol (MADCAP). This allows TCP/IP-based multimedia devices, such as video conferencing applications, to receive required IP addresses automatically.

- User-class support with client configurations based on class IDs. This allows clients to receive DHCP configuration based on client type. For example, a group of DHCP clients can be configured to automatically release their DHCP leases upon shutdown.

- Support for vendor-specific classes for DHCP allocation. This allows for the defining of vendor-specific options as an alternative to the potentially lengthy process of obtaining Internet Engineering Task Force (IETF) approval for a new standard option. These vendor classes are defined by specific vendors and are triggered by data bits that determine whether a given option class is standard or vendor-specific.

Determining the Number of DHCP Servers to Use

Although clustering your DHCP servers can reduce the need for additional redundant or backup DHCP servers, you must still consider the total number of servers you need to support your network. You should consider the location of routers on the network, whether a DHCP server is needed in each subnet, the number of clients using DHCP, and the bandwidth between each segment for which the DHCP Server service will be provided. With slower network links or dial-up links, a DHCP server is usually deployed on each side of these links to service clients locally. In addition, the size of a network is limited by the IP address subnet, such as the 254-node limit of a Class C subnet. You should also consider such issues as disk capacity and CPU speed for each server. For example, if more DHCP servers are needed because of the size of your network, you might be able to save money with smaller disks and less CPU capacity in the servers.

Finally, you must decide whether to cluster all of your DHCP servers or just certain servers.

Defining and Configuring Scopes

You must configure a scope for each physical subnet to define the parameters used by clients for the subnet, as shown in Figure 6-2. A scope has the following characteristics:

- A scope is a range of IP addresses from a single subnet that is provided by a DHCP server.

- You can exclude addresses from a scope for devices that need static IP addresses.

- A scope must be assigned a name when it is created.

- Lease durations for clients that receive dynamically allocated IP addresses can be set at the scope level.

- You can reserve IP addresses from a scope for devices that need the same IP addresses consistently assigned to them.

- A scope must be activated on the DHCP server before it can begin offering IP address leases to DHCP-enabled clients.

- The IP addresses used for virtual servers on a cluster must be excluded from any DHCP scope that they are contained in so that they are not distributed to clients.

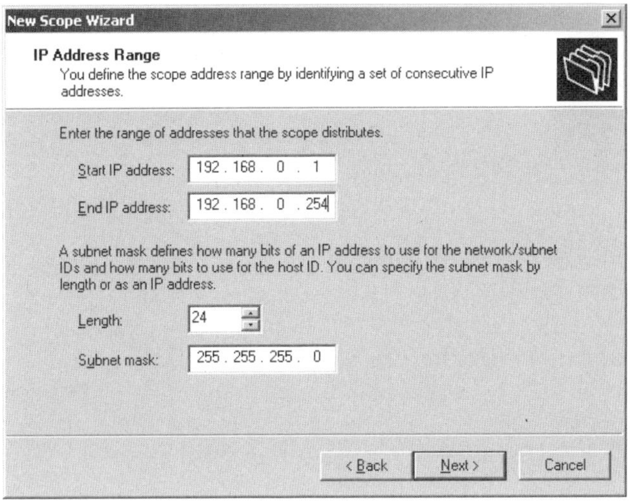

Figure 6.2   Defining DHCP scopes using the New Scope Wizard

Using Superscopes

You can group scopes into a single Superscope using an administrative feature of the Microsoft DHCP Manager tool. Superscopes are useful for dealing with the following DHCP Server service issues:

- Providing IP address leases for DHCP clients on a single physical network segment with multiple logical IP subnets.

- Supporting DHCP clients located remotely from BOOTP or DHCP relay agents.

- Enabling more hosts to be added to a network without affecting current scopes.

- Allowing for IP addresses on a network to be renumbered.

- Managing separate logical subnets on the same physical subnet with two DHCP servers.

When you implement DHCP on a cluster, you can implement scopes and superscopes in the same manner as with a stand-alone DHCP server configuration.

Reserving IP Addresses

You can reserve certain IP addresses for the computers or other devices on your network that require a specific IP address. This ensures that the computer or device is leased the same IP address each time one is requested. The alternative to this is to assign a static IP address to the computer or device and to exclude the IP address from the DHCP scope. The function of the device or computer and the layout of your network will determine which method you employ.

Using the DHCP Manager to reserve selected IP addresses for special-function devices on the network ensures that DHCP does not duplicate or reassign the address. Reservations are useful for the following types of network devices:

- Windows NT–based servers on a network that require static IP addresses, such as WINS servers.
- Print servers that use TCP/IP print services and require static IP addresses.
- DNS servers on a network.
- IP addresses used for Cluster Service nodes.

For each reservation, the Media Access Control (MAC), or physical, address of the DHCP client is used to associate the reserved IP address with a device.

IP Addressing Options for Clients

In addition to providing a lease for an IP address, DHCP can also be used to configure other TCP/IP information for the clients on your network. You must decide which of these options to configure and for which clients on your network the options should be applied. You can create options for all the clients on your network, for a specific subnet, or for individual clients. Here are the common client IP addressing options:

- Default Gateway (03–Router)
- DNS Server (05–Name Server)
- NetBIOS over TCP/IP (46–NetBIOS Node Type)
- WINS server (44–NetBIOS Name Server)

Cluster-Specific Considerations

When you create a DHCP resource, be sure to include the following dependent resources:

- Physical Disk
- IP Address
- Network Name

The IP Address resource must also be the one used to authorize the DHCP Server service in Active Directory so it can function correctly and provide IP address leases for clients on the network. Each address must be a static IP address rather than a dynamic IP address obtained from a DHCP server. It must also be excluded from any scopes defined on the same subnet for any DHCP servers on your network.

In addition, the database, audit, and backup paths that you specify for the resource must be located on the shared device that you used as a resource, as shown in Figure 6-3. For example, if the shared device is drive W, you must choose a database, audit, and backup path on drive W. You cannot use the *%SystemRoot%* environment variable as part of these paths, but other environment variables are acceptable.

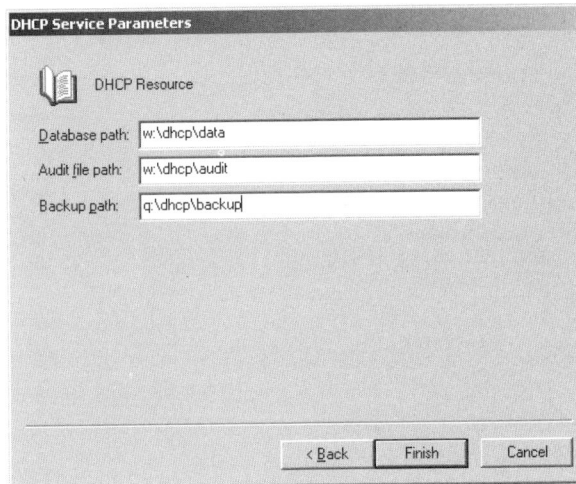

Figure 6.3   Assigning DHCP Server parameters for a resource

Steps for Installing a DHCP Cluster

Here are the steps you must perform to ensure a successful installation of DHCP Server:

1. Review the concepts associated with cluster resources.

2. Review resource groups and resource dependencies.

3. Review DHCP concepts such as scopes, leases, and options.

4. Determine the IP address range or ranges that DHCP will provide on your network.

5. Determine the hardware and software requirements for the DHCP cluster.

6. Install the cluster hardware and configure Cluster Service.

7. Install DHCP Server on a cluster node.

8. If you're using multiple scopes, configure any global options for the server that should be inherited by all scopes.

9. Create a new scope and assign an IP address range and any options such as WINS and DNS servers.

10. If needed, configure additional scope options.

11. If needed, add reservations for clients that require a reserved IP address assigned by DHCP.

12. Exclude IP address ranges that should not be leased for the scope.

13. Activate the scope.

14. If needed, configure and assign option classes.

15. If needed, define additional option types.

16. If needed, adjust the length of lease durations.

17. If you need to support more than one subnet, create and use superscopes as necessary to support your network DHCP configuration.

18. Authorize DHCP Server in Active Directory.

19. Set any DNS dynamic update policy needed for DHCP Server.

20. For routed networks, determine whether you need to implement DHCP or BOOTP relay agents. If you do, review possible relay agent configurations and related design issues.

21. If needed, create multicast scopes.

22. If you need to support BOOTP clients through DHCP, configure the BOOTP table.

23. Plan common cluster resource settings.

24. Use the New Group Wizard in Cluster Administrator to create a resource group for DHCP resources.

25. Use the New Resource Wizard in Cluster Administrator to create the Dependent Disk, IP Address, and Network Name DHCP cluster resources.

26. Use the New Resource Wizard in Cluster Administrator to create the DHCP resource and assign the required resource dependencies.

27. Configure the location of DHCP database, audit log, and backup database files so they are on a shared disk.

28. Verify the failover capabilities of the DHCP cluster.

29. Verify that DHCP Server is available to clients.

30. If necessary, disable automatic address configuration on Windows 2000 clients.

31. Use System Monitor to track DHCP Server performance.

32. If desired, set up local groups and users as DHCP administrators to control access to the DHCP cluster.

33. Troubleshoot and resolve any DHCP or cluster-related issues.

34. If needed, review the DHCP Server audit log for help in troubleshooting any problems.

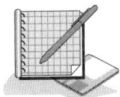

Practice: Implementing DHCP Server on a Cluster

In this practice, you will install and configure DHCP Server on cluster NodeA. You will then create a DHCP Cluster resource and activate the DHCP server for failover.

Note This practice assumes that you're implementing DHCP Server on a new cluster. Only the default group and resources should appear in Cluster Administrator.

Installing the DHCP Server Service

1. On NodeA, click Start, point to Settings, and then click Control Panel.

2. In the Windows Control Panel, double-click Add/Remove Programs, and then click Add/Remove Windows Components.

3. Under Components, scroll to and click Networking Services.

4. Click Details.

5. Under Subcomponents Of Networking Services, select Dynamic Host Configuration Protocol (DHCP), click OK, and then click Next.

6. If prompted, type the full path to the Windows 2000 Advanced Server distribution files and click Continue. The required files will be copied to your hard disk.

7. Click Finish to close the Windows Components Wizard.

8. Repeat this process on NodeB.

Creating a DHCP Resource Group

1. Open Cluster Administrator by clicking Start, pointing to Programs, pointing to Administrative Tools, and then clicking Cluster Administrator.

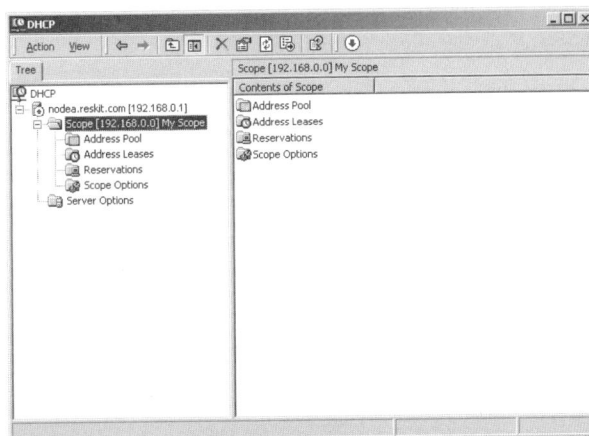

Figure 6.4 The DHCP console

2. In the console tree, double-click the Groups folder.

3. On the Action menu, click New and point to Group. The New Group Wizard will open.

4. Type *DHCP Group* in the Name field and *DHCP Resource Group* in the Description field. Click Next.

5. Click on NodeA in the Available Nodes list and click Add. Repeat this step to add NodeB.

6. Click Finish to complete the wizard.

Transferring a Physical Disk Resource

1. Click the Resources folder.

2. Right-click Disk W: and point to Change Group. A popup menu will appear listing all of the available groups in the cluster.

3. Click DHCP Group. A message box will appear asking if you are sure you want to change the group.

4. Click Yes. The Disk W: resource will be shown as part of the DHCP Group. Having the disk resource as part of the group will allow you to add a DHCP resource to the group.

Creating an IP Address Resource

1. Click the Groups folder.

2. Right-click DHCP Group, point to New, and click Resource.

3. In the New Resource dialog box, type in or indicate the information below:

Name   *IP address for DHCP*

Description   *IP address of DHCP resource*

Resource Type   *IP Address*

Group   *DHCP Group*

4. Click Next.

5. Both nodes should appear in the Possible Owners list. If they do not, add them to the list.

6. Click Next.

7. In the Dependencies dialog box, the Resource Dependencies list will be blank. Click Next.

8. In the TCP/IP Address Parameters dialog box, type in or indicate the following information:

   Address   *192.168.0.4*

   Subnet Mask   *255.255.255.0*

   Network   *Public Cluster Connection*

   You can leave NetBIOS enabled.

9. Click Finish.

10. A message box will appear stating that the IP Address resource was created successfully.

11. Click OK.

Creating a Network Name Resource

1. Click the Groups folder.

2. Right-click DHCP Group, point to New, and click Resource.

3. In the New Resource dialog box, type in or indicate the information below:

   Name   *Network name*

   Description   *Network name for DHCP resource*

   Resource Type   *Network Name*

   Group   *DHCP Group*

4. Click Next.

5. Both nodes should appear in the Possible Owners list. If they do not, add them to the list.

6. Click Next.

7. In the Dependencies dialog box, add the IP address for the DHCP resource to the Resource Dependencies list and click Next.

8. In the Network Name Parameters dialog box, type *CLUSTERDHCP*.

9. Click Finish. A message box will appear stating that the Network Name resource was created successfully.

10. Click OK.

Creating a DHCP Resource

1. Click the Groups folder.

2. Right-click DHCP Group, point to New, and click Resource.

3. In the New Resource dialog box, type in or indicate the information below:

    Name   *DHCP Resource*

    Description   *DHCP Cluster Resource*

    Resource Type   *DHCP*

    Group   *DHCP Group*

4. Click Next.

5. Both nodes should appear in the Possible Owners list. If they do not, add them to the list.

6. Click Next.

7. On the Dependencies page, add all of the listed resources to the Resource Dependencies list and click Next.

8. On the DHCP Service Parameters page, modify each path to match the following. (These paths will be created automatically.)

    Database path   *w:\dhcp\data*

    Audit file path   *w:\dhcp\audit*

    Backup path   *w:\dhcp\backup*

9. Click Finish. A message box will appear stating that the DHCP resource was created successfully.

10. Click OK.

Creating a New DHCP Scope

1. Open the DHCP console by clicking Start, pointing to Programs, pointing to Administrative Tools, and then clicking DHCP. (The DHCP console is the administrative tool for managing the DHCP Server service and configuring DHCP servers.)

2. If this is the first time you're running the DHCP console, you must add the nodes.

3. In the console tree, click the NodeA DHCP server in the left pane.

4. On the Action menu, click New Scope to open the New Scope Wizard.

5. Click Next to proceed to the Scope Name page.

6. Type *My Scope* in the Name field and *DHCP Scope for Cluster* in the Description field.

7. Click Next.

8. On the IP Address Range page, type in the following information. (The length and subnet mask values should be automatically filled in once you enter the range.)

Start IP Address   *192.168.0.1*

End IP Address   *192.168.0.254*

Subnet Mask   *255.255.255.0*

9. Click Next.

10. On the Add Exclusions page, type *192.168.0.1* in the Start IP Address field and *192.168.0.10* in the End IP Address field. Click Add to add this range to the list of exclusions.

11. Click Next to proceed to the Lease Duration page, and click Next again.

12. On the Configure DHCP Options page, select Yes, I Want To Configure These Options Now, and then click Next.

13. On the Router (Default Gateway) page, enter the same IP address that was used as the default gateway for NodeA. Click Next.

14. On the Domain Name And DNS Servers page, enter *reskit.com* in the Parent Domain field. Type *NodeA* in the Server Name field and click Resolve. The IP address for NodeA should appear in the IP Address field.

15. Click Add to add the IP address to the list.

16. Click Next to proceed to the WINS Servers page. Leave all fields empty and click Next.

17. Select Yes, I Want To Activate This Scope Now, and then click Next. Click Finish to complete adding a new DHCP scope.

Authorizing a DHCP Server in Active Directory

1. In the DHCP console tree, click DHCP.

2. On the Action menu, click Manage Authorized Servers.

3. In the Manage Authorized Servers dialog box, click Authorize.

4. Enter *NodeA* as the name of the DHCP server to be authorized, and then click OK. The DHCP server on NodeA should now start automatically.

Verifying the DHCP Cluster

1. If needed, right-click on the DHCP Group in Cluster Administrator and click Bring Online to bring the group online.

2. Right-click on DHCP Group and click Move to move the group to the other node. Each of the group resources will be moved from one node to the next with the group to which it belongs. You should see the entry in the Owner category change as the resource moves. You should also see the resources automatically come back online after they have been moved.

3. Open Microsoft Windows Explorer by clicking Start, pointing to Programs, pointing to Accessories, and then clicking Windows Explorer.

4. Double-click on My Computer in the Folders tree. The tree will expand and display the folders and disks available under My Computer.

5. Double-click on the disk or volume designated by *W:*. The tree will expand and display files and folders on this disk. Verify that the w:\dhcp\data, w:\dhcp\audit, and w:\dhcp\backup folders created earlier are present on the shared disk.

Monitoring a Clustered DHCP Installation

DHCP servers are usually critical components of a network implementation. A drop in server performance can have a major effect on a given network. The Windows 2000 operating system includes a set of performance counters for monitoring various types of DHCP server activity. These counters are available only if DHCP Server has been installed. You must use System Monitor to examine these counters. Table 6.2 lists the performance counters for DHCP Server that can be displayed using System Monitor.

Table 6.2   System Monitor Counters for DHCP Server

Counter	Description
Nacks/sec	The number of DHCP negative acknowledgment messages (DHCPNAKs) sent per second by the DHCP server to clients. A very high value might indicate potential network problems on servers or clients. A deactivated scope might result from an improperly configured server. Client computers moving between subnets might also result in a very high value. Mobile devices, such as laptops or portables, are a common cause of this problem.
Offers/sec	The number of DHCP offer messages (DHCPOFFERs) sent per second by the DHCP server to clients. Heavy traffic on the DHCP server is indicated by an instant or unexpected increase in this value.
Acks/sec	The number of DHCP acknowledgment messages (DHCPACKs) sent per second by the DHCP server to clients. An instant or unexpected increase in this value might indicate a large number of clients being renewed by the DHCP server. It might also signal that scope lease durations are not long enough.
Active queue length	The current length of the internal message queue for the DHCP server. This value represents the number of unprocessed messages received by the server. A large value might indicate heavy server traffic.
Conflict check queue length	The current length of the conflict check queue for the DHCP server. This queue acts as a place to hold messages that don't have responses while the DHCP server performs address conflict detection. A large value might indicate that server lease traffic is unexpectedly heavy or that the Conflict Detection Attempts setting is too high
Declines/sec	The number of DHCP decline messages (DHCPDECLINEs) received per second by the DHCP server from clients. Address conflicts between clients might result in a high value, indicating network problems. Enabling conflict detection on the DHCP server might help you troubleshoot the problem. Be sure to disable conflict detection once the problem is resolved in order to reduce server overhead.

Table 6.2   System Monitor Counters for DHCP Server *(continued)*

Counter	Description
Discovers/sec	The number of DHCP discover messages (DHCPDISCOVERs) received per second by the server. When a client queries the network for a new IP address lease from the DHCP server, these messages are sent by the client. This value might unexpectedly increase if a large number of clients are querying for an IP address lease simultaneously.
Duplicates dropped/sec	The number of duplicated packets per second dropped by the DHCP server. This number is affected when the same packet is sent to the server by multiple DHCP relay agents or network interfaces. A large value might indicate that clients are timing out too quickly or that the server is slow to respond.
Informs/sec	The number of DHCP inform messages (DHCPINFORMs) received per second by the DHCP server. Inform messages are used to flag moments when the DHCP server queries the Directory Service for the enterprise root or when the DHCP server is performing dynamic updates for the client.
Milliseconds per packet (avg)	The average time in milliseconds that the DHCP server takes to process each packet it receives. The value varies depending on the server hardware and its I/O subsystem. Instant or unexpected increases might indicate I/O subsystem problems such as too much processing overhead or a subsystem performance slowdown.
Packets expired/sec	The number of packets per second that expire and are dropped by the DHCP server. If a DHCP-related message packet is queued for more than 30 seconds, the packet is expired by the server. A large value for this counter might indicate that the server cannot process the packets while other packets are queued. A large value might also indicate that network traffic is too high for the server to manage.
Packets received/sec	The number of message packets received per second by the DHCP server. A large value indicates heavy DHCP traffic.
Releases/sec	The number of DHCP release messages (DHCPRELEASEs) received per second by the DHCP server from clients. This value is generated when a client using DHCP sends a release to the server. Releases can be sent manually using the ipconfig utility at the client or automatically during client shutdown. For the release to occur automatically during shutdown, the client must be configured with the Release DHCP Lease On Shutdown option. This value usually remains low because clients usually release their addresses automatically.
Requests/sec	The number of DHCP request messages (DHCPREQUESTs) received per second by the DHCP server from clients. An instant or unexpected increase in this number might indicate a large number of clients concurrently trying to renew their leases with the DHCP server. A large value might also indicate a short scope lease duration.

Lesson Summary

This lesson discussed the benefits and limitations of implementing DHCP on a cluster along with implementation considerations relating to software, hardware, the network, and the cluster. The lesson also described DHCP-specific implementation and planning considerations such as network layout, IP address scope, and IP addressing options for clients. Some of the options for monitoring and managing a DHCP cluster were discussed.

Lesson 3: Implementing WINS Server Clusters

This lesson discusses the steps for installing, configuring, and managing a WINS server on a cluster. It covers how to plan for the number of WINS servers, recommended hardware requirements, replication of WINS servers, network traffic, and fault tolerance. You'll also learn about the benefits and limitations of a WINS server cluster and how this approach compares to other methods of providing increased redundancy and availability for WINS servers. Finally, you'll learn some of the options for monitoring and managing WINS performance.

Overview of WINS Server Clusters

By implementing a WINS server, you allow clients on your network to use Network Basic Input/Output System (NetBIOS) names instead of TCP/IP addresses on a Windows network. Using WINS eliminates the need for broadcasts to resolve computer names to IP addresses. It also provides a dynamic database that maintains mappings of computer names to IP addresses instead of using the static LMHOSTS file to do this manually. This type of name resolution is appropriate for clients running Windows NT and earlier versions of Microsoft Windows operating systems. Because DDNS in Windows 2000 is the standard name resolution method, WINS services are required only to support legacy clients and NetBIOS-dependent applications.

The WINS server design consists of the following server types:

- A name server that records and resolves name resolution queries from clients. Each legacy WINS client is configured to query up to two name servers either statically or using DHCP. Windows 2000 clients can be configured to query more than two WINS servers. One WINS server is configured as the primary name server for resolving client queries, while a secondary WINS server is used in the event that a name resolution query fails.

- A replication hub or backup WINS server is configured to perform local or wide area replication of the WINS database between name servers.

A WINS cluster can be formed from either a name server or a replication hub. Both options provide greater redundancy, increased availability, and more efficient management of WINS traffic.

Benefits of Clustering a WINS Server

Other than the standard benefits of availability and redundancy with any clustered service, there are not many benefits to clustering WINS servers over replicating WINS servers. With clustering, the WINS database is stored on the shared device and supports failover for availability and redundancy. With WINS replication, availability and redundancy is provided with a replica of the WINS database that is stored on another WINS server. Some additional availability could be gained by clustering each WINS server, but this would increase the cost without adding much benefit. Perhaps the greatest benefit to clustering WINS can be gained by combining WINS services with an existing cluster that is set up for another application or service, such as DHCP. Both services can thus benefit from being clustered without the additional cost.

Limitations of Clustering a WINS Server

Although Windows 2000 supports clustering of WINS servers, you should carefully consider the advantages and disadvantages of clustering WINS. Because WINS is a legacy technology, you might be in the process of upgrading your infrastructure to an environment in which WINS is not needed. In a case in which the requirement for WINS servers is small, clustering WINS is simply not necessary. If you're looking to provide greater redundancy and availability for WINS, replication is a more effective solution because it also makes WINS fault tolerant. To ensure uninterrupted service, you can also configure your WINS clients with the address of a secondary WINS server as an alternative to clustering WINS.

Like DHCP, WINS will not failover from Windows 2000 to Windows NT 4 in a mixed-node cluster.

Implementation Considerations for Clustering WINS Servers

When you implement a WINS server on a cluster, you must consider many of the same questions that you would when implementing a stand-alone WINS server.

Determining the Number of Required WINS Servers

The number of WINS servers required for your network depends on both the number of WINS clients per server and the network topology. A single WINS server can process NetBIOS name resolution requests for 10,000 clients. However, when deciding how many WINS servers you need, you must also consider the location of routers on your network and the distribution of clients in each subnet. Also, the number of users per server depends on patterns of usage and the storage and processing capacity of the server.

Identifying Hardware and Storage Requirements

As with DHCP servers in a cluster, you might need to upgrade the hardware of your cluster nodes to support either a WINS name server or replication hub. Clustered WINS servers should have a hard disk with high-speed I/O that is dedicated to the WINS service. This helps to increase the database response and guarantees high clustering efficiency.

Designing the WINS Replication Partners

Part of planning WINS replication includes deciding whether WINS servers are configured as pull or push partners and setting partner preferences for each server. Replication can be performed either manually or automatically. Deciding whether to configure a WINS server as a pull partner, a push partner, or both depends on your network environment. Here are some guidelines:

- You should configure a push partner when servers are connected by fast links. Because push replication occurs when the configured number of updated WINS database entries is reached, a slow network link will cause your network to slow down at unscheduled intervals.

- You should configure a pull partner when you want replication to occur at specific intervals. This is recommended for slow links so you can control when replication occurs.

- You should configure each server to be both a push and pull partner whenever possible. This method allows automatic two-way replication to occur more efficiently between two servers.

Assessing Network Traffic

Although WINS can help reduce broadcast traffic on your network, it does create some additional traffic between servers and clients. You will need to estimate the impact of this traffic, especially on routed TCP/IP networks. The performance of a WINS server is also dependent on other network traffic. If the WINS server is located somewhere other than the local subnet and server requests need to travel through a router, this might cause delays on your network. You should also consider the effects of lower-speed and wide area links on replication traffic between WINS servers and WINS clients that register and renew NetBIOS names.

Planning for Fault Tolerance

When planning your WINS design for fault tolerance, you should consider the following situations in which the WINS service would no longer be available on your network:

- A hardware failure that results in WINS server downtime
- A power failure that results in WINS server downtime
- A network link or router failure that prevents clients from reaching a WINS server

The first step in planning for failure is to determine the maximum length of time that any given WINS server is unavailable to your network. Be sure to consider both planned and unplanned outages. Also, consider the impact on the client if its primary WINS server is not available.

Replication is the primary method of fault tolerance for WINS servers. By providing and assigning multiple WINS servers for clients, you can minimize the impact of a single WINS server being offline. Clustering of WINS servers can also be used to provide greater availability and redundancy in the case of a hardware failure.

Cluster-Specific Considerations

When you create a WINS resource, be sure to include the following dependent resources, as shown in Figure 6.5.

- Physical Disk
- IP Address
- Network Name

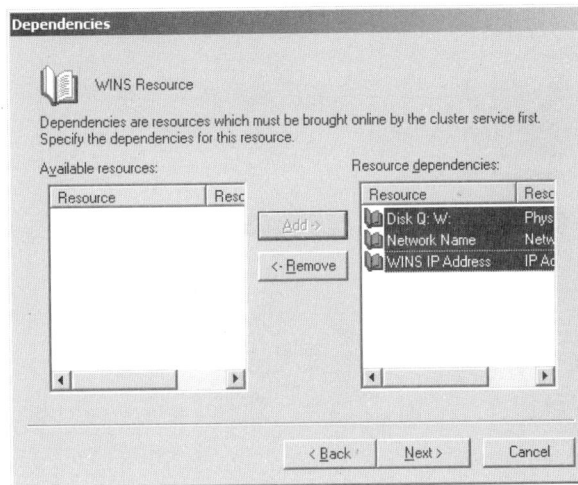

Figure 6.5   WINS resource dependencies

In addition, the database and backup paths that you specify for the resource must end with a backslash (\) and must specify a location on the dependent shared disk that you used as a resource. For example, if the dependent disk is drive W, you must choose a database and backup path on drive W. You cannot use the *%SystemRoot%* environment variable as part of these paths, but other environment variables are acceptable.

You should never use static WINS mappings for cluster Network Name resources. Doing so will prevent failover of that resource and its dependencies.

Steps for Installing a WINS Cluster

You must take the following steps to successfully install WINS on a cluster:

1. Review the concepts behind cluster resources.
2. Review resource groups and resource dependencies.
3. Review WINS concepts such as NetBIOS names, WINS servers, WINS clients, and replication partners.

4. Verify the need for a WINS server on your network and verify that the WINS server should be clustered.

5. Determine the number of WINS servers you need, the number that need to be clustered, and the hardware and software requirements for the clustered WINS servers.

6. Install the cluster hardware and configure Cluster Service.

7. Install WINS on each cluster node, as shown in Figure 6.6.

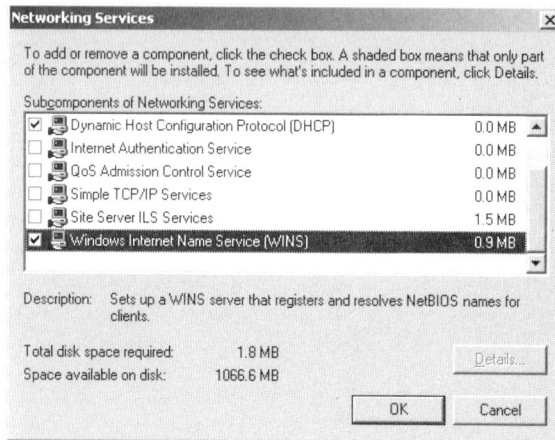

Figure 6.6 Installing WINS

8. If needed, modify WINS server defaults.

9. If needed, configure replication settings for both primary and secondary WINS servers using the following replication methods:

   - Push partner only

   - Pull partner only

   - Push/pull partner (recommended)

10. Plan common cluster resource settings.

11. Use the New Group Wizard in Cluster Administrator to create a resource group for WINS resources.

12. Use the New Resource Wizard in Cluster Administrator to create the Dependent Disk, IP Address, and Network Name WINS cluster resources.

13. Use the New Resource Wizard in Cluster Administrator to create the WINS resource and assign the required resource dependencies.

14. Configure the location of the WINS database and backup database files so they are on a shared disk.

15. Verify the failover capabilities of the WINS cluster.

16. Verify that the WINS service is available to clients.

17. If needed, filter the WINS database view of active registrations.

18. If needed, add and remove mappings in the WINS database.

19. Regularly back up, scavenge, and compact the WINS database.

20. Periodically view server statistics to monitor WINS server performance.

21. Update client configurations on your network to correctly specify both primary and secondary WINS servers based on your network configuration.

22. Depending on whether you configure network clients to obtain TCP/IP addresses statically or dynamically, you should

    ▪ Configure WINS settings in advanced TCP/IP properties for client network adapters

    ▪ Configure and enable WINS options for DHCP scopes so that DHCP provides IP addresses of WINS servers and NetBIOS names to clients that require them

23. If needed, verify registration of client NetBIOS names in WINS.

24. Troubleshoot and resolve any WINS or cluster-related issues.

Practice: Implementing WINS on a Cluster

In this practice, you will install and configure WINS on the cluster. You will then create a WINS cluster resource and activate the WINS server for failover.

Installing WINS

1. Open Windows Control Panel by clicking Start, pointing to Settings, and then clicking Control Panel.

2. Double-click Add/Remove Programs, and then click Add/Remove Windows Components.

3. Under Components, scroll to and click Networking Services.

4. Click Details.

5. Under Subcomponents Of Networking Services, select Windows Internet Name Service (WINS), click OK, and then click Next.

6. If prompted, type the full path to the Windows 2000 Advanced Server distribution files and click Continue. The required files will be copied to your hard disk.

7. Click Finish to close the Windows Components Wizard.

8. If needed, start the WINS service.

9. Repeat this process on NodeB.

Creating a WINS Resource Group

1. Open Cluster Administrator on either node by clicking Start, pointing to Programs, pointing to Administrative Tools, and then clicking Cluster Administrator.

2. In the console tree, double-click the Groups folder.

3. On the Action menu, click New and point to Group. The New Group Wizard will open.

4. Type in *WINS Group* in the Name field and *WINS Resource Group* in the Description field. Click Next.

5. Click on NodeA in the Available Nodes list and click Add. Repeat this step to add NodeB.

6. Click Finish to complete the wizard.

Transferring a Physical Disk Resource

1. Click the Resources folder.

2. Right-click Disk W: and point to Change Group. A popup menu will appear listing all of the available groups in the cluster.

3. Click WINS Group. A message box will appear asking if you're sure you want to change the group.

4. Click Yes. The Disk W: resource will be shown as part of the WINS Group. Having the disk resource as part of the group will allow you to add a WINS resource to the group.

Creating an IP Address Resource

1. Click the Groups folder.

2. Right-click WINS Group, point to New, and click Resource.

3. In the New Resource dialog box, type in or indicate the information below:

    Name   *WINS IP address*

    Description   *IP Address for WINS Resource*

    Resource   *Type IP Address*

    Group   *WINS Group*

4. Click Next.

5. Both nodes should appear in the Possible Owners list. If they do not, add them to the list.

6. Click Next.

7. In the Dependencies dialog box, the Resource Dependencies list will be blank. Click Next.

8. In the TCP/IP Address Parameters dialog box, type in the following information:

   Address   *192.168.0.5*

   Subnet Mask   *255.255.255.0*

   Network   *Public Cluster Connection*

9. Click Finish. A message box will appear stating that the IP Address resource was created successfully.

10. Click OK.

Creating a Network Name Resource

1. Click the Groups folder.

2. Right-click WINS Group, point to New, and click Resource.

3. In the New Resource dialog box, type in or indicate the information below:

   Name   *Network name*

   Description   *WINS Network Name resource*

   Resource Type   *Network Name*

   Group   *WINS Group*

4. Click Next.

5. Both nodes should appear in the Possible Owners list. If they do not, add them to the list.

6. Click Next.

7. In the Dependencies dialog box, add the WINS IP Address resource to the Resource Dependencies list, and then click Next.

8. In the Network Name Parameters dialog box, type *CLUSTERWINS*.

9. Click Finish. A message box will appear stating that the Network Name resource was created successfully.

10. Click OK.

Creating a WINS Resource

1. Click the Groups folder.

2. Right-click WINS Group, point to New, and click Resource.

3. In the New Resource dialog box, type in or indicate the information below:

   Name   *WINS resource*

   Description   *WINS Service resource*

   Resource Type   *WINS Service*

   Group   *WINS Group*

4. Click Next.

5. Both nodes should appear in the Possible Owners list. If they do not, add them to the list. Both nodes should be listed as possible owners to allow for failover of the WINS resource. If only one node is listed as the resource's possible owner, the resource cannot fail over.

6. Click Next.

7. On the Dependencies page, add all of the listed resource to the Resource Dependencies list, and then click Next.

8. On the WINS Service Parameters page, modify each path to match the following. (These paths will be created automatically.)

   Database path   *w:\wins\data*

   Backup path   *w:\wins\backup*

9. Click Finish. A message box will appear stating that the WINS resource was created successfully.

10. Click OK.

Verifying a WINS Cluster

1. If needed, right-click on the WINS Group and click Bring Online to bring the group online.

2. Right-click on the WINS Group and click Move to move the group to the other node. Each of the group resources will be moved from one node to the next with the group to which it belongs. You should see the entry in the Owner category change as the resource moves. You should also see the resources automatically come back online after they have been moved.

3. Open Windows Explorer by clicking Start, pointing to Programs, pointing to Accessories, and then clicking Windows Explorer.

4. Double-click on My Computer in the Folders tree. The tree will expand and display the folders and disks available under My Computer.

5. Double-click on the disk or volume designated by *W:*. The tree will expand and display files and folders on this disk. Verify that the w:\wins\data and w:\wins\backup folders created earlier are present on the shared disk.

WINS Performance Counters

You can also monitor WINS server performance using System Monitor. Table 6.3 lists WINS performance counters available for monitoring a WINS server.

Table 6.3   WINS Counters

Counter	Description
Group Conflicts/sec	The rate at which group registration received by the WINS server resulted in conflicts with records in the database.
Unique Conflicts/sec	The rate at which unique registrations/renewals received by the WINS server resulted in conflicts with records in the database.
Total Number of Conflicts/sec	The sum of the unique conflicts and group conflicts per second. Conflicts were seen by the WINS server at this total rate.
Group Registrations/sec	The rate at which the WINS server receives group registrations.
Unique Registrations/sec	The rate at which unique registration are received by the WINS server.
Total Number of Registrations/sec	The sum of the unique and group registrations per second. This is the total rate at which registration are received by the WINS server.
Group Renewals/sec	The rate at which group renewals are received by the WINS server
Unique Renewals/sec	The rate at which the WINS server receives unique renewals.
Total Number of Renewals/sec	The sum of the unique renewals and group renewals per second.
Queries/sec	The rate at which the WINS server receives queries.
Successful Queries/sec	Total number of successful queries per second.
Failed Queries/sec	Total number of failed queries per second.
Releases/sec	The rate at which the WINS server receives releases.
Successful Releases/sec	The total number of successful releases per second.
Failed Releases/sec	The total number of failed releases per second.

Lesson Summary

This lesson described the requirements for installing, configuring, and managing a WINS server cluster, including those relating to hardware, software, the network, and the cluster. The lesson also described WINS-specific implementation and planning considerations. Some of the performance counters for monitoring a WINS server were also identified.

Lesson 4: Implementing Clustered Internet Information Services

This lesson discusses installing and administering Internet Information Services (IIS) on a cluster. Although it introduces various IIS clustering technologies, the lesson primarily describes IIS server clusters. Specifically, it discusses the two types of IIS sites that can be clustered, Web or FTP, with respect to setting up IIS server clusters. In addition, the lesson offers guidelines for installing, implementing, and managing IIS server clusters.

IIS and Clustering Technologies

Both Network Load Balancing (NLB) and server clusters can be implemented with IIS. You can cluster up to 32 servers with NLB to provide high availability and scalability for IIS. Two or four connected servers in a server cluster can provide high availability and failover support for IIS. Whether you implement NLB for both high availability and scalability or a server cluster for high availability will depend on your needs and the available resources.

Web sites or FTP sites within IIS can be set up on a preferred server node, either manually or programmatically, to provide static load balancing in a server cluster. Client connections can also be distributed between multiple server nodes to provide NLB. In both cases, load balancing and fault tolerance are the primary goals of clustering IIS.

Both Cluster Service and the Microsoft Content Replication System (CRS) feature of Microsoft Site Server integrate seamlessly with IIS. The IIS metabase and other configuration settings can also be replicated manually from one server to others using the Iissync.exe command-line utility.

Installing IIS on a Cluster

After you install and configure Cluster Service on each node, you can easily implement IIS on your cluster. On a two-node cluster, both nodes should be configured as either domain controllers or member servers. Although IIS 5.0 is installed by default with Windows 2000 Advanced Server, you can customize the installation so that IIS is installed later. Either method is acceptable for setting up a IIS server cluster.

Use the following guidelines for installing IIS on a cluster:

- Verify that the cluster fails over correctly before you install IIS server instances on your cluster.

- Install Microsoft Distributed Transaction Coordinator (MS DTC) on your cluster before you install IIS server instances if you plan to implement Web applications that use transactions or that call MS DTC integrated applications.

- To set up MS DTC and install the MS DTC resource group on the cluster automatically, run Comclust.exe on each node.

- If your Web sites are not using transactions, it is not necessary to have a MS DTC resource dependency for an IIS virtual server instance.

- Create a folder on the cluster shared disk for each IIS virtual server. If possible, these folders should be created on a non-Quorum disk.

- Create a cluster resource group in Cluster Administrator for each IIS virtual server if you have the required Dependent Disk resources for each group.

- The dependent disk for MS DTC must be the same disk that was used for an IIS virtual server.

- All IIS virtual server resources must be created on the same node that owns the dependent Physical Disk resource where the virtual Web resides.

- Create an IP Address resource for your IIS virtual server in the same resource group as the Physical Disk resource where the virtual Web folders reside.

- Make the IP Address resource dependent on the Physical Disk resource used for the IIS virtual server.

- The IP Address resource should depend on the MS DTC resource, if one is being used.

- Create a Network Name resource for your IIS virtual server in the same resource group as the Physical Disk resource where the virtual Web folders reside. The Network Name resource must be dependent on the IP Address resource.

- Use the Internet Services Manager snap-in (shown in Figure 6.7) to create a new Web site or configure an existing Web site as the clustering Web site. Configure the Web site to use the IP address and folder on the shared disk associated with your IIS virtual server.

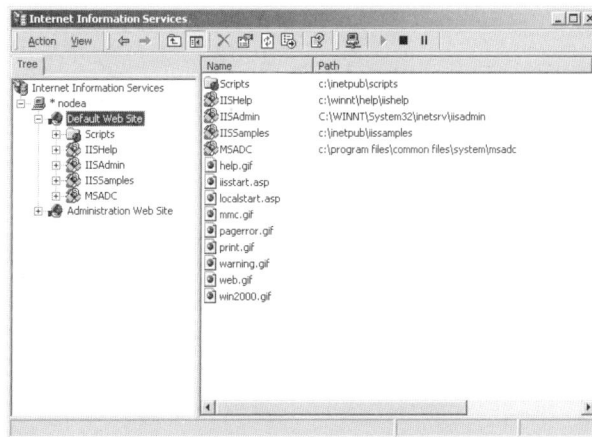

Figure 6.7   The Internet Services Manager snap-in

- Once a Web site is configured for clustering on one node, an identical Web site must be configured on the other cluster node. You can manually configure this Web site on the other node or use the iissync utility to automatically synchronize the two nodes.

- Make sure none of the Web sites on either node is set to the IIS virtual server IP address or to All Unassigned. If the default Web site is in its default configuration of All Unassigned, the IIS virtual server will not be accessible.

- Use Cluster Administrator to create a new IIS server instance. Set the Web site parameter to map to the IIS Web site configured for clustering. You can do this only after you have created the Web site and all of the required resources indicated above.

- Both nodes should be listed as possible owners for the IIS server instance in order to support failover. This is the default setting.

- The IIS server instance requires an IP Address resource dependency in order to support failover.

- A Network Name dependency is recommended for the IIS server instance in order to support failover when the resource is accessed using a network name.

- The IIS server instance should be dependent on the Physical Disk resource if your Web or FTP content is stored on the clustered disk. IIS will not be able to access your Web content after a failover if a node that does not have access to the cluster disk brings the IIS server instance online.

- You can optionally add a host entry to your DNS server that maps the IIS virtual server network name to the IIS virtual server IP address used to access the clustered Web site.

- Make sure the Web sites configured on each node are using anonymous user names and passwords that are usable by all nodes.

- All virtual Web directory paths should point to either a shared drive in the cluster or identical drive letters and paths on local disks.

- To stop and start clustered Web sites or FTP sites, you must use Cluster Administrator rather than the Internet Service Manager snap-in.

Installation and Management Considerations

The following considerations are related to installing and managing IIS on a cluster:

- Before you uninstall Cluster Service from a node, you must remove all IIS resources, including NNTP and SMTP. You will not be able to stop or start previously clustered IIS sites if the IIS resources are not removed. Type the following command at the Inetpub\AdminScripts command prompt to fix this problem for each previously clustered IIS resource:

```
adsutil.vbs set <service name>/<instance id>/ClusterEnabled 0
```

- Cluster Service does not support the use of Microsoft FrontPage Server Extensions on clustered Web sites.

- Cluster Service will attempt to automatically restart IIS if you use the Restart IIS command in the Internet Service Manager snap-in or if you use Iisreset.exe at the cluster. If you need to prevent Cluster service from automatically restarting IIS, take all IIS cluster resources off line using Cluster Administrator and then use the Internet Service Manager snap-in to restart IIS.

- Clustered ASP or FTP sessions cannot fail over to other nodes. However, if the affected node fails back before an ASP session times out, session information will not be lost unless the failure resulted from IIS stopping unexpectedly. With FTP sites, the session information is always lost. In most cases, a failover will require the user of the web or FTP site to reestablish the connection.

- You cannot use the Internet Service Manager snap-in to stop clustered IIS resources, such as NNTP and SMTP. When these resources are clustered, only Cluster Administrator can be used to stop them.

- You must set the ServerAutoStart metabase property to TRUE if your clustered Web sites are using host headers. Type the following command at the %SystemDrive%\inetpub\adminscripts command prompt to set this property, where *<instance id>* is the instance ID of the virtual host sites that are part of the cluster:

```
adsutil.vbs set w3svc/<instance id>/ServerAutoStart True
```

- To delete clustered IIS resources, use Cluster Administrator to remove the resources from the cluster, and then use the Internet Service Manager snap-in to delete the resources.

- Upgrades of IIS and rolling upgrades of IIS Cluster Service resources are supported. All clustered IIS resources must be taken offline during an IIS upgrade. However, clustered IIS resources can remain available to clients during a rolling upgrade. Windows 2000 Datacenter Server does not support upgrades, so a clean install of IIS is required.

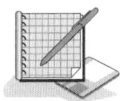

Practice: Implementing IIS on a Cluster

In this practice, you will install and configure IIS on a cluster and set up a Web site resource for failover. Once IIS is installed on both nodes and configured for failover, you'll bring the IIS resource and its dependencies online and test for correct failover capacity. To see a demonstration of this practice, run the IIS.exe animation located in the Media folder of the companion CD.

Installing the IIS Components

1. Open Cluster Administrator on NodeA by clicking Start, pointing to Programs, pointing to Administrative Tools, and then clicking Cluster Administrator.

2. Expand the console tree, and verify that both nodes are running correctly and that the cluster Physical Disk resource is running on NodeA.

3. Close Cluster Administrator.

4. Click Start, point to Settings, and then click Control Panel. Control Panel will open.

5. Double-click Add/Remove Programs, and then click Add/Remove Windows Components.

6. Under Components, scroll to and click Internet Information Services (IIS).

7. Click Details.

8. Under Internet Information Services (IIS), select Common Files Internet Information Services Snap-In, Internet Services Manager (HTML), and World Wide Web Server. Click OK, and then click Next. If prompted, type the full path to the Windows 2000 Advanced Server distribution files, and then click Continue. The required files will be copied to your hard disk.

9. Click Finish to close the Windows Components Wizard.

10. Repeat steps 1 through 9 to install IIS on NodeB.

Creating a New Web Folder on the Cluster Shared Disk

1. Open Cluster Administrator on NodeA by clicking Start, pointing to Programs, pointing to Administrative Tools, and then clicking Cluster Administrator.

2. Expand the console tree and verify that the cluster Physical Disk resource is running on NodeA.

3. From the Windows 2000 desktop on NodeA, double-click on the My Computer icon.

4. Double-click on the drive W: icon in the My Computer window.

5. From the File menu for the drive W: window, point to New and click Folder. A New Folder icon will appear in the window.

6. Change the name of the new folder to *inetpub* and press Enter.

7. Double-click on the inetpub folder to open a new window.

8. From the File menu in the Inetpub window, point to New and click Folder. A New Folder icon will appear in the window.

9. Change the name of the new folder to *wwwroot*.

10. Copy the default.htm file from the Samples folder on the companion CD to the wwwroot folder you just created.

Creating a New Web Site on the Cluster

1. Open Cluster Administrator on NodeA by clicking Start, pointing to Programs, pointing to Administrative Tools, and then clicking Cluster Administrator.

2. Expand the console tree and verify that the cluster Physical Disk resource is running on NodeA.

3. Open Internet Services Manager on NodeA by clicking Start, pointing to Programs, pointing to Administrative Tools, and then clicking Internet Services Manager.

4. Click NodeA in the left pane to expand the console tree.

5. Right-click on Default Web Site in the console tree and click Properties.

6. On the Web Site tab, change the IP address from All Unassigned to the IP address for the Public Cluster Connection for the node.

7. Click OK to accept the changes, and close the Default Web Site Properties dialog box.

8. Right-click on Default Web Site in the console tree, point to New, and click Site. This will open the Web Site Creation Wizard.

9. Click Next to continue past the welcome page of the wizard, and then type in *Clustered IIS Web site* for the description of the Web site. Click Next.

10. Leave the IP Address and Port settings as they are, and click Next.

11. Enter *w:\inetpub\wwwroot* for the Web site Home Directory path. Click Next.

12. Leave the Web site Access Permissions as they are, and click Next. Click Finish to complete the Web Site Creation Wizard.

13. Repeat steps 1 through 12 for NodeB.

Creating an IIS Resource Group

1. Open Cluster Administrator on NodeA by clicking Start, pointing to Programs, pointing to Administrative Tools, and then clicking Cluster Administrator.

2. Expand the console tree and verify that the cluster Physical Disk resource is running on NodeA.

3. In the console tree, double-click the Groups folder.

4. On the File menu, point to New and click Group. The New Group Wizard will open.

5. Type *Cluster IIS* in the Name field and *IIS Cluster Group* in the Description field. Click Next.

6. Click on NodeA in the Available Nodes list and click Add. Repeat this step to add NodeB.

7. Click Finish to complete the wizard.

Transferring a Physical Disk Resource

1. Click the Resources folder.

2. Right-click on Disk W: and point to Change Group. A popup menu will appear listing all of the available groups in the cluster.

3. Click the Cluster IIS group. A message box will appear asking if you're sure you want to change the group.

4. Click Yes. The Disk W: resource will be shown as part of the Cluster IIS group. Having the disk resource as part of the group will allow you to add an IIS Service Instance resource to the group.

Creating an IP Address Resource

1. Click the Groups folder.

2. Right-click on Cluster IIS, point to New, and click Resource.

3. In the New Resource dialog box, type in or indicate the information below:

   Name   *IIS IP Address*

   Description   *IIS IP Address Resource*

   Resource Type   *IP Address*

   Group   *Cluster IIS*

4. Click Next.

5. Both nodes should appear in the Possible Owners list. If they do not, add them to the list.

6. Click Next.

7. In the Dependencies dialog box, the Resource Dependencies list should be blank. Click Next.

8. In the TCP/IP Address Parameters dialog box, type the following information:

   Address   *192.168.0.7*

   Subnet Mask   *255.255.255.0*

   Network   *Public Cluster Connection*

9. Click Finish. A message box will appear stating that the IP Address resource was created successfully.

10. Click OK.

Creating a Network Name Resource

1. Click the Groups folder.
2. Right-click on Cluster IIS, point to New, and click Resource. The Resource dialog box will appear.
3. In the New Resource dialog box, type in or indicate the information below:

   Name   *IIS Name*

   Description   *IIS Network Name Resource*

   Resource Type   *Network Name*

   Group   *Cluster IIS*

4. Click Next.
5. Both nodes should appear in the Possible Owners list. If they do not, add them to the list.
6. Click Next.
7. In the Dependencies dialog box, add the IIS IP Address resource to the Resource Dependencies list and click Next.
8. In the Network Name Parameters dialog box, type *CLUSTERIIS*.
9. Click Finish. A message box will appear stating that the Network Name resource was created successfully.
10. Click OK.

Creating an IIS Server Instance Resource

1. Click the Groups folder.
2. Right-click on Cluster IIS, point to New, and click Resource.
3. In the New Resource dialog box, type in or indicate the information below:

   Name   *IIS Resource*

   Description   *Cluster IIS Resource*

   Resource Type   *IIS Server Instance*

   Group   *Cluster IIS*

4. Click Next.
5. Both nodes should appear in the Possible Owners list. If they do not, add them to the list.
6. Click Next.

7. On the Dependencies page, add all of the listed resources to the Resource Dependencies list and click Next.

8. On the Parameters page, select WWW for the resource and select Clustered IIS Web Site for the IIS Server.

9. Click Finish to close the wizard.

Verifying the IIS Cluster

1. Right-click on the Cluster IIS group and click Bring Online to bring the group online.

2. In the right pane, right-click on IIS Resource, and click Initiate Failure. The resource will fail and cause the group to fail over to the other node. You should see the entry in the Owner category change as each resource fails over. You should also see the resources automatically come back online after they have failed over.

3. Right-click on the Cluster IIS group and click Move to move the group back to the original node. Each group resource is moved from one node to the next with the group to which it belongs. You should see the entry in the Owner category change as the resource moves. You should also see the resources automatically come back online after they have been moved.

4. Open Internet Explorer by double-clicking the Internet Explorer icon on the Windows desktop.

5. Enter *http://192.168.0.7* on the address line, and press Enter. You should see the sample Web page displayed.

Lesson Summary

This lesson described how to install and administer Internet Information Services on a cluster. It offered guidelines for installing, implementing, and managing IIS server clusters, and it discussed issues related to Web site and FTP site configuration on a cluster.

Review

?

The following questions will help you review key information presented in this chapter. You'll find the answers in Appendix A, "Questions and Answers."

1. Is a folder called w:\cluster\dhcp\, where W: is the shared disk, a valid path for the DHCP database on a clustered DHCP server?

2. Which of the following characteristics identifies a cluster-unaware application?

   a. The application does not use the Cluster API.

   b. The application is managed as a Generic Application resource.

   c. The application can perform the necessary initialization and cleanup tasks.

   d. The application is highly available to cluster resources.

3. Is a folder called w:\cluster\wins, where W: is the shared disk, a valid path for the WINS database on a clustered WINS server?

4. Which of the following characteristics indicate that an application can be modified to become cluster-aware?

   a. The application's network protocol is TCP/IP.

   b. The application maintains data in a location that can be configured.

   c. The application supports transaction processing.

   d. The application does not use the Cluster API.

5. When you create a new WINS resource for a cluster using the New Resource Wizard, should you set both nodes as Possible Owners for the resource? Why?

6. Which of the following resources is a required dependency for an IIS server instance?

    a. IP Address

    b. Physical Disk

    c. Network Name

    d. MS DTC

7. Which technique provides the highest availability for a DHCP server, splitting scopes or clustering DHCP?

8. Which of the following cluster resources is a DHCP resource not dependent on?

    a. Physical Disk

    b. File Share

    c. IP Address

    d. Network Name

9. As the system administrator for your organization, you have been asked to deploy an application developed internally on a new cluster to increase its availability for clients. The application was previously deployed on a single server that all clients accessed directly and was not originally developed to be cluster-aware. After installing the application on each node, you add it to the cluster using the Generic Application resource type. You then test the application's ability to fail over to the second node in the cluster. Your tests show that the application behaves as expected. With this in mind, do you need to implement a custom resource DLL for this application?

10. Which of the following are valid steps for creating a WINS cluster?

    a. Authorize the WINS server in Active Directory

    b. Create a WINS resource

    c. Activate replication on a WINS cluster node

    d. Specify a path on the dependent disk for the WINS database

C H A P T E R   7

Troubleshooting Cluster Service

About This Chapter

This chapter describes a number of techniques for troubleshooting Cluster Service. It begins with general troubleshooting considerations and then addresses specific problems relating to resources, resource groups, nodes, and applications. The chapter also describes how to use the cluster log to interpret problems associated with the cluster. The cluster log is a text file created by Gluster Service that includes a variety of information about events and activities associated with the cluster. If you have a good understanding of the information in the cluster log, you can more easily administer your implementation of Cluster Service. The chapter concludes by describing backup and recovery processes for your cluster.

Before You Begin

To complete this chapter, you must have

- The necessary hardware as outlined in the section titled "About This Book" in the Introduction
- The Windows 2000 Advanced Server installation CD-ROM
- Cluster Service installed in a two-node Windows 2000 Advanced Server cluster
- The *Microsoft Windows 2000 Server Resource Kit* (or Internet access to obtain the necessary Resource Kit tools)

Lesson 1: General Troubleshooting

This lesson discusses general troubleshooting techniques for Cluster Service, including ways to address problems with installation, startup, SCSI devices, and network connectivity. For example, you can identify the source of many startup problems (such as problems involving the shared device, the network configuration, or the Cluster Service domain account) by monitoring the Microsoft Windows Event Log or Cluster Administrator for errors. This lesson also discusses ways to identify the source of failures that disrupt network or disk access, including interpreting cluster error messages and reviewing error logs.

After this lesson, you will be able to
- List common problems associated with a cluster installation
- Interpret common error messages and error codes

Estimated lesson time: 45 minutes

Troubleshooting Cluster Service Installation Problems

Cluster Service installation might seem simple compared with the installation of other network server applications, but Cluster Service is actually quite complex. A successful installation depends on many factors, including hardware compatibility, proper hardware configuration, and proper network configuration. Failure to meet the strict installation requirements usually leads to problems, so you must address the following issues before attempting installation:

- **Hardware compatibility**   As described earlier in this training kit, you should ensure that all nodes are configured using the same hardware and associated device drivers. This includes mirroring the configuration of various cards within the computers. Remember that Microsoft will support only installations of Cluster Service that use complete systems with HCL-certified hardware.
- **Disk space**   You must have enough space on both the system drive and the shared device. Although you need only a few megabytes to install Cluster

Service, this space must be on the local system disk. Data from applications that will be installed on the cluster will typically reside on the shared device.

- **Space for the system paging file** Insufficient space for the paging file can lead to system lockup during installation or to reduced system performance. You can check or update the paging file size and other Virtual Memory settings (shown in Figure 7.1) under the Performance options on the Advanced tab of the System utility in the Control Panel. The minimum is the amount of physical RAM plus 12 MB. The page files should be on local disks only, not on shared drives, network drives, or other remote or removable storage. This will ensure that the operating system has access to the page files. In addition, the system drive must have enough free space to hold a memory dump in the event of a system crash. You can use System Monitor for further troubleshooting of virtual memory problems.

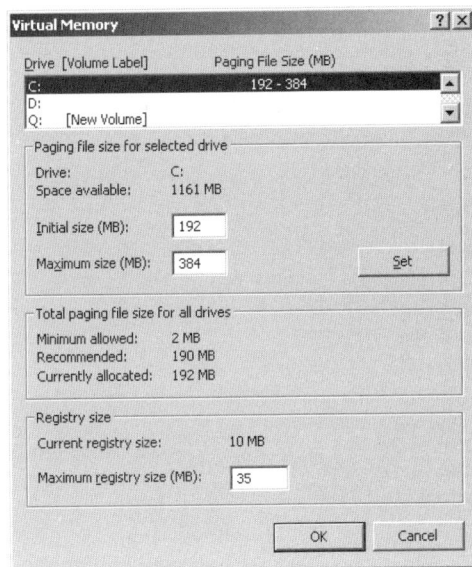

Figure 7.1 Virtual Memory settings

- **Domain accounts** Although a cluster node can be a domain controller or a member server, all nodes in a cluster must be members of the same domain. The domain account used for Cluster Service authentication must be the same on each node. Cluster Service setup must also be able to communicate with a domain controller during the installation process, and any other service that uses a domain account must use the same domain account on each node.

- **Installation login permissions** You must have administrative rights on each node in order to install Cluster Service. You can ensure this by using a Domain Admins account when you install the service.

- **Installation event log errors**   You should check the system and application event logs for errors before installing Cluster Service in order to verify the state of the system and identify any problems. You should also check the event logs after you complete the installation, especially if you encountered any installation problems. See Appendix C for a complete list of Cluster Service–related events.

- **Network configuration**   Cluster Service will not function properly if the network is improperly configured or malfunctioning. The Cluster Service setup will validate and use network connections during installation. You should verify that the network adapters are configured correctly with appropriate TCP/IP settings. Remember that IP addresses should be statically assigned rather than provided by a DHCP server. Also, verify that you are using the correct network adapter drivers. In some cases, a network adapter will appear to be working because the driver is similar but not an exact match to the correct driver. This might happen if the wrong driver is loaded because an OEM or integrated network adapter is using the same chip set as the standard driver. Loading an incorrect driver might only degrade performance, but it might also prevent the adapter from functioning. In addition, there might not be any errors in the system event log relating to the problem.

File and Print Sharing Problems

You might receive the following error message while installing Cluster Service:

Cluster Service Cannot Be Configured Because
LanManServer Could Not Be Started
The specified service does not exist as an
installed serviceError ID: 1060 (00000424)

This error occurs if file and printer sharing is not installed on the node on which you're installing Cluster Service. To fix this problem, simply install File And Printer Sharing For Microsoft Networks on the node. (See Figure 7.2.) Although you can install Cluster Service without file and printer sharing, you cannot configure Cluster Service without it.

Problems Joining the Cluster

When you install additional cluster nodes, you should verify that the first node you installed is running. You should also be sure to specify the correct cluster name to join. This will help ensure that the Quorum resource can give the new node the required information to join the cluster.

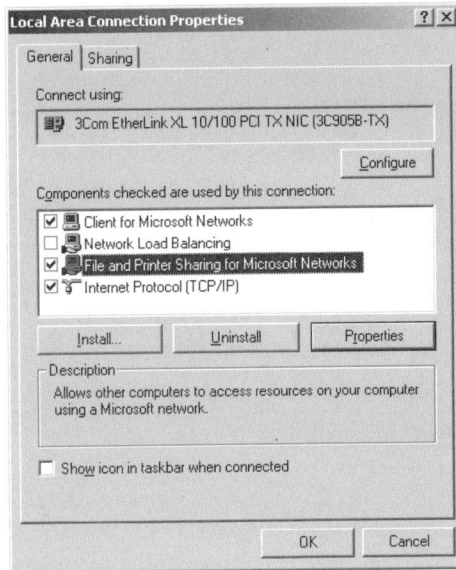

Figure 7.2   Installing File And Printer Sharing For Microsoft Networks

Troubleshooting Cluster Service Startup Problems

After installation, there are a number of reasons Cluster Service might fail to start: configuration problems, hardware-related problems, and network-related problems. To troubleshoot startup problems, you should first check the status of items on which Cluster Service depends.

When Cluster Service initially starts, it attempts to contact other cluster nodes if any exist. If other nodes are found, it attempts to join a cluster. If it is unable to join a cluster, it will attempt to form a cluster by locating and mounting a Quorum device.

Cluster Service performs the following steps at startup:

1. Authenticates the Cluster Service domain account.

2. Loads the local cluster database (clusdb).

3. Tries to contact other nodes using information from the local database.

4. Begins the join process if contact is successful.

5. If no other nodes are available, uses the information in the local database to mount the Quorum device and form a cluster.

6. Updates the local copy of the database using the latest checkpoint file and the Quorum log.

If you have problems with Cluster Service startup, the cause lies with one of these steps. Here are some general troubleshooting guidelines for determining the cause:

- If the entire cluster has failed, try to bring at least one node online. This will help with troubleshooting and might also allow you to keep resources available to users.

- If possible, check the event log on the failed node for errors. In many cases, you'll find a SCSI bus or connectivity-related problem.

- If possible, check the failed node for the existence of a recent Memory.dmp file. This file is sometimes created when a system crashes. You might need to contact Microsoft Product Support Services for help in interpreting this file.

- If one of the nodes has started, verify that all resources and groups are online.

- Check the cluster diagnostic log file for errors.

Problems can also occur when you apply service packs or hot fixes to the cluster. You should avoid applying a service pack or hot fix to both nodes at the same time unless the instructions tell you to. By updating one node at a time, you might be able to avoid unnecessary downtime for the cluster.

Cluster Service Domain Account Problems

If you have a problem with the domain account under which Cluster Service runs, the Service Control Manager (SCM) will not allow Cluster Service to load. If you have enabled diagnostic logging for Cluster Service, new entries will also not be written to the log. You should check the following items if you have a problem related to the Cluster Service domain account:

- Verify that the account is still a member of the local administrators group.

- Verify that the account has the appropriate rights on each node.

- Verify that the account is not disabled.

- Verify that the password has not expired for the account.

- Verify that a domain controller is available to authenticate the account.

If you promote a member server to a domain controller or demote a domain controller to a member server, you must update the rights. The following rights are required for the Cluster Service domain account:

- Lock Pages In Memory

- Log On As A Service

- Act As Part Of The Operating System

- Back Up Files And Directories

- Increase Quotas

- Increase Scheduling Priority
- Load And Unload Device Drivers
- Restore Files And Directories

All of these rights except Lock Pages In Memory, Log On As A Service, and Act As Part Of The Operating System are granted to the local Administrators group by default and are granted to the Cluster Service account when it is created during the installation process.

The local Administrators group is replaced by the Domain Local Administrators group when you promote a member server to a domain controller. This results in a loss of the local rights to Logon As A Service and Lock Pages In Memory for the Cluster Service account.

A local Administrators group is created and the Domain Local Administrators group is deleted when a domain controller is demoted to a member server. This new local Administrators account will not have the Cluster Service account as a member, so you must add it. Also, the Cluster Service account's Log On As A Service, Act As Part Of The Operating System, and Lock Pages In Memory rights are removed and must be regranted.

Event Log Errors

The application and system event logs play an important role in troubleshooting. The following cluster-related event log errors might occur when Cluster Service fails to start:

- **Event ID: 1000**   Cluster Service failed to start because an error was found in the local cluster database (clusdb).
- **Event ID: 1057**   Cluster Service failed to start because clusdb could not be opened.
- **Event ID: 1069**   Cluster Service failed to start because a Physical Disk resource failed.
- **Event ID: 1147**   Cluster Service failed to start because it could not find the Quorum log file.
- **Event ID: 7000**   Cluster Service could not start due to a problem with authenticating the Cluster Service account or because cluster logging was not configured properly.
- **Event ID: 7009**   Cluster Service timed out trying to connect, probably because of improperly configured cluster logging.
- **Event ID: 7013**   Cluster Service could not start due to a problem with authenticating the Cluster Service account.

For more cluster-related events, see Appendix C.

Problems Connecting to the Cluster Using Cluster Administrator

If Cluster Service starts but you cannot connect to the cluster using Cluster Administrator, you should first check the Services utility to verify that the service is running. If it is, the problem might be related to the cluster's Network Name or IP Address resources. There might also be problems with the Remote Procedure Call (RPC) service. Verify that the RPC service is running on both nodes. If it is, try connecting to a cluster node using the computer name. You can also try connecting using a period (.) instead of the cluster name, which will create a local connection and not require name resolution.

If you can make a local connection, verify that all of the resources are online and functioning properly. Network Name or IP Address resources might fail if a duplicate name or IP address is in use on the network. Also, a duplicate IP address on the network can cause communication problems or shut down the network adapter. Check the system event log for errors relating to this. Another possibility is that you have just started the system and you need to wait another 30 to 60 seconds for Cluster Service to start before trying to connect using Cluster Administrator.

Problems with the Local Cluster Database

Cluster Service might not start if clusdb is corrupted, inaccessible, or otherwise unavailable. The cluster database is a hive in the system registry found under HKEY_LOCAL_MACHINE\Cluster. By default, the file for this registry hive is located in the %SystemRoot%\Cluster\Clusdb folder.

You can use the following troubleshooting steps to find the source of the problem:

1. Verify that the Cluster Service domain account has full access to the clusdb file.
2. Verify that the clusdb file is not Read-Only.
3. Check the registry for the existence of the HKEY_LOCAL_MACHINE\Cluster key, shown in Figure 7.3.
4. If possible, restore the file from backup.
5. If one node in the cluster is still working, uninstall Cluster Service from the failed node, reinstall it, and then have the node rejoin the cluster. You should do this only if necessary because it can result in problems with some cluster resources. Afterwards, you might need to reconfigure cluster resources and reinstall applications on the cluster.
6. If none of the previous steps resolves the problem, your only remaining option (other than contacting Microsoft for support) might be to completely reinstall the cluster or use a disaster recovery method to restore the cluster from backup.

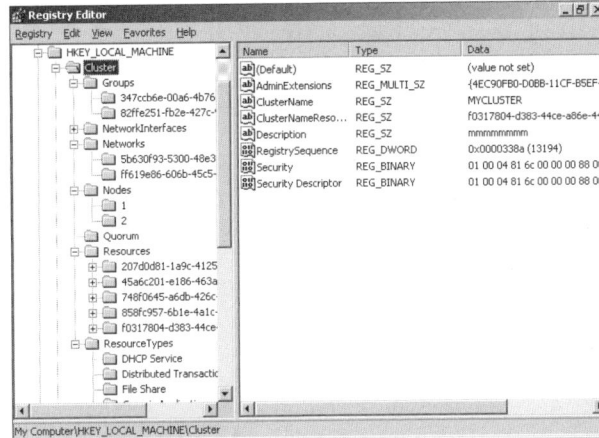

Figure 7.3   Viewing the local cluster database in the registry

Problems with RPC

Cluster Service uses RPCs to start and operate, so the RPC service must be running on both nodes. If you have problems with RPC, verify that the RPC service is running on both nodes and that there are no RPC-related errors, such as the service having failed to start, in the event log.

Problems with the Quorum Device

If the Quorum device does not come online, Cluster Service will not start. You can start Cluster Service with the *–fixquorum* switch to check the status of the Quorum device. Also, check the status of.the Quorum disk and attempt to bring it online if it has failed. You might also need to verify the Quorum location on the Quorum disk.

You can also check the System event log for disk errors. If the Quorum disk is coming online successfully but Cluster Service fails to start, the Quorum database might be corrupted. If so, you might want to restore it from backup. In addition, you might want to check the cluster log for errors if nothing else has identified the problem.

Troubleshooting Problems with Cluster SCSI Devices

The shared SCSI bus and the SCSI devices connected to it are crucial for proper operation of Cluster Service. At least one device must be available on the shared bus to act as the Quorum disk. In the event of a system failure or network communication problems, access to the Quorum disk is vital because it determines whether the cluster remains online. This section describes some general techniques for solving problems with cluster SCSI devices.

SCSI Configuration Problems

Verify that the SCSI host adapters are configured correctly and that each device on the bus has a unique ID number. On a two-node cluster, one adapter should be set to SCSI ID 6 and the other adapter to SCSI ID 7. Although other IDs will work, this configuration ensures that the host adapters have adequate priority on the bus.

You can use the host adapter utilities to establish whether the adapter can identify all disk devices on the SCSI bus. You should do this on both nodes, with only one node turned on at a time. If the adapters can identify the devices, you should verify that the operating system can see the drives. You can do this using Disk Management from the Computer Management MMC. As with the previous check, only one node should be turned on at a time when you verify that the operating system can see the drives. Also, you must start Cluster Service before performing this check; otherwise, the shared drives will not be online.

Physical Disk Resource Problems

Physical Disk resource problems are often hardware related. Cables, termination, or SCSI host adapter configuration problems can result in failure of a disk resource. You should verify that each SCSI cable is firmly connected and that there are no termination problems. Although the System event log might contain events related to a disk or a controller, the information might not be helpful in identifying or solving the problem. Therefore, you should start by verifying the shared SCSI bus and attached device configuration. Faulty cables and termination can also cause intermittent problems that are difficult to troubleshoot. Another consideration might be the BIOS or firmware versions on both the cards and drives that need to be updated or replaced.

Quorum Resource Failures

If Cluster Service is not starting because of a Quorum disk failure, there might be a problem with the SCSI device being used. If you have already tried starting Cluster Service with the *–fixquorum* startup option, you might need to change the Quorum drive settings. To modify the Quorum drive settings, right-click the cluster name at the root of the tree in the left pane of Cluster Administrator and select Properties to open the Cluster Properties window. This window has three tabs, one of which is for the Quorum disk properties. Figure 7.4 shows the Quorum tab. In addition to modifying Quorum disk properties, you can also redesignate the Quorum resource on the Quorum tab.

Problems Accessing a Shared Drive

If you get an error while attempting to access a shared drive using its drive letter, the node or drive you are trying to access might be offline. The drive might also be owned by another node in the cluster and should therefore be accessed from that node. Also, an error could indicate drive or controller problems.

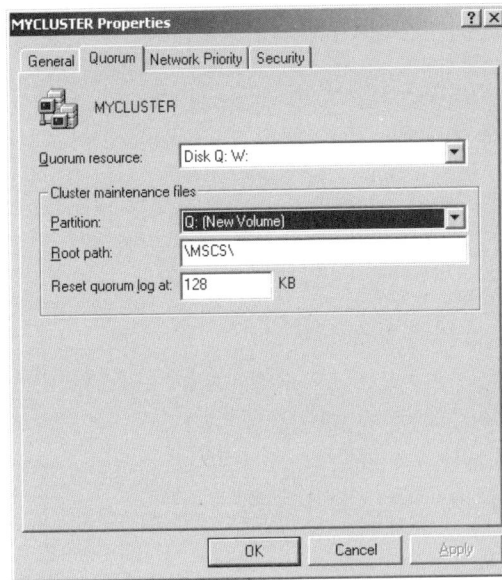

Figure 7.4   The Quorum tab of the Quorum disk Properties window

Note that Autochk, a companion program to Chkdsk that performs a disk check when the system starts up, will not perform a disk check on shared drives when the system starts. When Cluster Service brings a shared disk online, it performs a file system integrity check for each drive and automatically launches Chkdsk as necessary.

Event Log Errors

Some System event log errors relate to problems with the SCSI devices in a cluster. A problem might not manifest itself in the form of failures until multiple occurrences of these errors are present in the log. These events are generated by the device driver for the attached storage devices and not by the devices themselves. In addition, these events are not issued from the cluster software. See Appendix C for a full list of Cluster Service–related events. Here are some of those events:

- **Event ID: 9**   This error indicates that an I/O timeout has occurred in the storage system. This I/O timeout has no relation to the Cluster Service software. This error also causes the SCSI bus to be reset. The error might be caused by devices on the SCSI bus powering on or off, or it might indicate cabling, termination, or SCSI hardware configuration problems.

- **Event ID: 11**   This is a more serious error than an I/O timeout. It occurs with the SCSI driver or hardware itself rather than the cluster software. The error might result from a bad or corrupted device driver, a hardware or device failure, or problems with cabling or termination. In addition to checking general problems, you might also need to check the version of the SCSI controller BIOS and the device firmware revision for any updates. To check the SCSI device driver version, look in the %Systemroot%\System32\Drivers folder. Locate the version in the file properties, and verify with the manufacturer that you have the latest version.

- **Event ID: 15**   This error indicates that the device is not ready. It can result from SCSI host adapter problems, such as configuration problems. The Cluster Service software is probably not a factor. You should first check for updated drivers or firmware from the manufacturer. The device itself might not be functioning correctly. You might find Event ID 1038, 1036, or 1069 errors reported by Cluster Service in the event log along with this error.

You can use the following approaches to deal with SCSI device event log errors:

- Look for loose connections.
- Look for physical damage to cables or connector pins.
- Verify that the driver and firmware versions match those used on all servers in the cluster. Check with the manufacturer for updates.
- Make sure that your SCSI bus is properly terminated.
- Make sure that you do not have duplicate termination. For example, duplicate termination will occur if the controllers are terminated by software and the cables are terminated with physical connectors.
- Make sure that you have disabled the internal termination in the BIOS of the controller.
- Verify that the total cable length of the bus does not exceed the maximum SCSI length specified by the manufacturer.
- Check for duplicate SCSI IDs on the same bus.
- Verify that the automatic SCSI bus reset option is turned off for each controller.

Only One Node Can Connect to Cluster Drives

This problem has several possible causes. Use the following checklist to troubleshoot:

- Verify that the same drive letters are assigned to the drives on each node of the cluster.
- Verify that the SCSI devices have unique IDs.
- Verify that the second node is physically connected to the cluster drive. Make sure you restart each node after reconnecting the drive.
- Make sure SCSI controllers are configured correctly and that they are transferring data at the same rate.

Troubleshooting Network Connectivity Problems

Clients should be able to connect to clustered resources regardless of which node is the owner. There are several things you should check if clients are unable to connect to a clustered resource:

- Check for errors in the System event log of each node.
- Make sure that the resource group the client is trying to access has at least one IP Address resource and one Network Name resource.
- Verify that clients are using the correct IP address or network name to connect.
- Verify that the IP Address and Network Name resources the clients are connecting to are online.
- Check for network connectivity to the node that owns the resources.

Using the Ping Utility

You can use the TCP/IP Ping utility to verify network connectivity between clients and clustered resources. Running Ping from both the client and the cluster nodes can be helpful in troubleshooting problems. You run the utility from the command prompt using the following format:

```
PING <IP address or network name>
```

If the ping is successful, the device will respond; otherwise, you receive an error message, such as *Destination Host Unreachable*. Here are some examples of using the Ping utility to test network connectivity:

- Ping the IP address of the public network adapter on each node.
- Ping the IP address associated with a resource group or a virtual server.
- Ping the network name associated with a resource group or a virtual server.
- Ping the router or gateway between the client and the cluster if one is used.
- Ping the IP address of the client.

If you can successfully ping all of the items above, the problem might be somewhere else on the network. If you are unable to ping the client IP address from the server, there might be a client TCP/IP configuration or routing problem. If you cannot ping the network name of a group or a virtual server, you might have a name resolution problem. Name resolution problems might be associated with either a client configuration or a WINS problem.

If clients are unable to connect with the cluster, verify that Cluster Service is running and check the System event log for errors on each node. Also, check connectivity between cluster nodes and with other network devices. The problem is likely to be associated with the network or a client configuration if Cluster Service is running without any connectivity problems between nodes. In this case, you should verify that the client is using TCP/IP protocol and has a valid IP address on the network.

Intermittent Client Access Problems

If clients are having occasional problems accessing the cluster, the likely cause is improper network adapter configuration. In some cases, setting the network transmission speed to Autodetect might cause problems. Thus, it is a good practice to set network transmission speed to the actual speed of your network rather than have the network card detect it automatically.

In some cases, clients might not be able to access cluster resources immediately after you create a new IP Address resource or change the address of an existing resource. This delay can result if you are using WINS for name resolution on the network. The problem originates with delays during WINS replication and has no relation to Cluster Service. You might need to monitor or optimize your WINS implementation to alleviate the problem.

Network Interface Errors

Cluster Service determines the availability of network interfaces using a sophisticated algorithm, and it detects disconnected network cables and connectivity problems via the Plug and Play functionality in Windows 2000. Cluster Service also uses Internet Control Message Protocol (ICMP) echo requests as a secondary method of determining failures. It does not use ICMP echo requests as the primary method because they consume more network resources than other methods. You can view the current state of each network interface on a cluster using Cluster Administrator. (See Figure 7.5.)

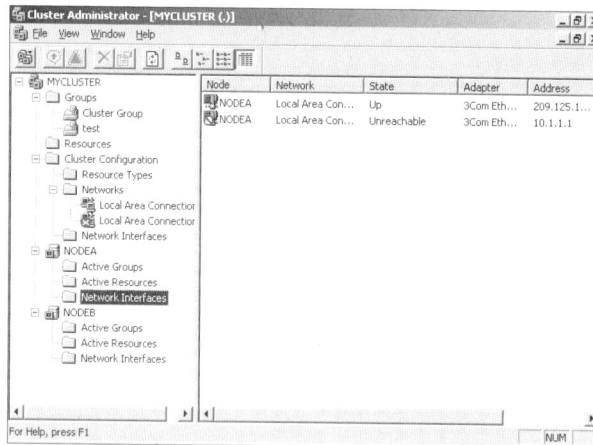

Figure 7.5   Viewing the network interface state in Cluster Administrator

The following are the network interface states returned by Cluster Service:

- **Unavailable**   The node that owns the network interface is down.
- **Failed**   The local interface cannot communicate with other interfaces on the network. This problem might be due to a network adapter, driver, cable, or port failure.
- **Unreachable**   The local interface cannot communicate with at least one other interface whose state is not failed or unavailable.
- **Up**   This is the normal operational state, in which the local interface can communicate with all other interfaces on the network whose states are not failed or unavailable.

You can also view the state of the private and public networks using Cluster Administrator. Here are the possible states for these two networks in a cluster:

- **Unavailable**   All interfaces defined on this cluster network are unavailable.
- **Down**   All network interfaces defined on this cluster network have lost communication with one another and with all known external hosts. This state also indicates that all connected network interfaces on each node are in the Failed or the Unreachable state. Thus, all IP Address resources that are defined and all resources that depend on those resources are not available to clients.
- **Partitioned**   One or more network interfaces are in the Unreachable state. However, at least two interfaces can still communicate with each other or with an external host. This state can occur only if the cluster has two or more healthy nodes.
- **Up**   This is the normal state, in which all network interfaces defined on this cluster network that are not Failed and not Unavailable can communicate.

Lesson Summary

This lesson described some ways to troubleshoot problems with clusters, including those related to installation, startup, network connectivity, and SCSI devices. While installing a cluster, you might need to respond to problems such as hardware compatibility, hardware configuration, and network configuration. If your cluster will not start correctly, you must identify the problem and respond in order to minimize downtime. You might also need to contend with cluster-related network and SCSI device issues.

Windows provides several tools for troubleshooting cluster-related problems, including the Windows Event Log, Cluster Administrator, cluster log files, and the network Ping utility. This lesson discussed how to use these tools to determine the cause of cluster failures. It also provided step-by-step procedures for identifying and resolving cluster installation, startup, network connectivity, and disk connectivity malfunctions.

Lesson 2: Troubleshooting Groups and Resources

This lesson discusses common problems associated with resource and resource group failures. These failures often occur when the failover process does not happen as expected. The lesson offers possible solutions to common resource and resource group problems and includes a troubleshooting section organized by individual resource type.

After this lesson, you will be able to

- Identify and resolve problems associated with resource groups
- Identify and resolve problems associated with resources
- List possible problems and their solutions by resource type

Estimated lesson time: 30 minutes

Troubleshooting Problems with Resource Groups

The following are potential problems that you might encounter with resource groups, along with solutions you can try.

A Resource Group Cannot Be Brought Online

In this situation, you see a warning symbol displayed next to the group in Cluster Administrator. Because Cluster Service attempts to bring all resources in a group online simultaneously, if one resource cannot come online, the entire group is affected. Therefore, you must examine each resource independently.

Here are some troubleshooting strategies:

- Verify access to the disk. If disk access is a problem, perform SCSI troubleshooting techniques as described in Lesson 1 in this chapter.
- Try moving the group to another node and bringing it online from there. If this is successful, verify that the first node can access each resource that is necessary to bring the group online.
- Try bringing each resource online individually. If none of the resources can be brought online, Cluster Service might not have the proper permissions to access the shared disk.
- Check for any hardware or configuration problems with any of the group's disk resources.
- Ensure that all resource dependencies are configured correctly.

A Resource Group Will Not Move or Fail Over to Another Node

All resources in the group must be able to be accepted by the other node. When a resource group will not move or fail over, the resources' Affect The Group option, which tells the group to fail over to the other node in the cluster, might not be selected. It's also possible that the group is actually failing over and immediately failing back. Cluster Service will allow the group to return to its preferred owner in the cluster if the preferred owner is defined and currently online.

Here are two ways to troubleshoot this situation:

- Verify that the node is listed as a Possible Owner of the resource in the group.
- Verify that the Affect The Group option is selected on each resource's property page.

A Resource Group Will Fail Over but Will Not Fail Back

In this situation, the failback properties of the resources and the group might not be configured properly or the node that you want the resource group to fail back to is not the preferred owner of the group.

You can try these approaches:

- Deselect the Prevent Failback check box in the group's Properties dialog box.
- If the Allow Failback option is selected, be sure to allow enough time for the failback to take place.
- Verify the aforementioned property selections for each resource in the group.
- Verify that the node you want to fail back to is the preferred owner of the group.

A Resource Group Has Failed and Has Not Restarted

This problem can occur when a node has been taken offline or when the group has exceeded its failover threshold settings.

Here are ways to troubleshoot :

- Verify that the node is online.
- Check the Possible Owners list of the group and each resource to ensure that there is more than one Possible Owner.
- Bring each resource online independently to try to determine which resource is causing the problem.

Clients Cannot Access a Failed Over Resource Group

In this case, the physical connection between the nodes might not be intact, so you can check the following:

- Ensure that the cabling is in working order.
- Ensure that the SCSI cabling has not failed.

Troubleshooting Problems with Resources

Here are some problems that you might encounter with resources, along with possible solutions.

A Resource Cannot Be Brought Online

- This can happen if the resource is not installed or configured properly or is not compatible with Cluster Service.

You can try these approaches:

- Verify that the application or service has been installed properly.
- Verify that the property settings are correct for the resource.
- Check to see whether this application can be configured to fail over in a cluster.

A Resource Will Not Fail Over

This problem is likely due to improper configuration of the cluster storage device. You should verify that the device and all cables are properly configured and in working order.

A Failed Resource Will Not Come Back Online

This problem can happen because of an offline resource dependency or because the resource has reached its failure threshold.

You can try these troubleshooting strategies:

- Check all dependencies to verify that they are online and configured correctly.
- If the failure threshold has been reached and the resource cannot be moved to another node, the resource's state has changed to Failed. You must bring it back online manually.
- Verify that the resource's Do Not Restart option is deselected.

A Resource Has Failed Over but Will Not Fail Back

The possible causes of this problem include:

- Cluster Service does not detect a heartbeat or is not sure that another node ever came online.
- An interconnect or SCSI cable has failed.
- The resource is set to fail back immediately.
- You are troubleshooting outside the allowable failback hours for the resource.

Here are some solutions to try:

- Verify that hardware and network connections are intact and working properly.

- View the failback policy on your cluster by using Cluster Administrator. The group might be configured to fail back only during certain hours.

Troubleshooting Client Access Problems

If clients cannot access a cluster resource, check for one of the following causes:

- The IP Address resource or Network Name resource associated with the resource's group is not online. Check the resource's dependencies, and verify that they are online. Ensure that the resource is dependent on either the IP Address resource or the Network Name resource. Try pinging the virtual server and the cluster node from the client computer.

- The client computer or the cluster node is not properly configured using WINS or DNS. Be sure that the cluster nodes employ some type of name resolution using WINS or DNS and that the clients are using the same form of name resolution.

- Improper DNS configuration is preventing the client from accessing the cluster using a different subnet. Both the client and the cluster nodes should be configured to use either WINS or DNS. If you choose DNS, be sure to add a cluster DNS address record in the DNS database.

- The public network or private network is down. Communication problems on the public network affect only client access to the cluster. As long as the private network between cluster nodes is not down, Cluster Service will function normally. However, a failure in communication on the cluster private network will cause resources that are configured for failover to fail over to the node that owns the Quorum resources. Cluster Service will be shut down on the other node.

- One of the nodes in the cluster might have lost connectivity. To determine whether a node has lost network connectivity, verify that the TCP/IP configuration settings are correct, check the WINS or DNS configuration, and verify that the static IP address is correct and that other network resources are not using it.

Troubleshooting by Resource Type

You can troubleshoot a cluster problem by resource type. This section lists the default resource types and common techniques for troubleshooting them.

Physical Disk Resource

If nodes cannot recognize the physical disk or are unable to bring the disk online, check the following:

- Determine whether the disk residing on the shared SCSI bus has been recently repartitioned. If the cluster has resources that reference this disk, the disk should not be repartitioned. But if you need to repartition the disk, you can remove any disk resources prior to the repartition. If the Quorum resource's disk must be repartitioned, the Quorum resource must relocated before the repartition.

- If any disk has been repartitioned, you should reboot both nodes in the cluster. The nodes will not recognize changes until they have been rebooted.

- Be sure that the drive letters for the disk that resides on the SCSI bus are consistent on all nodes of the cluster.

- Cluster Service stores the shared disk's signature in the registry, so you cannot restore a backup of Cluster Service to another computer. The disk signatures will not match, and Cluster Service will not be able to access the shared SCSI bus.

- Be sure that enough time has passed for the registry to be updated. When the second node in the cluster boots, its registry is updated. Disk signature information might be included in the registry. The update usually takes between 60 and 90 seconds.

IP Address Resource

An IP Address resource is one of the simpler resource types to troubleshoot because it has no dependencies and the TCP/IP address and the subnet mask are easy to troubleshoot using standard TCP/IP testing procedures.

The most common cause of IP Address resource problems is an improperly configured property. The incorrect property might be an IP address or a subnet mask.

You can test an IP Address resource using the Ping utility. You should test the resource's IP address from a computer on the same subnet mask and then test it from a computer on a remote subnet. If your physical network is functioning correctly (the local test is successful and the remote test is not), the problem might be an invalid subnet mask. Cluster Service does not verify whether an IP address resides in a specific subnet mask, so it is possible to configure an IP Address resource and bring it online even if the mask is incorrect.

If an IP address stops responding when an IP Address resource is taken offline, you might not have waited long enough for the resource to go offline. It can take up to 3 minutes for an IP Address resource to go fully offline.

The two main reasons that an IP address created and added to a group in the cluster might fail are:

- The IP address is not unique. Be sure that the IP address is different from every other IP address on the network and is not duplicated in any other group.

- The IP address is not static. IP addresses must be statically assigned and excluded from a DHCP scope. Otherwise, they must be reserved by a network administrator.

Network Name Resource

Network Name resources perform the same functions as NetBIOS names and host names. When a Network Name resource is not functioning properly, you can check several things:

- Check the IP Address resource. Network Name resources have an IP Address resource dependency, so you should verify that the IP Address resource is configured properly and is online.

- If the IP Address resource appears to be functioning normally, you can try pinging the network name. A successful ping to both the IP address and the network name indicates that TCP/IP is functioning properly. However, a 60-to-90-second delay in results being returned by the ping test for the network name might indicate a missing DNS database entry for the network name. In this case, the system where the ping test was performed should be configured to use a DNS server. Entries in a WINS server database for the network name do not prevent this delay in ping response because Ping checks DNS before checking WINS. You might get a more rapid response using the Net View command to test the network name because this command uses NetBIOS resolution prior to using DNS resolution. Use the following format at a command prompt to test the network name with the Net View command:

```
Net view \\network_name
```

- A problem can result when new Network Name resources are being constantly created and deleted, such as on a cluster test platform. Cluster Service automatically registers all Network Name resources with the WINS server specified for a node. If these WINS entries are then replicated to other servers, some WINS servers might have outdated cluster network name information because of delays in replication. If you are experiencing problems with a network name in a cluster where the network name has changed recently, check the WINS entries on the node that owns the Network Name resource. Then verify that the identified WINS server is being replicated. If you discover a problem, you might have to force a WINS database replication to occur, or delete any incorrect WINS database entries.

File Share Resource

File Share resources have dependencies on the Network Name resource and the Physical Disk resource. Be sure that each of these resources and any dependencies are properly configured and working correctly.

If you experience problems when you try to bring a File Share resource online, verify that the file share's directory exists. If it does, verify that it was created on an NTFS partition. If the directory resides on an NTFS partition, be sure that the directory can be accessed with the existing NTFS security permissions. If it cannot, the resource cannot be brought online.

If you have problems writing or saving to a File Share resource, the source might be NTFS security. NTFS permissions can restrict access to the file share. It is possible to create the file share with the proper access, only to have NTFS permissions restrict that access. Only the most restrictive permissions are granted to users accessing the file share.

If clients cannot attach to a File Share resource, the source of the problem is probably one of the following:

- Your WINS or DNS server might be configured incorrectly, so check your WINS or DNS configuration. If you're running WINS, be sure that the cluster and each node are registered and active in the database.

- The current security policies might not allow the client to access the share, so verify that the client has the right to log on to the share and is allowed to access the share. If the client can't do these things, you should enable the guest account.

Generic Service Resource

A Generic Service resource is easy to troubleshoot because the complicated work is done when you get the application to run as a service. If your Generic Service resource is not functioning properly, you can check the following:

- Check whether the service that the resource is trying to run is supported in a cluster. Some services, such as DNS, are not supported by the cluster and therefore cannot be configured as a Generic Service resource.

- If the service is required to log on with a specific account, you might try to log on with that account manually to make sure that the account is still active and that the password has not expired.

- If the Generic Service resource functions properly on one node but fails on the other node, check to make sure that any registry information pertaining to the service is being replicated properly.

Generic Application Resource

Check the following variables when you troubleshoot a Generic Application resource:

- A generic application does not require any dependent resources, but Generic Application resources often have a physical disk dependency. If there is a dependency, verify that the dependent resource is online and functioning properly.

- If the Generic Application resource functions correctly on one node but not on the other node, check the registry for information about the application. If information is stored in the registry, verify that the properties for registry replication have been configured correctly.

- Most programs can be installed as Generic Application resources, so it is possible to configure a malfunctioning program. To test your program, try running the program interactively and observe its behavior. Specifically, check the following:

- Is the program a Windows application? If so, the Allow Application To Interact With Desktop option on the Parameters tab of the Properties dialog box must be selected. If this option is deselected, the resource will be brought online but will run in the background because it does not have access to a window.

- Does the application resource continually restart and then fail? If so, one of two things is happening. If an application ends in an error, Cluster Service believes that the resource has failed and tries to restart the application. If the application ends normally, Cluster Service also believes that this is a failure. In both cases, the application will reach its failure threshold and be failed over to another node on the cluster or the resource will be placed in a failed state.

Print Spooler Resource

Check the following when you troubleshoot a Print Spooler resource:

- A Print Spooler resource has two dependencies, a Physical Disk resource and a Network Name resource. Verify that these dependent resources are online and functioning properly.

- Check the disk and the directory targeted by the Print Spooler resource. Be sure that they have not been restricted by NTFS permissions. Verify that the spool directory's disk is not full. Print jobs will hang if the disk is full.

- Be sure that the printer driver is installed on each node of the cluster. The driver might be absent if the printer is working correctly on one node of the cluster but not on the other.

- Check the LPR port mapping for the print device. The LPR port must be created for each cluster member. If the print spooler works from one cluster member but not the other, the mapping could be the problem.

IIS Server Instance

Check the following when you troubleshoot an IIS server instance:

- The IIS server instance resource's dependency is an IP Address resource. Verify that the IP Address resource is online and functioning properly.

- If the IIS server instance works correctly with the IP address but not with the domain name, the problem might be with DNS and name resolution. Verify that DNS is functioning properly.

- If the resource is designated as a WWW or FTP virtual root, access to the virtual root can be set to Read or Execute. However, in order for a client to run a program residing in the directory, the access must be set to Execute.

- If the IIS resource works correctly on only one node of the cluster, verify that the resource's directory is located on the shared disk. If the directory resides on a local disk, the directory must exist in the directory of each cluster node.

SQL Server Resource

Check the following when you troubleshoot a SQL Server resource:

- A SQL Server resource is dependent on two resources, a Network Name resource and a Physical Disk resource. Verify that these two resources are online and functioning properly.

- If the SQL Server resource functions properly on one node of the cluster but not the other, check the SQL Server account user name and password. These values should be identical on both nodes.

Distributed Transaction Coordinator Resource

Check the following when you troubleshoot a Distributed Transaction Coordinator resource:

- A Distributed Transaction Coordinator resource is dependent on a Physical Disk resource and a Network Name resource. Be sure that both of these resources are online and functioning properly.

- Check the transaction server to make sure it is functioning properly. The transaction coordinator accesses a database server, so verify that this server is operating properly.

Message Queue Server Resource

Check the following when you troubleshoot a Message Queue Server resource:

- The Message Queue Server resource is dependent on a Physical Disk resource and a Network Name resource. Verify that these resources are online and functioning properly.

- Make sure that MSMQ was not installed in workgroup mode. See Knowledge Base article Q254287 for more information.

- You might have installed a Cluster hot fix that has broken MSMQ. See Knowledge Base article Q257577 for more information.

- An encryption conflict is preventing MSMQ from coming online. See Knowledge Base article Q247585 for more information.

- Ensure that MSMQ is operating correctly.

- Some MSMQ settings can stall the message queue. This problem is related to the software and is not a cluster issue.

Lesson Summary

This lesson described common problems associated with resources and resource groups and suggested some approaches you can take to solve these problems. It also offered troubleshooting techniques for the default resource types.

Lesson 3: Troubleshooting Nodes and Applications

This lesson describes some common problems that occur when you work with nodes in a cluster and describes possible causes and remedies. It also discusses problems with the Quorum log, virtual servers, and applications.

After this lesson, you will be able to

- List and identify possible problems and solutions associated with clustered nodes
- List and identify possible problems and solutions associated with clustered applications

Estimated lesson time: 30 minutes

Troubleshooting General Node Problems

This section describes common problems associated with nodes and offers possible solutions.

Cluster Administrator Stops Responding on Failover

After a node has failed and Cluster Service has initiated failover, Cluster Administrator might not respond if it is performing an update. There are two ways to determine whether Cluster Administrator is running on the remaining node on the cluster. Check to see whether you can open Cluster Administrator, or look for the Cluadmin.exe process.

Cluster Administrator Cannot Connect to a Node

If Cluster Administrator cannot open a connection to a node, the node might not be running. Verify that the node is running, and confirm that Cluster Service and the RPC service are running.

A Node Cannot Detect the Network After a Cluster Service Failure

In this situation, you might have a problem with the node's network configuration. If you made any recent changes to any node, such as installing a new resource that requires a reboot, that change might have adversely affected the network configuration. Check the node to ensure that it is properly configured for the network.

Another possible cause of this problem is that the node is not properly configured for TCP/IP. Verify that both nodes in the cluster are properly configured. An improper TCP/IP configuration can result in inadequate failover protection.

Both Nodes are Functioning, but Resources Continually Fail Back

In this case, you might have a problem with the power supply. You should determine whether your power is failing, and if so, determine the cause. The solution might be to install an uninterruptible power supply (UPS).

Both Nodes Appear to Be Working Correctly, but One Node Cannot Access All Drives

In this case, the shared drive is not functioning properly. You can check the shared drive by trying to access it from another node. If the other node can access the drive, check the cabling between the drive and the node. If the cabling is not the problem, try rebooting your computer and then accessing the drive again. If you still cannot access the drive, check your cluster configuration.

Another possible cause of this problem is that the drive has completely failed. Try accessing the drive from another node to determine whether the drive is operating. To do this, you might have to reboot your computer. If you still cannot access the drive, you might have to replace it.

Node Performance Is Sluggish, and Then the Node Fails

You might have an overloaded CPU. Check the CPU performance usage to determine whether the CPU is running at, or close to, 100 percent. Too many resources might be assigned to that node. You might also want to check the size of your paging file and adjust it accordingly.

The Entire Cluster Is Down

To address this problem, try bringing one node online. If this is successful, clients will be able to access the cluster and you will limit the impact of a nonfunctioning cluster. Once one node is online, you can get log information and look at other information that can help you troubleshoot the problem.

A Single Node Is Down

If this happens, be sure that the necessary resources and groups have failed over to the other node in the cluster. Once the resources are running, begin troubleshooting the node that failed. Try bringing the node online and check the cluster and event logs for information relating to the failed node.

A Node Cannot Communicate on a Network

Here you might have a connection problem that results in resources not being able to fail over to the other node. To troubleshoot this problem, verify that the connection between the network and the nodes is operating properly. For example, if the nodes are connected to the network through a hub, you should verify that the hub is working correctly. Also, check all network cabling between the nodes.

When Resources Fail Over and the Nodes Do Not Detect One Another, There Is No Connectivity Between the Nodes or with the Cluster Storage Device

This problem can happen if the RPC service is not running. If the service is running, verify that the nodes have RPC connectivity.

One Or More Nodes Have Stopped Responding

If one or more nodes are not responding but have not otherwise failed, the problem might involve configuration, software, or driver issues. If both nodes are member servers rather than domain controllers, the domain controller might have become unavailable. Cluster Service uses RPC calls for much of its communication. If a domain controller is unavailable, the necessary authorizations become unavailable as well. Check the domain controller to ensure that it is working properly.

Troubleshooting Quorum Disk Problems

This section addresses common problems associated with the Quorum disk.

The Quorum Disk Has Failed

If the Quorum resource's disk fails, the resource cannot be brought online and Cluster Service will not start. You can start Cluster Service without the Quorum resource by using the special command-line parameter *–fixquorum*. Once Cluster Service starts, you can use Cluster Administrator to designate a new Quorum resource.

The Quorum Resource Will Not Start

The Quorum resource might not be physically connected to the server, so check all connections and cabling. Another possible cause of this problem is incorrect hardware configuration. If you are using SCSI, verify that the SCSI devices are properly terminated. Also, check the devices on the SCSI bus to ensure that they are connected and functioning properly.

The Quorum Log Is Corrupt

A number of factors might cause the Quorum log to become corrupted. When Cluster Service identifies a corrupted Quorum log, the following message will appear in the Windows 2000 system log:

The log file [name] was found to be corrupt.
An attempt will be made to reset it.

Cluster Service will attempt to reset the Quorum log. If it is unsuccessful, Cluster Service will not be able to start. If Cluster Service fails to start, an undetected corrupted Quorum log might be the cause. If this is the case, an ERROR_CLUSTER-LOG_CORRUPT message will appear in the System error log.

If Cluster Service is unable to reset the Quorum log, you must reset the Quorum log manually. Start Cluster Service at the command prompt using the Noquorum logging option, which will allow you to run Cluster Service temporarily. Cluster Service will bring the Quorum disk online, but logging will be disabled. You must correct the disk corruption and delete the Quorum log. ChkDsk will detect and correct the disk corruption. You must then shut down Cluster Service and restart it.

There is a potential problem associated with this procedure, however. The Quorum log stores cluster configuration changes until all nodes in the cluster are updated. Therefore, when you start Cluster Service without logging, recent configuration changes cannot be recorded and will not be propagated to the other nodes in the cluster. Even though a loss of data is possible, the Quorum log is already corrupted, so this solution is still reasonable.

Troubleshooting Virtual Server Problems

This section addresses some common problems associated with virtual servers.

Clients Can Detect Nodes but Not a Virtual Server

Virtual servers typically consist of at least three resources—the IP Address resource, the Network Name resource, and the application or service resource. You should verify that these resources are configured correctly and that they are online and functioning properly. Be sure that your virtual servers have unique IP addresses and names on the network.

Another possible cause of this problem is that one or more of the nodes in the cluster might be incorrectly configured to use WINS or DNS. Verify that this is not the case.

Clients Cannot Connect to Virtual Servers

First, verify that the resources the virtual server is dependent on are online and functioning properly. These include IP Address and Network Name resources. If these resources are not the problem, verify that TCP/IP is correctly installed and configured on each node in the cluster. Finally, verify that the name resolution technique used on your LAN is configured properly on the client.

Troubleshooting Problems with Applications and Services

If you're experiencing problems with applications or services, you should verify that the application or service is configured correctly and running properly. If the application or service resource has never worked, you might need to reinstall the resource. If the resource did work at one time, you should do the following:

- Determine whether the application or service is supported by Cluster Service.
- Check the resource installation.
- Make sure the resource was installed in the same directory on each node.

An Application Starts but Cannot Be Taken Offline

In this case, one of the application's dependent resources might still be online. Verify that all dependent resources are offline, and then try to take the application resource offline.

Lesson Summary

This lesson addressed problems associated with clustered nodes and applications and the Quorum disk. Because the Quorum resource is critical to the operation of a cluster, you should know the steps for making sure the Quorum resource is available for the cluster. This lesson also described how to troubleshoot virtual servers and their related resource types, IP Address and Network name.

Lesson 4: Using the Cluster Log for Troubleshooting

Many tools are available for determining why a resource has failed over. You can use the standard monitoring tools provided with Windows 2000 Advanced Server, such as Disk Administrator, Performance Monitor, or Event Viewer. You can also use the Cluster Service log file to determine the cause of a problem.

This lesson provides a general overview of the cluster log and offers techniques for using it to troubleshoot problems.

After this lesson, you will be able to

- Describe the cluster log and its location
- Interpret entries in the cluster log in order to troubleshoot a cluster

Estimated lesson time: 60 minutes

Overview of the Cluster Log

The cluster log is a file that contains information related to activity performed by a cluster. Any event or activity that takes place in a cluster, such as creating groups or resources or even forming or joining a cluster, is recorded in the cluster log. This diagnostic log is a complete record of Cluster Service events that occurred on a specific node. The cluster log records events that lead up to items recorded in the Windows Event Viewer. Therefore, when the cluster log and Event Viewer are used together, they provide a powerful troubleshooting solution.

Cluster logging is enabled by default in Windows 2000 Advanced Server but can be disabled. The cluster log file is at %windir%\cluster\cluster.log. Its size is limited to 8 MB. After the cluster log file reaches that limit, events are removed in the sequence that they were first entered, so the log will include only the latest activity.

To successfully interpret the cluster log, you must be familiar with the following:

- The layout of a cluster log entry
- Abbreviations used in cluster log entries
- State codes used in cluster log entries
- Problem-tracking tools

Cluster Log Entries

Each cluster log entry includes a number of items:

- The process ID and thread ID that issued the log entry. These IDs are concatenated and separated by a period.
- A timestamp, in Greenwich Mean Time (GMT), in the following format: yyyy/mm/dd-hh:mm:ss.sss.
- An event description.

The following is an example of a cluster log entry:

```
00000488.000004a8::2000/11/17-
23:54:46.019 [CS] Cluster Service started - Cluster Node Version 3.2195
00000488.000004a8::2000/11/17-
23:54:46.019          OS Version 5.0.2195
```

Here's how you interpret the information:

- The Process ID is 00000488.
- The Thread ID is 000004a8.
- The time of the recorded event is 46.019 seconds past 11:54 in the evening.
- The event that took place is *Cluster Service started.*
- The cluster node version is 3.2195
- The operating system (OS) version is 5.0.2195.

There are two types of log entries in the cluster: component event log entries and resource DLL log entries, as described in the upcoming sections.

Component Event Log Entries

As you know, Cluster Service is made up of several components, including the Database Manager and the Communications Manager. The events generated by the interaction among the components are logged in a component event log entry. Knowing how the components interact can help you in troubleshooting problems.

A component event log entry identifies a component and its state. It displays this information using an abbreviation between the timestamp and the event description that tells you one of the following:

- The component that wrote the event to the log
- The state of the node at the time the entry was written
- A combined component and state

The abbreviations used are listed in Table 7.1.

Table 7.1   Component Event Log Abbreviations

Abbreviation	Component or Node State
[API]	API Support
[ClMsg]	Cluster Messaging
[ClNet]	Cluster Network Engine
[CP]	Checkpoint Manager
[CS]	Cluster Service
[DM]	Database Manager
[EP]	Event Processor
[FM]	Failover Manager
[GUM]	Global Update Manager
[INIT]	The initial state of a node before it forms or joins a cluster
[JOIN]	The state that follows [INIT] when a node is attempting to join a cluster
[LM]	Log Manager
[MM]	Membership Manager
[NM]	Node Manager
[OM]	Object Manager
[RGP]	Regroup
[RM]	Resource Monitor

Here's an example of a component event log entry:

```
00000488.000006a8::2000/11/17-23:54:46.029 [DM]: Initialization
```

Here's how you interpret the information:

- The Process ID is 00000488.
- The Thread ID is 000006a8.
- The event was logged at 11:54:46.029 in the evening.
- The Database Manager component wrote the entry to the log.
- The event taking place was the initialization of the component.

Here's another example:

```
00000604.00000634::2000/11/18-
00:33:58.772 [NMJOIN] Processing request to
create new interface f1b84421-2ae2-4427-b667-
ffe8ff317967 for joining node.
```

You interpret the information as follows:

- The Process ID is 00000604.
- The Thread ID is 00000634.
- The event was logged at 12:33:58.772 in the morning.
- The Node Manager component wrote the entry to the log.
- A node attempted to join the cluster.
- The event description states that the cluster was processing the request to create a new interface for the node joining the cluster.

Notice the globally unique identifier (GUID) in the above entry (f1b84421-2ae2-4427-b667-ffe8ff317967), which identifies the resource that the component found. GUIDs help you determine a resource's identity when the resource's name is not given.

Resource DLL Log Entries

Resource DLL entries present information about resource groups. This information can be critical in the event of a failover. A resource DLL entry displays the resource type and the resource name between the timestamp and the event description.

Here is an example of a resource DLL log entry:

```
000004b8.000002a0::2000/11/19-
21:29:38.653 Physical Disk <Disk Q: W:>: [DiskArb]-------
DisksArbitrate -------.
```

Here's how you interpret the information in the entry:

- The Process ID is 000004b8.
- The Thread ID is 000002a0.
- The event was logged at 9:29:38.653 in the evening.
- The resource type is Physical Disk.
- The resource name is <Disk Q: W:>.
- The event description for this entry is [DiskArb]------- DisksArbitrate -------.

Status, Error, and State Codes

Some cluster log entries include status, error, or state codes or combinations of those codes.

Status Codes

Consider the cluster log example on the following page.

```
000004b8.00000278::2000/11/19-
21:29:38.282 Physical Disk <Disk Q: W:>: [DiskArb]
CompletionRoutine, status 0.
```

This log entry displays status 0. To find out what status 0 means, you use the Net helpmsg command-line utility:

```
Net helpmsg [status_number]
```

The status number 0 means that the operation completed successfully.

Error Codes

Consider the following cluster log example:

```
00000488.0000029c::2000/11/17-
23:56:44.740 [FM] FmpRmOfflineResource: RmOffline()for 45a6c201-e186-
463a-bff0-97970744e584 returned error 997
```

This log entry displays the error 997. Using the Net helpmsg command, you'll find that error 997 means that overlapped I/O operation is in progress.

State Codes

The state code is associated with a type of object. Five types of objects have state codes:

- Cluster nodes
- Cluster groups
- Cluster resources
- Network interfaces
- Networks

To determine the meaning of the state code, you must first identify the object associated with the cluster log entry. The object type is typically displayed with the GUID. If the object type is not displayed, you can use the GUID to identify the object.

In Windows 2000 Advanced Server, the resource name is logged with the resource's GUID when it is created. Therefore, you can look in the beginning of the cluster log to find the correct resource. However, if these entries have been overwritten, you can find the resource in the registry. See the practice later in this chapter for more information on finding a GUID in the registry.

Consider the following cluster log example:

```
00000488.0000068c::2000/11/17-23:55:21.640 [NM] Network 5b630f93-5300-
48e3-b9e4-49cc58b6d1c3 is now in state 3
```

This example tells you the following information:

- The object is a network.
- The object's GUID is 5b630f93-5300-48e3-b9e4-49cc58b6d1c3.
- The state is 3.

With the object type and the state, you can look up the meaning of the state code in Tables 7.2 through 7.6. For the example above, Table 7.6 tells you that a state code of 3 is defined as ClusterNetworkUp.

Table 7.2   Cluster Node State Codes

State Code	State
−1	ClusterNodeStateUnknown
0	ClusterNodeUp
1	ClusterNodeDown
2	ClusterNodePaused
3	ClusterNodeJoining

Table 7.3   Cluster Group State Codes

State Code	State
−1	ClusterGroupStateUnknown
0	ClusterGroupOnline
1	ClusterGroupOffline
2	ClusterGroupFailed
3	ClusterGroupPartialOnline

Table 7.4   Cluster Resource State Codes

State Code	State
−1	ClusterResourceStateUnknown
0	ClusterResourceInherited
1	ClusterResourceInitializing
2	ClusterResourceOnline
3	ClusterResourceOffline
4	ClusterResourceFailed
128	ClusterResourcePending
129	ClusterResourceOnlinePending
130	ClusterResourceOfflinePending

Table 7.5   Network Interface State Codes

State Code	State
−1	ClusterNetInterfaceStateUnknown
0	ClusterNetInterfaceUnavailable
1	ClusterNetInterfaceFailed
2	ClusterNetInterfaceUnreachable
3	ClusterNetInterfaceUp

Table 7.6   Network State Codes

State Code	State
−1	ClusterNetworkStateUnknown
0	ClusterNetworkUnavailable
1	ClusterNetworkDown
2	ClusterNetworkPartitioned
3	ClusterNetworkUP

Cluster Log Tracking Items

You can use several items in the cluster log file to help you track entries and find problems, as described below.

Timestamps

The timestamp of a cluster log entry is logged when an event occurs. One activity might include several events and therefore require many log entries. By checking the timestamps for periods of inactivity that are more than 1 second long, you can determine when a specific activity was completed. For example, notice that the second entry, shown in boldface font, has a timestamp that is out of order

```
00000604.0000068c::2000/11/18-
00:34:12.532 [GUM] GumSendUpdate:  Locker waiting
type 2 context 15
00000604.0000068c::2000/11/18-
00:34:12.522 [GUM] Thread 0x68c UpdateLock wait on Type 2
00000604.0000068c::2000/11/18-
00:34:12.532 [GUM] DoLockingUpdate successful, lock granted to 1
```

Timestamps can appear out of chronological order if the cluster log obtains the system time before it accesses the log file. Therefore, it is possible for another thread to obtain access to the log file and record its event before the initial thread.

GUIDs

Cluster Service doesn't always include the resource's display name when it refers to the resource. In the following example, the group 82ffe251-fb2e-427c-9f33-51f6d83f6bfe has just been created:

```
00000488.000006a8::2000/11/17-
23:55:19.257 [FM] Creating group 82ffe251-fb2e-427c-9f33-51f6d83f6bfe
```

Here you can see that the group has been initialized:

```
00000488.000006a8::2000/11/17-
23:55:19.257 [FM] Initializing group 82ffe251-fb2e-427c-9f33-
51f6d83f6bfe from the registry.
```

Here you can see that the display name for the group is Cluster Group:

```
00000488.000006a8::2000/11/17-
23:55:19.257 [FM] Name for Group 82ffe251-fb2e-427c-9f33-
51f6d83f6bfe is 'Cluster Group'.
```

And here you can see that the group is dependent on a resource with the GUID 858fc957-6b1e-4a1c-8474-d42a9cdc5340:

```
00000488.000006a8::2000/11/17-23:55:19.257 [FM] Group 82ffe251-fb2e-
427c-9f33-51f6d83f6bfe contains Resource 858fc957-6b1e-4a1c-8474-
d42a9cdc5340.
```

With just a GUID, it would be impossible to track this group or the resource that it is dependent on.

Resources

When a resource is created, all the information about it is recorded in the log. Consider the following log file entries when a resource is created. You can see that the Failover Manager created the resource and assigned a GUID to it:

```
00000604.00000534::2000/11/18-
00:00:00.211 [FM] Creating resource 858fc957-6b1e-4a1c-8474-
d42a9cdc5340
```

You can see here that the Failover Manager initialized the resource with values from the cluster's database:

```
00000604.00000534::2000/11/18-
00:00:00.211 [FM] Initializing resource 858fc957-6b1e-4a1c-8474-
d42a9cdc5340 from the registry.
```

The display name for the resource along with its GUID is shown here:

```
00000604.00000534::2000/11/18-
00:00:00.211 [FM] Name for Resource 858fc957-6b1e-4a1c-8474-
d42a9cdc5340 is 'Cluster IP Address'.
```

Here you can see that a list of Possible Owners for the resource has been created:

```
00000604.00000534::2000/11/18-
00:00:00.211 [FM] FmpAddPossibleEntry: adding node 1 as possible host
for resource 858fc957-6b1e-4a1c-8474-d42a9cdc5340.
00000604.00000534::2000/11/18-
00:00:00.211 [FM] FmpAddPossibleEntry: adding node 2 as possible host
for resource 858fc957-6b1e-4a1c-8474-d42a9cdc5340.
```

And here the Failover Manager notes that the resource's dependencies have been created:

```
00000604.00000534::2000/11/18-
00:00:00.211 [FM] All dependencies for resource 858fc957-6b1e-4a1c-
8474-d42a9cdc5340 created.
```

All of the above entries are created from the information you supplied when you used the Resource Wizard to create a resource. The cluster log is appended when each step of the wizard is completed.

Process and Thread IDs

Process and thread IDs can help you trace activity and actions in Cluster Service so that, for instance, you can determine why a process is requiring too much processor time to complete.

A new process is started when an executable file is run. This new process receives a process ID. Therefore, you can trace the activities of a process using this ID.

A thread executes code inside a process. Each process has a primary thread that performs the work for the process. However, if more work needs to be performed, additional threads might be created or spawned to help. Each thread created receives a unique ID. It is possible to use multiple threads to complete a single operation, such as creating a group or a resource. In these cases, tracing thread IDs can become misleading.

Global Update Manager Updates and Sequence Numbers

A Global Update Manager (GUM) update entry is created when a change is made to the cluster database. GUM update entries can contain sequence numbers, types, and contexts. Consider the following GUM entry:

```
000004b8.000001dc::2000/11/19-
21:32:51.688 [GUM] GumSendUpdate: Dispatching seq 11494
type 0 context 8 to node 1
```

This example tells you the following information:

- The sequence number is 11494.
- The type is 0.
- The context is 8.

Using the list of GUM update entries below, you'll find that type 0 refers to the Failover Manager. The three types of GUM update entries are:

- Type 0: FailoverManager
- Type 1: GUMUpdateRegistry
- Type 2: GUMUpdateMembership

When a change is made to the database, all the nodes in the cluster must receive the same information. GUM entries use a unique sequence number to identify each transaction. However, one transaction might consist of several actions and result in several entries with the same sequence number. Using the sequence number in the GUM update entry, you can track the changes in the log files of both nodes in the cluster.

Quorum Locks and gdwQuoBlockingResources

If a component cannot gain access to the Quorum resource, the Quorum resource might be locked. A lock (also called a Quorum lock) means that the Quorum resource is unavailable to components other than the component that holds the lock.

Cluster Service uses two types of locks:

- **Shared locks**   A shared lock is acquired in shared mode. Dependencies acquire a shared mode lock if they require access to the Quorum resource. This lock guarantees that the Quorum resource will remain online while it is needed.

- **Exclusive locks**   An exclusive lock is acquired in exclusive mode. It is acquired when Cluster Service takes the Quorum resource offline. Once this lock is acquired, only the holder of the lock can access the Quorum resource.

These two types of locks function differently. Giving priority to one type of lock over another could cause problems, so Cluster Service solves lock managing issues by implementing the *gdwQuoBlockingResources* global variable, which is a count of the existing shared locks. The *gdwQuoBlockingResources* variable changes as follows:

- When a shared lock is acquired, the count increases by 1.
- When a shared lock is released, the count decreases by 1.
- When the count reaches 0, Cluster Service is allowed to acquire an exclusive lock on the Quorum resource.

Requests for exclusive locks are queued behind existing shared locks.

InterlockedIncrement and InterlockedDecrement Entries

If a request is received to take the Quorum resource offline and the value of the *gdwQuoBlockingResources* count is greater than 0, a pair of entries called InterlockedIncrement and InterlockedDecrement appears in the log along with the count of existing shared locks. If the Quorum resource cannot be taken off-line, the resource preventing this will be bracketed between these entries.

Practice: Examining the Cluster Log

In this practice, you will open the cluster logs on your cluster and then identify important parts of the cluster log using the log provided.

Opening the Cluster Log

1. From the Windows 2000 Start menu, point to Settings and then click Control Panel.

2. Double-click the System icon.

3. Click the Advanced tab.

4. Click the Environment Variables button.

5. In the System Variables box, find the Cluster Log variable. Note the path listed under the value for the cluster log.

6. From the Windows 2000 Start menu, point to Programs, point to Accessories, and then click Windows Explorer.

7. Find the path in step 5, and open your cluster log.

Identifying Cluster Log Entries

For this part of the practice, you must refer to the sample cluster log located on the accompanying CD-ROM in the \ClusterLog folder. The correct answers to this practice are listed in Appendix A.

1. What is the cluster version number?

2. What is the operating system version?

3. Locate the following entry, and identify what kind of entry it is:

   `00000488.000006a8::2000/11/17-23:54:46.029 [EP] Initialization...`

4. Look at the entry in the previous question. Which component logged the entry?

   `00000488.000006a8::2000/11/17-23:54:46.029 [EP] Initialization...`

5. What information is contained in the abbreviation [NMJOIN]?

6. What kind of entry is this?

   ```
   0000050c.00000164::2000/11/19-
   21:33:20.168 Network Name <Cluster Name>: Registered server name
   MYCLUSTER on transport \Device\NetBt_If13.
   ```

7. Look at the entry in the above question. What is the display name of the resource in this entry, and what kind of resource is it?

8. What is the sequence number of this log entry?

   ```
   000004b8.00000680::2000/11/20-19:51:54.134 [GUM] GumSendUpdate:
   completed update seq 11678    type 0 context 8
   ```

9. What is the type and context indicated in this entry?

   ```
   000004b8.00000680::2000/11/20-19:51:54.134 [GUM] GumSendUpdate:
   completed update seq 11678    type 0 context 8
   ```

10. What does the following group of entries describe?

    ```
    000004b8.000001dc::2000/11/19-
    21:30:58.655 [FM] Initializing resource 348202f0-011e-47f3-8d73-
    88e77a2bf77b from the registry.
    000004b8.000001dc::2000/11/19-
    21:30:58.655 [FM] Name for Resource 348202f0-011e-47f3-8d73-
    88e77a2bf77b is 'test1'.
    000004b8.000001dc::2000/11/19-
    21:30:58.655 [FM] FmpAddPossibleEntry:
    adding node 1 as possible host for resource 348202f0-011e-47f3-
    8d73-88e77a2bf77b.
    000004b8.000001dc::2000/11/19-
    21:30:58.655 [FM] FmpAddPossibleEntry: adding node 2 as possible
    host for resource 348202f0-011e-47f3-8d73-88e77a2bf77b.
    000004b8.000001dc::2000/11/19-
    21:30:58.655 [FM] All dependencies for resource 348202f0-011e-
    47f3-8d73-88e77a2bf77b created.
    ```

Lesson Summary

This lesson explained how to use the cluster log file for troubleshooting Cluster Service problems. The cluster log, located in the %windir%\cluster folder, includes entries associated with a variety of Cluster Service activities. These entries are in addition to the high-level information presented in the Windows Event Viewer. By interpreting the entries in the cluster log and reviewing the entries in the Event Viewer, you can get detailed information to aid you in the troubleshooting process.

Lesson 5: Implementing Disaster Recovery Methods

Planning and implementing a disaster recovery strategy is a vital part of using any technology, including clustering. A complete backup of a cluster must include data from each node and the data from the cluster shared device. At a minimum, the Windows system state must be backed up in order for you to be able to restore Cluster Service and the Quorum data. While Windows 2000 Backup is the primary tool, several additional tools are available for providing disaster recovery. These include Regback, Clusrest, an emergency repair disk, and command-line switches for starting Cluster Service. This lesson discusses how to use these tools separately or in combination to provide backup and recovery for your cluster.

After this lesson, you will be able to

- Describe how to develop a cluster server disaster recovery plan
- List the tools used in backing up and restoring data associated with a cluster
- Take the necessary steps for backing up and restoring a Cluster Service implementation

Estimated lesson time: 60 minutes

Planning a Cluster Backup and Recovery Strategy

The first step in planning a disaster recovery strategy for a cluster is creating a complete and accurate backup strategy. A failure on your cluster might include one or more nodes or even the cluster disk itself. Your backup and recovery strategy must address all of the components of a cluster. The following should be included in your backup strategy:

- Documentation of the cluster configuration
- Documentation of which resource registry keys map to which resources

A resource registry key can be identified only by the GUID associated with the resource. Therefore, the following information is crucial for recovering from a disaster:

- A catalog of the backup
- A safe location for storage of backup media
- An emergency repair disk for each node
- Documentation of restore procedures
- A schedule for completing your backups with the least amount of impact on cluster performance

The emergency repair disk contains information about your current Windows system settings. You can use this disk to repair a node if it does not start or if system files are damaged or erased. You can also use it to restore Windows 2000 Advanced Server to the node.

Backing Up and Restoring Quorum Data

The cluster database, or hive, is a set of registry keys stored under HKEY_LOCAL__MACHINE in the Windows 2000 Registry. The following information about the physical and logical elements in a cluster is stored in this database:

- A list of cluster objects
- A list of cluster properties
- Cluster configuration data

A continuously updated copy of the cluster database is stored on each node and on the Quorum disk. The data is kept consistent via global updates and periodic consistency checks on each node.

Recovering from a Missing or Damaged Quorum Log

If Cluster Service is not starting because the Quorum log is missing or damaged, you might be able to recover. If you have a recent backup of the Quorum log file, you can try starting Cluster Service using the following procedure:

1. Type *clussvc –debug –noquorumlogging* at the command prompt.
2. Copy the Quorum log file backup to the MSCS directory on the Quorum drive.
3. Stop Cluster Service.
4. Restart Cluster Service normally from the Cluster Administrator or by typing *net start clussvc* at the command prompt.

If you do not have a recent backup of the Quorum log file, use the procedure above without copying the backup Quorum log. However, keep in mind that in this case the system will attempt to create a new Quorum log file based on possibly stale information in the cluster hive. If no Quorum log is found, Cluster Service assumes a new installation and creates a new Quorum log using local system information. Any updated cluster information will be added as other nodes are brought online.

Backing Up and Restoring Cluster Application Data

Generally, you should use the same procedures for backing up and restoring cluster application data that you would for backing up and restoring application data outside the cluster. Some applications have built-in backup programs that you can use to back up cluster application data. Whether you use an application's backup program, the default Windows 2000 backup, or a third-party backup tool, you must make sure that the backup program is capable of backing up the Quorum data. In addition to application data, the backup should include the clustering software, the cluster administrative software, the Quorum, and the system state data. Once the cluster Quorum disk has been backed up from one node, it does not need to be backed up from the remaining nodes.

Cluster Service has a method of keeping track of application data, called checkpointing. Checkpointing allows changes to application data stored in the registry to be propagated to the registries on each node in the cluster. Since checkpoints are included in backups created by Windows 2000 Backup only when the system state is saved, this information must be backed up.

Tools for Cluster Backup and Restore

Several Windows 2000 tools or utilities support backup and restore functionality for a cluster. These tools must be used together in order to provide a complete backup and restore of all cluster components.

Windows 2000 Backup

Using Windows 2000 Backup, you can back up and restore the following cluster configuration information:

- Cluster registry snapshot files
- Quorum log file
- Registry checkpoint files for each resource
- Crypto checkpoint files for each resource

This information is backed up only if you select the option to back up the system state. Also, you cannot back up the local cluster registry hive, clusdb, using this method. You must use the Regback.exe utility instead (as described later).

To restore a cluster using Windows 2000 Backup (see Figure 7.6), you must first stop Cluster Service on all nodes except the one on which you are running the restore. At a minimum, you must restore the system state as part of the restore process. The restore process creates a temporary folder under the Winnt\Cluster folder called Cluster backup. If the Quorum data then needs to be restored, you must use the Clusrest.exe tool to restore this data from the temporary folder to the Quorum disk.

You complete the restore process by restarting Cluster Service on the newly restored node and then restarting the other nodes if needed. If you have added or changed any cluster disk resources since the last backup, these will not be recognized by the restored cluster database. Even if the restore operation is completely successful, these resources will remain offline. To resolve this, you must delete the Physical Disk resources and replace them with newly created disk resources.

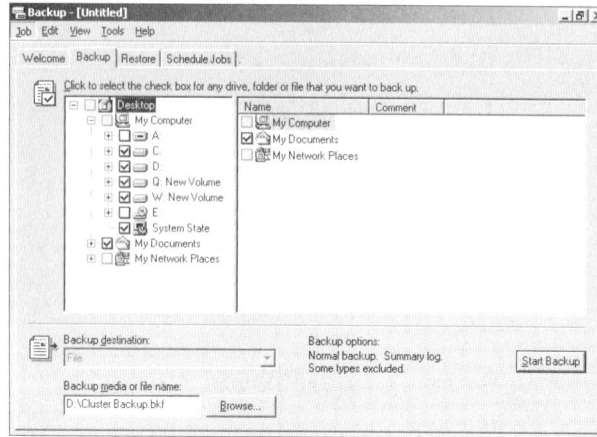

Figure 7.6   Windows 2000 Backup

Clusrest.exe

After you restore a node using Windows 2000 Backup, you must use the Clusrest.exe utility to restore the Quorum data to the Quorum disk. This utility is in the Windows 2000 Resource Kit; you can also download it from Microsoft's Web site. Depending on the reason for the restore, you might not need to restore the Quorum disk. For example, if a node has failed but the Quorum data has not been compromised, you only need to restore data to the node. To run Clusrest.exe, enter *clusrest* at the command prompt.

Restoring Quorum data sets the cluster back to the most recent backup date. Since this operation might result in data loss, you should attempt it only if the Quorum disk is compromised. You must also make sure that another node with a more current database does not take ownership of the Quorum before you update the Quorum data from the restored node. This will cause the restore to fail.

Regback.exe

Regback.exe is another tool found in the Windows 2000 Resource Kit. You can use it alone or in conjunction with your emergency repair disk to back up and restore the cluster configuration information stored in the system registry and the cluster registry hive (Clusdb).

Type the following at the command prompt to back up the cluster configuration information. (Note: The filename and path must be valid, as in C:\Clusbak.)

```
regback <filename> machine cluster
```

To restore the cluster registry, take the following steps:

1. Stop Cluster Service on both nodes.

2. On NodeA, click Start, click Run, and then type *regedt32*.

3. Locate and click the following registry key:

`HKEY_LOCAL_MACHINE\Cluster`

4. On the Registry menu, point to Unload Hive.

5. Rename %SystemRoot%\Cluster\Clusdb and %SystemRoot%\Cluster\Clusdb.log as Clusdb.old and Clusdb.log.old, respectively.

6. Rename your cluster registry backup file, Filename, as Clusdb, and copy it to the %SystemRoot%\Cluster directory.

7. Repeat steps 1 through 6 on NodeB to replace the cluster registry hive (Clusdb) on that computer.

8. On NodeA, in Administrative Tools, click Services.

9. Type *–ResetQuorumLog* in the Parameters box of Cluster Service.

10. Start Cluster Service on NodeA.

11. Open Windows Explorer, and delete the Quolog.log file and all the Chkxxx.tmp files from the Mscs folder on the Quorum drive. The cluster will re-create the Quorum log and checkpoint file.

12. Start Cluster Service on NodeB

Practice: Backing Up and Restoring a Cluster

In this practice, you will perform a complete backup of a cluster node. Although the complete backup can be restored, you will restore only the system state to the cluster node. Optionally, you can restore the Quorum data to the Quorum disk using the Clusrest.exe utility.

Verifying That a Node Owns the Quorum Resource

1. Choose the node that you think owns the Quorum resource, and log in with administrative permissions.

2. From the Start menu, point to Programs, point to Administrative Tools, and click Computer Management.

3. If needed, expand the Computer Management tree in the left pane to show items under Storage, and then click Disk Management.

4. Search the list of disk volumes in the right pane for the disk containing the Quorum resource. This disk should be identified by the drive letter Q:

5. Repeat steps 2 through 4 on the second node if the first node is not identified as the owner of the Quorum resource.

Backing Up a Cluster Node

1. If needed, log in to the node identified as the owner of the of the Quorum resource with administrative permissions.

2. From the Start menu, point to Programs, point to Accessories, point to System Tools, and then click Backup. This will open Windows 2000 Backup.

3. On the Welcome tab, click the Backup Wizard button to start the Backup Wizard.

4. Click Next, select the Back Up Everything On My Computer option, and click Next again.

5. On the Where To Store The Backup window, choose File as the backup media type and choose a name and location for your backup file. Verify that the location has sufficient space to store the backup image. Optionally, you can use a tape device if your system is set up for one.

6. Click Next and then click Finish to begin the backup.

7. Once the backup is completed, click Close to close the progress window.

Starting the Node in Safe Mode

1. From the Start menu, point to Shutdown, choose the Restart option, and click OK to restart the node.

2. When a line of text appears at the bottom of the screen prompting you to press F8 for startup options, press F8. The Windows 2000 startup menu appears.

3. Use the arrow keys to select Directory Services Restore Mode, and then press Enter.

Restoring the System State on a Cluster Node

1. Shut down the second node. From the Start menu, point to Shutdown, choose the Shutdown option, and click OK to shut down the node.

2. Log in to the node that is still active, using administrative permissions.

3. From the Start menu, point to Programs, point to Accessories, point to System Tools, and point to Backup. This will open Windows 2000 Backup.

4. On the Welcome tab, click the Restore Wizard button to start the Restore Wizard.

5. Click Next and expand the What To Restore tree in the left pane to display each of the backup items.

6. Select the System State check box.

7. Click Next, click Finish, and then click OK to accept the file to restore from and begin the restore. If the backup file is not shown, you must browse for it in the location where it was saved.

8. Once the restore is completed, click Close to close the progress window.

9. You will be prompted to restart. Click OK to restart the system.

10. Once the system has restarted successfully, restart the other cluster node.

Restoring the Quorum Data (Optional)

1. Locate Clusrest.exe in the Windows 2000 Resource Kit, or download it from Microsoft's Web site. Make sure that Clusrest.exe is available on the node that owns the Quorum disk.

2. From the Start menu, point to Run, type *command*, and then click OK to open a command prompt.

3. If necessary, change to the directory where Clusrest.exe is located. On the command line, type *clusrest* and press Enter.

4. Press the Y key to continue. This will start the restore process. It might take a few minutes for the restore to complete. During this time, a flashing cursor will appear below the command line. Once the restore is completed, the next command line will appear.

5. Type *exit* and then press Enter to exit the command window.

Verifying Cluster Service

1. From the Start menu, point to Programs, point to Administrative Tools, and click Cluster Administrator.

2. In the left pane of Cluster Administrator, click MYCLUSTER to expand the tree if needed and verify that both nodes and all resources are online.

Lesson Summary

This lesson discussed disaster recovery for your cluster and introduced several tools for backing up and restoring the nodes and the shared device in a cluster, including Windows 2000 Backup, Regback, Clusrest, Emergency Repair Disk, and command-line switches for starting Cluster Service. Using these tools, you can provide backup and recovery for cluster nodes, cluster shared devices, and applications running on your cluster.

Review

The following questions will help you review key information presented in this chapter. You'll find the answers in Appendix A, "Questions and Answers."

1. While installing Cluster Service on a node, you receive an error indicating that LanManServer Could Not Be Started. What is causing the error?

   a. The SCSI bus is not configured correctly.

   b. File and Printer Sharing is not installed on the node.

   c. A network adapter is not configured correctly.

   d. You are not logged in with administrative permissions.

2. What are the four possible states for a cluster network interface?

3. Which of the following are possible reasons that a group will not come online?

   a. A resource dependency is not online.

   b. Cluster Administrator is currently open on the other node.

   c. The group's disk resource has hardware configuration problems.

   d. A resource dependency is not configured properly.

4. You are testing a new virtual server's IP Address resource. As part of your troubleshooting process, you decide to take the group offline. However, the IP address seems to still be in use. How is this possible?

5. Which of the following are possible causes for the Quorum resource not starting?

   a. The SCSI devices are not properly terminated.

   b. The resource is not physically connected to the server.

   c. The Quorum log is corrupt.

   d. A node in the cluster failed.

6. A client can detect both nodes in your cluster but cannot detect any virtual servers. What are possible reasons for this?

7. Which of the following information is displayed in all cluster log entries?
    a. Event description
    b. Component abbreviation
    c. Process ID
    d. Timestamp

8. Explain how the tracking of process and thread IDs can be helpful.

9. Under which of the following conditions should you start Cluster Service with the *–noquorumlogging* switch?
    a. When you back up the Quorum log
    b. When you restore the system state to a node
    c. When you recover from a missing or damaged Quorum log
    d. When you back up the local Quorum database

10. What Cluster Service information can and cannot be backed up using Windows 2000 Backup?

C H A P T E R   8

Installing and Supporting Exchange Server 2000 in a Clustered Environment

About This Chapter

This chapter describes how to plan and implement an installation of Microsoft Exchange Server 2000 on a cluster. It also describes how to configure the appropriate resource types to complete the installation. This chapter also discusses administering and maintaining an Exchange Server installation.

Before You Begin

To complete this chapter, you must have

- The necessary hardware as outlined in the section titled "About This Book" in the Introduction
- The Windows 2000 Advanced Server installation CD-ROM
- Cluster Service installed in a two-node Windows 2000 Advanced Server cluster
- The Exchange Server 2000 installation CD-ROM

Lesson 1: Planning an Exchange Server 2000 Installation

This lesson describes how to plan for an Exchange Server 2000 installation on a cluster. The available architecture, load planning, and performance are discussed.

After this lesson, you will be able to

- Describe the architecture of Exchange Server when it is deployed on a cluster

Estimated lesson time: 45 minutes

Exchange Server 2000 and Cluster Service

Before you implement Exchange Server on a cluster, you should understand how Exchange Server interacts with Cluster Service. Specific resource types for implementing Exchange Server are installed as a part of the setup process. You will need to implement the available Exchange resources based on the implementation model required by your organization—either active/active or active/passive.

Exchange Server 2000 Architecture

Exchange Server 2000 is fully cluster-aware and supports active/active clustering, which means that it can simultaneously run multiple instances within the cluster. Two specific features in Exchange Server 2000 enable this capability:

- The Exchange 2000 resource DLL, exres.dll
- Support for multiple storage groups and virtual servers on a single node

Running Exchange Server 2000 in a clustered environment is similar to running it on a stand-alone system. Therefore, many of the concepts involved in managing a stand-alone implementation can be applied to a clustered environment.

Exchange Virtual Servers

The Exchange Virtual Server (EVS) is an important concept to understand if you plan to deploy Exchange on a cluster. An EVS is a cluster group that acts as a stand-alone server. Exchange therefore views each EVS as a separate instance of Exchange.

An EVS consists of the following:

- IP Address resource
- Network Name resource
- Physical Disk resource
- Exchange resources

Clients use the IP Address resource and the Network Name resource to enable them to connect to the cluster. This is typical of a standard cluster virtual server. The Physical Disk resource stores the Exchange databases, message tracking logs, and Simple Mail Transport Protocol (SMTP) queues. Storing this data on the disk resource allows it to be shared with all nodes in the cluster in case of a failover. Properties such as preferred owner, failover, and failback are set on the EVS Group. This group is the basic unit of failover.

Exchange allows each resource group or EVS to host multiple storage groups. However, the maximum number of storage groups allowed per node is four. Be sure to take this into account when you plan your Exchange Server environment. For example, if NodeA has two storage groups and NodeB has one storage group, during a failover either node can support the existing storage groups. But if NodeA has three storage groups and NodeB has two, neither node can support all the existing storage groups in the event of a failure.

Exchange Resources

A collection of Exchange resources resides in the EVS. Each resource has its own dependencies and possible owners. Each resource represents a different component of Exchange. The Exchange-specific resources are as follows:

- **System Attendant**   This resource controls the creation and deletion of resources in the EVS. The IsAlive call to this resource checks with the Service Control Manager to determine whether the System Attendant is running.

- **Information Store**   This resource comes online once the storage group has been loaded and all transaction logs have been reviewed. The IsAlive call to this resource checks with the Service Control Manager to determine whether the Information Store is running.

- **Protocols (SMTP, HTTP, IMAP, POP3)**   The IsAlive call to this resource calls the specific protocol and waits for its response banner. If the timeout period passes and the banner has not returned, the ISAlive call fails and Cluster Service assumes that the specific protocol is unavailable. The protocols cannot be set to reject all connections from all servers because doing so would cause the protocol to reject its own IsAlive call. Each EVS must accept connections from its designated IP Address resource.

  When an EVS is taken offline, all instances of SMTP are stopped and restarted. However, if the Do Not Restart option on the property page is selected, the protocol will not restart.

  An Exchange cluster supports connectivity using the SMTP, X.400, and Routing Group connectors only. Therefore, be sure to plan and arrange your Exchange cluster so that it uses the proper connectors.

- **Routing**   The IsAlive call to this resource checks with the Service Control Manager to determine whether the Routing Service is running.

- **Message Transfer Agent (MTA)**   While online, the MTA serves all EVSs in the cluster. The MTA is originally created on the first EVS in the cluster. However, if that EVS is not the last EVS in the cluster, the MTA is deleted and moved to the next EVS. The IsAlive call to this resource checks with the Service Control Manager to determine whether the MTA is running.

- **MSSearch/Content Indexing**   Content indexing for EVSs is provided by the MSSearch resource. The IsAlive call to this resource returns a pointer to the data structure of the database that is currently being indexed. A valid pointer indicates that the resource is working properly.

Cluster Support

The Exchange resources support clustering, but the level of support varies. Table 8.1 lists the Exchange-specific resources and the level of clustering, if any, that they support.

The following terms describe the level of clustering functionality:

- **Active/passive**   Only one instance of the resource can run in a cluster at a time.

- **Active/active**   Multiple instances of the resource can run concurrently in the cluster.

Table 8.1   Exchange Server 2000 Resource Types

Resource	Functionality	Notes
System Attendant	Active/active	Multiple virtual servers per node.
Information Store	Active/active	After failover, each node is limited to four storage groups.
Message Transfer Agent	Active/passive	One instance per cluster; the MTA will be in only one cluster group.
POP3	Active/active	Multiple-protocol virtual servers per node.
IMAP	Active/active	Multiple-protocol virtual servers per node.
SMTP	Active/active	Multiple-protocol virtual servers per node.
HTTP	Active/active	Multiple-protocol virtual servers per node.
Network News Transfer Protocol	Not supported	
Key Management Service	Not supported	
Full-Text Indexing	Active/active	
Instant Messaging	Not supported	
Chat	Active/passive	Does not require a System Attendant resource in the virtual server.
Conferencing Services	Not supported	

Performance

Exchange Server 2000 on a cluster differs from Exchange Server 2000 on a stand-alone server in two major ways:

- Cluster Service makes IsAlive calls to resources to determine whether resources are working properly.
- Each EVS acts as a stand-alone server, so messages between separate EVSs are transported by SMTP.

The failover policy for an EVS can affect the availability of the server. Therefore, it is important to have a short failover time. Failover can be planned or unplanned, as described below.

In a planned failover

- The information store removes the storage groups from the node and stops the virtual servers.
- The resources are failed over.
- The Information Store on the remaining node assumes the storage groups and starts the protocols needed for another IP address.

In an unplanned failover

- Cluster Service determines that one node is not available or is not responding.
- The remaining node assumes the storage groups that failed over and reads the transaction logs in an effort to synchronize the databases.
- The protocols needed for another IP address are brought online.

You can increase the performance and reliability of your storage resources by placing the transaction logs on a different drive than the storage groups.

Domain controllers require a lot of processing power and computer resources, so Microsoft recommends against installing a clustered Exchange environment on a domain controller.

When you plan your Exchange environment, be sure to consider the resources required for Cluster Service as well as those required for Exchange 2000.

Preparing to Install Exchange Server 2000

Before you can install Exchange Server 2000 on a cluster, you must update the forest and domain. This includes adding groups and setting permissions. Normally, if the account used to install Exchange is a member of the SchemaAdmin and EnterpriseAdmin Groups, the forest and domain will be updated automatically. However, with a clustered implementation, you must perform these operations manually.

Note For purposes of this training kit, both nodes in the cluster are assumed to be domain controllers. However, this configuration might use too much of the system's resources for a production implementation. It is also assumed that no previous versions of Exchange have been installed on either node.

Preparing the Forest

To install Exchange 2000, you must extend the Windows 2000 Active Directory schema to include Exchange-specific information. The Setup program includes a command line argument named ForestPrep for this purpose. As part of the ForestPrep process, new objects are created in Active Directory and the designated Exchange administrator account is given permissions on these objects. Once the process is completed, the designated Exchange administrator will have sufficient rights to install an Exchange 2000 server on your network.

Take the following steps to prepare your Active Directory forest:

1. Make sure that the Windows 2000 Service Pack 1 has been installed on both cluster nodes. Exchange 2000 cannot be installed until this service pack has been installed.

2. Load the Exchange 2000 CD-ROM in your CD-ROM drive.

3. Click Start, and then click Run.

4. In the Open dialog box, click Browse, navigate to
   CD_drive_letter\setup\i386\setup, and type /forestprep after the path.
   (*CD_drive_letter* is the letter of your CD-ROM drive.) Click OK.

5. On the welcome page of the Microsoft Exchange 2000 Installation Wizard, click Next.

6. On the End User License Agreement page, read the agreement, and if you agree to the license terms, click I Agree and then click Next.

7. On the Product Identification page, enter the 25-digit CD key located on the back of the CD package, and then click Next.

8. On the Component Selection page, verify that the action listed next to Exchange 2000 Server is ForestPrep, and click Next.

9. On the Installation Type page, click Create An Exchange 2000 Organization.

10. On the Organization Name page, type a name for your new organization. Once you enter a name, you cannot change it.

11. On the Exchange 2000 Administrator Account page, type the name of the user or group that is responsible for installing Exchange 2000. This account will have permission to create all levels of Exchange 2000 administrator accounts. Be sure to use the same account that was used to install Cluster Service. Click Next.

12. You will see a dialog box informing you that setup will install a cluster-aware version of Exchange. Click OK.

13. On the Completion page, click Finish.

Preparing the Domain

After completing the ForestPrep process, you must update the domain in which Exchange will be installed. Setup includes a second command-line argument, called DomainPrep, for this purpose. Two new domain groups are created by DomainPrep: a Windows 2000 global security group named Exchange Domain Servers, which contains the computer accounts of all Exchange servers in the domain, and a Windows 2000 domain local security group named Exchange Enterprise Servers, which consists of every Exchange Domain Servers group in your organization. The Public Folder proxy container is also created by DomainPrep. You must run DomainPrep against each domain that will host the Exchange Server.

Complete the following steps to update your domain using DomainPrep:

1. Load the Exchange 2000 CD-ROM in your CD-ROM drive. DomainPrep can be run on any computer that is running Windows 2000 Server in the domain.

2. Click Start, and then click Run.

3. In the Open dialog box, click Browse, navigate to *CD_drive_letter*\setup\i386\setup, and type /domainprep after the path. (*CD_drive_letter* is the letter of your CD-ROM drive.) Click OK.

4. On the welcome page of the Microsoft Exchange 2000 Installation Wizard, click Next.

5. On the End-User License Agreement page, click I Agree, and then click Next.

6. On the Product Identification page, type your product key.

7. On the Component Selection page, make sure that the action listed next to Exchange 2000 Server is DomainPrep, and click Next.

8. A dialog box will appear informing you that the setup program will install a cluster-aware version of Exchange. Click OK.

9. On the Completion page, click Finish.

Preinstallation Checklist

Once the forest and domains have been updated, you must complete additional configuration steps before actually installing Exchange. Here are the preinstallation requirements:

- NNTP and SMTP must be installed on each node of your cluster. Microsoft Internet Information Server (IIS) 5 is installed by default with Windows 2000 Advanced Server, but NNTP is not installed with IIS.

- A Domain Name System (DNS) server must be available for the domain that the cluster resides on.

- Exchange 2000 must be installed using the same account that Cluster Service was installed with. In this chapter, this account will be referred to as the *installation account*. It must be a member of the Domain Admins security group.

- The installation account must be a member of the Built-In Administrators Group on each node of the cluster. If the Exchange server you are installing is not the first server in the organization, you must grant Exchange full Administrator privileges to the Cluster Service account.

- Completion of the ForestPrep stage of the Exchange setup requires that the installation account be a member of the Domain Admins, Schema Admins, and Enterprise Admins Groups.

- You must install Exchange 2000 at the same location on each computer and on the shared disk. The default installation folder determines where the binary files are stored; these files do not need to be shared. However, the Exchange databases do need to be shared and therefore should reside on the shared disk.

- The Exchange shared data folder on the shared disk must be empty.

- You must install the same build of Exchange on both nodes. You cannot install the beta release of Exchange 2000 on one node and the release version on the other node.

- The minimum components you can install are Microsoft Exchange Messaging and Collaboration and Microsoft Exchange System Management.

Lesson Summary

This lesson described the Exchange Server architecture and Exchange Virtual Servers and explained some performance considerations for when you use Exchange with Cluster Service. It also addressed exchange resources and the level of cluster support that each provides and explained how to prepare the forest and domain for your Exchange Server installation. Finally, the preinstallation requirements were presented.

Lesson 2: Installing Exchange Server 2000 on a Cluster

This lesson describes how to install Exchange Server 2000 on a cluster and how to configure resources on Exchange. It concludes by explaining how to test the clustered Exchange installation.

After this lesson, you will be able to

- Install Exchange Server on a cluster
- Configure Exchange Server using Cluster Administrator
- Test an Exchange implementation using Microsoft Outlook Express

Estimated lesson time: 60 minutes

Installing Exchange Server 2000

Prior to installing Exchange Server, you should verify that the Active Directory schema has been extended, the necessary security groups have been created, and the domain has been prepared.

Note You must complete the Exchange installation on the first node of the cluster before attempting to install Exchange on the second node.

The following steps are required to complete an Exchange installation on a cluster (a new installation, not an upgrade from an earlier version). To see a demonstration of this practice, run the Exchange.exe animation located in the Media folder on the companion CD.

1. Log in to NodeA of the cluster using the installation account.
2. Start Microsoft Exchange 2000 Setup.
3. On the welcome page, click Next.
4. On the End User License Agreement page, read the license agreement, and if you agree to the terms, click I Agree and then click Next.
5. On the Product Identification page, enter the 25-digit CD key located on the back of the product CD-ROM, and click Next.
6. On the Component Selection page, make sure that the actions listed next to the following components are correct:

    Action   Component

    Typical   Microsoft Exchange 2000

    Install   Microsoft Exchange Messaging and Collaboration Services

    Install   Microsoft Exchange System Management Tools

7. You can also change the drive location of the installation by clicking Microsoft Exchange 2000 and then clicking Change Folder. But for our purposes, keep

the default location. Click Disk Information to display information about available drive space on each drive. The Exchange 2000 binary files are installed to the local drive by default. Close the Disk Information window.

8. On the Licensing Agreement page, read the per-seat licensing agreement. To continue, select the appropriate option and click Next.

9. On the Component Summary page, click Next.

10. A message box will appear, informing you that the setup program will install a cluster-aware version of Exchange. Click OK.

11. On the Completing Microsoft Exchange 2000 page, click Finish, and then restart the computer.

12. When the Exchange 2000 installation is completed on the first node, repeat the process on the second node.

Configuring the Exchange Server 2000 Resources Using Cluster Administrator

After you install Exchange 2000 on both nodes in the cluster, you must configure it. Only the binary files have been installed at this point. The configuration will complete the installation process. You'll configure Exchange Server 2000 using Cluster Administrator. To correctly configure Exchange, you must create a resource group, create three separate resources, and transfer a disk resource. The three resources you must create are

- An IP Address resource
- A Network Name resource
- An Exchange 2000 System Attendant resource

Creating a Resource Group for Exchange Server 2000

To create a new resource group for Exchange, take these steps:

1. Open Cluster Administrator.

2. Right-click Groups, point to New, and click Group.

3. In the Name box, type *Exchange Group*.

4. In the Description box, type *Group for Exchange resources*.

5. Click Next.

6. In the Preferred Owners dialog box, add NodeA to the Preferred Owners list. (The list should not contain both nodes in the cluster. If both nodes are made preferred owners of the group and one node stops working, the entire resource will go offline, causing Exchange Server to repeatedly fail over and fail back.)

7. Click Finish. A message box will appear, stating that the group was created successfully.

8. Click OK.

Creating an IP Address Resource

Within the new resource group, create a new IP Address resource as follows:

1. Right-click Exchange Group, point to New, and click Resource.

2. In the Resource dialog box, type *Exchange IP Address* in the Name box, type *IP Address of Exchange Server* in the Description box, select IP Address as the resource type, and select Exchange Group as the group.

3. Click Next.

4. Both nodes should appear in the Possible Owners list. If they do not, add them to the list.

5. Click Next.

6. In the Dependencies dialog box, the Resource Dependencies list should be blank. Click Next.

7. In the TCP/IP Address Parameters dialog box, type the following information:

   Address   *192.168.0.5*

   Subnet Mask   *255.255.255.0*

   Network   *Public Cluster Connection*

   Leave the Enable NETBios for this address selected.

8. Click Finish. A message box will appear stating that the IP Address resource was created successfully.

9. Click OK.

Creating a Network Name Resource

Using the IP Address resource you just created, add a Network Name resource to the Exchange Group as follows:

1. Right-click Exchange Group, point to New, and click Resource.

2. In the New Resource dialog box, type *Exchange network name* in the Name box, type *network name for Exchange* in the Description box, select Network Name as the resource type, and select Exchange Group as the group. Click Next.

3. Both nodes should appear in the Possible Owners list. If they do not, add them to the list.

4. Click Next.

5. In the Dependencies dialog box, add the Exchange IP Address resource to the Resource Dependencies list and click Next.

6. In the Network Name Parameters dialog box, type *EXCHANGETEST*.

7. Click Finish. A message box will appear, stating that the Network Name resource was created successfully.

8. Click OK.

9. Right-click Exchange Group, and then click Bring Online.

Transferring the Disk Resource to the Exchange Group

This training kit assumes that there is only one shared drive in the cluster. To transfer this drive to the Exchange Group or to create a new shared drive resource and add it to the group, take these steps:

1. Click the Resources folder.

2. Right-click Disk W: and point to Change Group. On the popup menu that lists all of the available groups in the cluster, click Exchange Group.

3. A message box will appear, asking if you are sure you want to change the group. Click Yes.

Creating the System Attendant Resource

When Exchange was installed on this node, specific resource types were added to the cluster. The only resource you must create is the System Attendant resource. When Exchange is first started, additional resources will be created automatically (as described below). To create the System Attendant resource, follow these steps:

1. Right-click Exchange Group, point to New, and click Resource.

2. In the New Resource dialog box, type *Exchange System Attendant* in the Name box and in the Description box, select Microsoft Exchange System Attendant as the resource type, and select Exchange Group as the group. Click Next.

3. Both nodes should appear in the Possible Owners list. If they do not, add them to the list. Click Next.

4. In the Dependencies dialog box, add the Exchange Network Name and Physical Disk resources to the Resource Dependencies list and click Next.

5. In the Data Directory dialog box, verify the location of the data files (for example, W:\Exchsrvr) and then click Next. This location should be on the shared disk.

6. Bring the service online by right-clicking Exchange Group and clicking Bring Online. Bringing the group online might take a while because the Exchange System Attendant creates all the virtual servers required when Exchange is used in a cluster. The additional servers are as follows:

   - Exchange Information Store instance
   - Exchange Message Transfer Agent instance
   - Exchange Routing Service instance
   - SMTP virtual server instance
   - Exchange HTTP virtual server instance

- Exchange IMAP4 virtual server instance
- Exchange POP3 virtual server instance
- Exchange MS Search instance

Testing the Exchange Implementation

You test your new Exchange implementation by creating a new user account and then using this account to send yourself test e-mail while Exchange is running on NodeA and then after it is moved to NodeB.

Creating a New User Account

To test the Exchange installation, you need a new account that you'll use to send yourself e-mail. This account must be associated with an account in Exchange.

1. From the Windows 2000 Start menu, point to Programs, point to Microsoft Exchange, and click Active Directory Users And Computers.

2. If reskit.com is not expanded, click the plus sign to expand it. Right-click Users, point to New, and click User.

3. In the First Name text box, type *Test*. In the Last Name text box, type *Mail*. In the User Logon Name text box, type *testmail* and then click Next.

4. Type a password in the Password text box, and type the password again in the Confirm Password text box. Select the Password Never Expires option, and click Next.

5. Make sure that the Create An Exchange Mailbox option is selected, accept the defaults listed, and click Next.

6. Click Finish.

7. Add this account to the Domain Admins Group.

Configuring Outlook Express

In the default Outlook Express e-mail program, you'll use the new account you just created. Here's how to configure Outlook Express to use the clustered Exchange server:

1. Log on to NodeB with the newly created account.

2. From the Windows 2000 Start menu, point to Programs, and then click Outlook Express.

3. The Internet Connection Wizard will open. Select the I Want To Set Up My Internet Connection Manually or I Want To Connect Through A Local Area Network (LAN) option. Click Next.

4. Select the I Want To Connect Through A Local Area Network (LAN) option, and then click Next.

5. On the Local Area Network Internet Configuration page, accept the defaults and click Next.

6. On the Set Up Your Internet Mail Account page, select No and click Next.

7. On the Completing The Internet Connection Wizard page, click Finish.

8. On the Your Name page, type *Test Mail* and click Next.

9. On the Internet E-mail Address page, select the I Already Have An E-Mail Address That I'd Like To Use option.

10. In the e-mail address box, type *testmail@reskit.com* and click Next. This is the e-mail address of your newly created account.

11. On the E-mail Server Names page, select POP3 from the drop-down list, type *ExchangeTest* in the Incoming Mail Server text box, type *ExchangeTest* in the Outgoing Mail Server text box, and click Next.

12. On the Internet Mail Logon page, if the account name is not filled in, type *TestMail*. Type the password in the Password box, select the Remember Password option, and click Next.

13. On the Congratulations page, click Finish.

Sending Test E-Mail

Now that Outlook Express has been configured to use the clustered Exchange server, you can test the installation by sending a test e-mail:

1. Click New Mail.

2. On the To line, type *testmail*. On the Subject line, type *test*, and in the body of the message, type *test*.

3. Click Send.

4. Click Send/Receive. The test e-mail will appear in your inbox.

5. Return to Cluster Administrator on NodeA.

6. Right-click Exchange Group, and click Move Group. All resources in the group should now move to NodeB.

7. Return to NodeB.

8. Repeat steps 1 through 4, but type *testb* both on the Subject line and in the body of the message.

9. If you have two e-mail messages in the inbox, both nodes were able to process.

Lesson Summary

This lesson explained how to install and configure Exchange 2000 on a cluster and how to test the Exchange implementation using Outlook Express to send e-mail to a user account.

Lesson 3: Administering and Maintaining Exchange Server 2000

This lesson discusses administering and maintaining Exchange Server 2000 on a Windows 2000 cluster. Exchange Server 2000 is administered using Exchange System Manager and the Active Directory Users and Computers consoles. Common tasks include managing administrative groups, routing groups, address lists, and policies. This lesson describes appropriate practices for maintaining Exchange Server 2000 in a cluster, such as performing backups and monitoring performance. It also discusses the differences between performing maintenance and administrative functions on Exchange Server in a cluster and performing them on a stand-alone Exchange server.

After this lesson, you will be able to

- Administer a clustered installation of Exchange Server 2000
- Describe the key tasks for maintaining a clustered Exchange server

Estimated lesson time: 30 minutes

Administering Exchange Server 2000

Generally, administering Exchange Server 2000 on a cluster is identical to administering it on a single-server platform. Because the Exchange System Manager is fully cluster-aware, you can perform any Exchange administrative tasks without considering the cluster. However, you should not run the Exchange System Manager program locally on a cluster node. If a failover occurs while it is running on a cluster node, the Exchange System Manager can lock up and cause problems with your Exchange server. Therefore, you should run it only on computers that are not part of your clustered Exchange server.

Like many other Windows 2000 programs, Exchange Server 2000 is administered using Microsoft Management Console (MMC) snap-ins. The Exchange System Manager and the Active Directory Users and Computers consoles are the two primary snap-ins used for administering Exchange.

The Exchange System Manager (shown in Figure 8.1) is installed when you run the Microsoft Exchange 2000 Installation Wizard if you select Microsoft Exchange System Management Tools on the Component Selection screen. You can also install the Exchange System Manager on any computer running Windows 2000 by installing SMTP. Windows 2000 Professional also requires the Windows 2000 Administration Tools to be installed. Using the Exchange System Manager, you can connect to any Windows 2000 domain controller and extract information from Active Directory.

The Active Directory Users and Computers snap-in is installed automatically when a Windows 2000 server is promoted to a domain controller. You can also install the Windows 2000 Administrative Pack on a computer running Windows 2000 that is not a domain controller to facilitate remote administration of Active Directory.

Active Directory lets you perform administrative tasks across multiple Exchange servers from a single point of control.

Exchange System Manager

Exchange Server configuration is done centrally through the Exchange System Manager. When you open the Exchange System Manager, it connects to the closest available domain controller to obtain configuration information. You can configure address lists, connectors, policies, protocols, public folders, and servers using the Exchange System Manager.

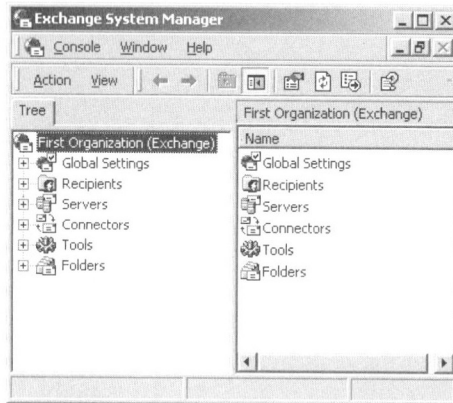

Figure 8.1   The Exchange System Manager

Administrative Groups and Routing Groups

In Exchange 2000, servers can be organized into administrative or routing groups. Routing groups are based on a physical grouping of servers for routing, while administrative groups are based on a logical grouping of servers for administering permissions. Both groups are optional and are not visible in the Exchange System Manager unless you enable them.

Address Lists

Address lists in Exchange 2000 provide a method of organizing mail-related objects in Active Directory. Default address lists are created automatically based on Active Directory object attributes. You can also create custom address lists based on any grouping you desire. Management using the Exchange System Manager is simple because address list membership is updated automatically as Active Directory changes. Address lists help to streamline searches for users, groups, or contacts. In addition, they are supported by all versions of Outlook. However, this feature is not supported by Outlook Express.

Policies

Policies allow you to apply configuration settings to a group of objects. System policies are primarily used to apply configuration changes to mailbox stores, public folders, and servers. Recipient policies are primarily used to apply configuration changes to users, groups, and contacts.

Maintaining Exchange Server 2000

System maintenance is a crucial part of Exchange Server 2000 administration. You should follow the same guidelines on a clustered Exchange server that you would on a stand-alone system. Your system maintenance plan should include the following practices:

- Periodic backup
- Monitoring performance
- Monitoring event logs
- Setting up performance and failure notifications

Using Windows 2000 Backup

You can use the Windows 2000 Backup program to back up and restore the Exchange 2000 Server Information Store. Backups are important for protecting your clustered Exchange server from both accidental loss and hardware failures from which the clustering technology does not protect your system.

Monitoring Performance

To monitor the performance of your clustered Exchange servers, you can use the Windows System Monitor, performance logs, or the Alerts snap-in. System Monitor is shown in Figure 8.2. These utilities provide detailed statistics on resources used by software components, such as the Windows operating system, Exchange, or Cluster Service. Performance can be displayed in graphs and recorded in logs or reports. The Messenger service notifies users when a particular performance counter reaches, surpasses, or falls below a predefined threshold.

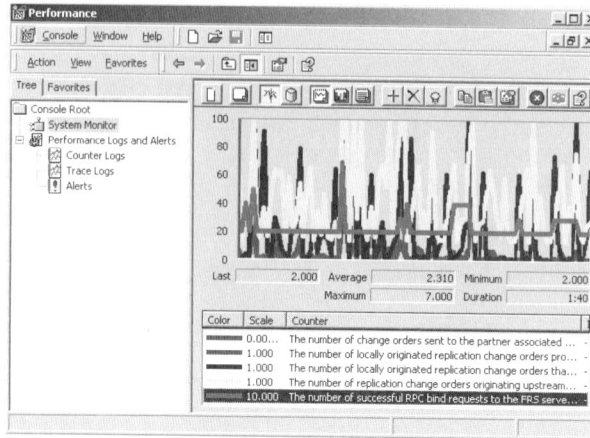

Figure 8.2   Monitoring performance using System Monitor

You should run System Monitor only on remote computers to monitor performance on your clustered Exchange server. Use the Microsoft Exchange Server network name rather than individual node names when you add performance counters. Running System Monitor on a cluster node or tracking node statistics will not give you accurate readings of the cluster's performance.

Regular system monitoring is vital to maintain the efficiency and effectiveness of your clustered Exchange server. You should monitor the following as part of your system monitoring plan:

- **Windows Event Log**   Events are logged in the event log of the cluster node. These events are replicated to the remaining cluster node's event logs.

- **Processor**   Monitoring the usage level of the processor is one of the best ways to determine the efficiency of your clustered Exchange server. If the processor is at close to maximum output for an extended period, you might need a processor upgrade. Generally, a usage level of 75 percent or greater indicates that a processor upgrade is needed. You should refrain from adding more users to the server until this upgrade is performed. Otherwise, the performance of both the cluster and Exchange Server might degrade.

- **Disk I/O**   Disk input and output (I/O) is determined by the number of reads and writes made to the hard drive. Disk operations performed by Windows 2000, Cluster Service, and Exchange Server all contribute to disk I/O traffic. Monitoring disk I/O can give you valuable information about the efficiency of your physical storage.

- **Memory**   It is important to monitor physical memory (RAM) usage to determine whether you have sufficient RAM to support your clustered Exchange server. Insufficient RAM on a cluster node might result in greater use of virtual memory, thus slowing the operating speed of your system. However, RAM on a cluster is dynamically allocated or released to each cluster node as needed. Therefore, RAM requirements will be smaller than for a stand-alone Exchange server. In addition, the amount of physical storage required for virtual memory will also be less than for a stand-alone Exchange server because the memory is located on each separate node.

- **Physical Storage**   On a clustered Exchange server, the physical storage of the shared disk containing the Exchange data store must be monitored as the number of mail users and other Exchange objects increases. Monitoring physical storage on the nodes is not crucial, but it could become a factor in situations in which virtual memory increases or if the node is a domain controller. You must make sure that sufficient disk space is available to store mail and handle additional users.

Managing Exchange-Related Services

You should use only Cluster Administrator to stop or start Exchange-related services on a clustered Exchange server. By default, the startup for these services is set to manual rather than automatic to allow the Cluster Resource Manager to start them in order of dependency. Therefore, you should never use the Services application or a *net start* or *net stop* command to stop or start these services. Doing so will cause the Cluster Resource Manager to see the resource as failed and might result in unpredictable consequences when the Cluster Resource Manager tries to either restart or fail over the cluster resource the service belongs to. When a service needs to be shut down for maintenance, you should fail over the entire Microsoft Exchange Server cluster group rather than stop any services.

Lesson Summary

This lesson described how to administer and maintain Exchange Server 2000 on a Windows 2000 cluster and discussed how it differs from administering and maintaining Exchange on a stand-alone server. Some of the crucial components in administering Exchange Server 2000 were introduced, including administrative groups, routing groups, address lists, and policies. This lesson also explained ways to maintain Exchange Server 2000 in a cluster, such as performing backups and monitoring performance.

Review

?

The following questions will help you review key information presented in this chapter. You'll find the answers in Appendix A.

1. Which of the following is not considered an Exchange resource?

    a. EVS

    b. System Attendant

    c. Information Store

    d. Routing

2. Why does Microsoft recommend that you not install Exchange Server 2000 on a domain controller?

3. What two things must you do before you install Exchange Server 2000?

    a. Extend the Active Directory schema using the DomainPrep argument.

    b. Extend the Active Directory schema using the ForestPrep argument.

    c. Add domain groups using the DomainPrep argument.

    d. Add domain groups using the ForestPrep argument.

4. The Exchange Group is owned by only one node. Why?

5. Which of the following are requirements for installing Exchange Server 2000 on a cluster?

    a. Exchange and Cluster Service must be installed using the same account.

    b. NNTP must be installed on both nodes in the cluster.

    c. The cluster's domain must have a DNS server available.

    d. IIS does not need to be installed on the nodes of the cluster.

6. An EVS requires a Physical Disk resource. What are the responsibilities of the Physical Disk resource?

7. Which of the following are the primary tools for administering an Exchange server?

   a. System Monitor

   b. Exchange System Manager

   c. Active Directory Sites and Services

   d. Active Directory Users and Computers

8. Why is it unwise to run Exchange System Manager on a cluster node?

9. Which of the following mail programs support Exchange Server 2000 address lists?

   a. Outlook Express

   b. Outlook 97

   c. Microsoft Mail

   d. Outlook 2000

10. When should the Services application be used to stop or start Exchange-related services on a clustered Exchange 2000 server?

C H A P T E R   9

Installing and Supporting SQL Server 2000 in a Clustered Environment

About This Chapter

This chapter describes how to install and support Microsoft SQL Server 2000 in a clustered environment. Before you start the SQL Server setup process, you must address a number of issues, including hardware considerations that affect performance, and the appropriate clustering configuration based on your organization's needs and the SQL Server license you have purchased. The chapter also describes cluster-specific functionality in the SQL Server setup program and some common support and maintenance concerns for a clustered installation of SQL Server.

Before You Begin

To complete this chapter, you must have

- The necessary hardware as outlined in the section titled "About This Book" in the Introduction
- The Windows 2000 Advanced Server installation CD-ROM
- Cluster Service installed in a two-node Windows 2000 Advanced Server cluster
- The SQL Server 2000 installation CD-ROM

Lesson 1: Planning a Clustered SQL Server Installation

This lesson describes how to plan for a clustered SQL Server 2000 installation. It explains the available configuration models and lists preinstallation requirements.

After this lesson, you will be able to

- Compare and contrast the two configuration models supported by SQL Server, active/active and active/passive.
- List the planning considerations for a clustered SQL Server installation.

Estimated lesson time: 30 minutes

Configuration Models

Before you deploy SQL Server 2000, you must decide on an active/active or active/passive configuration. Your choice will depend on your organization's needs as well as the licensing model required for SQL Server.

Active/Active

The active/active configuration (shown in Figure 9.1) lets you run at least one SQL Server instance on each node in the cluster and still provide failover support. Typically, the default instance is installed on one node and a second, named instance, is installed on the second node. Each node maintains its own copies of the master, model, msdb, tempdb, and user databases for the instance associated with the node.

In addition, for each instance, a virtual server is created for use by Cluster Service. Each virtual server's primary node is responsible for accessing and changing its own databases. These databases are stored on a dedicated shared drive for the given instance. Thus, if you're using an active/active configuration with one instance of SQL Server on each node, you need at least two shared drives managed by the cluster. In the event of a failover, the remaining node is responsible for the activities of both virtual servers.

Active/Passive

The active/passive configuration (shown in Figure 9.2) provides optimal performance in the event of a failover because only one instance of SQL Server is installed on the cluster, with one node at a time running SQL Server. However, the executable files associated with SQL Server are installed on each node in the cluster. The data associated with the instance of SQL Server is installed on the shared drive, allowing both nodes to access it. Because only one instance of SQL Server is configured, only one virtual server is used. The primary node controls access to the SQL Server data, while the secondary node assumes these responsibilities only during a failover.

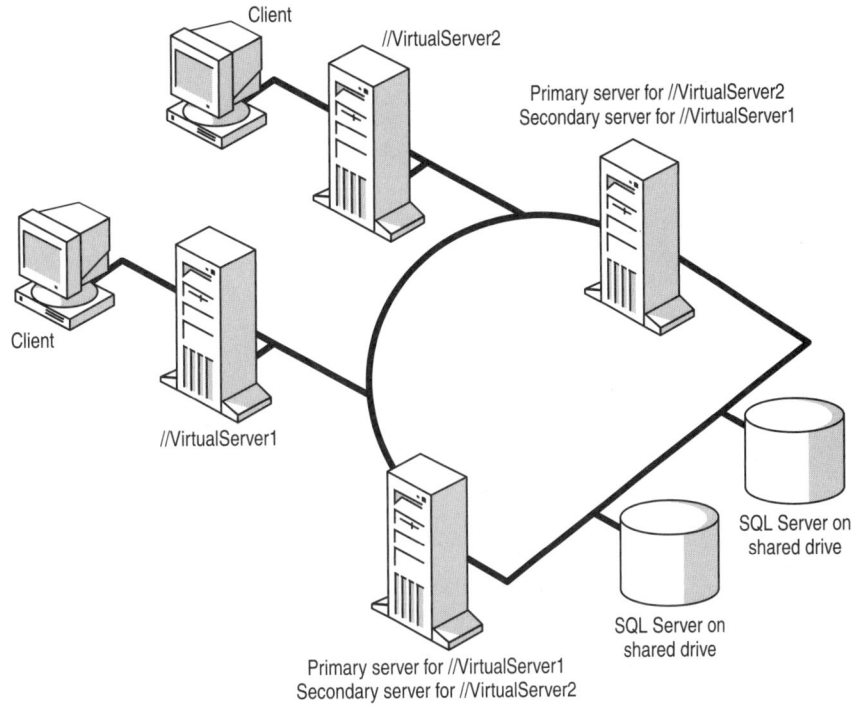

Figure 9.1   Active/active failover configuration

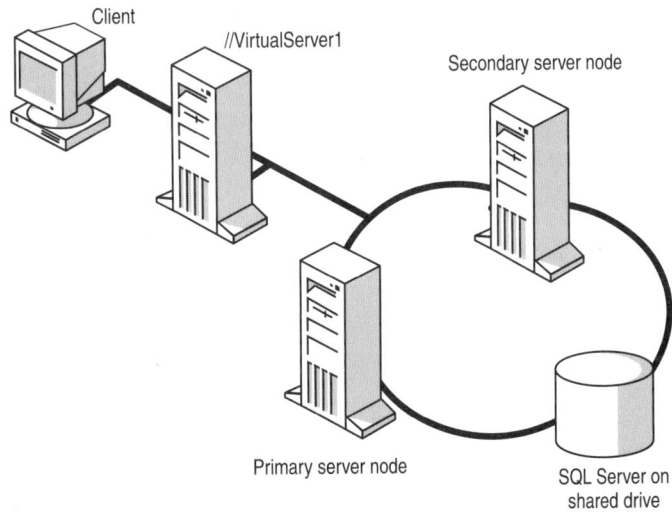

Figure 9.2   Active/passive failover configuration

Cluster Support

A cluster can support multiple instances of SQL Server 2000. Multiple instancing enables easier installation, configuration, and maintenance of SQL virtual servers. Clients can connect to the separate instances of SQL Server much like they access SQL Server databases that reside on separate computers. You might consider implementing multiple instances to provide different departments in your organization with separate data stores based on their needs. For example, the sales department might need a SQL Server instance for inventory control, while the human resources department might need an instance of SQL Server to manage employee training and certification records. Up to 16 instances of SQL Server 2000 can be installed on a cluster.

SQL Server 2000 Failover Clusters

SQL Server installs the required files on the nodes specified during setup. This means that you don't need to run setup on each node in the cluster. The SQL Server executable and binary files are installed on the local disk drive of each node in the cluster. Therefore, the drive letters must match on both nodes. This is important because the SQL Server executable must be able to be started from the same location on each node. The installation will also enter the necessary SQL Server information in the registry of each node.

You associate the SQL Server virtual server name with the instance of SQL Server during setup. The cluster group that maintains the SQL Server databases will be associated with that virtual server. There can be only one database group per SQL Server instance and one SQL Server instance per virtual server.

Aside from the SQL Server cluster resources and group, only the database files fail over. The other files and information needed to operate SQL Server are located on the node itself. Therefore, if a failover occurs, the healthy node in the cluster will already have the necessary files and information to operate and maintain the SQL Server instance.

The limit of 16 instances of SQL Server per computer is enforced on a cluster because the nodes share registry information and SQL files. There can be only one default instance of SQL Server per cluster. Remember that each instance of SQL Server must be identified by a unique name or must be the default instance.

When an application attempts to connect to an instance of SQL Server, it must specify the virtual server name and the instance of SQL Server that it wants to connect to. If the SQL Server instance is the default instance, the instance name can be omitted. For example, consider the following scenario:

- Cluster Administrator creates a failover cluster with two nodes, NodeA and NodeB.
- Each node maps the drive letter C to a local hard drive.

- There is one shared disk in the cluster.

- Cluster Administrator creates ClusterGroupA and adds the shared drive as a resource. This group is assigned to NodeA.

The SQL Server System Administrator can then run Setup to install a default instance of SQL Server on NodeA, specifying a SQL Server virtual server name of *VirtualServerX* and specifying that the database files be placed on the drive in ClusterGroupA. Setup will install the SQL Server executable files on the local drives of both NodeA and NodeB and place the database files in ClusterGroupA.

Applications attempting to connect to the default instance need only specify the virtual server name *VirtualServerX*. The default instance normally runs on NodeA. If NodeA fails, however, Cluster Service will transfer ownership of ClusterGroupA to NodeB and restart the default instance on NodeB. Applications will still connect to the default instance by specifying the virtual server name *VirtualServerX*.

Planning and Performance

Before you create a failover cluster, you should consider the following issues:

- If your memory is greater than 3 GB of physical RAM and you're using the Windows 2000 Address Windowing Extensions (AWE) API to take advantage of this memory, you must ensure that the same amount of memory is available at all times. In the case of a failover, the remaining node must have the same amount of RAM as the failed node. If the remaining node has less memory, the SQL Server instance or instances might fail to start.

- The Total Max Server Memory values for all instances should be less than the least amount of physical RAM available to any of the virtual servers in the cluster.

- You should use a cluster File Share as your snapshot folder when you configure a Distributor for replication on a cluster. This will provide high availability because the distribution database will still be available for continued replication when a failure occurs.

- A cluster File Share resource can also be used for additional storage of snapshot files or as the location where Subscribers find a snapshot when creating publications. This will make the snapshot files available to every node of the cluster and to any Subscribers that need to access them.

- You must install a server certificate with the fully qualified DNS name of the virtual server on each node in the cluster in order to use encryption. You must then select the Force Protocol Encryption check box in the SQL Server Network utility.

- The BUILTIN/Administrators account should never be removed from SQL Server. Because the IsAlive thread runs under the context of the Cluster Service account, it will no longer be able to create a trusted connection if you remove the BUILTIN/Administrators account. The account allows access to SQL Server through the local administrator group on each node. Thus, the Cluster Service account can gain access to SQL Server because it is a member of the local administrators group. Removing the BUILTIN/Administrators account results in a loss of access to the virtual server.

Failover Performance

You should consider the following points when you optimize your SQL failover cluster:

- **Data loss during a failover**   You must disable write-caching within your disk controller if the controller is not external to your nodes; otherwise you could lose data during a failover.
- **Write-back caching**   If you have a host controller in your cluster and write-back caching is enabled, performance will be affected. External disk arrays can synchronize with the cache correctly, even across a SCSI bus, because they are not affected by failover clustering.
- **File shares**   Cluster drives that are used for file shares can affect cluster recovery times or even cause a failure due to resource problems.

SQL Server Virtual Servers

For each instance of SQL Server that you deploy on your cluster, you must create a virtual server. A SQL Server virtual server has the following characteristics:

- It has a cluster resource group with one or more Physical Disk resources. Only one virtual SQL Server is allowed per cluster resource group.
- Each virtual server uses one Network Name resource by which it is identified.
- In the event of a failover, SQL Server 2000 uses specific registry keys and service names to correctly interact with the cluster during the failover.
- You must provide a unique name for each instance of SQL Server running on a cluster, including the default instance. This will prevent a conflict of service names and registry keys if more than one instance fails over to a single server. There cannot be a duplicate named instance of SQL Server running on a node of a cluster, including stand-alone installations.
- To connect to a clustered instance of SQL Server, you must use the Virtual_SERVER\Instance-name string rather than the computer name. SQL Server 2000 does not listen on the IP address of the local servers, so you cannot access an instance of SQL Server using the computer name. Clustered SQL Server 2000 listens only on the IP address for the virtual server.

- Each virtual server requires one or more IP addresses in order for clients to connect.

- Each virtual server needs at least one instance of SQL Server 2000, a SQL Server resource, a SQL Server Agent resource, and a Fulltext resource.

- All IP addresses and the network name are removed from the cluster resource group when a SQL Server 2000 instance is uninstalled from within a virtual server.

- Even though you can run a cluster with different versions of Windows 2000 and Windows NT 4, a SQL Server virtual server will always appear on the network as a single server running Windows 2000 Advanced Server, Windows 2000 Datacenter Server, or Windows NT 4 Enterprise Edition Server.

Microsoft Distributed Transaction Coordinator

Microsoft Distributed Transaction Coordinator (MS DTC), shown in Figure 9.3, is a component of SQL Server that is required for distributed queries, two-phase commit transactions, and some replication functionality. MS DTC must be configured for running in clustered mode. To do this, you run the Cluster Application Wizard (Comclust.exe) on each node.

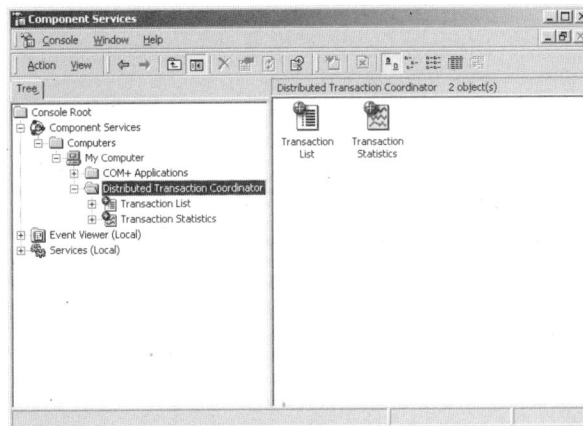

Figure 9.3   **Microsoft Distributed Transaction Coordinator**

The following configuration changes are made when MS DTC is installed on a cluster using the Cluster Application Wizard:

- An MS DTC resource is created if the resource group for SQL Server contains a Physical Disk resource and a Network Name resource.

- An MS DTC log file is created on the shared cluster disk specified for the Physical Disk resource belonging to the SQL Server resource group.

- Required MS DTC Registry entries are copied to the shared cluster Registry.

Only one node can run the MS DTC service at a time when MS DTC is running in clustered mode. However, MS DTC can be used by any process running on any node of the cluster. When a process runs on a cluster node, a call is made to the MS DTC proxy, which automatically forwards the call to the MS DTC service on whichever node it is running.

The MS DTC service is automatically restarted on another node in the cluster whenever a failover occurs. To determine the outcome of recent and pending transactions, the restarted MS DTC service reads the MS DTC log file on the shared cluster disk. The outcome of these transactions is decided by resource managers that have reconnected to MS DTC and performed recovery. New transactions can be initiated by applications that have reconnected to MS DTC.

Note   The MS DTC service, MS DTC proxy, and Component Services administrative tools are installed by default as part of the Windows 2000 setup. Thus, they should already be present on each node of a cluster when SQL Server 2000 is installed.

Preinstallation Checklist

Before you install SQL Server 2000, you should verify the following:

- Network Interface Cards (NICs) and SCSI controllers do not share Interrupt Requests (IRQs).
- The cluster's hardware is on the Microsoft Hardware Compatibility List (HCL).
- WINS is configured according to Knowledge Base article Q258750, "Recommended Private Heartbeat Configuration on Cluster Server."
- The shared disk's drive letters are the same on both nodes.
- NetBIOS has been disabled for all private network cards.
- The system logs have been cleared and are free of error messages.

Lesson Summary

This lesson discussed how to plan and implement a clustered SQL Server 2000 installation. It described the active/active and active/passive configuration models, and it explained how SQL Server 2000 on a cluster differs from a stand-alone instance. It listed requirements for setting up and maintaining SQL virtual servers and explained how to implement MS DTC. Finally, it provided clustered SQL Server pre-installation guidelines.

Lesson 2: Installing SQL Server on a Cluster

This lesson describes how to install SQL Server 2000 on a cluster. It includes step-by-step procedures and describes the setup options. Before you install SQL Server, you should review the pre-installation checklist presented at the end of Lesson 1 and also complete the following tasks:

- Verify that the cluster is installed and operating properly.
- Choose the SQL Server tools and features that you want to use and ensure that they are supported with clustering.
- Determine whether the tools and features selected will affect the cluster.

After this lesson, you will be able to

- Install and configure a clustered instance of SQL Server 2000

Estimated lesson time: 45 minutes

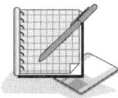

Practice: Installing SQL Server 2000

In this practice, you will install SQL Server 2000 Enterprise Edition. To see a demonstration of this practice, run the SQL.exe animation located in the Media folder of the companion CD.

1. Using the SQL Server installation CD-ROM, start the Setup program on NodeA.
2. On the splash screen that appears, click SQL Server 2000 Components.
3. On the Install Components screen, click Install Database Server.
4. On the SQL Server Installation Wizard welcome page, click Next.
5. On the Computer Name page, specify where you want to install SQL Server. You have three options:
   - Local Computer
   - Remote Computer
   - Virtual Server

   The Virtual Server option is available only when Setup is run on a Windows 2000 clustered computer. This option should be selected. If it is not, select it. When the Virtual Server option is selected, you can enter the name of the new virtual server on which SQL Server will reside in your cluster.
6. Type *VIRSQL* in the text box and click Next.
7. On the User Information screen, type the appropriate user information and click Next.

8. Read the licensing agreement, and if you agree, click Yes.

9. On the Failover Clustering page, type *192.168.0.6* as the IP address and choose Public Cluster Connection as the network to use. This page lets you define the virtual server for a cluster. You can add or remove IP addresses that are designated for your virtual servers.

10. Click Add, and the information will move to the list box at the bottom of the screen. Click Next.

11. On the Cluster Disk Selection page, click the W: and click Next. This page allows you to designate which group will be associated with the SQL virtual server. Only the groups that already contain the shared cluster disk will be listed.

12. A warning will appear saying that you have chosen the Quorum disk. Click Yes. Selecting the Quorum disk will cause the following warning to appear: *It is strongly recommended that you not use the Quorum group with SQL Server.*

    In this practice, we are selecting the Quorum disk. This is generally not recommended, but if you have a small cluster, it might be the only disk available. If you must use the Quorum disk, you should use the cluster only for testing purposes or to experiment with SQL Server failover clustering. (Selecting the Quorum resource is not recommended because the Quorum resource requires that all nodes in the cluster are able to access it. Therefore, you cannot stop certain nodes from accessing the SQL Server data files.)

13. On the Cluster Management page, verify that both nodes are listed in the Configured Nodes list. This page presents SQL Server's view of a cluster. You can specify which nodes of the cluster SQL Server will be installed on. Click Next.

14. On the Remote Information page, type in *Administrator* as the user and type the account's password for this node. Click Next.

15. On the Instance Name page, make sure that the default option is selected, and then click Next.

16. On the Setup Type page, make sure that Typical is selected.

17. If the default destination folder for the data files is Q:\Program Files\Microsoft SQL Server, change the destination folder to W:\Program Files\Microsoft SQL Server. Click Next.

18. On the Services Accounts page, select the Use The Same Account For Each Service option.

19. In the Service Settings box, select the Use A Domain User Account option.

20. In the User Name box, type *Administrator*.

21. Type the account's password in the Password box.

22. If the Domain box is empty, type *RESKIT* and click Next.

23. On the Authentication page, select the Mixed Mode (Windows Authentication And SQL Server Authentication) option and type a password for the sa account in the Password box.

24. Confirm the password, and click Next.

25. On the Start Copying Files page, click Next.

26. On the Choose Licensing Mode page, select the Processor License For option and type *1* in the text box. You can use this licensing mode as long as your server cluster is set up in an active/passive configuration.

27. Click Continue.

28. On the Setup Complete page, click Finish.

Creating the SQL Server Group

1. On the Windows desktop, point to Programs, point to Administrative Tools, and click Cluster Administrator.

2. Click Groups.

3. Right-click Groups, point to New, and click Group.

4. Type *SQL Server Group* in the Name box, and click Next.

5. Assign both nodes as Possible Owners, and click Next. The SQL Server Group will be created.

Transferring Resources

1. In the left pane of Cluster Administrator, click Resources.

2. Right-click the SQL Server Agent resource, point to Change Group, and click SQL Server Group.

3. A message box will ask whether you're sure you want to change the group. Click Yes.

4. In the Move Resources dialog box, click Yes.

5. Close Cluster Administrator.

Configuring MS DTC

If you want to use distributed queries, two-phase commit transactions, or certain replication features, you must configure MS DTC on your cluster, as follows:

1. On the Windows desktop, click Start, and click Run.

2. Type *command* and click OK.

3. At the command prompt, type *comclust* and press Enter.

4. Repeat steps 1 through 3 on the remaining cluster node.

5. Close the command window.

Verifying the SQL Server Installation

1. On the Windows desktop, click Start, point to Programs, point to Administrative Tools, and click Cluster Administrator.

2. Open the SQL Server Group.

3. The following resources should be listed in the group:
   - SQL IP Address (VIRSQL)
   - SQL Network Name (VIRSQL)
   - Physical Disk
   - MSDTC
   - SQL Server
   - SQL Server Agent
   - SQL Server Fulltext

   SQL Server creates these resources from the information you provided during the setup stage of the installation.

Testing the SQL Server Installation

1. If you are not currently logged on to NodeB, do so.

2. On the Windows desktop, click Start, point to Programs, point to Microsoft SQL Server, and click Enterprise Manager.

3. Expand Microsoft SQL Servers, expand SQL Server Group, and right-click VIRSQL.

4. If Connect is not disabled, click Connect.

5. Close SQL Enterprise Manager.

6. On NodeA, from the Windows desktop, click Start, point to Programs, point to Administrative Tools, and click Cluster Administrator.

7. Move the SQL Server Group to NodeB.

8. Repeat steps 1 through 5, moving the SQL Server group back to NodeA.

Lesson Summary

This lesson walked you through the installation of SQL Server 2000 on a cluster and described the various setup options.

Lesson 3: Managing and Supporting a Clustered SQL Server Installation

This lesson discusses how to manage and support SQL Server 2000 on a cluster. It also describes how to use the SQL Server management tools that require special handling when run on a cluster. These include full-text queries, SQL Server Enterprise Manager, Service Control Manager, SQL Profiler, Query Analyzer, and SQL Mail. The lesson explains how to add and remove cluster nodes that have been configured for SQL Server failover clustering and discusses methods for troubleshooting problems with a SQL Server cluster such as connection problems and disk or network failures.

After this lesson, you will be able to

- Describe how the primary components of SQL Server interact with Cluster Service
- Manage a clustered instance of SQL Server
- List common SQL Server clustering problems and possible solutions

Estimated lesson time: 30 minutes

Failover Clustering Considerations

SQL Server 2000 management is essentially the same when it is set up for failover clustering. However, you should note some usage considerations that will affect the way you implement and operate some of the SQL Server tools and features. These considerations are outlined below.

Fulltext Queries

You should consider the following when you perform Fulltext queries using the Microsoft Fulltext Search service:

- Fulltext queries require that the same system account be used on each node that SQL Server runs on.
- Only the SQL Server Enterprise Manager can be used to change the SQL Server start-up account. Changing the start-up account in the Windows 2000 Services application will prevent full-text queries from running.

SQL Server Enterprise Manager

SQL Server Enterprise Manager is shown in Figure 9.4. You should consider the issues listed on the following page when you use SQL Server Enterprise Manager on a clustered SQL Server.

- Only SQL Server Enterprise Manager can be used to change the SQL Server start-up account. Changing the start-up account in the Windows 2000 Services application might prevent SQL Server from running.

- You can view the cluster disks for the local virtual server only when you create or alter databases.

- The browsing capability in SQL Server Enterprise Manager does not support failover. When the connection is lost due to a failover, a *Communication Link Failure* error message will appear. You must close the browse window and open a new one to make any further changes, run queries, or edit the grid. Any changes you made to the data while the original window was open will be lost.

- On a clustered SQL Server, SQL Server, Fulltext, and SQL Server Agent services will not restart automatically after you change the properties of the SQL Server service account. You must restart these services manually using the Windows Cluster Administrator utility.

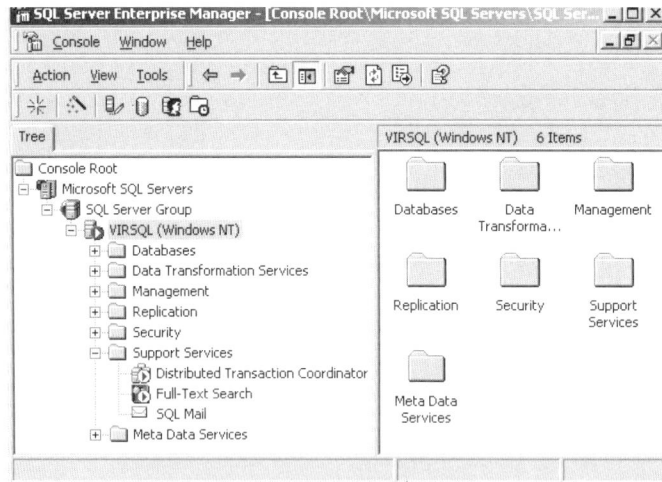

Figure 9.4   **SQL Server Enterprise Manager**

Service Manager

You should use SQL Server Service Manager (shown in Figure 9.5) only to stop or start a clustered instance of SQL Server. You cannot use it to pause a clustered instance of SQL Server. Only the Service Manager and Cluster Administrator should be used to start SQL Server and related services. Using the Windows 2000 Services snap-in or Net Start from the command line to stop or start these services on a cluster will result in errors.

Figure 9.5   **SQL Server Service Manager**

SQL Profiler

If a failover occurs on a cluster node on which you're running a SQL Profiler trace, the trace will stop collecting data. You must either restart the trace when the node comes back online or start another trace on the node that the cluster failed over to in order to continue tracing.

Query Analyzer

If a failover occurs while a query is running, execution will stop. You must restart the query when the server comes back online.

SQL Mail

You should consider the following points when you use SQL Mail on a clustered SQL Server:

- An instance of SQL Server 2000 must be running using the same account on all nodes in order for SQL Mail to work when a node fails over.

- A MAPI profile with identical name and settings must be set up on each cluster node.

Managing SQL Server on a Cluster

There are some additional management and maintenance issues you should consider when you run SQL Server 2000 on a cluster. You might want to change or repair your existing setup, add more nodes, run a clustered instance of SQL Server as a stand-alone instance, remove a node from a clustered instance, or recover from a failure in the cluster. This section will explain how to perform these types of management and maintenance tasks.

Adding a Node to an Existing Virtual Server

If you chose to maintain an existing virtual server during SQL Server setup, you can expand the cluster with additional nodes later. Depending on your cluster setup, you can add up to three additional nodes to an existing virtual server that is configured to run on only one node.

Removing a Node from an Existing Cluster

Each node in a virtual SQL Server is considered a peer to other nodes and can be removed at any time. You can also add a removed node, such as a failed node that was rebuilt, to the cluster at any time. The removal process does not uninstall the SQL Server instance from an unavailable node. If an instance of SQL Server 2000 is still available when a removed node comes back online, the Setup program removes this instance from the node and installs a new instance.

Running a Clustered Instance of SQL Server as a Stand-Alone Instance

Cluster Service usually controls an instance of SQL Server on a cluster. However, there are several reasons why it might be necessary to run a stand-alone instance of SQL Server on your cluster. For example, you might need to run an instance of SQL Server in single-user mode to perform maintenance or administrative tasks. Both IP Address and Network Name resources must be online in order for you to connect to a clustered instance of SQL Server 2000 in stand-alone mode using sockets.

You can also connect using Named Pipes if both IP Address and Network Name resources cannot be online. To do this, you must create an alias on the client side to communicate with the pipe name to which the instance of SQL Server is listening. To find out the pipe name, you can use the SQL Server Network utility.

Recovering from a Cluster Failure

A clustered SQL Server instance might fail due to either a hardware failure or some other failure where the system can be recovered without replacing hardware. In either case, it might be necessary to recover a SQL Server cluster node. Your first recovery task is to remove the clustered SQL Server instance from the failed node:

1. Start the SQL Server 2000 Setup program.
2. On the welcome page, click Next.
3. On the Computer Name page, click Virtual Server, specify the name of the server you want to remove the clustered instance from, and then click Next.
4. On the Installation Selection page, click Upgrade and remove components from or add components to an existing instance of SQL Server.

5. Enter the name of the instance to remove, or click Default if you used a default instance name. Click Next.

6. On the Existing Installation page, click Uninstall Your Existing Installation and then click Next.

7. On the Remote Information page, specify the password for the administrator account used on all nodes in the cluster. Click Next.

8. You should see a message indicating that the instance was successfully uninstalled. Click OK.

9. On the Setup Complete page, click Finish.

Be sure to read any SQL Server Installation Wizard messages that appear after the installation completes. You must also reboot if instructed to do so. Failure to follow any of these directions might prevent SQL Server from running correctly on one or more nodes in the cluster.

If the node failure was caused by a hardware failure in a two-node cluster, the SQL Server instance should have failed over to the second node and the cluster should still be functioning. After you have removed the failed node, use the following steps to recover the failed node:

1. From the healthy node, use Cluster Administrator to evict the failed node from the cluster.

2. Install new hardware to replace the failed hardware in the failed node.

3. If necessary, reinstall the Windows operating system on the failed node.

4. Install Cluster Service on the node and join the existing cluster.

5. Run the SQL Server Installation Wizard on the second node and add the first node back to the failover cluster.

If the node failure was caused by a node being down or offline, the failed node should have failed over to a working node and the cluster should still be functioning. In this case, you might be able to bring the node back online without having to go through a lengthy recovery process. However, if recovery is necessary, the recovery process will be different from the recovery process for a hardware failure. As before, you must remove the failed node. You then use the following steps to recover the failed node:

1. Resolve the problem with the failed node.

2. Ensure that Cluster Service is running without errors on all nodes that remain online.

3. Run the SQL Server Installation Wizard on a running node and add the failed node back to the cluster.

Modifying Service Accounts

When a cluster node goes down or offline, you should not modify the SQL Server service accounts. This includes not changing a password. If the password needs to be changed for some reason, you must reset it using SQL Server Enterprise Manager once all nodes are back online.

The service accounts for SQL Server should always have administrative permissions on each node in a cluster. If a service account is not an administrator of the cluster, the administrative shares cannot be deleted on any nodes of the cluster. In order for SQL Server to function, the administrative shares must be available to the cluster.

Troubleshooting SQL Server Clusters

This section covers some of the troubleshooting techniques for solving common problems with using clustered SQL Server, connecting to SQL Server clusters, and using extended stored procedures and COM objects in a cluster.

Table 9.1 lists common problems and possible solutions.

Table 9.1   SQL Server 2000 Troubleshooting

Problem	Solution
After migrating to another node, SQL Server can no longer log in to the network.	Verify that the SQL Server service account passwords are identical on all nodes. If you changed the SQL Server service account password on one node, you must change it on all other nodes. This will be done automatically if you make changes using SQL Server Enterprise Manager, however.
SQL Server is unable to access the cluster shared disks.	Make sure the drive letters used for the shared disks are the same on each node.
You want to prevent a failover from occurring when a service such as Fulltext Search or SQL Server Agent fails.	Use Cluster Administrator to configure specific services so that the SQL Server group is prevented from failing over. For example, to prevent a failover when the Fulltext Search service fails, deselect the Affect The Group check box on the Advanced tab of the Fulltext Properties dialog box. This will not prevent Fulltext Search from restarting if SQL Server causes a failover for some other reason.
SQL Server service will not start automatically.	SQL Server service cannot be started automatically when it is configured for clustering. You must use Cluster Administrator to configure SQL Server to automatically start when Cluster Service starts.
During SQL Server setup, the error message *All cluster disks available to this virtual server are owned by other node(s)* is displayed.	The drive and path you selected for installing SQL data files is not owned by the local node. Use Cluster Administrator to move the disk resource to the local node.

Table 9.1   SQL Server 2000 Troubleshooting *(continued)*

Problem	Solution
During SQL Server setup, this error message is displayed: *Unable to delete SQL Server resources. They must be manually removed. Un-installation will continue.*	This message is displayed if SQL Server setup is unable to delete all of the SQL Server resources when it removes an instance of SQL Server. You must uninstall the instance you were trying to remove on every node in the cluster.
The operating system error log for clustering cannot be enabled.	Cluster Service uses the operating system cluster error log to record information about the cluster. This error log is usually used to debug cluster configuration problems. Set the system environment variable *CLUSTERLOG=<path to file>* to enable this log. For example, CLUSTERLOG=c:\winnt\cluster\cluster.log will enable the cluster log to be written to the c:\winnt\cluster folder. On Windows 2000, this log is on by default.

Using Named Pipes

You might need to use Named Pipes to connect to SQL Server if the network Name and IP Address resources are unavailable. To do so, you must create an alias using the Client Network utility:

1. Use Cluster Administrator to determine which node has the instance of SQL Server running, and stop SQL Server.
2. Use Net Start to start SQL Server manually on this node.
3. Run the SQL Server Network utility (shown in Figure 9.6) on the node.

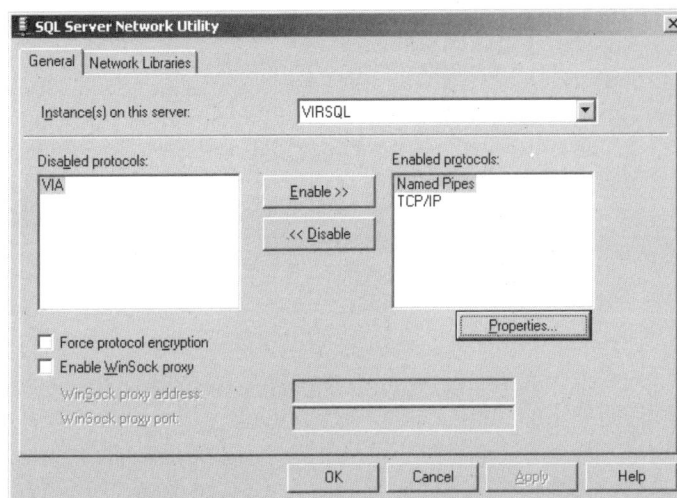

Figure 9.6   **The SQL Server Network utility**

4. Verify that the pipe name is similar to\\.\pipe\$$VIRSQL\sql\query, as shown in Figure 9.7.

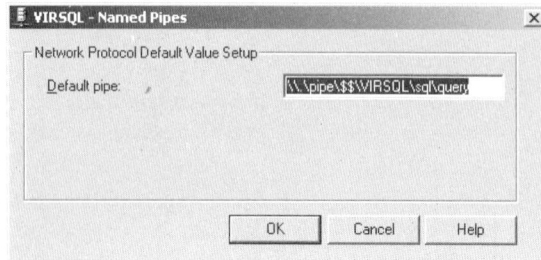

Figure 9.7   **Verifying the default pipe name**

5. Start the Client Network utility on the client computer from which you are trying to connect to the server.

6. Create an alias for connecting using Named Pipes. Use the pipe name identified for the server.

7. Connect to this instance using the alias.

Using Extended Stored Procedures and COM Objects

Any extended stored procedures you use on your cluster must be installed on the shared cluster disk so that you can access them in the event of a failover. Also, if COM components are used by the extended stored procedure, these must be registered on each node of the cluster. In order for a component to be created, the registry on the active node must contain the information for loading and executing the COM component.

Lesson Summary

This lesson described techniques for managing and supporting SQL Server 2000 on a cluster, including using management tools such as SQL Server Enterprise Manager, Query Analyzer, and SQL Profiler. This lesson also discussed adding and removing SQL Server cluster nodes. It offered techniques for identifying and resolving common usage issues as well as procedures for connecting to SQL Server using Named Pipes. Finally, it discussed using extended stored procedures and COM objects.

Review

The following questions will help you review key information presented in this chapter. You'll find the answers in Appendix A, "Questions and Answers."

1. How many virtual servers are available in an active/passive clustered SQL Server installation?

   a. 2

   b. 1

   c. 1 on each node

   d. 0

2. In a SQL Server 2000 cluster, what components will fail over when a failure occurs?

3. Which installation program is used to install the Microsoft Distributed Transaction Coordinator (MS DTC) service on a cluster node?

   a. Cluster Wizard (comclust.exe)

   b. Cluster Service Configuration Wizard (cluscfg.exe)

   c. Windows 2000 Setup

   d. SQL Server 2000 Setup

4. What name do you use when you connect to a clustered instance of SQL Server 2000?

5. Which installation program is used to install MS DTC on a clustered virtual server?

   a. Cluster Wizard (Comclust.exe)

   b. Cluster Service Configuration Wizard (Cluscfg.exe)

   c. Windows 2000 Setup

   d. SQL Server 2000 Setup

6. Why is using the Quorum resource to store the SQL Server data files not recommended?

7. What do you do on the Failover Clustering page of the SQL Server Installation Wizard?

   a. Add IP addresses

   b. Choose cluster groups

   c. Set virtual server names

   d. Select nodes to configure

8. What actions must you perform after you make changes to the SQL Server
   service account in order for the changes to take affect?

9. Which of the following methods should you use to start SQL Server on a
   cluster?

   a. From the Windows 2000 Services snap-in

   b. Using *net start MSSQLServer* from a command prompt

   c. Using SQL Server Service Manager

   d. Using Cluster Administrator

10. On a clustered SQL Server, how can you prevent a failover from occurring
    when a service such as Fulltext Search or SQL Server Agent fails?

C H A P T E R   1 0

Introduction to Network Load Balancing

About This Chapter

This chapter describes Network Load Balancing (NLB), the second clustering technology offered by Microsoft, and shows you how to implement an NLB cluster. It explains which types of server applications work best in an NLB cluster, as well as which network hardware and configurations to use. You'll learn how to set up and configure an NLB cluster in a variety of networking environments, the most common of which is a Web farm. This chapter also describes how an NLB cluster solution can scale to the demands of the largest Web sites on the Internet.

Before You Begin

To complete this chapter, you must have

- The necessary hardware as outlined in the section titled "About This Book" in the Introduction

Lesson 1: NLB Overview

This lesson explains the basics of NLB. You'll learn how NLB can provide a scalable solution for many TCP/IP-based server applications. The lesson also discusses the advantages of NLB compared to other load-balancing solutions. Finally, you'll learn what type of server applications work well with NLB.

After this lesson, you will be able to

- Describe the NLB clustering technology
- List the implementation configurations available with NLB

Estimated lesson time: 30 minutes

What Is NLB?

NLB provides TCP/IP applications with increased scalability and availability. It allows you to run Windows 2000 Advanced Server on up to 32 physical servers that respond to TCP/IP requests. One of the most common uses for NLB is to distribute Web requests among a cluster of Internet server applications such as Microsoft Internet Information Server (IIS). NLB is also commonly used for deploying multiple terminal servers for client access.

The core of NLB is a driver named *Wlbs.sys*, which operates between the network adapter driver and the TCP/IP protocol. (See Figure 10.1.) This driver is loaded on each server in the cluster. Using a statistical mapping algorithm, the driver determines which server handles each incoming request. The name of the driver, *Wlbs.sys*, comes from NLB's predecessor, Windows Load Balancing Service (WLBS). WLBS was originally designed to run on Microsoft Windows NT 4. You'll see occasional references to WLBS in NLB for reasons of backward compatibility.

NLB is considered a clustering technology. While Cluster Service provides for availability, NLB provides for scalability and availability. Certain applications, such as Web servers, streaming media servers, Terminal Services, and Virtual Private Network (VPN) servers, lend themselves well to NLB. In a typical scenario, you might find an NLB cluster of Web servers accessing a back-end SQL Server database that uses Cluster Service.

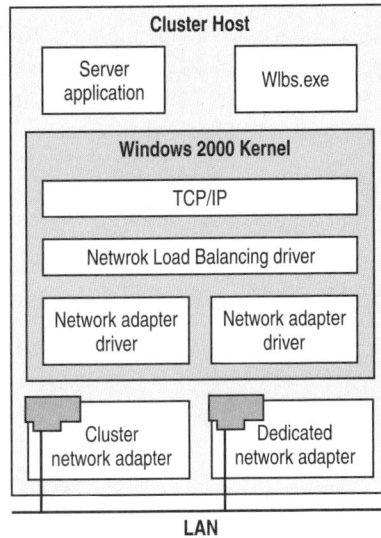

Figure 10.1   The NLB driver runs between the network adapter driver and TCP/IP.

Why Use NLB?

Here are the main benefits of using NLB:

- **Scalability**   NLB scales the performance of server-based applications by distributing requests across servers in the cluster. As the traffic to your network applications increases or as your applications require more server power, you can add new servers to the cluster. Windows 2000 Advanced Server supports up to 32 servers in a cluster; you can add or remove servers from the cluster without having to shut down the cluster.

- **Availability**   Because an NLB cluster automatically detects the failure of a server, requests will continue to be processed as long as at least one server is available. Within 10 seconds of a server failing, NLB will reroute requests to available servers.

- **Load balancing**   Requests to applications in an NLB cluster are load-balanced based on the NLB configuration. Configurable port rules determine which servers in the cluster get what percentage of the load. When all the servers in the cluster share requests, each individual client's request is processed faster.

- **Remote management**   NLB includes a remote control application called Wlbs.exe. Using this program, a system administrator can remotely manage servers in the NLB cluster. We'll discuss Wlbs.exe in more detail in the next lesson.

Other technologies that are similar to NLB fall short in some key areas. For example, round-robin DNS (RRDNS) distributes the workload among available servers, but if one of the servers goes down, the DNS server will continue to send requests to that server until the system administrator removes it from the address list. Third-party hardware products designed for load balancing are available, but these solutions introduce additional costs and can potentially create single points of failure. Because NLB is a distributed application, there is no single point of failure. Even if you lose all but one of your servers, the NLB cluster will still function. In addition, NLB requires no special or proprietary hardware, so an NLB solution can save you a lot of money.

The NLB architecture also maximizes throughput by using the broadcast subnet to deliver incoming requests to all servers in the cluster. This eliminates the need to reroute incoming requests, which can be a lengthy process. Instead, requests are filtered on each server and are accepted or rejected based on the NLB settings. As network and server performance increases, the ability to increase throughput also increases. NLB has demonstrated 200-MB throughput in realistic customer scenarios with e-commerce loads of more than 800 million requests per day.

As stated earlier, NLB is backward compatible with its predecessor, WLBS, so you can have a mixed environment of WLBS and NLB in the same cluster. This allows you to do rolling upgrades from Windows NT to Windows 2000 Advanced Server. In addition, Microsoft has made some significant enhancements to NLB in Windows 2000:

- NLB is now integrated with the networking architecture of Windows 2000. It appears as an optional LAN service rather than as a virtual network interface card (NIC). The service is automatically installed when you install Windows 2000 Advanced Server. To enable NLB, you simply set properties for the service.
- You can configure NLB when you perform an unattended installation.
- You can make changes to the NLB properties without causing a server reboot. After you make changes, the service will be back up and running after a delay of 15 to 20 seconds.

Lesson Summary

This lesson described the NLB clustering technology, which can scale TCP/IP applications and make them highly available. It also compared NLB with other load-balancing solutions, such as RRDNS, as well as hardware-based solutions that can introduce a single point of failure. You also learned that NLB is a driver that forwards network packets between the network card driver and TCP/IP.

Lesson 2: The NLB Architecture

In this lesson, you'll learn how to configure your cluster for different types of server applications. The lesson will also compare the use of unicast vs. multicast mode. You'll learn how servers in your cluster communicate with each other to determine the health of the NLB cluster, and you'll learn about the remote control program (Wlbs.exe), which enables you to remotely control and configure an NLB cluster.

After this lesson, you will be able to

- Describe how NLB load balances requests to an IP address
- List the primary NLB configuration properties and describe when to use them
- Compare and contrast unicast and multicast mode

Estimated lesson time: 45 minutes

Architecture Overview

NLB uses a distributed software architecture, which means that a copy of the NLB driver runs in parallel on each cluster server. The drivers expect to be on a single subnet to concurrently detect network traffic for the cluster's primary IP address. The primary IP address is a single IP address on which all of the clusters listen. This IP address is configured in the TCP/IP settings just like any IP address would be. Normally, you would expect to receive an error from Windows 2000 about an IP address conflict if you tried to assign the same IP address to multiple servers. When you have NLB enabled on an NIC, this error will not occur if everything is configured correctly. You can also assign additional IP addresses to the cluster to allow for a multi-homed NLB cluster.

IP Addresses

NLB deals with two types of IP addresses: a primary IP address and a dedicated IP address. The primary IP address is the virtual IP address on which all of the servers in the cluster listen for requests. The dedicated IP address is used for network traffic that is intended for a particular server in the cluster. For example, a request coming in for a Web server in the cluster will come in on the primary IP address. If you want to connect to a specific server in the cluster for administrative purposes, you use the dedicated IP address. By default, all IP addresses on the server are considered primary IP addresses. (See Figure 10.2 for the relationship between the primary and dedicated IP addresses.) In the NLB properties dialog box, you can configure only one IP address as the dedicated IP address. When you type the IP addresses in the TCP/IP Properties section, you must type the dedicated IP address first so that all of the outgoing requests will use that IP address.

Cluster with Primary (Virtual) IP 192.168.0.3

Cluster server	Cluster server
Server application	**Server application**
Windows 2000 kernel	**Windows 2000 kernel**
TCP/IP	TCP/IP
NLB driver	NLB driver
NCI driver	NCI driver
NIC	**NIC**
Dedicated IP 192.168.0.1	Dedicated IP 192.168.0.2

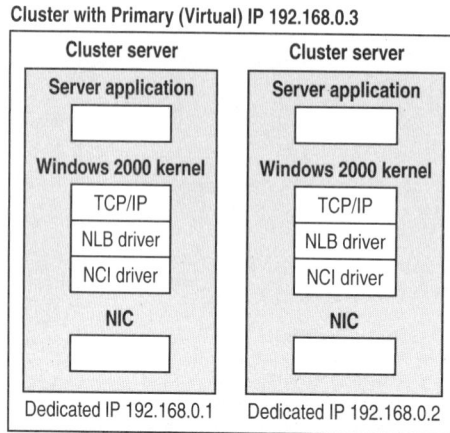

Figure 10.2   The primary and dedicated NLB IP addresses

Host Priority

Each server in the cluster requires a unique host ID, which is a unique identifier of the server in the cluster and establishes a default handling priority for requests that are not specifically load balanced by port rules. The ID with the lowest number represents the highest priority, with values ranging from *1* to *32*. There might also be gaps in the numbering sequence (such as when one of the servers in the cluster is offline).

Initial State Parameter

Typically, the Initial State parameter is configured so that NLB starts when the server boots. But this might not be desirable in some situations, such as when an application running on the server experiences a delay before it starts responding to requests. A better solution in this case might be to run an application such as Microsoft Cluster Sentinel to monitor your application and then start NLB when the application starts responding to requests. Cluster Sentinel is available with the Windows 2000 Resource Kit.

Port Rules

Port rules, which are configured for a range of ports, define how requests are sent to servers in the cluster. A port rule is basically a filter on a specific port or range of ports. By selecting a protocol and a filtering mode for a given range of ports, you can define how requests are balanced between servers in your cluster.

For example, you might have four servers in your cluster, three that are required to handle HTTP (port 80 and 443 for SSL) requests and one that is required to handle SMTP (port 25) requests. You can set up three of the servers to handle a 33 percent share of the HTTP load and the other server to handle 0 percent. You set up the server that handles 0 percent of HTTP requests to handle the highest priority SMTP requests and the other servers to handle SMTP requests with lower priorities. Using this configuration, during normal operations the three Web servers will handle all of the HTTP requests and the other server will handle all of the SMTP requests. If your main SMTP server fails, the server that is to handle the next-highest priority requests will pick up the requests until the main SMTP server comes back online. Ultimately, you could lose up to three servers and still handle HTTP and SMTP requests. If you were to change the load weight on your main SMTP server to handle 1 percent of the requests, you could even lose all three of your primary Web servers and still handle HTTP requests. Keep in mind that if you configure your SMTP server to handle 1 percent of the requests, your main SMTP server will always serve 1 out of every 100 HTTP requests, and this might not be desirable. While this isn't a very realistic scenario, it does show the range of configuration options that NLB offers.

The following sections describe the port rules in greater detail.

Port Range

The port range simply specifies what port or range of ports the rule should apply to. If you use the same beginning and ending port in the range, the rule will apply to only one port. Port numbers ranging from 0 to 65,535 are currently supported. You cannot have two port ranges that overlap. If you do, NLB will alert you with a message when the changes are applied. Note that port ranges you configure must be the same on every server in your NLB cluster.

Protocol

The protocol parameter specifies which protocol (TCP, UDP, or both) should be filtered in the port range. Only requests for the specified protocol are affected; other requests are handled by the default filtering mode in the Host Priority setting.

Filtering Mode

There are the three filtering modes, as described below. (Note that the filtering mode must be the same on each server in the cluster for a particular port.)

- **Multiple hosts**   This mode is appropriate when multiple servers will handle a request. Web servers are typically configured with this option. Two settings in this mode control what server in the NLB cluster handles requests, Load Weight and Affinity:

    - **Load Weight**   This parameter specifies the percentage of requests that a server should handle, ranging from *0* to *100*. (The total need not equal 100 percent.) The fraction of requests is computed based on the number of servers that are online in the NLB cluster. To prevent a server from handling any requests, you can set this value to *0*. Alternatively, you can use the equal parameter to specify that all servers handle the same number of requests.

- **Affinity**   Affinity in this case is defined as the relationship between a client and a particular server in your NLB cluster. This setting is important in situations where a client maintains a session with a server. For example, if you're browsing a Web site and retrieving static pages, state is not important. But if you're on an e-commerce site and you store items in your shopping cart, state is very important. If you get one server on one request and another server on another request, the servers might not be able to share your state between them. As a result, the e-commerce site will fail to work properly because the contents of your shopping cart will be lost when you are sent to another server. Figure 10.3 shows an example of such an e-commerce session, where server 1.1.1.4 is processing the transaction.

  You can use one of three affinity settings. The None setting causes every client request to be directed to a server based on the load weight; client requests will likely span physical servers in the NLB cluster. The Single setting causes NLB to maintain state for a particular client IP address. When NLB sees that IP address, the request is sent to the same server every time. This helps maintain state for the client. The Class C setting means that as long as all of the client's proxy servers are on the same class C subnet, state will be maintained. (When users might be accessing a server through a proxy, the user's address can change if every request does not come through the same proxy server.)

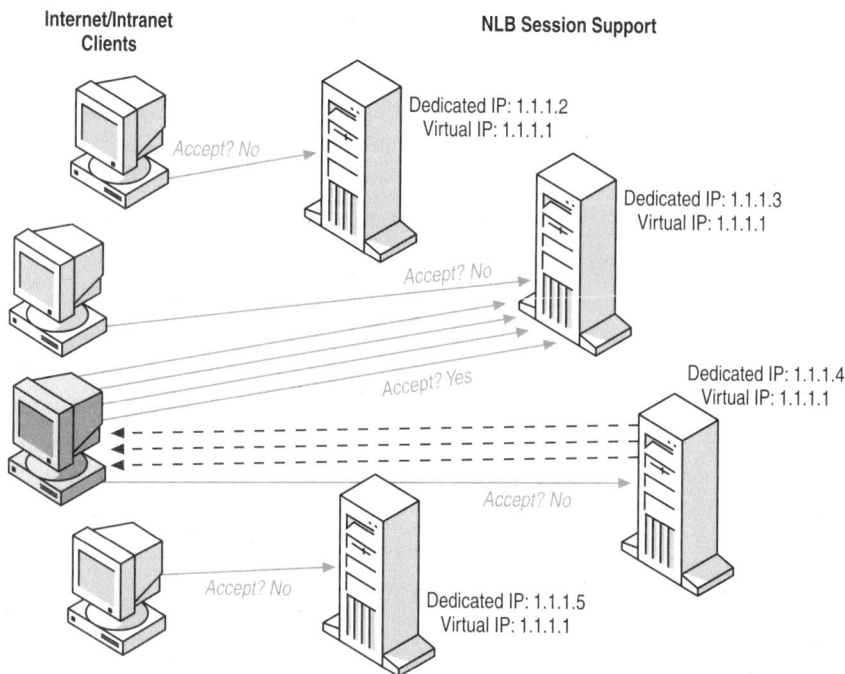

Figure 10.3   NLB session support

When you use Single or Class C affinity, you must keep two things in mind. First, if all of your clients are connected through the same proxy server, all of the requests will end up on the same server; they will not be load balanced. Second, some large companies or ISPs might have proxy servers that span multiple Class C IP addresses that a Single client uses. In this case, state might be lost between requests. The best and most scalable solution is to set the affinity to None and manage state in the server application. Note that affinity also involves some cluster overhead; therefore, if affinity is not required for the server application, it is best to set the value to None.

- **Single host** This mode is appropriate when one server will handle requests, such as when you're using an SMTP server. You can select this mode and set the handling priority so that another server in the cluster will handle requests if the main SMTP server fails. The lower the handling priority number, the higher the server's priority. Each server in the NLB cluster must have a unique priority.

- **Disabled** This mode prevents requests from reaching a server in your cluster. It essentially builds a firewall against incoming requests that you don't want to respond to—for example, if you're getting requests for FTP when you don't have an FTP server running. In this case, requests will not be passed to your cluster for processing.

Unicast Mode vs. Multicast Mode

NLB uses layer 2 Media Access Control (MAC) unicast or multicast mode to concurrently distribute incoming network traffic among the servers in the cluster. NLB can operate in either unicast or multicast mode. All servers in the cluster must operate in the same mode.

Unicast Mode

The default operation mode in NLB is unicast. This mode reassigns the MAC address of the network adapter. Once the address is reassigned, all cluster servers will respond to the same IP address and incoming packets will be received by all cluster servers. Once received, the packets are passed to the NLB driver. The driver filters the packets and passes some packets to the TCP/IP stack based on the port rules. The MAC address is based on the cluster's primary IP address (which helps ensure that the address is unique). For example, if the IP address listed in the NLB properties is 192.168.0.5, the unicast MAC address is 02-BF-192-168-0-5. NLB automatically edits a registry setting and then reloads the network adapter's driver, effectively modifying its address without restarting the server.

If the cluster servers are connected to a switch rather than to a hub, the common MAC address will create a conflict because switches expect to see a unique MAC address on each of the switch ports. NLB solves this problem by modifying the source MAC address of the outbound packets. A MAC address of 02-BF-192-168-0-1 is set to 02-n-192-168-0-1, where n is the server's priority in the cluster. This value is shown in the NLB Properties dialog box. This process keeps the switch from learning the actual MAC address of the cluster and enables inbound packets to be delivered to all switch ports. If the cluster servers are connected directly to a hub, you can disable this behavior and avoid the flooding of upstream switches. To disable source address masking, set the NLB registry parameter MaskSourceMAC to 0. You can also limit switch flooding by using an upstream layer 3 switch. The main difference between a layer 2 and a layer 3 switch is that a layer 2 switch switches packets at the layer 2 (MAC) address and a layer 3 switch switches packets at the layer 3 (IP) address. The switching ability gives you some of the same capabilities that a router offers.

Because all servers in the cluster share the same MAC address, communication between them is impossible. For example, you cannot connect to a file share or open the Event Viewer from one server in the cluster to another. This is because the packets are sent to the MAC address, which in this case is the address of both the sender and receiver. These packets are looped back to the sender by the network stack and never reach the wire.

Unicast mode does not affect communication between the cluster and the outside world. Each cluster server receives all network traffic because the servers respond to the same MAC address. Traffic for the dedicated IP address is never load balanced and is thus automatically delivered to its intended server. Because the switch does not know the MAC address of the cluster adapter, all of this traffic is sent to every port on the switch. If many requests are made to the dedicated IP address, an excess of network traffic might occur on the cluster network and hinder performance.

To solve server-to-server communication problems and performance problems when you connect from outside the cluster to a dedicated server IP address, you can add a second network card to each server in your cluster. In this configuration, the NLB cluster is connected to the public network, receiving client requests. The other adapter is then part of a local network that is used mainly for communication between cluster servers and back-end database servers. It is typically good practice when you use unicast mode to install two network cards in each server in the cluster.

Multicast Mode

Multicast mode assigns a layer 2 multicast address to the cluster adapter rather than changing the MAC address. For example, a cluster server with an IP address of 192-168-0-1 has a multicast address of 03-BF-192-168-0-1. Each server has a unique MAC address and therefore does not require an additional network adapter. This configuration also alleviates the performance penalty involved when the cluster receives a large amount of traffic to a dedicated IP address. Note that some routers do not accept Address Resolution Protocol (ARP) responses from NLB. In this case, you must add a static ARP entry to the router for each virtual IP address.

Switch Flooding

Switch flooding means that a packet of data is sent to all ports on the switch. This is typically undesirable because it causes unnecessary network traffic. Normally, you want the packet to be sent just to the port on the switch that includes the MAC address for which the packet of data is intended. Switch flooding occurs when the switch does not know where the packet should go because it does not recognize the MAC address.

NLB causes switch flooding by design, however. When you use NLB, you want all of your servers to receive all of the packets sent to the cluster. The NLB driver causes switch flooding in unicast mode by changing the MAC address for outgoing packets so the switch never learns the MAC address of each network card. Multicast mode often causes switch flooding as well, but you can typically alleviate this by manually programming the switch so that only the ports that are connected to servers in the cluster get the data packets. Switch flooding is the most efficient approach for an NLB cluster because each server needs to receive all of the packets sent to the cluster in order to filter the packets and decide which packets it should accept. Because NLB causes switch flooding by design, it is not desirable to have other computers share a switch with the cluster.

Using a Hub vs. a Switch

The use of a hub is often desirable when you connect servers in the cluster. Hubs simply broadcast data to all ports and are as efficient as switches when used in an NLB cluster. If you need to connect other computers that are not members of the cluster, you can put a switch upstream from the hub. Remember that when you use unicast mode with a hub, you should change the MaskSourceMAC registry value to 0, which will prevent the flooding of upstream switches. This change prevents NLB from modifying outgoing packets because hubs do not require unique MAC addresses for each port.

Using Multiple Network Cards

In most cases, it is desirable to use two network cards in each server in the NLB cluster, and it might be necessary when you require your NLB cluster to be configured for unicast mode and server-to-server communication. The second network adapter will handle all outgoing connections to the server and can be on a separate switch because it doesn't receive any packets intended for the cluster. This second network card also provides an efficient means of communicating with back-end servers such as a database. This second adapter becomes the dedicated adapter and is therefore configured with the dedicated IP address. Figure 10.4 shows the connections when two network cards in each NLB cluster server are used. It shows an NLB cluster running in unicast mode. Each node is configured with the MaskSourceMAC registry value set to *0*. Cluster adapters plug in to the hub and share a common MAC address, while the dedicated adapters plug in to the switch and maintain their own unique MAC address.

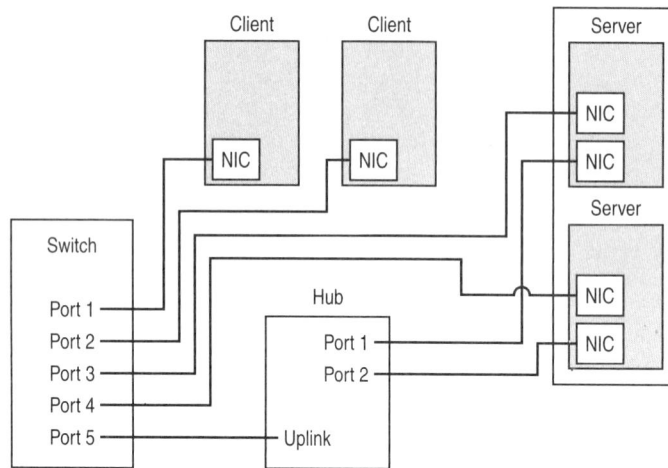

Figure 10.4   An NLB cluster in unicast mode with a hub

Using Unicast vs. Multicast

There is no clear-cut answer to the question "Should I use unicast or multicast?" It really depends on your hardware and your network configuration. If all of the switches and routers work with multicast, multicast is a good choice. Unicast, however, is probably easier to set up because it typically doesn't require you to make any hardware configuration changes. However, some NICs won't let NLB change the MAC address, which means you would have to buy a new NIC or use multicast instead. When you use two NICs, unicast and multicast will perform about the same, but if your hardware and network is not configured properly, multicast can cause switch flooding and hinder the performance of your network. The bottom line is that you should figure out which mode is supported by your hardware and try different configurations to see which mode is the easiest to configure and maintain.

How NLB Works

NLB is essentially a network driver that is installed on each of the servers in the NLB cluster. The cluster presents a virtual IP address for client requests. The client request actually goes to all the servers in the cluster, but only one server responds to the request. Which server responds depends on the server priority, port rules, load weight, and affinity. Figure 10.5 depicts client requests being broadcast to all the servers in the NLB cluster and being accepted by only one server per request.

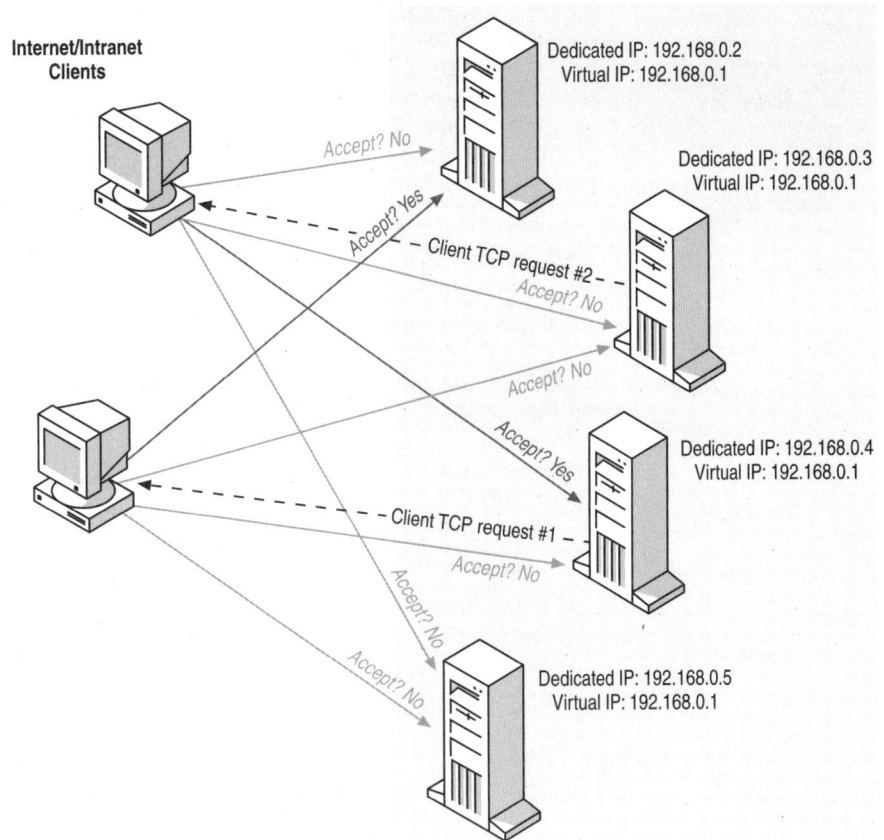

Figure 10.5   NLB managing client requests

Convergence

The servers in the NLB cluster send heartbeat messages to one another to determine the health of the cluster. By default, each server in the cluster broadcasts its heartbeat message every second; the message contains the state of the server, its configuration, and port rule information. The heartbeat message is very small—only a packet of data. If during a 5-second window any server recognizes that another server has not sent its heartbeat messages or that a new server has been added, the server will enter a process known as *convergence*. In addition, if a new server attempts to join the cluster, it sends out messages that trigger convergence. The convergence process accomplishes the following tasks:

- Determines which servers are still part of the NLB cluster
- Selects the new default server based on the priority of all the servers
- Recalculates the load weight factor based on the number of servers

Convergence typically takes about 10 seconds. The cluster continues to handle client request during the convergence process as long as the requests were bound for servers that are still alive. If a request was bound for a server that is not alive, the client might experience a delay of up to 10 seconds. You can adjust the number of missed messages required to start convergence and the number of milliseconds between heartbeat messages by editing the registry. Under the key HKEY_LOCAL_MACHINE\System\CurrentControlSet\Services\WLBS\Parameters, edit the AliveMsgPeriod parameter with the number of milliseconds between heartbeat messages, the AliveMsgTolerance parameter with the number of missed heartbeats, or both. Keep in mind that the shorter the time between heartbeats, the greater the network overhead.

Figure 10.6 depicts a healthy cluster with all servers running. (NLB is configured for multiple hosts, each taking an equal share of the requests.)

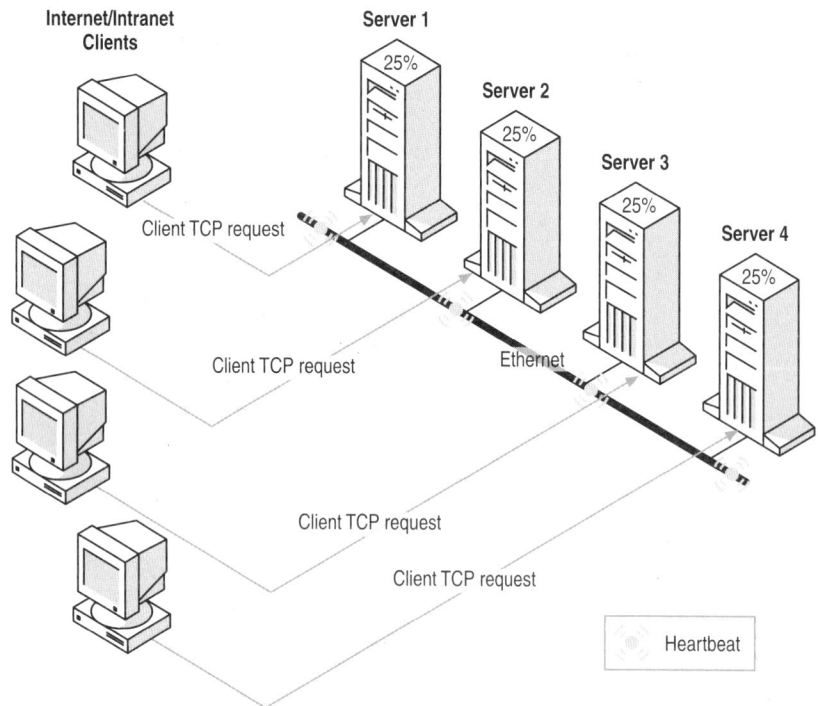

Figure 10.6   A healthy NLB cluster

Figure 10.7 depicts the same cluster with one of the servers offline. (NLB is configured for multiple hosts, each taking an equal share of the requests. After convergence, NLB redistributes the requests equally across all of the servers, leaving out the server that did not respond during the convergence process.)

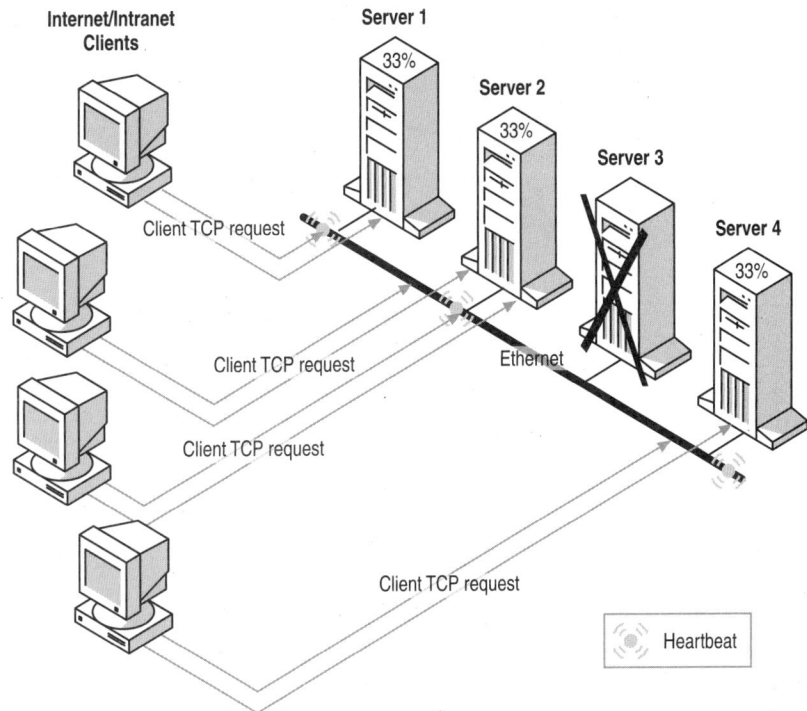

Figure 10.7   Same NLB cluster with one server offline

Remote Control

To simplify management of an NLB cluster, NLB includes a remote control program called Wlbs.exe. The program allows system administrators to remotely manage the cluster as well as query the status of the cluster or a particular server in the cluster. Wlbs.exe can be run from any server in the cluster or from any computer on the same network that is running Windows 2000 Server, Windows 2000 Advanced Server, or Windows 2000 Datacenter Server. Connections to the remote system are made using the UDP protocol on port 2504 to the cluster's primary IP address. The program can also be incorporated into scripts to automate NLB cluster control. Developers can also write programs to monitor and manage the NLB cluster such as Cluster Sentinel, available with the Windows 2000 Resource Kit.

You can carry out the following operations remotely:

- Start, stop, suspend, or resume a server in the cluster or the entire cluster
- Enable or disable a port range
- Display cluster status

Remote control commands are password protected, and you can enable or disable the remote control functionality on the cluster. If remote control is enabled, you should use a firewall on the remote control port to prevent unauthorized access.

NLB Performance Considerations

NLB requires some processing power from each server to maintain the cluster. You must consider this extra power when you're designing a cluster or adding bandwidth or more servers to the cluster.

Processor Load

You must consider CPU usage when you design an NLB cluster. Two types of CPU overhead are associated with NLB:

- **Filtering overhead**   This overhead consists of the processor cycles required to handle requests. Filtering overhead increases with higher network traffic to the cluster. For example, when NLB serves Web pages, it filters packets on each server to distribute the workload between the servers. Thus, any processing required, such as the processing required for an Active Server Pages (ASP) page, is divided between the clusters based on each request from a client browser. The processor cycles required to filter the requests, however, are run in parallel on all the servers. Therefore, the more clients you have requesting pages, the more processor cycles it will take from each server to filter the requests. There is no easy formula for calculating how much processor power it will take to filter cluster packets because many factors come into play. For example, when a client first connects to a Web server, more processor cycles are required to filter the packets than to return the page of content. Thus, one 10-KB page takes less processor power to serve than 10 1-KB pages. To give you an idea of the percentage of processor power required for NLB filtering overhead, a 500-MHz server would require about 5.5 percent of the CPU cycles at a transfer rate of 100 Mbps serving 10-KB Web pages.

- **Transfer overhead**   This overhead consists of the processor cycles the NLB driver uses to forward packets through the network stack. NLB runs as a driver between the network adapter driver and TCP/IP, so it forwards all packets that flow through the network card. This process requires some CPU cycles, but only to process packets for the server, not for the whole cluster. Therefore, the amount is a fixed percentage regardless of the number of servers you add to the cluster. To give you an idea of the percentage of processor power required for NLB transfer overhead, a 500-MHz server would require about 12 percent of the CPU cycles at a transfer rate of 100 Mbps serving 10-KB Web pages.

Saturation

As demand on your servers grows, you could theoretically continue to add servers to the cluster to keep up until you reach NLB's maximum of 32. But you must consider the network traffic going to the servers because as network traffic grows, so does the time it takes to filter that traffic. If servers are being added because they're serving processor-intensive applications, adding more servers might make sense. If servers are being added along with bandwidth, it might be wise to consider breaking the cluster into two or more clusters.

For example, if a company rolls out a new Web site that includes many new processor-intensive features, it would make sense to add new servers to the cluster. However, if the company is simply getting more requests and is trying to keep up with demand, it would be important to consider how many CPU cycles might be required to keep up with the newly added bandwidth. Very large Web sites that run 20 to 30 servers in a cluster typically use a RRDNS server to hand off requests to a number of clusters. This divides the network traffic between the clusters (if the network is configured properly), and each server spends fewer CPU cycles filtering requests.

Lesson Summary

In this lesson, you learned how to configure an NLB cluster for different types of applications and networking environments. The lesson provided details about filtering modes as well as when to select multiple hosts, a single host, or none. Unicast and multicast modes were explained, along with performance differences between using single vs. multiple network cards. The lesson explained the convergence process and discussed ways to configure it for special situations. It also introduced the remote control program. Finally, it covered performance considerations for an NLB cluster and how to determine the number of servers to have in a cluster based on network bandwidth and CPU usage.

Lesson 3: When to Use NLB

This lesson will discuss different scenarios for using NLB clustering. You'll learn how an NLB solution allows an organization to easily add more servers to a cluster to meet increased demand. You'll also learn about issues specific to e-commerce when you configure an NLB cluster. Finally, you'll learn about Microsoft Terminal Services in an NLB scenario.

After this lesson, you will be able to

- Describe when and why you should implement NLB in various business scenarios

Estimated lesson time: 45 minutes

Scenarios for Using NLB

NLB allows clustering of up to 32 nodes, so it is ideal for high availability and scalability of TCP/IP-based services. Services that are stateless (meaning that each instance of a connection is not dependent on another connection from the same client) generally work well with NLB. Although NLB includes support for state, a more robust solution is to have the server software manage the state.

For example, IIS is required to maintain state for a given user, as in the case of an e-commerce site. There are a number of ways to keep track of state. IIS uses sessions to manage state for a user in memory. Because session data is stored in server memory, other servers do not have access to it. A robust solution would probably use a back-end database that all the servers in the cluster could access to store the session data. Other types of applications, such as streaming media servers, typically don't need to manage state at all and are therefore great candidates for an NLB cluster. VPN services and Terminal Services are also applications that are typically used in an NLB cluster.

Scenario 1: Multi-Homed IIS

Consider an ISP that hosts about 200 customer Web sites that all serve static content. These sites vary greatly in the number of client requests they receive and are currently running on four multi-homed nonclustered servers. The Web administrator manually installs new customer Web sites on whichever server exhibits the least demand. A few of the Web sites often get an excessive amount of traffic, causing the server's usage to run above 90 percent for extended periods of time. The current servers are also getting older and components are starting to fail, causing outages for clients.

After hearing from the sales team that the ISP is about to lose a customer due to server outages and poor site performance, the company decides to buy new hardware, create a plan to maintain high availability, and allow the system to scale to meet the increasing service requirements. The ISP opts for four new high-powered servers and use of an NLB cluster rather than hosting Web sites on individual boxes, for two main reasons: The first reason is availability. In the past, when a server went down, so did a number of customer Web sites. Second, during periods of high traffic, some of the servers would run at 100 percent utilization for an extended period while other servers would be virtually idle. NLB can distribute requests across the cluster, allowing the Web farm to handle the extra load when required. (See Figure 10.8.) Furthermore, NLB will allow the ISP to easily add new clients to the existing cluster by simply replicating the Web site to all the servers, adding a new IP address to the cluster adapters, and creating a new site in IIS on each server. This can all be done without the need to reboot the servers. Even if one server were to need a reboot for some reason, no hosted site would go down. Also, if the servers were to reach an unacceptable level of utilization, a new server could be easily added to the cluster by replicating the server and its data and then adding it to the cluster.

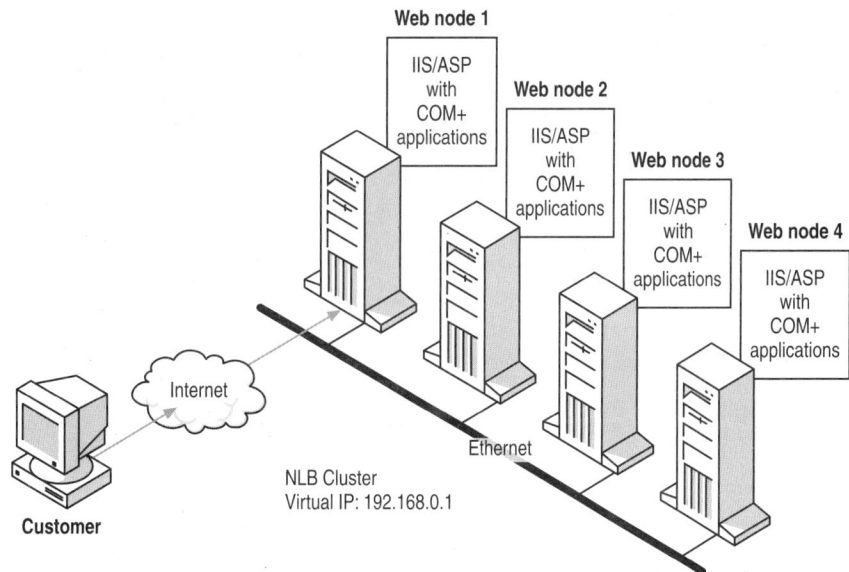

Figure 10.8 A simple NLB Web cluster configuration

All of the Web sites being hosted are serving static Web pages, so the ISP sets the affinity to None to decrease the CPU load required to analyze the requests in more detail. Because IIS is the only server responding to client requests, only a rule for port 80 is added to port rules. As an added measure to ensure availability, the ISP implements Cluster Sentinel to monitor client Web sites.

Scenario 2: IIS and COM+ Applications Accessing a Back-End Database

This scenario is an extension of the previous one. The ISP has already implemented its NLB cluster, and it is running smoothly. The sales team reports that a potential client is interested in having its Web site hosted and would like to include e-commerce abilities. The ISP has been considering offering this service, so it contacts a consulting company to help develop the e-commerce site and assess the hardware and software requirements. It hopes that this first site will serve as a prototype that can be applied to future sites for existing clients or other prospective clients.

The ISP decides to run Microsoft SQL Server 2000 Enterprise Edition for the data store and Microsoft Exchange 2000 as the e-mail solution. The e-commerce application will consist of ASP and COM+ applications that run on the NLB cluster servers. SQL Server and Exchange will run using Cluster Service to ensure availability. Even though it is advisable to run the SQL server and Exchange server in their own cluster, due to budget constraints the ISP decides that SQL Server will run on one node of the cluster and Exchange will run on the other and that each will fail over to the other server. This failover solution is acceptable because there won't be much load on the servers early on and they have enough memory to run simultaneously. (See Figure 10.9.) In the future, as demand grows, the COM+ applications can be separated into their own clusters.

The developers decide to use a hybrid solution to manage state. Some state information will be managed on the server, and the more critical state information will be managed using SQL Server. Because some state information will be managed on the server, Class C affinity, which maintains state for all clients from a given Class C IP address range, will be enabled on all servers in the NLB cluster so that even clients browsing from large corporations and ISPs who are using proxy servers can hold state while browsing. In this scenario, in addition to configuring port 80, you must configure a port 443 rule because customers using the e-commerce site will require secure connections so SSL will be implemented. SSL also requires that affinity be set to Single or Class C, so this port rule will also be set to Class C.

Scenario 3: Terminal Services

Windows 2000 Terminal Services allows Windows-based applications access to desktop computers that cannot run Windows 2000. It also allows corporations to manage deployment and support of software on a few powerful servers rather than on many desktops. Using Windows 2000 Terminal Services, administrators can deploy the latest Windows-based applications, in which applications run entirely on the server. Applications are installed only once on the server, and clients automatically have access to the new or upgraded software.

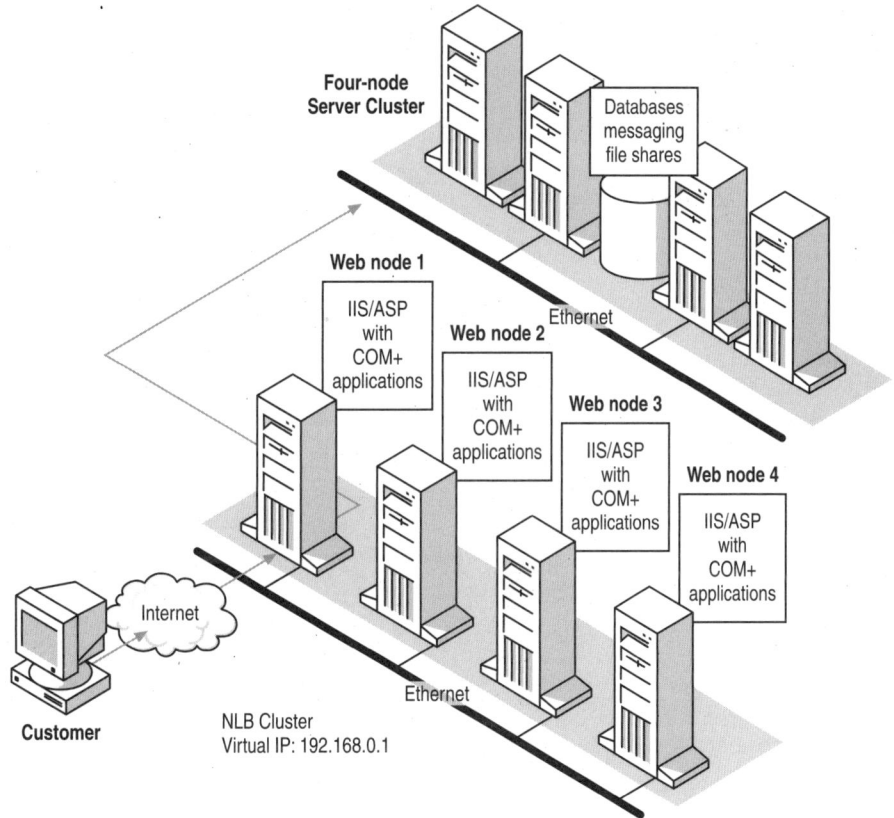

Figure 10.9   An NLB configuration using a back-end database

You can use NLB to scale a Terminal Services solution to handle a large number of clients. As in other NLB scenarios, statelessness is an important consideration because clients can connect to any servers in your cluster. For example, applications that enter data into a back-end database work well in an NLB cluster. (See Figure 10.10.) If each of your users is guaranteed to have a static IP address, an affinity setting of Single will ensure that the user will always connect to the same server. However, if you have roaming users who do not have static IP addresses, you cannot guarantee that they will connect to the same server. If you have an NLB cluster that requires users to connect to the same server every time, you'll achieve scalability but not availability because if a server in your cluster goes down, any users who need to connect to that server will also be down. It is advisable to have any user information stored on a back-end file server. That way, if a user is disconnected from the server and is forced to connect to another server in the cluster, that user will still have access to his or her data.

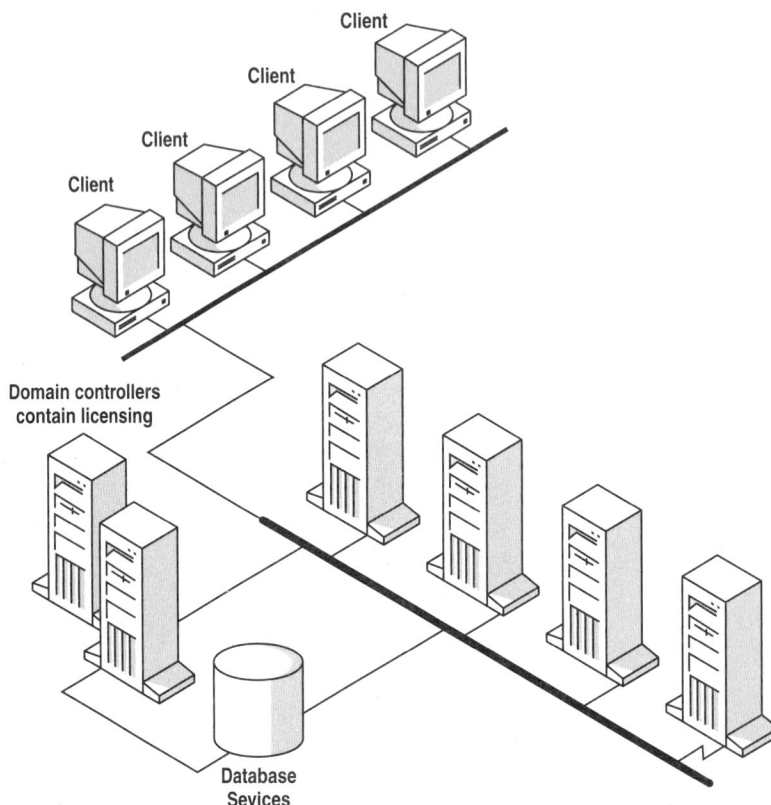

Figure 10.10   A Terminal Services NLB configuration

You should consider a number of issues before you use NLB with Terminal Services. Say, for example, that a user is working on a Microsoft Word document and suddenly gets disconnected from Terminal Services. Normally, that user's session would still remain active, and when the user reconnected, he or she could pick up right at the same spot. If the user ended up connecting back to another server, that would involve creating a new session and the document would not be available to the user. Even if the .doc file itself were stored on a file server, that document would probably be locked by the other session. In this scenario, the user would have to wait until the other session timed out before regaining access to the document, and any unsaved changes would likely be lost. Setting the NLB cluster's affinity to Single solves this problem unless the server goes down altogether. Keep in mind that if you have dial-up users and they get disconnected from their ISP, they will probably get a different IP address upon reconnect. You should have a moderate time-out of around 30 minutes for your Terminal Services sessions so that dropped sessions can be resumed and so that if a user is reconnected to another server, the original session will time out in a reasonable amount of time, freeing up those resources on the server.

Lesson Summary

This lesson presented a few scenarios for effectively using NLB. You learned about two ways to set up and configure an NLB cluster for IIS, both with and without a back-end database. You also learned about affinity with regard to IIS and SSL. Finally, you saw a scenario that used Terminal Services in an NLB cluster.

Review

?

The following questions will help you review key information presented in this chapter. You'll find the answers in Appendix A, "Questions and Answers."

1. What issues should you consider when you add servers to an existing NLB cluster?

2. What IP address is unique for each server in an NLB cluster?

   a. Virtual IP address

   b. Primary IP address

   c. Multi-homed IP address

   d. Dedicated IP address

3. Why is it typically undesirable to have the NLB server's cluster adapter on the same switch as the primary adapter of other computers when you use unicast mode?

4. Which statement below is most accurate?

   a. Unicast mode with a single network card is the most efficient networking solution for an NLB cluster.

   b. Multicast with a single network card is the most efficient networking solution for an NLB cluster.

   c. Unicast and multicast with two network cards perform about the same, but unicast is more compatible with most networks.

   d. Unicast and multicast with two network cards perform about the same, but multicast is more compatible with most networks.

5. When you use NLB in unicast mode, why is it desirable to connect the dedicated cluster adapters to the network using a switch rather than a hub?

6. If one server in the NLB cluster fails to hear from another server, how many seconds will it wait by default before it starts the convergence process?

   a. 10 seconds

   b. 1 second

   c. 5 seconds

   d. 11 seconds

7. Why can't NLB clustering guarantee that your server application will respond to requests? What should you do to ensure that your server application is responding to all requests?

8. In which scenario should you set affinity to None?

   a. When you implement SSL on a Web server

   b. When a Web server is managing state in a database on a back-end server

   c. When clients are connecting to Terminal Services on the local network

   d. When you're using an SMTP server in an NLB cluster

9. If you're running an e-commerce site using IIS and NLB clustering, do you need to always set affinity to Single or Class C to preserve state? Why or why not?

10. What process of NLB requires more CPU power as the number of requests increases?

    a. Filtering

    b. Convergence

    c. Transferring

    d. Routing

C H A P T E R   1 1

Implementing Network Load Balancing

About This Chapter

This chapter describes how to implement Network Load Balancing (NLB) on multiple computers in a cluster. Unlike with Cluster Service, you can include more than two servers in an NLB cluster when you're using Microsoft Windows 2000 Advanced Server. The NLB software is installed automatically with Windows 2000 Advanced Server, so this chapter will focus on enabling and configuring NLB. You use the default Web site included with Microsoft Internet Information Services (IIS) to verify your NLB installation. Sample Web pages are included with this training kit for this purpose. This chapter also includes information on optimizing and troubleshooting an NLB implementation.

Before You Begin

To complete this chapter, you must have

- The necessary hardware as outlined in the section titled "About This Book" in the Introduction

- The sample default.asp pages on the CD-ROM that accompanies this training kit

- The Windows 2000 Advanced Server installation CD-ROM

Lesson 1: Deployment Considerations

This lesson describes issues you must consider before implementing NLB, including hardware requirements, server capacity, and application requirements. A preconfiguration checklist is also included.

After this lesson, you will be able to

- Describe issues you must consider before implementing NLB
- List the hardware requirements for NLB

Estimated lesson time: 30 minutes

System Requirements

Before enabling and configuring NLB on your servers, you should verify that the existing server and network environment can support NLB. The following are the NLB system requirements:

- Windows 2000 Advanced Server
- TCP/IP protocol
- Fiber Distributed Data Interface (FDDI), Ethernet, or Gigabit Ethernet
- Cluster hosts residing on the same physical subnet
- 1.5 MB of free hard disk space
- Between 250 KB and 4 MB of available RAM (depending on network load and the parameters set in the Network Load Balancing properties dialog box)

Here are some additional considerations for planning an environment that will support NLB:

- A server cannot be a member of a server cluster and a member of an NLB cluster simultaneously.
- Load-balancing on a token ring network is not supported by NLB.
- NLB can operate on a mixed-version cluster. It is possible for an NLB cluster to have some servers operating on Windows NT 4 and some servers operating on Windows 2000 Advanced Server.
- Only one network adapter per host is necessary, but an additional network adapter is recommended. The extra adapter on each host will be responsible for separating client requests from network traffic that is unrelated to NLB, such as content replication information or access to server-based databases.

Planning an NLB Configuration

The following sections discuss configuration issues you must consider as you plan an NLB cluster implementation.

Network Risks

The network risks involved in implementing Cluster Service are also applicable here. These include internal and external causes of failure, such as software and power outages. You can increase the availability of your NLB cluster by

- Reducing the number of possible points of failure
- Developing backup plans (such as implementing Cluster Service, using uninterruptible power supplies, and having redundant access to the WAN)
- Load balancing appropriate applications
- Ensuring that the servers are properly configured to run the applications residing on them

NLB provides increased availability of your cluster and its applications. However, it does not protect your data in all circumstances. For instance, NLB cannot restore data in the event of a hard drive crash. However, if you are mirroring data between Web sites that are clustered with NLB, the content can be made available to users even if one server fails. Be sure to account for this in your implementation.

Cluster Size

Cluster size is defined as the number of cluster hosts that participate in the cluster. Cluster size depends on the number of computers required to meet an application's anticipated load. For example, if you need three computers to run IIS for your e-commerce Web site, your NLB cluster will consist of three cluster hosts, each running NLB.

A good general rule is to add servers to the cluster until the client load can be easily handled without causing the cluster to become overloaded. The maximum cluster size is 32 servers. The type of application you're clustering will affect the number of hosts that are required. You should make sure that the remaining servers can handle the applications from a failed host.

If your cluster is approaching saturation on your network, you can add another cluster on a different subnet. You must use Round Robin DNS (RRDNS) to direct clients to the clusters. You can then add clusters as needed. RRDNS directs clients to cluster IP addresses rather than individual servers, thus allowing uninterrupted access if a server fails.

If you need to deploy two or more clusters and you use network switches, you might consider placing each cluster on its own switch. This configuration will allow incoming cluster traffic to be handled separately by each cluster.

Server Capacity

You should plan your server capacity based on the types of applications you'll cluster and their predicted load requirements. For instance, a file server is extremely disk intensive and thus requires a large amount of disk space as well as fast I/O access. Each application's documentation can help you determine how to configure your cluster.

While it might be possible to handle the predicted client load with a few large powerful servers, it might be better to deploy many less powerful servers. This configuration will distribute the load more widely so that a failover will have less impact.

NLB Models

The four models for configuring NLB are described below. There is no limit, other than physical slots available, on the number of network adapters a host can have, and it is possible for different hosts to have a different number of adapters. One important thing to remember is that NLB does not support a mixed environment. All the hosts in the cluster must run in either unicast mode or multicast mode; otherwise, the cluster will not operate correctly. The next few sections will provide more information about unicast mode and multicast mode.

Single Network Adapter in Unicast Mode

This model works best when communication between cluster hosts is not required and a limited amount of traffic will be directed to the cluster hosts.

The advantages of this model are as follows:

- Only one network interface card (NIC) is required.
- Configuration is easy.
- All routers are supported.

The disadvantages are as follows:

- Cluster hosts cannot communicate with each other.
- Performance might suffer bacause all communication will be directed through the single NIC.

Multiple Network Adapters in Unicast Mode

This model works best when communication between cluster hosts is necessary. It is also useful when a large volume of outside traffic will be directed to the cluster hosts.

The advantages of this model are as follows

- It can enhance performance because network traffic will be directed to the appropriate NIC.

- It allows for intracluster communication.
- All routers are supported.

The disadvantage is that a second NIC is required.

Single Network Adapter in Multicast Mode

This model works best when intracluster communication is necessary and limited outside traffic will target the cluster hosts.

The advantages of this model are as follows:

- Only one NIC is required.
- It allows for intracluster communication.

The disadvantages are as follows:

- Performance might suffer because there is only one NIC.
- Some routers might not support this mode.

Multiple Network Adapters in Multicast Mode

This model works best when intracluster communication is necessary and a large amount of outside traffic will target the cluster hosts.

The advantages of this model are as follows:

- Network performance is better.
- It allows for intracluster communication.

The disadvantages are as follows:

- A second NIC is required.
- Some routers might not support this mode.

Application Requirements

In order for an application to run on an NLB cluster, it must meet the following conditions:

- Clients must be configured to connect using TCP/IP.
- The application must use TCP or UDP ports.
- Multiple instances of an application must be able to run concurrently. If those instances must share data, you must have a way to handle data synchronization.
- If session state is required, the application must use Single or Class C affinity or must provide a way to maintain session state that can be accessed from anywhere in the cluster.

Most applications configured to use the TCP/IP protocol with an associated port can be load balanced. Table 11.1 lists the types of applications supported by NLB.

Table 11.1   TCP/IP Application Ports Supported by NLB

TCP/IP protocol	Port	Type of application
HTTP	80	Web server
HTTPS	443	Traffic encryption
FTP	20, 21,1024 65535	File transfer (FTP)
TFTP	69	TFTP servers
SMTP	25	Mail transport

Applications that are not compatible with NLB have one or both of the following characteristics:

- **They bind to the computer name.**   Both Dfs (Distributed File System) and Exchange Server behave in this way.
- **They require that a file be continuously open for writing.**   In an NLB cluster configuration, multiple instances of an application should not have files being written to concurrently. However, this is allowed if the application is designed to handle data synchronization.

Router Considerations

If you're planning to have clients access the cluster through a router, you must decide which mode to use, unicast or multicast. Multicast is supported by some routers, while unicast is supported by all routers. If you want to use a router and multicast mode, the router must be able to accept an ARP reply that has two MAC addresses in it: one address that indicates where the ARP reply was received from and one address inside the ARP structure. If your router does not meet this requirement, you might still be able to use it with NLB, but you must create a static ARP entry in the router.

Preinstallation Checklist

Before installing and configuring NLB, you must do the following:

- Choose an NLB model.
- Decide on the cluster's full Internet name.
- Get the IP address and subnet mask for your cluster. This will be the primary IP address.
- Choose the mode of operation, unicast or multicast.

- Decide whether to enable remote operation.
- If you're enabling remote operation, choose a password for your remote operation.
- Determine each host's priority ID.
- Determine what the cluster's initial state should be.
- Determine the necessary port range.
- Determine which protocols will be covered.
- Determine the filtering mode.
- Choose an affinity setting.
- Determine how to set load weight.
- Determine the handling priority.

Lesson Summary

This lesson discussed planning considerations for an NLB cluster, including hardware and additional system requirements. It also described and compared the four configuration models available for NLB. Finally, it discussed planning issues such as server capacity, cluster size, and application requirements, and it provided a preinstallation checklist.

Lesson 2: Installing and Configuring NLB

This lesson discusses the installation and configuration of NLB. It walks you through setting up an NLB cluster, recommends some best practices for implementing an NLB cluster, and discusses maintenance and upgrades.

After this lesson, you will be able to

- Configure NLB for use on multiple servers in a cluster
- Test an NLB configuration using the default Internet Information Web site

Estimated lesson time: 45 minutes

Installing NLB

The NLB driver is installed automatically with Windows 2000 Advanced Server or Datacenter Server. It is an optional service and can be enabled at any time. NLB is compatible with most Ethernet and FDDI network adapters, so no hardware changes are required to install and operate it.

Configuring NLB

The settings you specify in the Network Load Balancing properties dialog box determine how NLB handles client requests. The three kinds of parameters you must set—cluster parameters, host parameters, and part rules—are described in this section.

Cluster Parameters

The cluster parameters determine the behavior of the cluster. Unless otherwise stated, they should match in each node in the cluster. The cluster parameters are as follows:

- **Primary IP Address and Subnet Mask**   The primary IP address is the IP address of the cluster. The subnet mask is the subnet mask of the primary IP address. All of the hosts in the cluster should use this IP address.

- **Full Internet Name**   This is the full Internet name of the cluster. For example, our cluster would be cluster.reskit.com. Use this name on all hosts in the cluster.

- **Network Address**   This parameter is generated automatically based on the computer's IP address.

- **Multicast Support**   This parameter specifies multicast mode or unicast mode.

- **Remote Password and Confirm Password**   These parameters specify the password to be used to access the cluster from remote locations.

- **Remote Control**   This parameter indicates whether remote operations are enabled.

Host Parameters

The host parameters determine how each host in the cluster behaves. They can be configured for use by the current node in the NLB cluster. Some of these parameters will vary between nodes in the cluster. The host parameters are as follows:

- **Priority ID**   The priority ID determines the sequence in which the cluster hosts will handle network traffic for the ports that are not addressed in the port rules. The host with the highest priority handles all of the network traffic; when that host goes offline, the host with the next highest priority takes over. The highest priority is 1.

- **Initial State**   The initial state determines whether the NLB service will start automatically. This parameter also designates whether the cluster host should join the cluster right after the computer's startup.

- **Dedicated IP Address and Subnet Mask**   The dedicated IP address is the cluster host's own unique IP address. The subnet mask is the subnet associated with the IP address.

Port Rules

The port rules, listed below, determine how the cluster traffic will be distributed among the cluster hosts. They must be the same on every host of the cluster; otherwise, the cluster cannot complete the convergence process. The rules apply to all nodes in the cluster. For more information about convergence, see Chapter 10.

- **Port Range**   The port range designates the TCP/UDP ports that the port rule covers. The default range is 1 through 65.535.

- **Protocols**   This parameter specifies which protocols the port rule should cover. It can cover TCP, UDP, or both.

- **Filtering Mode**   The filtering mode determines which cluster hosts, if any, will support the network traffic received by the ports designated in the port range.

- **Affinity**   The Affinity setting is used for associating client requests with cluster hosts. The affinity parameter determines which Affinity setting, if any, to use.

- **Load Weight**   Load weight determines the percentage of load-balanced traffic that the specific cluster should handle.

- **Equal Load Distribution**   Equal load distribution means that all load-balanced traffic should be distributed equally across all hosts in the cluster.

- **Handling Priority**   When the single host filtering mode is selected, the handling priority parameter becomes available. The handling priority determines the sequence in which the cluster hosts will handle network traffic.

Remote Cluster Control

Once NLB is installed, you can control the cluster's operations and parameter settings using the remote control tool, Wlbs.exe, which can be found in the system32 folder. The tool's name comes from Windows Load Balancing Service (WLBS), the predecessor to NLB in Windows 98. WLBS is still used in Windows 2000 because of backward compatibility issues. WLBS runs in a command window and can run Wlbs.exe on any cluster host or any remote Windows 2000 computer that can access the cluster. From these locations, you can control the operations of the cluster. However, you cannot change the cluster's parameters from a remote computer. You must be on a cluster host in order to do this or you must use Terminal Services to administer your host.

Remote Access

You can protect your NLB cluster from unauthorized remote access by requiring a password. You assign this password on the Cluster Parameters tab of the Network Load Balancing properties dialog box. If the password option is enabled, the password must be typed in after all cluster commands. If the password is not typed in, a prompt for the password will appear. If you plan to allow remote access to your cluster via the Internet, you might consider using a firewall for additional security.

Practice: Configuring NLB

This practice will walk you through setting up an NLB cluster with IIS. It assumes the following:

- You have at least two computers in your NLB cluster.

- Cluster Service has not been installed on the computers.

- The computers are not running any additional software, such as Microsoft SQL Server 2000 or Microsoft Exchange 2000 Server.

- Each machine has at least one network adapter, and the adapter or adapters are configured as shown in Chapter 2 (in the practice in the section titled "Configuring the Network Adapters").

- The first cluster host should have the following TCP/IP settings:

  IP Address   192.168.0.1

  Subnet Mask   255.255.255.0

- The second cluster host should have the following TCP/IP settings:

  IP Address   192.168.0.2

  Subnet Mask   255.255.255.0

- IIS has been installed on both computers.

Enabling NLB

First, you'll enable the NLB networking component that was automatically installed on your Windows 2000 Advanced Server. To see a demonstration of this practice, run the NLB.exe animation located in the Media folder on the companion CD.

1. On the Windows Desktop, right-click My Network Places and click Properties.

2. In the Networking And Dialog Connections dialog box, right-click Public Cluster Connection and click Properties.

3. In the Components list, click Network Load Balancing. If Network Load Balancing does not appear in the list, it has been removed from the system and you must reinstall it.

Configuring NLB Parameters

Next you'll configure NLB properties to enable the service to load balance requests to an IP address.

1. Click Properties. The Cluster Parameters tab should be selected; if not, click it. Type in the following values:

   Primary IP Address   *192.168.0.8*

   Subnet Mask   *255.255.255.0*

   Full Internet Name   *cluster.reskit.com*

   Select the Multicast Support option, type in the remote password twice, and select the Remote Control option.

2. Click the Host Parameters tab and type in or specify the following values:

   Priority (Unique Host ID) *1*

   Initial Cluster State   *Active*

   Dedicated IP Address   *192.168.0.1*

   Subnet Mask   *255.255.255.0*

   Increment your priority for each cluster host. Be sure to use each host's specific IP address for the dedicated IP address entry.

3. Click the Port Rules tab and type in or specify the following:

   Port Range   *1 to 65,535*

   Protocols   *Both*

   Filtering Mode   *Multiple Hosts*

   Affinity   *Single*

   Load Weight   *Equal*

4. Select the default rule and click Remove.

5. Click OK.

Configuring TCP/IP

You'll continue the configuration by adding the load-balanced IP address to each server in the cluster.

1. From the Windows desktop, right-click My Network Places and click Properties.

2. Right-click on Local Area Connection (or whichever item represents your LAN connection), and then click Properties.

3. Select Internet Protocol (TCP/IP).

4. Click Properties.

5. Click Advanced.

6. In the IP Addresses area on the IP Settings tab in the Advanced TCP/IP settings, click Add.

7. Type in the following information:

   IP Address   *192.168.0.8*

   Subnet Mask   *255.255.255.0*

8. Click Add.

9. In the Advanced TCP/IP Settings dialog box, click OK.

10. In the Internet Protocol (TCP/IP) Properties dialog box, click OK.

11. In the Public Cluster Connection Properties dialog box, click OK.

12. Repeat steps 1 through 9 on each host of the cluster, making appropriate changes.

Verifying NLB

You'll use the sample pages included with this training kit and the default Web site to verify that your NLB configuration is operating correctly.

1. On the CD-ROM, locate the Samples\NodeA folder. Copy the default.asp page from this folder to the c:\inetpub\wwwroot folder on NodeA.

2. Repeat step 1 for the second node, using the Samples\NodeB folder. Copy the default.asp page to the c:\inetpub\wwwroot folder on NodeB. Be sure to copy it from the correct folder.

3. From a remote machine on the same subnet, open Internet Explorer. (You cannot perform this test using either of the nodes in the cluster because by default they will resolve automatically to the local server.)

4. On the address line, type *http://192.168.0.8/default.asp* and press Enter.

5. The test page will display the name of the node that responded to the request, as shown here:

```
This page presented by: NodeA
```

6. Close Internet Explorer.

7. Return to the NLB cluster.

8. On NodeA, from the Windows desktop, right-click My Network Places and click Properties.

9. In the Networking And Dialog Connections dialog box, right-click Public Cluster Connection and click Properties.

10. In the Components list, click Network Load Balancing.

11. To change the priority of this host so that NodeB will respond to client requests, click the Host Parameters tab and enter *3* in the Priority (Unique ID) field.

12. Click OK.

13. Close the Networking And Dialog Connections dialog box.

14. Check the Windows Event Viewer for an event verifying that NodeB (host 2) has been converged.

15. Return to the remote machine and open Internet Explorer.

16. Type *http://192.168.0.8/default.asp* and press Enter.

17. The test page will display the name of the node that responded to the request, as shown here:

```
This page presented by: NodeB
```

18. Close Internet Explorer.

Starting and Stopping NLB Remotely

Next, you'll use the NLB command-line tool Wlbs.exe to manage nodes in your cluster. The actions you can perform include stopping and starting NLB on a remote server.

1. From NodeA, on the Windows desktop, click Start and then click Run.

2. In the Open text box, type *command*.

3. At the command prompt, type the following:

```
wlbs stop 192.168.0.8:2 /PASSW password
```

This command line specifies that WLBS should use the cluster with the address of 192.168.0.8 and direct the appropriate command (*stop*, in this case) to the host with priority 2 (which is NodeB). WLBS will report that the cluster operation has stopped.

4. At the command prompt, type the following:

```
wlbs start 192.168.0.8:2 /PASSW password
```

WLBS will report that the cluster operation has started.

Recommended Practices

Here are the recommendations for your environment and network configuration:

- Use at least two network adapters whenever possible. The second one will increase network performance and speed up access to server-based databases. Using two network adapters will also enable communication between clusters.

- When you use two or more network adapters, make sure that NLB is enabled on the public adapter (the adapter connected to the outside) only.

- The only protocols that should be present on the public adapter are NLB and TCP/IP.

- Make sure that the cluster parameters and port rules are set identically on all hosts in the cluster.

- The host parameters on each cluster host should be unique.

- Make sure that a port rule is in effect for all ports used by the load-balanced application.

- Make sure that the port rule appears in the list of rules before you close the properties dialog box.

- Make sure that the application (such as IIS) that is being load-balanced is running correctly on all cluster hosts. NLB cannot start applications.

- Be sure to type in both the dedicated IP address and the cluster IP address in the Internet Protocol (TCP/IP) Properties dialog box on the public adapter on each host of the cluster.

- In the Internet Protocol (TCP/IP) Properties dialog box, make sure that the dedicated IP address is listed above the cluster IP address.

- Use static IP addresses for both the dedicated IP address and the cluster IP address. Do not use DHCP addresses.

- Verify that all hosts in the cluster reside on the same subnet and make sure that clients cannot access the subnet.

- Make sure that all nodes in the cluster are in either unicast mode or multicast mode. Remember that NLB does not support a mixed-mode cluster.

- Remember that the NLB command-line executable is named *Wlbs.exe*.

- Remember that the NLB driver is installed automatically during the Windows 2000 Advanced Server installation, so you only have to enable it on the system on which you want to deploy NLB.

Managing Server Applications

Server applications can be load balanced without being modified. However, you must remember that the system administrator is responsible for starting the load-balanced applications on the cluster hosts. Once started, the applications must be monitored for correct operation. You cannot use NLB to do this; it simply controls which hosts are operational. You must have a separate application monitor for monitoring the current condition of the application. If a problem occurs with the application, the monitor will contact NLB and tell it how to respond.

Maintenance and Rolling Upgrades

You can do maintenance, such as replacing failed hardware, on an NLB cluster without interrupting its normal operations. The load assigned to this computer will automatically be distributed among the remaining hosts in the cluster. After the necessary maintenance is completed, the host can rejoin the cluster and assume its load responsibility.

You can perform rolling upgrades on your cluster without interrupting service to your clients. After you upgrade a specific host, it will rejoin the cluster.

Lesson Summary

This lesson discussed the installation and configuration of NLB and explained the configuration parameters. The practice walked you though the installation, configuration, verification, and remote operation of NLB. Finally, the lesson discussed basic maintenance and management considerations.

Lesson 3: Optimizing and Troubleshooting NLB

This lesson will discuss how to optimize and troubleshoot your NLB cluster.

After this lesson, you will be able to

- Change the cluster configuration to improve performance
- Troubleshoot your cluster installation

Estimated lesson time: 30 minutes

Optimizing an NLB Cluster

You can configure NLB on Windows 2000 Advanced Server or Datacenter Server so that it can benefit from the operating system's adaptable architecture and ability to allocate resources as needed. You can also make other configuration choices to enhance its performance, as detailed in the following sections.

Paging File Size and Location

The size and location of your paging file can greatly affect cluster performance. You can to minimize your paging file's effect on performance as follows:

- Place the paging file on an independent, fast, low-use drive.
- Determine the amount of physical memory on the computer. Set your paging file size to the appropriate number. (Some applications, such as Exchange 2000, require that you multiply the amount of physical memory by 2 to set the paging file size.)

Network Performance

If your cluster hosts are connected to a switch, all incoming network traffic will be sent to all the ports in the cluster. Therefore, to increase network performance, you should set parameters to avoid flooding the switch ports, thereby conserving switch bandwidth. A second network adapter is highly recommended for this configuration.

To avoid switch flooding, take the following steps:

1. Connect each host's network adapter to a hub.
2. Connect the hub to a switch port.
3. If multicast mode is currently being used, disable its use on the Cluster Parameters tab of the Network Load Balancing properties dialog box.
4. From the Windows desktop, click Start, click Run, and type *regedt32* in the Open text box. Open the following key:

   HKEY_LOCAL_MACHINE\System\CurrentControlSet\Services\WLBS\Parameters

5. Set the registry key, MaskSourceMAC, to *0*.

6. Reboot the computer.

Additional TCP/IP Services

If you're considering implementing WINS, DHCP, or DNS on your cluster, first consider the implications of doing so. These services use additional system resources and might require additional overhead. If you choose to implement them anyway, be sure that your cluster hosts can handle the necessary load appropriately.

Troubleshooting NLB

Many common problems with NLB are related to the configuration settings in the Network Load Balancing properties dialog box. This section discusses the problems and offers solutions.

A Remote Command Is Unsuccessful When You Use the Dedicated IP Address But Succeeds When You Use the Priority ID

The cluster host might have more than one dedicated IP address. For example, each adapter might have its own dedicated IP address. Make sure you're using the correct IP address when you work with remote commands. The correct IP address is the one listed on the Host Parameters tab of the Network Load Balancing properties dialog box.

When You Issue a Remote Command from an Outside Computer, One or Both of the Cluster Hosts Do Not Respond

This problem has three possible causes. First, you might be unable to access the network adapter from a remote computer. If more than one adapter is in the cluster host, they might be on different subnets. Therefore, if you issued a remote command from the incorrect subnet, the command might not have been able to reach NLB. If this is the case, make sure that you can access the network adapters from a remote computer and verify that the remote computer is on the correct subnet.

A second possible cause is that you're sending the remote commands to a secondary IP address. Remote commands must be sent to the cluster's primary IP address. You can locate this address on the Cluster Parameters tab of the Network Load Balancing properties dialog box.

The third possible cause is that the UDP control ports are protected by a firewall. By default, NLB uses UDP ports 1717 and 2504 at the cluster's IP address. Make sure that the appropriate ports have not been blocked by a firewall or router. If you want to designate another port, you can do so by changing a port rule.

When NLB Is Running, a TCP/IP Application Running on One of the Cluster Hosts Does Not Work Properly

One or more of the ports used by the application is being load-balanced by mistake. If you accepted the default port range or specified a large port range, the port used by the application might have been included. Make sure that the port rules include only ports that are needed by the load-balanced applications.

While NLB Is Running, a Load-Balanced Program Does Not Operate Properly

This problem has several possible causes. First, some of the ports used by the application might not be load balanced. The applications might require more than one port in order to correctly perform its necessary functions. If all the ports are not load balanced, the application will not operate properly. Verify that the port rules include all ports used by the application and that the affinity is enabled and set to Single or Class C.

A second possibility is that the application is not running on all cluster hosts. Remember that NLB does not start applications; you must start the applications manually. Verify that the application is running on all cluster hosts.

A third possibility is that you might not be able to load balance this application. Applications must meet specific requirements in order to be load balanced. Make sure your application meets the requirements for NLB listed in Lesson 1 of this chapter.

A fourth possibility is that the application is not configured to use TCP/IP. NLB requires that load-balanced applications be configured to use TCP/IP.

Finally, a firewall might be masking client traffic. If this is the case, NLB will think that all connections are coming from the same client. If the affinity setting is Single, the same cluster host is responding to all network traffic. To solve this problem, you can disable address translation on your proxy server or change your affinity setting to None. If you want to provide session support, you might need to set the affinity to Single.

The Default Cluster Host Is Handling All Network Traffic and Applications Are Not Being Load Balanced

If network traffic is not affected by a port rule, it is sent to the default cluster host. Therefore, if an application is not being load balanced it means that the port being used by the application is not covered by a port rule. You should make sure that the ports required by the application are covered in the port rules.

The Cluster Host Can Ping a Computer Outside of the Cluster, But It Cannot Browse the Computer or Use Telnet

In this case, the TCP/IP configuration has been set up incorrectly. If you are using one network adapter in your cluster host, you must enter the IP addresses in the correct order. If they are not in the correct order, outside computers will respond to the incorrect IP address. Make sure that you entered the cluster IP address in the Internet Protocol (TCP/IP) Properties dialog box and verify that the cluster host's dedicated IP address appears in the list before the cluster's IP address. You can also avoid this problem by using multiple adapters.

Network Traffic Is Being Handled in an Unexpected Manner

Network traffic might be causing a large amount of collisions or might not consistently arrive at its intended destination. In this situation, the switch and the unicast network address are conflicting with each other. If you're using a switch to connect the hosts in your cluster configuration, NLB must be set to use multicast mode. If you cannot change the mode to unicast, you must connect your cluster hosts in some other way, perhaps with a hub or coaxial cable. Otherwise, you'll have to switch to multicast mode using the Cluster Parameters tab of the Network Load Balancing properties dialog box.

When You Try to Ping the Cluster's IP Address from an Outside Network, You Get No Response

If you have multiple adapters in your cluster hosts, try to ping the cluster host's dedicated IP address from outside your router. If this is unsuccessful, the problem is not related to NLB. If you have a single adapter in your cluster hosts, there are three possible causes of the problem.

First, if the NLB mode is set to multicast and you're using a router, the router might be having difficulty resolving the MAC address that it is receiving. Try pinging the cluster's IP address from a client that resides on the same subnet as the cluster. Then try pinging each cluster host's dedicated IP address from outside the router. If both of these tests are successful, the problem is with the router. You must switch to unicast mode or make configuration changes to allow the router to understand the multicast MAC addresses.

Another possible cause of the problem is that the proxy you're using doesn't have ARP support or that ARP support is not enabled. Routers must be able to accept proxy ARP responses. This is true no matter which mode NLB is set to use. Make sure that the proxy you're using has ARP support and that it is enabled. If you want to disable ARP support, you must set a static ARP entry to do this.

The final possibility is that if NLB is set to use unicast mode, the network adapter was unable to change its MAC address. This is not a problem in multicast mode. Either replace your network adapter or change the mode setting on the Cluster Parameters tab of the Network Load Balancing properties dialog box.

NLB Reports That Convergence Is Finished, But There Is More Than One Default Host

The problem might be caused by cluster hosts residing on different subnets, which means that they're not accessible on the same network. You should make sure that intracluster communication is possible. This might require the addition of another NIC or reconfiguring your network architecture based on whether you're using unicast or multicast mode. For example, you might consider using a hub when unicast mode is enabled.

Another possible cause is that the cluster is using a different MAC address from the one used by NIC in the server. This happens when the cluster's primary IP address has not been assigned to the TCP/IP properties. In this situation, TCP/IP does not detect address conflicts and therefore allows multiple clusters to exist. Make sure that the primary cluster IP address is the same on all cluster hosts and verify that it is listed in the Internet Protocol (TCP/IP) properties dialog box.

Finally, there might be more than one cluster on the same subnet. Using different primary IP address on the different cluster hosts allows you to create multiple clusters on the same subnet. If you intended to create more than one cluster, this is not a problem.

The Cluster Hosts Begin to Converge But Never Complete the Convergence

The port rules might be incompatible or might not match. Check the port rules on all cluster hosts and make sure that the rules are the same on each host.

After You Install NLB and Restart the System, You Get an Error Message Stating That *The System Has Detected an IP Address Conflict with Another System on the Network...*

The primary IP addresses on the cluster hosts might not match. Check the primary IP address on the Cluster Parameters tab of the Network Load Balancing properties dialog box. Make sure that the same primary IP address is used on all cluster hosts.

Another possible cause of the problem is that the network adapter was unable to change its network address. This can occur when NLB is running in unicast mode. To solve this problem, you can replace the current network adapter or you can change the NLB mode to multicast.

One or More of the Cluster Hosts Is Having Trouble with the Network

One possible cause of this problem is that when the computer was turned on, the NLB driver was not loaded correctly—perhaps because the dependency driver was unable to load or is corrupt. NLB might be corrupt as well. To solve this problem, log on to the computer with a user that has administrative rights and run the *wlbs* query command. If an error is returned, check the event log to determine the driver's problem.

The second possibility is that the problem is related to the network, not to NLB. Try to determine whether NLB is at fault. Disable NLB by deselecting the NLB option in the Properties dialog box of My Network Places, and try to reproduce the problem. If you can, the problem is not related to NLB.

The third possible cause is that if you're using a switch to connect the hosts in your cluster, the NLB mode might be set to unicast, which can cause erratic behavior. Verify that the NLB mode is set to multicast on the Cluster Parameters tab of the Network Load Balancing properties dialog box.

You're Using a Switch to Connect the Hosts in Your Cluster, and the Cluster Communications Are Being Interrupted

If you recently changed the mode from unicast to multicast, the switch might be inadvertently using the cluster's MAC address. Restart the switch.

NLB Is Installed, But You Receive an Error Message Stating That It Is Not

The NLB query command was performed by a user who did not have administrative rights. Log on as a user with administrative rights and run the query command again.

Lesson Summary

This lesson presented some optimization techniques you can use when you create your NLB cluster. It also discussed issues related to TCP/IP services and network performance. The lesson presented common problems with NLB, most of them related to improper configuration, and offered solutions.

Review

?

The following questions will help you review key information presented in this chapter. You'll find the answers in Appendix A, "Questions and Answers."

1. Which NLB model is the best choice for a cluster when intracluster communication is necessary and the amount of outside traffic targeting the cluster hosts is limited?

    a. Single network adapter in unicast mode

    b. Multiple network adapters in unicast mode

    c. Single network adapter in multicast mode

    d. Multiple network adapters in multicast mode

2. Why is a second network adapter recommended?

3. Which of following requirements must an application meet in order to be load balanced?

    a. The clients must be able to connect using TCP/IP.

    b. The application must use TCP or UDP ports.

    c. Multiple instances of an application must be able to run concurrently.

    d. The application must bind to a computer name.

4. What do the port rules determine?

5. Which of the following must be configured for NLB to operate properly?

    a. Cluster parameters

    b. TCP/IP

    c. Host parameters

    d. Port rules

6. What is the difference between the primary IP address and the dedicated IP address?

7. Which of the following are recommended practices when you create an NLB cluster?

    a. The host parameters on each cluster host should be identical.

    b. The port rules on each cluster host should be identical.

    c. The same primary IP address should be used on all cluster hosts.

    d. The same dedicated IP address should be used on all cluster hosts.

8. After you enable remote access to your cluster, how do you limit unauthorized access by remote users?

9. Which of the following can hurt the performance of your NLB cluster?

    a. Paging file size

    b. Cluster hosts connected to a switch

    c. WINS

    d. Microsoft Exchange

10. What steps are required to install the NLB driver as part of a default Windows 2000 Advanced Server installation?

A P P E N D I X   A

Questions and Answers

Chapter 1
Introduction to Microsoft Clustering Technologies

Page 27

1. You are the administrator for a new Internet startup. Management has asked you to recommend the best technology for the internal e-mail system. Because the e-mail system will be used 24 hours a day by internal staff members and remote sales personnel—a total of 567 users—the server must be available as much as possible. Which clustering technology should you implement, and why?

   Cluster Service is the best choice for this scenario. Two servers running Windows 2000 Advanced Server, acting together in a cluster, provide the necessary redundancy to ensure high availability. Because of the limited, and therefore manageable, number of users, NLB is not appropriate in this situation.

2. What is a cluster? (Choose all appropriate answers.)

   a.   A group of individual servers that act as a backup for one another

   b.   A group of individual servers that work together as a single computer

   c.   A group of individual servers with the same name and IP address

   d.   A group of individual servers that have the same components and resources

   Answer: a, b, c. A cluster includes a number of individual servers that are grouped together and act as single server. The servers present the same name and IP address to network clients. Depending on the cluster model you implement, one node can act as a live backup for another node in the event of a failure.

3. You have recently been hired as a network administrator for an insurance company. The company is currently running Windows NT 4 servers for its database and e-mail needs. Management has decided to implement a secure Web site that will provide claim information to the adjustors in the field. This Web site will also be used to process client applications submitted by agents in real time. The company has more than 500 offices across the United States. Each office has at least four agents, who each process an average of 35 applications a day. If the Web site meets expectations, management might open the site to clients for instant access to their records, new application submission, finding a local agent, and so on. You have decided to use Windows 2000 Advanced Server for the Web site. Further, you have decided to use Cluster Service for increased availability. Should you also use NLB in this scenario?

While the internal version of the Web site might not warrant using NLB, you might need NLB when the site is opened for public use, in order to handle the demand. It is difficult to predict the load caused by Internet use. So, at the very least, you should plan for using NLB.

Page 28

4. What is a node?

   a. The name of a cluster

   b. The SCSI hard drive where the cluster information is stored

   c. A server in a cluster

   d. The component of Cluster Service that manages Cluster Service resources

Answer: c. A node is a single physical server in a cluster.

5. You have been asked to implement a cluster for your organization's e-mail server. Which operating systems support Cluster Service?

Only Windows 2000 Advanced Server and Windows 2000 Datacenter Server support the two available clustering technologies. Windows 2000 Advanced Server supports two nodes in a cluster, while Windows 2000 Datacenter Server supports up to four nodes.

6. How do cluster-unaware applications communicate with Cluster Service?

   a. Resource DLLs

   b. Cluster APIs

   c. Communications Manager

   d. Heartbeats

Answer: a. Cluster-unaware applications are not normally in communication with Cluster Service. Resource DLLs allow a cluster-unaware application to interact with Cluster Service in order to provide a basic level of functionality, such as the ability to fail over.

7. You have been asked to evaluate your company's network. A previous administrator implemented a cluster to host your company's Web server. However, management is worried that the upcoming marketing campaign will result in a dramatic increase in visitors to the Web site. NLB has not been implemented. Should you consider NLB?

Yes. NLB is a separate service that can be implemented under certain conditions. Since management has announced the marketing campaign, you can expect increased load due to company clients responding to the campaign. NLB is probably the best solution to handle the increased load.

Page 29

8. What implementation models are supported by Cluster Service?

a. Shared Device

b. Shared Nothing

c. Shared Everything

d. Mixed

Answer: a, b. The Shared Device model allows applications to obtain exclusive access to certain shared resources, such as a hard drive or a printer. The Shared Nothing model, which is the default, allows applications to have access to all shared resources in a cluster at all times and is controlled by the Quorum resource.

9. Describe when failovers and failbacks occur.

A failover occurs when a resource goes offline and the group it belongs to is moved to another node. A failback occurs when a resource group that was previously moved as a result of a failover is moved back to the original node. Only resources can fail. Resource groups can be moved from one node to another.

10. Your organization has asked you to implement a cluster using Cluster Service for its e-commerce Web site. You have decided to implement a solution that uses two nodes, one that hosts all the resources in the cluster and one that acts as a live backup in the event of a failure. Which configuration model does this represent?

a. Model A

b. Model B

c. Model C

d. Model D

e. Model E

Answer: b. Model B provides for a live backup node, or hot spare.

Chapter 2
Preparing Windows 2000 Server for Cluster Service

Page 50

1. Which network protocols are supported by the private network used by Cluster Service?

Cluster Service supports only the TCP/IP protocol, so TCP/IP should be the only protocol implemented on the private network. NetBIOS can be used by the public network to accept requests from clients, but it is not supported by the Cluster Service private network. No other network protocols are supported by the Cluster Service private network.

2. When you decide to make a server in the cluster a domain controller, which of the following is *not* true?

a. There will be added overhead when the server is configured as a domain controller.

b. All servers in the cluster must be domain controllers.

c. The server must have Active Directory installed.

d. The server must have access to both a DHCP server and a DNS server.

Answer: b. Servers in a cluster can be either domain controllers or member servers. They must have access to both a domain controller and a DNS server.

3. Why is using DHCP to obtain the TCP/IP settings for the public adapters in a cluster not recommended?

If the DHCP server fails and the lease address expires, the cluster will not be accessible. Therefore, it is not recommended that a DHCP server be used to provide IP addresses to the public network in a cluster because a failure of the DHCP server could result in a failure of the cluster.

4. Which of the following are true of the shared device when you use Windows 2000 Advanced Server?

   a. The shared device can be only one drive.

   b. The shared device can be more than one drive.

   c. The shared device must be a SCSI device.

   d. The shared device must be physically connected to all servers in the cluster.

   Answer: b, d. The shared device comprises one or more drives that are physically connected to all servers in the cluster. The shared device can be a SCSI or Fibre Channel device.

5. You have four network adapters in your cluster configuration—two per node. How are the adapters configured?

   The public adapters are connected to the LAN and the private adapters are connected to each other. To support Cluster Service, the private network adapters must be connected to the private network between cluster nodes. To support client access, the public network adapters must be connected to the LAN.

Page 51

6. When you use Windows 2000 Advanced Server and Cluster Service, which of the following drive types are supported for the shared device?

   a. SCSI

   b. EIDE

   c. ATA

   d. Fibre Channel

   Answer: a, d. The shared device supports only SCSI and Fibre Channel technologies.

7. Cluster Service requires three IP addresses associated with your LAN. Where are these IP addresses assigned?

   They are assigned at each public adapter and at the cluster itself. The cluster must have a public IP address available on the LAN in order to support client access. Each node of the cluster must have a public IP address for access from the LAN.

8. When you use a SCSI drive for the shared device, which of the following is *not* a requirement?

   a. A unique identification number.

   b. Each disk must be configured as Basic.

   c. Each disk must use a removable drive.

   d. Partitions must be in NTFS format.

   Answer: c. The shared device cannot use removable drives. The disks in the shared device must be configured as Basic disks and formatted as NTFS. Each disk must also have a unique SCSI ID.

9. What resides on the shared device?

   Shared data and the Quorum resource

10. Which of the following should you consider for a node in a cluster that will be used for file services?

    a. Large hard drives with fast access rates

    b. A large amount of virtual memory

    c. Multiple processors

    d. Network adapters that provide fast throughput

    Answer: a, d. If your cluster will be used primarily as a file server, you should consider using hardware configurations that provide fast disk access, plenty of storage space for files, and high network throughput. However, because a file server typically doesn't require much memory or processing power, you can consider trading drive and network access for memory and processor speed.

Chapter 3
Installing and Configuring Cluster Service

Page 82

1. When the Internal Communications Only (Private Network) option is selected for a network adapter, what is the result?

   Cluster Service uses this network adapter for node-to-node communication only. The Internal Communications Only (Private Network) option specifies that the adapter should be used only for Cluster Service communication between nodes.

2. Which command-line option does the Cluster Service setup program use for an unattended installation?

    a. *-u*

    b. *-s*

    c. *-a*

    d. *-i*

    Answer: a. The Cluster Service setup program uses *-u*, for "unattend," to automate the installation process.

3. Why should the private connection be listed first?

    When more than one adapter can be used for node communication, the adapter listed first has the highest priority. Cluster Service will attempt to use the first adapter listed for node-to-node communication.

4. Which of the following applications is used to install Cluster Service?

    a. Sysprep.exe

    b. Cluscfg.exe

    c. Setup Manager

    d. Winnt.exe

    Answer: b. Cluscfg.exe is used to perform unattended installation and also to run the Cluster Service Configuration Wizard for manual installations.

5. Where can you find the Cluster Verification utility?

    It is included in the Windows 2000 Resource Kit. It can also be found on the Microsoft Web site, under Resource Kit Tools.

Page 83

6. Which of the following must exist before you install Cluster Service?

    a. Three network adapters per node

    b. An IP address for the cluster

    c. A unique domain name for the cluster

    d. A domain account with administrative permission for Cluster Service

    Answer: b, d. The IP address and the domain user account must be created before you install Cluster Service. The name for the cluster is created during the installation and cannot exist on the network before you start the installation. The cluster does not require its own domain, although you might want to configure it so.

7. Which wizard page is displayed during the installation of the first node but not during the installation of the second node?

The Network Connections page

8. When you configure the Cluster Service account, which of the following user rights are required in addition to administrative permission?

a. Log on as a service

b. Act as part of the operating system

c. Back up files and directories

d. All of the above

Answer: d. In addition to administrative permission, the account needs a number of additional user rights, including all the ones listed above.

9. In order to perform a rolling upgrade to Windows 2000 Advanced Server, which Windows NT operating system and service pack must you have installed on the existing cluster nodes?

Windows NT 4 Server Enterprise Edition with Service Pack 4 or later

10. Which of the following operating systems that uses MSCS supports a rolling upgrade to Windows 2000 Datacenter Server?

a. Windows 2000 Advanced Server

b. Windows NT 4 Enterprise Edition, Service Pack 5

c. Windows NT 4 Enterprise Edition, Service Pack 6

d. None of the above

Answer: d. Windows 2000 Datacenter Server does not support rolling upgrades.

Chapter 4
Administering and Managing a Cluster

Page 118

1. You have been asked to port a legacy application that was developed in-house to reside on a new cluster. The application was not developed to be cluster-aware. Which resource type can you use to provide basic failover capability to increase the availability of this application?

The Generic Application resource type

2. Which of the following can be performed in Cluster Administrator?

   a. Connecting to a cluster

   b. Identifying a failover

   c. Initiating resource failure

   d. Transferring ownership of a group or resource

   Answer: All of the above. All of the items are common tasks that can be performed in Cluster Administrator.

3. Every new cluster includes the default resource group, Cluster Group. Which two resources are automatically included in this group?

   IP Address and Network Name

4. Which of the following statements about dependencies are true?

   a. A dependent resource and all of its dependencies must be in the same group.

   b. All resources, regardless of dependencies, are brought online and offline together.

   c. A dependent resource is taken offline before its dependencies.

   d. A dependent resource is brought online after its dependencies.

   Answer: a, c, d. Cluster Service ensures that the resources are brought online and taken offline in the order of the dependency list.

5. Which two resources are required to create a virtual server?

   IP Address and Network Name

Page 119

6. Which of the following property types is not associated with resources?

   a. General

   b. Advanced

   c. Dependency

   d. Failback

   Answer: d. Failback is a property of a group, not a resource.

7. Besides global groups, which two groups, when installed on a domain, can be given access to administer the cluster?

The Local Administrators group on the node and Domain Users.

8. Which of the following cannot be set using the New Resource Wizard?

    a. Pending timeout settings

    b. Resource name

    c. The node the resource will run on

    d. Resource type

    Answer: a. The pending timeout settings must be set on the resource's property page.

9. What state is a node in if it is currently supporting resources but not allowing new resources to come online?

    Paused. A paused node still supports its currently running resources, but unlike the Up state, it does not allow new resources to come online.

10. Which of the following are valid resource types?

    a. Physical Disk

    b. IP Address

    c. Print Share

    d. File Share

    Answer: a, b, d. Print Spooler is a valid resource type, but Print Share is not.

Chapter 5
Managing and Supporting a Cluster

Page 152   1. Describe what Dfs is and what it is used for.

Distributed file system (Dfs) is used to link shared folders residing on different servers to a single hierarchical namespace. Dfs provides load sharing and data availability. With Dfs, users do not need to know the physical location of the data because access to that data is transparent. Dfs also provides a consistent naming convention and can support multiple file protocols and mapping of servers.

2. Which of the following issues should you consider when you implement Dfs?

   a. Users accessing the shared resources will be distributed across multiple sites.

   b. Your organization uses internal and/or external Web sites.

   c. Redistributing shared resources can improve Network Load Balancing performance.

   d. All of the above.

   Answer: d. You should consider all of the items when you implement Dfs.

3. Which of the following statements about file shares is true?

   a. Normal shares are the most flexible, and their security terms are easy to understand.

   b. Subdirectory shares are available in Windows NT 4 Service Pack 4.

   c. Dfs root shares are available in Windows NT 4 Service Pack 4.

   d. A normal share allows administrators to create directories that host a large number of shares.

   Answer: a. Subdirectory shares are available in Windows NT 4 Service Pack 5 and later. Dfs root shares are available only in Windows 2000. A subdirectory share allows administrators to create directories for large numbers of shares.

4. Which disk management wizard is used to replace cluster disks?

   The Create Partition Wizard

5. In Windows 2000, printers do not need to be locally defined on each node in the cluster. Why? (Choose all that apply.)

   a. The port configuration is stored in the Cluster Registry.

   b. The cluster nodes share the port configuration.

   c. The printer driver files can be shared between the nodes.

   d. Cluster Service provides failover of the print server.

   Answer: a, b. The printers do not need to be locally defined because the port configuration is stored in the Registry, allowing all the cluster nodes to share it.

page 153

6. How do System Monitor and the Print Queue object help you?

   System Monitor provides performance information about system components. You can use it with the Print Queue object to track the performance of a local or remote printer. The information you receive will help you determine whether there is a performance problem with the printer.

7. Which of the following Physical Disk resource properties are not required?

a. Name

b. Description

c. Possible Owners

d. Required Dependencies

e. Disk

Answer: b, d. The Physical Disk description property is not required in order for the resource to operate. The Physical Disk resource also has no required dependencies, so entries for that property are not required.

8. What are the required dependencies for a Physical Disk resource?

None. The Physical Disk resource does not require any dependencies.

9. From which of the following can a Physical Disk resource be created?

a. A disk partition shared in the cluster

b. A tape drive shared in the cluster

c. A disk drive shared in the cluster

d. The disk where the Quorum resource resides

Answer: c, d. A Physical Disk resource can be created only for an entire cluster shared disk. It can be created for a partitioned drive, but the resource must be created with the entire disk, partitions and all. Tape drives cannot be used for Physical Disk resources.

10. In what situation must all nodes be possible owners of a Physical Disk resource?

When the Quorum resource resides on the disk

Chapter 6
Implementing Applications and Network Services on a Cluster

Page 193

1. Is a folder called w:\cluster\dhcp\, where W: is the shared disk, a valid path for the DHCP database on a clustered DHCP server?

Yes. The DHCP database must be stored in a folder on the cluster's shared disk. You can specify the name of the folder when you create a DHCP resource.

2. Which of the following characteristics identifies a cluster-unaware application?

   a. The application does not use the Cluster API.

   b. The application is managed as a Generic Application resource.

   c. The application can perform the necessary initialization and cleanup tasks.

   d. The application is highly available to cluster resources.

   Answer: a, b, d. A cluster-unaware application can be managed as a Generic Application resource, it does not use the Cluster API, and it is highly available to the cluster's resources. It might not be able to perform the initialization and cleanup tasks that are usually associated with Cluster Service.

3. Is a folder called w:\cluster\wins, where W: is the shared disk, a valid path for the WINS database on a clustered WINS server?

   No. Although the folder location specified is on the required shared disk, the path does not end with the required backslash. W:\cluster\wins\ would be the correct location.

4. Which of the following characteristics indicate that an application can be modified to become cluster-aware?

   a. The application's network protocol is TCP/IP.

   b. The application maintains data in a location that can be configured.

   c. The application supports transaction processing.

   d. The application does not use the Cluster API.

   Answer: a, b, c. These characteristics indicate that an application is capable of becoming cluster-aware.

5. When you create a new WINS resource for a cluster using the New Resource Wizard, should you set both nodes as Possible Owners for the resource? Why?

   Yes. Both nodes should be set as Possible Owners of the resource so the resource can fail over.

Page 194

6. Which of the following resources is a required dependency for an IIS server instance?

   a. IP Address

   b. Physical Disk

   c. Network Name

   d. MS DTC

   Answer: a. Only an IP Address resource is a required dependency for the IIS Service Instance resource. A Physical Disk resource is optional and is needed only to support failover of Web sites or FTP sites on a shared disk. A Network Name resource is needed only if you want to have clients access the resource by using a network name. The MS DTC resource is needed only to support transactions on a Web site.

7. Which technique provides the highest availability for a DHCP server, splitting scopes or clustering DHCP?

   Clustering DHCP. Splitting DHCP scopes does provide some increased availability, but it provides less than a DHCP cluster does because in the event of a failure, the entire DHCP database stays online when you use a clustered implementation. With a split scope implementation, in the event of a failure part of the available range of IP addresses will not be available.

8. Which of the following cluster resources is a DHCP resource not dependent on?

   a. Physical Disk

   b. File Share

   c. IP Address

   d. Network Name

   Answer: b. The DHCP resource is dependent on a Physical Disk, IP Address, and Network Name resource. It does not require a File Share resource.

9. As the system administrator for your organization, you have been asked to deploy an application developed internally on a new cluster to increase its availability for clients. The application was previously deployed on a single server that all clients accessed directly and was not originally developed to be cluster-aware. After installing the application on each node, you add it to the cluster using the Generic Application resource type. You then test the application's ability to fail over to the second node in the cluster. Your tests show that the application behaves as expected. With this in mind, do you need to implement a custom resource DLL for this application?

Probably not. Cluster-unaware applications do not need a custom re-source DLL, which would make them cluster-aware, if they are able to function normally on the cluster. If the application were unable to restart on the second node after a failover, you would probably need to create a custom resource type for it.

10. Which of the following are valid steps for creating a WINS cluster?

a. Authorize the WINS server in Active Directory

b. Create a WINS resource

c. Activate replication on a WINS cluster node

d. Specify a path on the dependent disk for the WINS database

Answer: b, d. Creating a WINS resource and specifying a path on the de-pendent disk for the WINS database are valid steps for creating a WINS cluster. Only DHCP servers need to be authorized in Active Directory. Replication is not required for creating a WINS cluster.

Chapter 7
Troubleshooting Cluster Service

Page 234

1. What is the cluster version number?

3.2195

2. What is the operating system version?

5.0.2195

3. Locate the following entry, and identify what kind of entry it is:

`00000488.000006a8::2000/11/17-23:54:46.029 [EP] Initialization...`

A component event log entry

4. Look at the entry in the previous question. Which component logged the entry?

`00000488.000006a8::2000/11/17-23:54:46.029 [EP] Initialization...`

The Event Processor

Page 235

5. What information is contained in the abbreviation [NMJOIN]?

The message is from the Node Manager. A node is trying to join the cluster.

6. What kind of entry is this?

`0000050c.00000164::2000/11/19-`
`21:33:20.168 Network Name <Cluster Name>: Registered server name`
`MYCLUSTER on transport \Device\NetBt_If13.`

A resource DLL entry

7. Look at the entry in the above question. What is the display name of the resource in this entry, and what kind of resource is it?

The display name of the resource is Cluster Name. The resource is a Network Name resource.

8. What is the sequence number of this log entry?

```
000004b8.00000680::2000/11/20-19:51:54.134 [GUM] GumSendUpdate:
completed update seq 11678    type 0 context 8
```

11678

9. What is the type and context indicated in this entry?

```
000004b8.00000680::2000/11/20-
19:51:54.134 [GUM] GumSendUpdate: completed update seq 11678    type 0 context 8
```

Type 0 is a function of the Failover Manager. Context 8 is ResourceState.

10. What does the following group of entries describe?

```
000004b8.000001dc::2000/11/19-
21:30:58.655 [FM] Initializing resource 348202f0-011e-47f3-8d73-
88e77a2bf77b from the registry.
000004b8.000001dc::2000/11/19-
21:30:58.655 [FM] Name for Resource 348202f0-011e-47f3-8d73-
88e77a2bf77b is 'test1'.
000004b8.000001dc::2000/11/19-
21:30:58.655 [FM] FmpAddPossibleEntry:
adding node 1 as possible host for resource 348202f0-011e-47f3-
8d73-88e77a2bf77b.
000004b8.000001dc::2000/11/19-
21:30:58.655 [FM] FmpAddPossibleEntry: adding node 2 as possible
host for resource 348202f0-011e-47f3-8d73-88e77a2bf77b.
000004b8.000001dc::2000/11/19-
21:30:58.655 [FM] All dependencies for resource 348202f0-011e-
47f3-8d73-88e77a2bf77b created.
```

A resource being created. The resource's display name is test1, and its GUID is 348202f0-011e-47f3-8d73-88e77a2bf77b. Node 1 and node 2 are possible owners of the resource.

Page 244

1. While installing Cluster Service on a node, you receive an error indicating that LanManServer Could Not Be Started. What is causing the error?

   a. The SCSI bus is not configured correctly.

   b. File and Printer Sharing is not installed on the node.

   c. A network adapter is not configured correctly.

   d. You are not logged in with administrative permissions.

   Answer: b. This error occurs if File and Printer Sharing is not installed on the node on which you are installing Cluster Service.

2. What are the four possible states for a cluster network interface?

   Unavailable, Failed, Unreachable, and Up.

3. Which of the following are possible reasons that a group will not come online?

   a. A resource dependency is not online.

   b. Cluster Administrator is currently open on the other node.

   c. The group's disk resource has hardware configuration problems.

   d. A resource dependency is not configured properly.

   Answer: a, c, and d. Resource dependencies must be online and properly configured in order for a group to come online.

4. You are testing a new virtual server's IP Address resource. As part of your troubleshooting process, you decide to take the group offline. However, the IP address seems to still be in use. How is this possible?

   The resource might not be fully offline. An IP Address resource can take up to 3 minutes to go fully offline.

5. Which of the following are possible causes for the Quorum resource not starting?

   a. The SCSI devices are not properly terminated.

   b. The resource is not physically connected to the server.

   c. The Quorum log is corrupt.

   d. A node in the cluster failed.

   Answer: a, b. The Quorum resource will not start if the SCSI devices are not properly terminated or if the resource does not have a physical connection to the server.

Page 245

6. A client can detect both nodes in your cluster but cannot detect any virtual servers. What are possible reasons for this?

   The virtual server might not have its own IP Address or Network Name resources, or if these resources exist, they might not be online. Another reason that a client might not detect a virtual server is that the nodes were not configured to use WINS or DNS properly.

7. Which of the following information is displayed in all cluster log entries?

   a. Event description

b. Component abbreviation

c. Process ID

d. Timestamp

Answer: a, c, and d. All cluster log entries contain a process ID, a thread ID, a timestamp, and an event description. A component abbreviation is contained only in a component event log entry.

8. Explain how the tracking of process and thread IDs can be helpful.

Process and thread IDs can help you trace activity and actions that occur in Cluster Service. Tracing these IDs can be helpful when you're trying to determine why a process is requiring a lot of time to complete.

9. Under which of the following conditions should you start Cluster Service with the *–noquorumlogging* switch?

a. When you back up the Quorum log

b. When you restore the system state to a node

c. When you recover from a missing or damaged Quorum log

d. When you back up the local Quorum database

Answer: c. The *–noquorumlogging* switch is used with the *–debug* switch to restore or re-create the Quorum log while Cluster Service is starting.

10. What Cluster Service information can and cannot be backed up using Windows 2000 Backup?

The Cluster Registry snapshot files, the Quorum log file, the registry checkpoint files for each resource, and the crypto checkpoint files for each resource can be backed up using Windows 2000 Backup. The local cluster registry hive, clusdb, cannot be backed up using this method.

Chapter 8
Installing and Supporting Exchange Server 2000 in a Clustered Environment

Page 266

1. Which of the following is not considered an Exchange resource?

a. EVS

b. System Attendant

c. Information Store

d. Routing

Answer: a. An EVS is not one of the Exchange resources discussed in Lesson 1.

2. Why does Microsoft recommend that you not install Exchange Server 2000 on a domain controller?

A domain controller requires many computer resources and much processing power. Exchange also requires many resources, so it is not a good idea to put so much demand on one machine.

3. What two things must you do before you install Exchange Server 2000?

   a. Extend the Active Directory schema using the DomainPrep argument.

   b. Extend the Active Directory schema using the ForestPrep argument.

   c. Add domain groups using the DomainPrep argument.

   d. Add domain groups using the ForestPrep argument.

   Answer: b, c. While the schema must be extended before an installation, the ForestPrep process will do this. The forest and domain must be prepared before you install Exchange 2000 on a cluster.

4. The Exchange Group is owned by only one node. Why?

   If both nodes were listed as preferred owners of the group, when one node failed, the group would fail over and fail back repeatedly. This would cause the Exchange Group to be unavailable and would negate the use of Cluster Service.

5. Which of the following are requirements for installing Exchange Server 2000 on a cluster?

   a. Exchange and Cluster Service must be installed using the same account.

   b. NNTP must be installed on both nodes in the cluster.

   c. The cluster's domain must have a DNS server available.

   d. IIS does not need to be installed on the nodes of the cluster.

   Answer: a, b, and c. You must install Exchange using the Cluster Service account. Ensure that NNTP is installed on both nodes of the cluster. Verify that a DNS server is available for the cluster's domain.

6. An EVS requires a Physical Disk resource. What are the responsibilities of the Physical Disk resource?

   It is responsible for storing the Exchange databases, message tracking logs, and SMTP queues.

Page 267

7. Which of the following are the primary tools for administering an Exchange server?

   a. System Monitor

   b. Exchange System Manager

   c. Active Directory Sites and Services

   d. Active Directory Users and Computers

   Answer: b, d. The Exchange System Manager and Active Directory Users and Computers are used for administering Exchange Server. System Monitor is used to monitor performance, and Active Directory Sites and Services is used to manage a different area of Active Directory.

8. Why is it unwise to run Exchange System Manager on a cluster node?

   If a failover occurs while the Exchange System Manager is running on a cluster node, it can potentially lock up.

9. Which of the following mail programs support Exchange Server 2000 address lists?

   a. Outlook Express

   b. Outlook 97

   c. Microsoft Mail

   d. Outlook 2000

   Answer: b, d. Only Outlook 97, 98, and 2000 support Exchange 2000 address lists. Outlook Express and Microsoft Mail do not.

10. When should the Services application be used to stop or start Exchange-related services on a clustered Exchange 2000 server?

   Never. Doing so will cause the Cluster Resource Manager to see the resource as failed and might result in unpredictable consequences when the Cluster Resource Manager tries to restart or fail over the cluster resource that the service belongs to.

Chapter 9
Installing and Supporting SQL Server 2000 in a Clustered Environment

Page 289

1. How many virtual servers are available in an active/passive clustered SQL Server installation?

   a. 2

   b. 1

   c. 1 on each node

   d. 0

   Answer: b. The active/passive configuration allows only one virtual server.

2. In a SQL Server 2000 cluster, what components will fail over when a failure occurs?

   Other than the resources and the group, only the database files fail over. The other files and information needed to operate SQL Server are located on each node, so they do not need to fail over.

3. Which installation program is used to install the Microsoft Distributed Transaction Coordinator (MS DTC) service on a cluster node?

a. Cluster Wizard (comclust.exe)

b. Cluster Service Configuration Wizard (cluscfg.exe)

c. Windows 2000 Setup

d. SQL Server 2000 Setup

Answer: c. The MS DTC service, MS DTC proxy, and Component Services administrative tools are installed by default as part of the Windows 2000 setup. Thus, they should already be present on each node of a cluster when SQL Server 2000 is installed.

4. What name do you use when you connect to a clustered instance of SQL Server 2000?

You must use the Virtual_SERVER\Instance-name string rather than the computer name when you connect to a clustered instance of SQL Server.

5. Which installation program is used to install MS DTC on a clustered virtual server?

a. Cluster Wizard (Comclust.exe)

b. Cluster Service Configuration Wizard (Cluscfg.exe)

c. Windows 2000 Setup

d. SQL Server 2000 Setup

Answer: a. The Cluster Wizard is used to install and configure MS DTC on a clustered virtual server.

Page 290

6. Why is using the Quorum resource to store the SQL Server data files not recommended?

Because the Quorum resource requires that all nodes in the cluster be able to access it. It is impossible to stop certain nodes from accessing the SQL data files, if the data resides on the same disk as the Quorum resource.

7. What do you do on the Failover Clustering page of the SQL Server Installation Wizard?

a. Add IP addresses

b. Choose cluster groups

c. Set virtual server names

d. Select nodes to configure

Answer: a. The Failover Clustering page allows you to add and remove IP addresses.

8. What actions must you perform after you make changes to the SQL Server service account in order for the changes to take affect?

On a clustered SQL Server, SQL Server, Fulltext Search, and SQL Agent services will not restart automatically after you make changes to the properties of the SQL Server service account. You must restart these services manually using the Windows Cluster Administrator utility.

9. Which of the following methods should you use to start SQL Server on a cluster?

   a. From the Windows 2000 Services snap-in

   b. Using *net start MSSQLServer* from a command prompt

   c. Using SQL Server Service Manager

   d. Using Cluster Administrator

   Answer: c, d. You should use only SQL Server Service Manager or Cluster Administrator to start the SQL Server service.

10. On a clustered SQL Server, how can you prevent a failover from occurring when a service such as Fulltext Search or SQL Server Agent fails?

   You can use Cluster Administrator to configure specific services so that the SQL Server group is prevented from failing over. For example, to prevent a failover when the Fulltext Search service fails, deselect the Affect The Group check box on the Advanced tab of the Fulltext Properties dialog box. This will not prevent Fulltext Search from restarting if SQL Server causes a failover for some other reason.

Chapter 10
Introduction to Network Load Balancing

Page 314

1. What issues should you consider when you add servers to an existing NLB cluster?

   First, you must consider why you're adding the servers. If network traffic has increased, you must be sure that the added bandwidth will not saturate your network or the CPUs in the servers. You should also make sure the servers have the same configuration. All the servers must use the same operations mode—unicast or multicast. You cannot mix the two. Also, make sure that each server has a unique host priority. It is also a good idea to check the event log after adding a server to the NLB cluster to make sure there are no errors.

2. What IP address is unique for each server in an NLB cluster?

   a. Virtual IP address

   b. Primary IP address

   c. Multi-homed IP address

   d. Dedicated IP address

   Answer: d. Each server is given a unique IP address for outbound requests.

3. Why is it typically undesirable to have the NLB server's cluster adapter on the same switch as the primary adapter of other computers when you use unicast mode?

   Unicast mode causes switch flooding, which creates unnecessary traffic on the network.

4. Which statement below is most accurate?

   a. Unicast mode with a single network card is the most efficient networking solution for an NLB cluster.

   b. Multicast with a single network card is the most efficient networking solution for an NLB cluster.

   c. Unicast and multicast with two network cards perform about the same, but unicast is more compatible with most networks.

   d. Unicast and multicast with two network cards perform about the same, but multicast is more compatible with most networks.

   Answer: c. The two modes perform about the same, but some routers and switches are not compatible with multicast mode and might need additional configuration in order to work properly.

5. When you use NLB in unicast mode, why is it desirable to connect the dedicated cluster adapters to the network using a switch rather than a hub?

   A switch will perform better on the dedicated adapter because packets are switched only to the port to which the specific dedicated adapter is connected. In most situations, a switch performs better than a hub.

Page 315

6. If one server in the NLB cluster fails to hear from another server, how many seconds will it wait by default before it starts the convergence process?

   a. 10 seconds

   b. 1 second

   c. 5 seconds

   d. 11 seconds

Answer: c. By default, the server will wait 5 seconds or five 1-second cycles.

7. Why can't NLB clustering guarantee that your server application will respond to requests? What should you do to ensure that your server application is responding to all requests?

NLB clustering does not guarantee that your server will respond to requests properly because, for example, the NLB server might be functioning properly but the Web service might not be running. In this case, the server in the NLB cluster will not respond to a request. Using a program such as Cluster Sentinel, you can check to make sure that the Web server is responding to requests. If it is not, you can remove it from the cluster and alert the system administrator.

8. In which scenario should you set affinity to None?

   a. When you implement SSL on a Web server

   b. When a Web server is managing state in a database on a back-end server.

   c. When clients are connecting to Terminal Services on the local network

   d. When you're using an SMTP server in an NLB cluster

   Answer: b. When state is managed on a back-end server, each server does not keep state information local, so there's no need to use Single or Class C affinity. When you use SSL on a server, affinity is required to manage the state of the SSL connection. When you implement Terminal Services in an NLB cluster, you should use Single or Class C affinity in case the user disconnects from the session on the server and later wants to reconnect. On a LAN, you'll probably want to set affinity to Single so that all the clients on the same class C subnet don't end up connecting to one server. When you use SMTP in an NLB cluster, you set the filtering mode to Single rather than Multiple because you will run only one SMTP server at a time on the cluster.

9. If you're running an e-commerce site using IIS and NLB clustering, do you need to always set affinity to Single or Class C to preserve state? Why or why not?

   You can set affinity to None on your cluster even if your e-commerce site requests state for the user. State can be managed in a back-end database that all the servers in the cluster access. The problem comes when you run SSL, which most e-commerce sites do. SSL requires state to operate properly, so you must typically set affinity to Single or Class C to preserve state.

10. What process of NLB requires more CPU power as the number of requests increases?

    a. Filtering

b. Convergence

c. Transferring

d. Routing

Answer: a. As network traffic increases, the number of CPU cycles required to filter requests increases on all servers in the NLB cluster.

Chapter 11
Implementing Network Load Balancing

Page 338

1. Which NLB model is the best choice for a cluster when intracluster communication is necessary and the amount of outside traffic targeting the cluster hosts is limited?

    a. Single network adapter in unicast mode

    b. Multiple network adapters in unicast mode

    c. Single network adapter in multicast mode

    d. Multiple network adapters in multicast mode

    Answer: c. If you expect a limited amount of outside traffic and you require the cluster hosts to be able to communicate with each other, this is the best model to use.

2. Why is a second network adapter recommended?

    It can improve network performance and speed up access to back-end databases.

3. Which of following requirements must an application meet in order to be load balanced?

    a. The clients must be able to connect using TCP/IP.

    b. The application must use TCP or UDP ports.

    c. Multiple instances of an application must be able to run concurrently.

    d. The application must bind to a computer name.

    Answer: a, b, c. A load-balanced application must connect using TCP/IP, must use TCP or UDP ports, and must have multiple instancing abilities. If the application binds to a computer name, it cannot be load balanced.

4. What do the port rules determine?

    How cluster traffic will be distributed among the hosts in the cluster

5. Which of the following must be configured for NLB to operate properly?

    a. Cluster parameters

    b. TCP/IP

c. Host parameters

d. Port rules

Answer: All of the above

Page 339

6. What is the difference between the primary IP address and the dedicated IP address?

   The primary IP address is the IP address of the cluster. The dedicated IP address is the unique IP address of the cluster host.

7. Which of the following are recommended practices when you create an NLB cluster?

   a. The host parameters on each cluster host should be identical.

   b. The port rules on each cluster host should be identical.

   c. The same primary IP address should be used on all cluster hosts.

   d. The same dedicated IP address should be used on all cluster hosts.

   Answer: b, c. The port rules and primary IP address should be identical. The host parameters and dedicated IP address should be unique on each cluster host.

8. After you enable remote access to your cluster, how do you limit unauthorized access by remote users?

   You can assign a password in the Remote Password box on the Cluster Parameters tab of the Network Load Balancing properties dialog box.

9. Which of the following can hurt the performance of your NLB cluster?

   a. Paging file size

   b. Cluster hosts connected to a switch

   c. WINS

   d. Microsoft Exchange

   Answer: a, b, c. The paging file size, a switch cluster connection, and WINS could negatively affect the NLB cluster's performance.

10. What steps are required to install the NLB driver as part of a default Windows 2000 Advanced Server installation?

    None. The NLB driver is automatically installed during the installation of Windows 2000 Advanced Server and Datacenter Server. You simply have to enable and configure it on the server in order for it to work.

A P P E N D I X   B

Cluster.exe Command Reference

This appendix describes the options and parameters supported by the Cluster.exe command-line utility. Cluster.exe allows you to configure the following five primary cluster categories:

- Cluster
- Cluster Node
- Cluster Group
- Cluster Resource
- Cluster ResourceType

The categories and their associated arguments are described below.

Cluster

When you configure options on the cluster itself, use the following syntax:

```
CLUSTER [cluster name] /option
```

The cluster name is optional. If you do not specify a cluster name, Cluster.exe will attempt to connect to the cluster running on the node on which you're running Cluster.exe. Table B.1 describes the Cluster options.

Table B.1   Cluster Command Options

Option	Description
/Rename:cluster name	Renames a cluster.
/Version	Displays the Cluster Service version number.
/QuorumResource:resource name [/Path:path] [/Maxlogsize:size]	Changes the name of the Quorum resource or the location or size of the Quorum log.
/List:[domain name]	Displays a list of clusters in the domain to which the computer belongs or displays a specified domain.
/? or /Help	Displays the cluster syntax.

Cluster Node

To configure options on a specific node in the cluster, use the following syntax:

```
CLUSTER [cluster name] NODE [node name] /option
```

The cluster name is optional. The node name is optional only when you use the /Status command. If no node name and no options are specified, the command defaults to /Status. Table B.2 describes the Cluster Node options.

Table B.2   Cluster Node Options

Option	Description
/Status	Displays the cluster node status (Up, Down, or Paused).
/Pause	Pauses a node.
/Resume	Resumes a paused node.
/Evict	Evicts a node from a cluster.
/Properties [propname=propvalue]	Displays the node properties. Use propname=propvalue to set the value of specific node properties. Note: You can only change the node's description using this option.
/PrivProperties [propname=propvalue]	Displays private node properties. Use propname=propvalue to set the value of specific private node properties. (There are no private properties on cluster nodes by default, but software vendors can add them to extend Cluster Service functionality.)
/? Or /Help	Displays the Cluster Node syntax.

Cluster Group

To configure options on a group in the cluster, use the following syntax:

```
CLUSTER [cluster name] GROUP [group name] /option
```

The cluster name is optional. The group name is optional only when you use the /Status command. If you do not specify a group name when you use the /Status command, Cluster.exe displays the status for all groups. Table B.3 describes the Cluster Group options. If no group name and no option are specified, the command defaults to the /Status option.

Table B.3   Cluster Group Options

Option	Description
[group name] /Status	Displays the status of a group (Online, Offline, or Partially Online).
/Status [/Node:node name]	Displays all the groups that are online on a particular node.
/Create	Creates a group.
/Delete	Deletes a group.
/Rename:new group name	Renames a group.
/MoveTo [:node name] [/Wait[:timeout in seconds]]	Moves a group to another node.
/Online [:node name] [/Wait[:timeout in seconds]]	Brings a group online.
/Offline [:node name] [/Wait[:timeout in seconds]]	Takes a group offline.
/Properties [propname=propvalue]	Displays a group's properties. Use propname=propvalue to set the value of specific group properties. (See Table B.4 for more information.
/PrivProperties [propname=propvalue]	Displays private properties of a group. Use propname=propvalue to set the value of specific private group properties. (There are no private group properties by default, but software vendors can add them to extend the Cluster Service functionality.)
/ListOwners	Displays a list of preferred owners.
/SetOwners:node list	Specifies the preferred owner.
/? Or /Help	Displays the Cluster Group syntax.

Cluster Group Property Names

Table B.4 describes the common Cluster Group property names, their uses, and valid settings.

Table B.4   Common Cluster Group Property Names

Property Name	Description
Description	Describes a group.
PersistentState	Describes the last known persistent state of a group (True = online; False = offline).
FailoverThreshold	Specifies the number of times Cluster Service will attempt to fail over a group before it concludes that the group cannot be brought online anywhere in the cluster.
FailoverPeriod	Specifies the interval, in hours, during which Cluster Service will attempt to fail over a group.
AutoFailbackType	Set to ClusterGroupPreventFailback (0) to prevent failback. Set to ClusterGroupAllowFailback (1) to allow failback.
FailbackWindowStart	Specifies the start time, on a 24-hour clock, for failback of a group to its preferred node. Values must be between 0 (midnight) and 23 (11:00 P.M.) local time for the cluster.
FailbackWindowEnd	Specifies the end time, on a 24-hour clock, for failback of a group to its preferred node. The valid values are as shown for FailbackWindowStart.

Cluster Resource

To configure options on a resource in the cluster, use the following syntax:

```
CLUSTER [cluster name] RESOURCE [resource name] /option
```

The cluster name is optional. The resource name is optional only when you use the /Status command. Table B.5 describes the Cluster Resource options.

Table B.5   Cluster Resource Options

Options	Description
/Status	Displays the status of a resource (Online, Offline, or Failed).
/Create /Group:group name /Type:res-type [/Separate]	Creates a new resource in a specified group. Use /Separate to specify that the resource should run in a separate Resource Monitor.
/Delete	Deletes a resource.
/Rename:new resource name	Renames a resource.
/AddOwner:node name	Adds a node name to the Possible Owners list.
/RemoveOwner:node name	Removes a node name from the Possible Owners list.
/ListOwners	Displays a list of Possible Owners.
/MoveTo:group	Moves the resource to a different group.
/Properties [propname=propvalue]	Displays the resource properties. Use propname=propvalue to set the value of specific resource properties.
/PrivProperties [propname=propvalue]	Displays the private resource properties. Use propname=propvalue to set the value of specific private resource properties. (See Table B.6 for more information.)
/Fail	Initiates resource failure.
/Online [/Wait[:timeout in seconds]]	Brings the resource online.
/Offline [/Wait[:timeout in seconds]]	Takes the resource offline.
/ListDependencies	Lists the dependencies for a resource.
/AddDependency:resource	Adds a dependency for a resource.
/RemoveDependency:resource	Removes a dependency for a resource.
/? Or /Help	Displays the Cluster Resource syntax.

Note When you use the /Online or /Offline argument, */Wait:timeout in milliseconds* specifies how long Cluster.exe should wait before canceling the command if the command does not complete successfully. By default, Cluster.exe waits indefinitely or until the resource state changes.

Cluster Resource Property Names

Table B.6 describes the common Cluster Resource Property names, their uses, and valid settings.

Table B.6   Common Cluster Resource Property Names

Property Name	Description
Description	Changes the text that describes a resource.
DebugPrefix	Specifies the appropriate debugger for the resource. (For more information, see the Microsoft Platform SDK.)
SeparateMonitor	Indicates whether a resource shares a Resource Monitor. Valid values are *True* and *False*.
PersistentState	Describes the last known persistent state of a resource. Because a resource cannot be online if its group is not online, it makes no sense to save the resource's PersistentState property unless the resource is offline.
LooksAlivePollInterval	Specifies the recommended interval, in milliseconds, that Cluster Service should poll a resource to determine whether it appears operational. If a resource does not have a value for the LooksAlivePollInterval property, a default value will be taken from the LooksAlivePollInterval property for the resource type.
IsAlivePollInterval	Specifies the interval, in milliseconds, that Cluster Service will poll a resource to determine whether it is operational. If a value is not specified, a default value will be taken from the IsAlivePollInterval property for the specific resource type. IsAlivePollInterval cannot be set to 0.

(continued)

Property Name	Description
RestartAction	Describes the action to perform if the resource fails. The choices are:
	ClusterResourceDontRestart (0): Do not restart following a failure.
	ClusterResourceRestartNoNotify (1): If the resource exceeds its restart threshold within its restart period, Cluster Service will not attempt to fail over the group to another node.
	ClusterResourceRestartNotify (2): If the resource exceeds its restart threshold within its restart period, Cluster Service will attempt to fail over the group to another node.
	The default, ClusterResourceRestartNotify, allows the resource to affect the group, which can cause the group to fail over to another system.
RestartThreshold	Specifies how many times Cluster Service will attempt to restart the resource during the RestartPeriod before failing over the group.
RestartPeriod	Specifies the amount of time allowed for the restart attempts to reach the RestartThreshold before Cluster Service fails over the group.
PendingTimeout	Specifies the amount of time a Pending Online or Pending Offline resource has to resolve its status before Cluster Service takes the resource Offline or assigns it Failed status. The default value is 3 minutes.

Cluster Resource Private Properties

Some resources store private properties. For example, to see the disk signature for the Disk L: resource, type the following at the Windows command prompt:

```
cluster resource "disk l:" /priv
```

Cluster ResourceType

To configure options on a ResourceType in the cluster, use the following syntax:

```
CLUSTER [cluster name] RESOURCETYPE [resource type display name] /
option
```

The cluster name is optional. The resource type name is optional only when you use the /List command. Table B.7 describes the Cluster ResourceType options. The default is /List if no option and no resource type are specified.

Table B.7   Cluster ResourceType Options

Options	Description
/List	Lists the available installed resource types.
/Create /DllName:dllname /Type:type name /Isalive:interval /LooksAlive:internal	Creates a resource type.
/Delete [/Type]	Deletes a resource type. If Cluster Service cannot access the resource DLL, specify the resource type name with the /Type option instead of specifying the resource type display name.
/Properties [propname=propvalue]	Displays the resource type properties. Use propname=propvalue to set the value of specific resource type properties.
/PrivProperties [propname=propvalue]	Displays the resource type private properties. Use propname=propvalue to set the value of specific private resource type properties. (There are no private properties by default, but software vendors can add private resource type properties to their resource types to extend the Cluster Service functionality.
/? Or /Help	Displays the Cluster ResourceType syntax.

Cluster ResourceType Property Names

Table B.8 describes the common ResourceType property names, their uses, and valid settings.

Table B.8   Common ResourceType Property Names

Property Name	Description
Name	Changes the display name of a resource type.
Description	Changes the text that describes a resource type.
DllName	Specifies the name of the DLL for a specific resource type.
DebugPrefix	Specifies the appropriate debugger for the resource type. (For more information, see the Microsoft Platform SDK.)
AdminExtensions	Describes one or more class identifiers (CLSIDs) for Cluster Administrator extensions.
LooksAlivePollInterval	Specifies the interval, in milliseconds, that Cluster Service will poll resources of a particular resource type to determine whether they appear operational.
IsAlivePollInterval	Specifies the interval, in milliseconds, that Cluster Service will poll resources of a particular resource type to determine whether they are operational.

Cluster.exe Command Abbreviations

Table B.9 lists the optional command abbreviations supported by Cluster.exe.

Table B.9   Cluster.exe Command Abbreviations

Command	Abbreviation	Command	Abbreviation
AddDependency	AddDep	QuorumResource	Quorum
DllName	Dll	RemoveDependency	RemoveDep
ListDependencies	ListDep	Rename	Ren
MoveTo	Move	Resource	Res
Online	On	ResourceType	ResType
Offline	Off	Status	Stat
PrivProperties	Priv	Version	Ver
Properties	Prop or Props		

APPENDIX   C

Error Messages

This appendix describes common error messages generated by Cluster Service and other sources.

Cluster Service Error Messages

Table C.1 describes error messages generated by Cluster Service.

Table C.1

Event ID	Description	Problem	Solution
1000	Cluster Service suffered an unexpected fatal error at line ### of source module %path%. The error code was 1006.	Messages such as this can appear when a fatal error causes Cluster Service to terminate on the node that experienced the error.	Check the System event log and the cluster diagnostic log file for more information. Cluster Service might have to restart after the error. The error might indicate serious problems with hardware or other causes.
1002	Cluster Service handled an unexpected error at line 528 of source module G:\Nt\Private\ Cluster\Resmon\Rmapi.c. The error code was 5007.	If this message appears right after you install Cluster Service, you can ignore it if Cluster Service starts and successfully forms or joins the cluster. Otherwise, it can indicate a corrupt Quorum log file or other problem.	Ignore the error if the cluster appears to be working properly. Otherwise, you can try creating a new Quorum log file using the *-noQuorumlogging* or *-fixQuorum* parameters (as documented in the *Cluster Service Administrator's Guide*).
1006	Cluster Service was halted because of a cluster member-ship or communication error. The error code was 4.	Nodes might have lost the ability to communicate with each other, thus affecting cluster membership.	Check network adapters and connections between nodes. Check the System event log for errors. A network prob-lem might be preventing reliable communication between cluster nodes.

(continued)

Table C.1 *continued*

Event ID	Description	Problem	Solution
1007	A new node, <ComputerName>, has been added to the cluster.	There is no problem. The Cluster Service setup program ran on an adjacent computer, and the node was admitted for cluster membership.	No action is required.
1009	Cluster Service could not join an existing cluster and could not form a new cluster. It has terminated.	Cluster Service started and attempted to join a cluster. The node might not be a member of an existing cluster because of eviction by an administrator. Also, because a cluster already exists with the same cluster name, the node could not form a new cluster with the same name.	Make sure you have the correct cluster name. If this is not the problem, remove Cluster Service from the affected node and reinstall it.
1010	Cluster Service is shutting down because the current node is not a member of any cluster. You must reinstall Cluster Service to make this node a member of a cluster.	Cluster Service tried to run but found that it is not a member of an existing cluster, perhaps because of eviction by an administrator or an incomplete attempt to join a cluster.	Remove Cluster Service from the affected node and reinstall it.
1011	The cluster node <ComputerName> has been evicted from the cluster.	An administrator evicted the specified node from the cluster.	If you want the node to be a part of the cluster, you must rejoin it. Otherwise, uninstall Cluster Service.
1012	Cluster Service did not start because the version of Windows NT is incorrect. Cluster Service runs only on Windows NT Server Enterprise Edition, with Service Pack 3 or later.	This error can occur if you force an upgrade using the installation disks, which effectively removes any service packs installed.	Make sure that the cluster node is running on Windows NT Server Enterprise Edition, with Service Pack 3 or later.
1015	No checkpoint record was found in the log file W:\Mscs\ Quolog.log; the checkpoint file is invalid or was deleted.	Cluster Service had difficulty reading data from the Quorum log file. The log file might be corrupted.	If Cluster Service fails to start because of this problem, try starting it manually using the *noQuorumlogging* parameter. If you need to adjust the Quorum disk designation, use the *fixQuorum startup* parameter when you start Cluster Service. Both of these parameters are covered in the *Cluster Service Administrator's Guide*.

Event ID	Description	Problem	Solution
1016	Cluster Service failed to obtain a checkpoint from the cluster database for the log file W:\Mscs\Quolog.log.	Cluster Service had difficulty establishing a checkpoint for the Quorum log file. The log file might be corrupt, or there might be a disk problem.	You might need to recover from a corrupt Quorum log file or run chkdsk on the volume to check for file system corruption.
1019	The log file D:\Cluster Service\ Quolog.log was found to be corrupt. An attempt will be made to reset it, or you can use Cluster Administrator to adjust the maximum size.	The Quorum log file for the cluster was found to be corrupt. The system will attempt to solve the problem.	The system will try to solve this problem, but this error might also indicate that you should increase the cluster property for maximum size (on the Quorum tab). You can fix this problem manually by using the *-noQuorumlogging* parameter.
1021	Insufficient space is left on the Quorum device for the Quorum log files, so changes to the cluster registry cannot be made.	Available disk space is low on the Quorum device.	Free some space on the Quorum device by removing data or unnecessary files. If necessary, designate another disk as the Quorum device.
1022	Insufficient space is left on the Quorum device, so Cluster Service cannot start.	Available disk space is low on the Quorum device.	Free some space on the Quorum device by removing data or unnecessary files so that the cluster can operate. If necessary, use the *-fixquorum* startup option to start one node. Bring the Quorum resource online and adjust free space, or designate another disk as the Quorum device.
1023	The Quorum resource was not found. Cluster Service has terminated.	The device designated as the Quorum resource could not be found. The device might have failed at the hardware level, or the disk resource corresponding to the Quorum drive letter might not match or might no longer exist.	Use the *-fixquorum* startup option for Cluster Service. Troubleshoot the problem with the Quorum disk. If necessary, designate another disk as the Quorum device and restart Cluster Service before starting other nodes.

(continued)

Table C.1 *continued*

Event ID	Description	Problem	Solution
1024	The registry checkpoint for Cluster resource <resourcename> could not be restored to registry key <registrykeyname>. The resource might not be functioning correctly. Make sure no other processes have open handles to registry keys in this registry subkey.	The registry key checkpoint imposed by Cluster Service failed because an application or process has an open handle to the registry key or subkey.	Close any applications that might have an open handle to the registry key so that it can be replicated as configured with the resource properties. If necessary, contact the application vendor about the problem.
1034	The disk associated with the cluster disk resource <resourcename> could not be found. The expected signature of the disk was <signature>.	Cluster Service attempted to mount a Physical Disk resource in the cluster. The cluster disk driver could not locate a disk with this signature. The disk might be offline or might have failed. This error can also occur if the drive has been replaced or reformatted or if another system continues to hold a reservation for the disk.	Determine why the disk is offline or nonoperational. Check cables, termination, and power for the device. If the drive has failed, replace the drive and restore the resource to the same group as the old drive. Delete the old resource. Restore data from a backup and adjust resource dependencies within the group to point to the new disk resource. If the disk was removed from the cluster, the resource should be deleted. If the disk was replaced, the resource must be deleted and re-created to bring the disk online. If the disk has not been removed or replaced, it might be currently inaccessible because it is reserved by another cluster node.
1035	The cluster Disk resource %1 could not be mounted.	Cluster Service attempted to mount a Disk resource in the cluster but could not complete the operation. This might be due to a file-system problem, a hardware issue, or a drive-letter conflict.	Check for drive-letter conflicts, file-system issues in the System event log, and hardware problems.

Event ID	Description	Problem	Solution
1036	The cluster Disk resource <resourcename> did not respond to a SCSI inquiry command.	The Disk resource did not respond to the issued SCSI command. This usually indicates a hardware problem.	Check the SCSI bus configuration and the configuration of SCSI adapters and devices. This problem might indicate a misconfigured or failing device.
1037	The cluster Disk resource %1 has failed a file-system check. Please check your disk configuration.	Cluster Service tried to mount a Disk resource in the cluster. A file-system check was necessary and failed during the process.	Check cables, termination, and device configuration. If the drive has failed, replace the drive and restore data. You might also need to reformat the partition and restore data from a current backup.
1038	Reservation of cluster disk Disk W: has been lost. Please check your system and disk configuration.	Cluster Service had exclusive use of the disk and lost the reservation of the device on the shared SCSI bus. The disk might have gone offline or failed, another node might have taken control of the disk, or a SCSI bus reset command might have been issued on the bus that caused a loss of reservation.	Check whether another node currently has control of the resource or if the SCSI bus was reset. If the drive failed, you will need to replace it.
1040	The cluster generic service <ServiceName> could not be found.	Cluster Service tried to bring the specified generic service resource online but could not locate it.	Remove the generic service resource if the service is no longer installed. The parameters for the resource might be invalid. Check the generic service resource properties, and confirm the correct configuration.
1041	The cluster generic service <ServiceName> could not be started.	Cluster Service tried to bring the specified generic service resource online. The service could not be started at the operating system level.	Remove the generic service resource if it is no longer installed. The parameters for the resource might be invalid. Check the generic service resource properties to confirm the correct configuration. Make sure the service account has not expired, that it has the correct password, and that it has the necessary rights for the service to start. Check the system event log for any related errors.

(continued)

Table C.1 *continued*

Event ID	Description	Problem	Solution
1042	The cluster generic service <resourcename> failed.	The service associated with the generic service resource failed.	Check the generic service properties and service configuration for errors. Check the system and application event logs for errors.
1043	The NetBIOS interface for the IP Address resource has failed.	The network adapter for the specified IP Address resource has experienced a failure. As a result, the IP Address resource is either offline or the group has moved to a surviving node in the cluster.	Check the network adapter and network connection for problems. Fix the network-related problem.
1044	The cluster IP Address resource %1 could not create the required NETBIOS interface.	Cluster Service tried to initialize an IP Address resource but could not establish a context with NetBIOS. The problem might be related to a network adapter or network adapter driver.	Make sure the network adapter is using a current driver. If the adapter is embedded, find out whether a specific OEM version of the driver is required. If you have many IP Address resources defined, make sure you haven't reached the NETBIOS limit of 64 addresses. If you have IP Address resources defined that do not need NETBIOS affiliation, use the IP Address private property to disable NETBIOS for the address. This option, available in Service Pack 4, helps conserve NETBIOS address slots.
1045	The cluster IP Address resource <IP address> could not create the required TCP/IP interface.	Cluster Service tried to bring an IP address online. The resource properties might specify an invalid network address or a malfunctioning adapter. This error can occur if you replace a network adapter with a different model and continue to use the old or inappropriate driver. As a result, the IP Address resource cannot be bound to the specified network.	Fix the network adapter problem, or change the properties of the IP Address resource to reflect the proper network address for the resource.

Event ID	Description	Problem	Solution
1046	The cluster IP Address resource %1 cannot be brought online because the subnet mask parameter is invalid. Please check your network configuration.	Cluster Service tried to bring an IP Address resource online but could not do so. The subnet mask for the resource is blank or is otherwise invalid.	Correct the subnet mask for the resource.
1047	The cluster IP Address resource %1 cannot be brought online because the IP address parameter is invalid. Please check your network configuration.	Cluster Service tried to bring an IP Address resource online but could not do so. The IP Address property contains an invalid value, possibly because you created the resource incorrectly using an API or the command-line interface.	Correct the IP Address properties for the resource.
1048	The cluster IP address <IP address> cannot be brought online because the specified adapter name is invalid.	Cluster Service tried but failed to bring an IP address online. The resource properties might specify an invalid network or a malfunctioning adapter. This error can occur if you replace a network adapter with a different model. As a result, the IP Address resource cannot be bound to the specified network.	Fix the network adapter problem, or change the properties of the IP Address resource to reflect the proper network for the resource.
1049	The cluster IP Address resource <IP address> cannot be brought online because that address is already present on the network. Please check your network configuration.	Cluster Service tried to bring online an IP address that is already in use on the network. The resource therefore cannot be brought online.	Resolve the IP address conflict, or choose another address for the resource.
1050	The cluster Network Name resource %1 cannot be brought online because the name %1 is already present on the network. Please check your network configuration.	Cluster Service tried to bring a Network Name resource online, but the name is already in use on the network, so the resource cannot be brought online.	Resolve the conflict, or choose another network name.

(continued)

Table C.1 *continued*

Event ID	Description	Problem	Solution
1051	The cluster Network Name resource <resourcename> cannot be brought online because it does not depend on an IP Address resource. Please add an IP address dependency.	Cluster Service tried to bring the Network Name resource online but found that a required dependency was missing. Cluster Service requires an IP address dependency for Network Name resource types. Cluster Administrator presents a pop-up message if you try to remove this dependency without specifying another like dependency.	Replace the IP address dependency for this resource. This error might also indicate problems within the Cluster Registry. Check other resources for possible dependency problems.
1052	The cluster Network Name resource <resourcename> cannot be brought online because the name could not be added to the system.	Cluster Service tried to bring a Network Name resource online, but the attempt failed.	Check the System event log for errors. Check the network adapter configuration and operation. Check the TCP/IP configuration and name resolution methods. Check WINS servers for database problems or invalid static mappings.
1053	The cluster File Share resource <resourcename> cannot be brought online because the share could not be created.	Cluster Service tried to bring the share online, but the attempt to create the share failed.	Make sure the Server service is started and functioning properly. Check the path for the share. Check ownership and permissions on the directory. Check the system event log for details. If diagnostic logging is enabled, check the log for an entry about the share. Check ownership related to this failure. Use the Net Helpmsg <errornumber> command with the error code found in the log entry.
1054	The cluster File Share resource %1 could not be found.	The share corresponding to the named File Share resource was deleted using a mechanism other than Cluster Administrator. This can occur if you select the share with Explorer and choose Not Shared.	You should delete shares or take them offline only by using Cluster Administrator or Cluster.exe. Try re-creating the share manually and then taking it offline using Cluster Administrator or Cluster.exe.

Event ID	Description	Problem	Solution
1055	The cluster File Share resource <sharename> has failed a status check.	Cluster Service periodically monitors the status of cluster resources (using Resource Monitors). In this case, a file share failed a status check. Someone might have attempted to delete the share using Windows NT Explorer or Server Manager instead of Cluster Administrator, or there might be a problem with the Server service or access to the shared directory.	Check the System event log for errors. Check the cluster diagnostic log (if it is enabled) for status codes that might be related to this event. Check the resource properties for proper configuration. Also, make sure the file share has proper dependencies defined for related resources.
1056	The cluster database on the local node is in an invalid state. Please start another node before starting this node.	The cluster database on the local node might be in a default state from the installation process, or the node might not be properly joined with an existing cluster.	Make sure another node of the same cluster is online before you start this node. Upon joining with the cluster, the node will receive an updated copy of the official cluster database, which should solve this problem.
1057	The CLUSDB service could not be opened.	Cluster Service tried to open the CLUSDB registry hive but could not do so. As a result, Cluster Service cannot be brought online.	Check the cluster installation directory for a file called CLUSDB. Make sure the registry file is not held open by any applications and that permissions on the file allow Cluster Service access to this file and directory.
1058	The Cluster Resource Monitor could not load the DLL %1 for resource type %2.	Cluster Service tried to bring a resource online that requires a specific resource DLL for the resource type. The DLL is missing or corrupt or is an incompatible version, so the resource cannot be brought online.	Check the cluster installation directory for the named resource DLL. Make sure the DLL exists in the proper directory on both nodes.

(continued)

Table C.1 *continued*

Event ID	Description	Problem	Solution
1059	The Cluster Resource DLL %1 for resource type %2 failed to initialize.	Cluster Service tried to load the named resource DLL, which failed to initialize. The DLL might be corrupt or might be an incompatible version. As a result, the resource cannot be brought online.	Check the cluster installation directory for the named resource DLL. Make sure the DLL is in the proper directory on both nodes and is the proper version. If the DLL is Clusres.dll, this is the default resource DLL that comes with Cluster Service. Make sure the version/date stamp is equivalent to or later than the version in the Service Pack you're using.
1061	Cluster Service successfully formed a cluster on this node.	This informational message indicates that an existing cluster of the same name was not detected on the network, so this node elected to form the cluster and own access to the Quorum disk.	No action is needed.
1062	Cluster Service successfully joined the cluster.	When Cluster Service started, it detected an existing cluster on the network and was able to successfully join the cluster.	No action is needed.
1063	Cluster Service was successfully stopped.	Cluster Service was stopped manually by the administrator.	No action is needed.
1064	The Quorum resource was changed. The old Quorum resource could not be marked as obsolete. If there is a partition in time, you might lose changes to your database because the node that is down will not be able to get to the new Quorum resource.	The administrator changed the Quorum disk designation without all cluster nodes being present.	When other cluster nodes attempt to join the existing cluster, they might not be able to connect to the Quorum disk or participate in the cluster because their configuration indicates a different Quorum device. You might need to use the *-fixquorum* option to start Cluster Service on these nodes and make configuration changes.
1065	The Cluster resource %1 failed to come online.	Cluster Service tried to bring the resource online, but the resource could not reach an online status. The resource might have exhausted the timeout period allotted for it to reach an online state.	Check any parameters related to the resource, and check the event log for details.

Event ID	Description	Problem	Solution
1066	The Cluster Disk resource <resourcename> is corrupted. Running Chkdsk /F to repair problems.	Cluster Service detected corruption on the disk resource and started Chkdsk /F on the volume to repair the structure. Cluster service automatically performs this operation only for cluster-defined Disk resources (not local disks).	Scan the event log for additional errors. The disk corruption might indicate other problems. Check related hardware and devices on the shared bus and ensure proper cables and termination. This error might indicate failing hardware or a deteriorating drive.
1067	The cluster Disk resource %1 has corrupt files. Running Chkdsk /F to repair problems.	Cluster Service detected corruption on the indicated Disk resource and started Chkdsk /F on the volume to repair the structure. Cluster Service automatically performs this operation only for cluster-defined Disk resources (not local disks).	Scan the event log for additional errors. The disk corruption might indicate other problems. Check related hardware and devices on the shared bus and ensure proper cables and termination. This error might indicate failing hardware or a deteriorating drive.
1068	The cluster File Share resource <resourcename> failed to start. Error 5.	The file share cannot be brought online. The problem might be caused by permissions to the directory or disk in which the directory resides, or it might be related to permission problems within the domain. Error 5 means "Access Denied."	Confirm that the Cluster Service account has access rights to the directory to be shared. Make sure a domain controller is accessible on the network. Make sure dependencies for the share and for other resources in the group are set correctly.
1069	The Cluster resource "Disk G:" failed.	The named resource failed, and Cluster Service logged the event. In this example, a Disk resource failed.	For Disk resources, check the device for proper operation. Check cables, termination, and log files on both cluster nodes. For other resources, check resource properties for proper configuration and make sure dependencies are configured correctly. Check the diagnostic log (if it is enabled) for status codes corresponding to the failure.

(continued)

Table C.1 *continued*

Event ID	Description	Problem	Solution
1070	The cluster node attempted to join the cluster but failed with error 5052.	The cluster node attempted to join an existing cluster but was unable to complete the process. This problem can occur if the node was previously evicted from the cluster.	If the node was previously evicted from the cluster, you must remove and reinstall Cluster Service on the affected server.
1071	Cluster node 2 attempted to join but was refused. Error 5052.	Another node attempted to join the cluster, but this node refused the request.	If the node was previously evicted from the cluster, you must remove and reinstall Cluster Service on the affected server. Look in Cluster Administrator to see whether the other node is listed as a possible cluster member.
1073	Cluster Service was halted to prevent an inconsistency within the cluster. Error 5028.	Cluster Service on the affected node was halted because of an inconsistency between cluster nodes.	Check connectivity between systems. This error might indicate configuration or hardware problems.
1077	The TCP/IP interface for the cluster IP Address resource <resourcename> has failed.	The IP Address resource depends on the proper operation of a specific network interface as configured in the resource properties. The network interface failed.	Check the system event log for errors. Check the network adapter for proper operation and replace the adapter if necessary. Confirm that the proper adapter driver is loaded for the device, and check for newer versions of the driver.
1080	Cluster Service could not write file W:\Cluster Service\ Chk7f5.tmp. This might indicate that the disk is low on space or some other serious condition.	Cluster Service attempted to create a temporary file in the Cluster Service directory on the Quorum disk. Lack of disk space or other factors prevented successful completion of the operation.	Check the Quorum drive for available disk space. The file system might be corrupted or the device might be failing. Check file system permissions to ensure that the Cluster Service account has full access to the drive and directory.
1093---	Node %1 is not a member of cluster %2. If the name of the node has changed, you must reinstall Cluster Service.	Cluster Service attempted to start but found that it was not a valid member of the cluster.	Cluster Service might need to be reinstalled on this node. If the problem is the result of a server name change, evict the node from the cluster (from an operational node) before reinstalling.

Event ID	Description	Problem	Solution
1096	Cluster Service cannot use network adapter %1 because it does not have a valid IP address assigned to it.	The network configuration for the adapter has changed, so Cluster Service cannot use the adapter for the network that was assigned to it.	Check the network configuration. If a DHCP address was used for the primary address of the adapter, the address might have been lost. For best results, use a static address.
1097	Cluster Service did not find any network adapters with valid IP addresses installed in the system, so the node is unable to join a cluster.	The network configuration for the system must be corrected to match the same connected networks as the other node of the cluster.	Check the network configuration, and make sure it agrees with the working node of the cluster. Make sure the same networks are accessible from all systems in the cluster.
1098	The node is no longer attached to cluster network <network_id> by adapter <adapter>. Cluster Service will delete the network interface <interface> from the cluster configuration.	Cluster Service observed a change in network configuration that might have been caused by a change in adapter type or by removal of a network. The network will be removed from the list of available networks.	No action is needed.
1100	Cluster Service discovered that the node is now attached to cluster network <network_id> by adapter <adapter>. A new cluster network interface will be added to the cluster configuration.	Cluster Service noticed a new network that is accessible to the cluster nodes and has added the new network to the list of accessible networks.	No action is needed.
1102	Cluster Service discovered that the node is attached to a new network by adapter <adapter>. A new network and network interface will be added to the cluster configuration.	Cluster Service noticed the addition of a new network. The network will be added to the list of available networks.	No action is needed.
1104	Cluster Service failed to update the configuration for one of the node's network interfaces. The error code was <errorcode>.	Cluster Service attempted to update a cluster node but could not perform the operation.	Use the Net Helpmsg <errorcode> command to find an explanation of the underlying error. For example, error 1393 indicates that a corrupted disk caused the operation to fail.

(continued)

Table C.1 *continued*

Event ID	Description	Problem	Solution
1105	Cluster Service failed to initialize the RPC services. The error code was %1.	Cluster Service attempted to use the required RPC services but could not do so.	Use the Net Helpmsg <errorcode> command to find an explanation for the underlying error. Check the System event log for other RPC-related errors or performance problems.
1107	The cluster node <node name> failed to make a connection to the node over network <network name>. The error code was 1715.	Cluster Service attempted to connect to another cluster node over a specific network but could not do so. This error is a warning message.	Make sure that the specified network is available and functioning correctly. If the node experiences this problem, it might try other available networks to establish the connection.
1109	The node was unable to secure its connection to cluster node %1. The error code was %2. Check that both nodes can communicate with their domain controllers.	Cluster Service attempted to connect to another cluster node but could not establish a secure connection. This might indicate domain connectivity problems.	Make sure the networks are available and functioning correctly. This might be a symptom of larger network problems or domain security issues.
1115	An unrecoverable error caused the join of node <node name> to the cluster to be aborted. The error code was <errorcode>.	A node attempted to join the cluster but was unable to do so.	Use the Net Helpmsg <errorcode> command to get further information about the error. For example, error code 1393 indicates that a disk structure is corrupted and nonreadable. Such an error code might indicate a corrupted Quorum disk.

Other Error Messages

Table C.2 describes relevant error messages generated by sources other than Cluster Service.

Table C.2

Event ID	Source	Error Message	Problem	Solution
9	Disk	The device \Device\ ScsiPort2 did not respond within the timeout period.	An I/O request was sent to a SCSI device but was not serviced within the timeout period. The device timeout was logged by this event. You might have a device or controller problem.	Check SCSI cables, termination, and adapter configuration. Excessive recurrence of this event message might indicate a serious problem that might lead to data loss or corruption. If necessary, contact your hardware vendor for troubleshooting help.
101	W3SVC	The server was unable to add the virtual root "/" for the directory <path> because of the following error: The system cannot find the path specified. The data is the error.	The World Wide Web Publishing service could not create a virtual root for the IIS Virtual Root resource. The directory path might have been deleted.	Re-create or restore the directory and contents. Check the resource properties for the IIS Virtual Root resource, and make sure the path is correct. This problem can occur if you had an IIS Virtual Root resource defined and then uninstalled on Cluster Service without first deleting the resource. In this case, you can evaluate and change virtual root properties using the Internet Service Manager.
1004	DHCP	The DHCP IP address lease <IP address> for the card with network address <media access control address> has been denied.	This system uses a DHCP-assigned IP address for a network adapter. The system attempted to renew the leased address, but the DHCP server denied the request. The address might already be allocated to another system. The DHCP server might also have a problem, which can affect network connectivity.	Correct the DHCP server problems or assign a static IP address. For best results within a cluster, use statically assigned IP addresses.

(continued)

Table C.2 *continued*

Event ID	Source	Description	Problem	Solution
1005	DHCP	DHCP failed to renew a lease for the card with the network address <MAC Address>. The following error occurred: The semaphore timeout period has expired.	This system uses a DHCP-assigned IP address for a network adapter. The system attempted to renew the leased address but was unable to. Network operations on this system might be affected.	A connectivity problem might be preventing access to the DHCP server that leased the address, or the DHCP server might be offline. For best results within a cluster, use statically assigned IP addresses.
2511	Server	The Server service was unable to re-create the share <sharename> because the directory <path> no longer exists.	The Server service tried to create a share using the specified directory path. This problem can occur if you create a share (outside of Cluster Administrator) on a cluster shared device. If the device is not exclusively available to this computer, the Server service cannot create the share. Also, the directory might no longer exist or there might be RPC-related issues.	Correct the problem by creating a shared resource using Cluster Administrator, or correct the problem with the missing directory. Check the dates of RPC files in the system32 directory. Make sure they match the service pack in use or any hotfixes applied.
4199	TCP/IP	The system detected an address conflict for IP address <IP address>, with the system having the network hardware address <media access control address>. Network operations on this system might be disrupted as a result.	Another system on the network might be using one of the addresses configured on this computer.	Resolve the IP address conflict. Check the network adapter configuration and any IP Address resources defined within the cluster.

Event ID	Source	Description	Problem	Solution
5719	Netlogon	No Windows NT Domain controller is available for domain <domain>. The following error occurred: There are currently no logon servers available to service the logon request.	A domain controller for the domain could not be contacted, so proper authentication of accounts could not be completed. This can occur if the network is disconnected or disabled through system configuration.	When you boot with the "No Net" hardware profile, this event is expected and can be ignored. Otherwise, solve the connectivity problem with the domain controller and restart the system.
7000	Service Control Manager	Cluster Service failed to start because of the following error: The service did not start because of a logon failure.	The Service Control Manager attempted to start a service (possibly ClusSvc). It could not authenticate the service account, possibly because of a failure to contact a domain controller or because account credentials are invalid. This error might be seen with Event 7013.	Check the service account name and password and make sure that the account is available and that credentials are correct. Or try running Cluster Service from a command prompt (if you're currently logged on as an administrator) by changing to the %systemroot%\Cluster directory (or the directory on which you installed the software) and typing *ClusSvc -debug*. If the service starts and runs correctly, stop it by pressing Ctrl+C and troubleshoot the service account problem. This error might also be due to network connectivity being disabled through the system configuration or hardware profile. Cluster Service requires network connectivity.

(continued)

Table C.2 *continued*

Event ID	Source	Description	Problem	Solution
7013	Service Control Manager	Logon attempt with current password failed with the following error: There are currently no logon servers available to service the logon request. (The description of this error message can vary based on the actual error. For example, another error listed in the event detail might be: "Logon Failure: unknown username or bad password."	The Service Control Manager attempted to start a service (possibly ClusSvc). It could not authenticate the service account with a domain controller.	The service account might be in another domain, or this system might not be a domain controller. The node can be a nondomain controller, but it must access a domain controller within the domain as well as the domain that the service account belongs to. Inability to contact the domain controller can occur because of a problem with the server, the network, or other factors. The problem is not related to the cluster software and must be resolved before you start Cluster Service. This error can also occur if network connectivity is disabled through the system configuration or hardware profile. Cluster Service requires network connectivity.
7023	Service Control Manager	The Server service terminated with the following error: "The Quorum log could not be created or mounted successfully."	Cluster Service tried to start but could not gain access to the Quorum log on the Quorum disk. This might be because of problems gaining access to the disk or problems joining a cluster that has already formed.	Check the disk and Quorum log for problems. If necessary, check the cluster log file for more information. Other events in the System event log might provide more information.

Glossary

A

active/active A type of cluster in which each node is capable of managing the resource groups specified in the cluster. When one node fails, the other takes control of the resources. All nodes dynamically assume one another's role.

active/passive A type of cluster in which specific resource groups are assigned to certain nodes as the resource's primary nodes. If the primary node fails, the resource fails over to the other node, which becomes active. When the failed node returns online, it resumes control of the resource.

adapter A network interface card (NIC) added to a PC that allows the PC to perform a specialized function, such as accessing a monitor or a communications line.

Address Resolution Protocol (ARP) A protocol for determining a host's Ethernet address from its Internet address.

affinity A relationship between client requests from a Single client address or a Class C network of clients and one of the cluster hosts. Affinity ensures that requests from the specified clients are always handled by the same host. The relationship lasts until convergence occurs (that is, until the membership of the cluster changes) or until the affinity setting is changed. There is no timeout—the relationship is based only on the client IP address.

application programming interface (API) A set of routines that an application uses to request and carry out lower-level services performed by the operating system.

array A collection of data accessed by an index or an element number.

Asynchronous Transfer Mode (ATM) A communications protocol for high-speed data communications.

atomic The property of a transaction that ensures that the transaction will execute completely or not at all.

B

BIOS Basic input/output system. A set of routines that works closely with the hardware to support the transfer of information between elements of the system, such as memory, disks, and the monitor.

boot partition The volume, formatted for an NTFS or FAT file system, that has the Windows NT operating system and its support files. The boot partition can be the same as the system partition. *See also* partition; FAT file system; NTFS.

Boot Protocol (BOOTP) A protocol used for booting diskless workstations.

Bootstrap Protocol A TCP/IP network protocol, defined by RFC 951 and RFC 1542, that is used to configure systems. DHCP is an extension of BOOTP. *See also* DHCP.

C

cache A special memory subsystem in which frequently used data values are duplicated for quick access. A memory cache stores the contents of frequently accessed RAM locations and the addresses where these data items are stored. When the processor references an address in memory, the cache checks to see whether it holds that address. If it does, the data is returned to the processor; if it does not, a regular memory access occurs. A cache is useful when RAM accesses are slow compared with the microprocessor speed because cache memory is always faster than main RAM memory. Some applications designate a certain amount of hard disk space as a disk cache. The application uses this space as temporary storage for files and data.

caching In DNS name resolution, a local cache where information about the DNS domain name space is kept. When a resolver request arrives, the local name server checks both its static information and the cache for the name–to–IP address mapping. *See also* DNS; IP address; mapping.

Checkpoint Manager A component that monitors changes to the key while the resource is online and writes a checkpoint to the Quorum disk if there is a change to the registered key.

Client Network Utility A tool for managing the client Net-Libraries and for defining server alias names. It can also be used to set the default options used by DB-Library applications.

cluster Two or more independent computer systems that are addressed and managed as a single system.

cluster activity The sum of all events that take place in a cluster. Cluster activity includes major blocks of activity such as the initialization, joining, and forming of operations.

Cluster Administrator A client application included with Cluster Service that is used to configure a cluster and its nodes, groups, and resources.

cluster API A collection of functions that are implemented by the cluster software and used by a cluster-aware client or server application, a cluster management application, or a resource DLL (to manage the cluster itself, the cluster nodes, cluster resources, or the configuration database).

cluster-aware application A client application that can run on a cluster node and can be managed as a cluster resource.

cluster log The place where the Quorum resource stores log data, which is maintained by the clustering software. If the nodes in the cluster cannot communicate with each other, only one of them is allowed to continue operating. In this situation, the Quorum resource, which can be owned by only one node, is used to determine which node can continue operating.

cluster management application Application that communicates with Cluster Service on a node. This type of application accesses Cluster Service through a standard API using RPC communication over the TCP/IP protocol.

cluster parameters Parameters that specify the behavior of the cluster. These include primary IP address, subnet mask, full Internet name, multicast support, remote control password, and confirm password parameters.

Cluster Service A software component implemented as a Windows 2000 Advanced Server and Datacenter Server service that controls all aspects of cluster operation and manages the configuration database. Every node in a cluster runs a copy of Cluster Service.

cluster-unaware application A client application that can run on a cluster node but cannot be managed as a cluster resource.

Cluster Verification tool A tool included in the Windows 2000 Resource Kit that verifies that two-node cluster systems are set up properly.

Communications Manager A tool for managing communication with all other nodes of the cluster.

Component Load Balancing (CLB) A technology that allows COM+ components to be load balanced. *See also* load balancing

Component Object Model (COM) An object-oriented programming model that defines how objects interact within a single application or between applications. In COM, client software accesses an object through a pointer to an interface—a related set of functions called *methods*—on the object.

Computer Browser service A service that maintains an up-to-date list of computers and provides the list to applications when requested. The service provides the computer lists displayed in the My Network Places, Select Computer, and Select Domain dialog boxes and, for Windows 2000 Server only, in the Server Manager window.

configuration Modification of the a client's initial setup.

Configuration Database Manager A component that maintains the cluster configuration database.

D

Database Manager A component that maintains the cluster configuration database. Also known as the Configuration Database Manager.

datagram A packet of data and other delivery information that is routed through a packet-switched network or transmitted on a LAN.

default gateway In TCP/IP, the intermediate network device on the local network that has knowledge of the network IDs of the other networks on the Internet. It forwards the packets to other gateways until the packet is eventually delivered to a gateway connected to the specified destination. *See also* gateway; network ID; packet.

dependency A relationship of reliance between two resources that requires them to run in the same group on the same node. Typically, an application is dependent on the disks that contain its data resources.

dependency tree A diagram that depicts the dependency relationships between resources. To create a dependency tree, first list all the resources in a particular group, and then draw arrows from each resource to each resource on which the resource directly depends.

DHCP *See* Dynamic Host Configuration Protocol (DHCP)

DHCP Server resource type A resource type that you can use to provide DHCP Server services from a cluster.

dismount To remove a removable tape or disc from a drive.

Distributed file system (Dfs) A Windows 2000 service consisting of software residing on network clients and servers that transparently links shared folders located on different file servers into a single namespace for improved load sharing and data availability.

Distributed Lock Manager (DLM) A traffic cop that locks cluster resources so that only one node accesses a resource at any instant and keeps the data in synchronization if needed.

DNS *See* Domain Name Service (DNS)

DNS name server In the DNS client-server model, a server containing information about a portion of the DNS database, which makes computer names available to client resolvers querying for name resolution across the Internet. *See also* Domain Name Service (DNS).

domain A group of computers that share a database and have a common security policy; the basic unit of a Windows NT Server LAN. Can also refer to an Internet domain name.

domain controller For a Windows NT Server or Windows 2000 Server domain, the server that authenticates domain logons and maintains the security policy and the security accounts master database for a domain. Domain controllers manage user access to a network, which includes logging on, authentication, and access to the directory and shared resources.

domainlet A small, lightweight domain that contains no user accounts or global catalog servers.

Domain Name Service (DNS) The naming service used on the Internet to provide standard naming conventions for computers using the IP protocol .

dynamic Occurring immediately and concurrently.

Dynamic Host Configuration Protocol (DHCP) An industry-standard TCP/IP protocol that assigns IP configurations to computers. The DHCP server computer makes the assignments and the client computer calls the server computer to obtain the address.

E

Encrypting File System (EFS) A new feature in Windows 2000 that protects sensitive data in files stored on disk using NTFS. It uses symmetric key encryption in conjunction with public key technology to provide file security. It runs as an integrated system service, which makes it easy to manage, difficult to attack, and transparent to the file owner and to applications.

encryption The process of making information indecipherable to protect it from unauthorized viewing or use, especially during network transmission or when it is stored on a transportable magnetic medium.

Ethernet A widely implemented LAN, from which the IEEE 802.3 standard for contention networks was developed. Ethernet uses a bus topology where network nodes are connected by either thin or thick coaxial cable or by twisted-pair wiring. Information on an Ethernet network is sent in variable-length frames containing delivery and control information and up to 1,500 bytes of data.

EULA End-User License Agreement.

Event Log Manager A component that ensures that each node of a cluster has the same event log entries.

Event Processor A component that connects all of the components of Cluster Service, handles common operations, and controls Cluster Service initialization.

Exchange Information Store An Exchange core component that stores users' mailboxes and folders. *See also* public information store; private information store.

Exchange Message Transfer Agent (MTA) A core Exchange component that routes messages to other Exchange MTAs, information stores, connectors, and third-party gateways.

Exchange System Attendant A core maintenance service included with Exchange.

Exchange Virtual Server (EVS) A cluster group that contains a Physical Disk resource, an IP Address resource, a Network Name resource and the Exchange 2000 resources.

F

failback The process of moving resources, either individually or in a group, back to their preferred node after the node has failed and come back online.

failback policy A configuration setting specifying whether resource groups should fail back. You must manually configure your group to fail back after failing over; otherwise, it will continue to run on the alternate node after the failed node comes back online.

failback timing The process of moving resources, either individually or in a group, back to their preferred node after the node has failed and come back online.

failover The process of taking resources, either individually or in a group, offline on one node and bringing them back online on another node. The offline and online transitions occur in a predefined order, with resources that are dependent on other resources taken offline before and brought online after the resources on which they depend.

failover clustering A mechanism that provides a server with a backup partner in case of emergency. If one system fails, the partner takes over.

Failover Manager A component that works with the Resource Manager to manage resources and resource groups and to initiate failover operations.

failover policy A configuration setting that an administrator can set using Cluster Administrator to specify how failover operations will be performed.

failover time The amount of time it takes a resource to complete the failover process. *See also* failover.

FAT file system A method for managing disk storage. A file allocation table (FAT) file system is used by an operating system to keep track of the status of various segments of disk space used for file storage.

fault tolerance The ability of a system to respond to an event such as a power failure so that information is not lost and operations will continue without interruption.

Fiber Distributed Data Interface (FDDI) A standard for high-speed fiber-optic LANs.

Fibre Channel A transmission channel that provides data transfer at one gigabit per second by mapping common transport protocols and merging networking and high-speed input and output in a single connection.

File Share resource A file share accessible by a network path that is supported as a cluster resource by a resource DLL provided with Cluster Service. Also known as an SMB share.

file sharing The use by more than one user of computer files on networks that store files on a central computer or a server. When a single file is shared by many people, access can be regulated through such means as password protection, security clearances, or file locking to prohibit changes to a file by more than one person at a time.

File Transfer Protocol (FTP) The Internet standard high-speed protocol for transferring files from one computer to another.

filtering mode A configuration setting for a port rule that determines load-balancing policy for the range of ports covered by the port rule. The three filtering modes are multiple host, single host, and disabled.

firewall A system or combination of systems that enforces a boundary between two or more networks and keeps hackers out of private networks. Firewalls serve as virtual barriers to passing packets from one network to another.

G

gateway A network software product that allows computers or networks running dissimilar protocols to communicate, providing transparent access to a variety of foreign database management systems (DBMS). A gateway moves specific database connectivity and conversion processing from individual client computers to a single server computer. Communication is enabled by translating up one protocol stack and down the other. Gateways usually operate at the session layer.

Generic Application resource An application that is supported as a cluster resource by a resource DLL provided with Cluster Service.

Generic Service resource A Windows NT service that is supported as a cluster resource by a resource DLL provided with Cluster Service.

Global Update Manager A component that provides a global update service used by other components within Cluster Service.

globally unique identifier (GUID) An identifier that uniquely ID identifies an object. It is expressed in the form *xxxxxxxx-xxxx-xxxx-xxxx-xxxxxxxxxxxx*. An example is F29F85E0-4FF9-AB91-08002B27 B3D9

group/resource group A collection of dependent or related resources that are managed as a single unit. Typically, a group contains all of the resources needed to run a specific application or service. When a group contains a Network Name and IP Address resource, it can be accessed by clients as a virtual server. Operations such as failover that are performed on a group affect all of its members. *See also* virtual server.

H

handling priority A configuration setting in single-host filtering mode that specifies a host's priority for handling all of the cluster's network traffic for that port rule. Handling priority overrides host priority for the range of ports covered by the port rule.

Hardware Compatibility List (HCL) A list of devices supported by an operating system. For example, the Windows 2000 HCL lists the devices supported by Windows 2000. You can download the latest version of that HCL from *www.microsoft.com*.

heartbeat A message that is sent at regular intervals by Cluster Service on one node to Cluster Service on the other nodes to detect failure.

host The main computer in a system of computers or terminals that are connected by communication links.

host parameters Parameters that define how each host functions within the cluster and in load balancing. They include host priority, initial value, dedicated IP address, and subnet mask parameters.

hot swapping A process whereby the user can add and remove hardware components without turning off the computer.

hub A central connecting device in a network that joins communication lines in a star configuration.

I

Input/Output (I/O) Read or write actions that your computer performs. The computer performs a "read" when you type information on your keyboard or select and choose items using your mouse. Also, when you open a file, your computer reads the disk on which the file is located to find and open it. Your computer performs a "write" when it stores, sends, prints, or displays information. For example, it performs a write when it stores information on a disk, displays information on your screen, or sends information through a modem or to a printer.

IDE hard drive Integrated Device Electronics hard drive. A type of disk-drive interface in which the controller electronics reside on the drive itself, eliminating the need for a separate adapter card.

IEEE Institute of Electrical and Electronics Engineers.

IIS Virtual Root resource A virtual-root designation used with Microsoft Internet Information Services (IIS) that supports the WWW, FTP, and Gopher services. IIS virtual roots are supported as cluster resources by a resource DLL provided with Cluster Service. IIS Virtual Root resources can have dependencies on IP Address, Network Name, and Physical Disk resources. Cluster Service does not support virtual roots containing access information.

Internet Control Message Protocol (ICMP) A network-level Internet protocol that provides error correction and other information relevant to IP packet processing.

Internet Protocol (IP) The part of TCP/IP that is responsible for addressing and sending TCP packets over the network.

Interrupt request (IRQ) A method by which a device can request to be serviced by the device's software driver. The system board uses a programmable interrupt controller to monitor the priority of the requests from all devices.

intracluster communication Communication between the hosts of a cluster.

IP address Internet Protocol address. A unique address that identifies a host on a network. It identifies a computer as a 32-bit address that is unique across a TCP/IP network.

IP Address resource A 32-bit number in dotted decimal format that represents an IP address and is supported as a cluster resource by a resource DLL provided with Cluster Service.

IPX/SPX Internetwork Packet Exchange/Sequenced Packet Exchange. These transport protocols are used in Novell NetWare networks. Windows NT implements IPX through NWLink.

IsAlive check A more thorough check than LooksAlive, which tests SQL Server by logging in and performing a simple query on the system catalogs. *See also* LooksAlive check.

L

legacy Any feature in a computer system based on older technology for which compatibility is maintained in other system components. In the context of Windows 98, a legacy feature is a non–Plug and Play feature.

load balancing A technique for scaling performance by distributing load among multiple servers. Network Load Balancing (NLB) distributes load for networked client/server applications in the form of client requests that it partitions across multiple cluster hosts.

load weight A configuration setting for the multiple-host filtering mode within a port rule that specifies the percentage of load-balanced network traffic that this host should handle; allowed values range from *0* to *100*. The actual fraction of traffic handled by each host is computed as the local load weight divided by the sum of all load weights across the cluster.

local area network (LAN) A group of computers and other devices dispersed over a relatively limited area and connected by a communications link that enables them to interact.

Log Manager A component that writes changes to the recovery log stored on the Quorum resource.

LooksAlive check A simple check that verifies that the SQL Server resource is running.

M

MAC address A unique 48-bit number assigned to the NIC by the manufacturer. MAC addresses (which are physical addresses) are used for mapping in TCP/IP network communication. *See also* Media Access Control (MAC); Address Resolution Protocol (ARP).

mapping In TCP/IP, the relationship between a host or computer name and an IP address, used by DNS and NetBIOS name servers on TCP/IP networks. In Windows Explorer, an assignment of a relationship between a driver letter and a network drive. In Windows NT License Manager, the relationship between users and computers in license groups. *See also* DNS; IP address.

MBps Megabytes per second.

Media Access Control (MAC) A layer in the network architecture that deals with network access and collision detection.

Membership Manager A component that tracks which nodes are members of the cluster. The manager writes entries to the log during initialization, form operations, and join operations, and when cluster membership changes.

messaging application program interface (MAPI) An open and comprehensive messaging interface used by programmers to create messaging and workgroup applications such as electronic mail, scheduling, calendaring, and document management applications.

Microsoft Management Console (MMC) A general-purpose management display framework for hosting administration tools.

Microsoft Message Queue Server resource A resource type that allows you to use Microsoft Message Queue Server (MSMQ) in an MSCS cluster.

mount To place a removable tape or disc into a drive.

multicast mode A configuration setting that instructs NLB to add a multicast MAC address to the cluster adapters on all hosts in a cluster. The adapters' existing MAC addresses are not changed. *See also* unicast mode.

Multicast Address Dynamic Client Allocation Protocol (MADCAP) A component of the Windows 2000 DHCP service that is used to support dynamic assignment and configuration of IP multicast addresses on TCP/IP-based networks. Formerly known as Multicast DHCP.

N

Named Pipes An interprocess communication (IPC) protocol that allows one process to communicate with another local or remote process.

NetBEUI NetBIOS Extended User Interface. A LAN transport protocol provided with Windows 98.

NetBIOS Network basic input/output system. A software interface for network communication.

NetLogon Service In Windows NT Server, a service that performs authentication of domain logons and keeps the domain's directory database synchronized between the primary domain controller (PDC) and the other backup domain controllers (BDCs) of the domain.

network Two or more connected computers. Networks are used for sharing resources such as documents, programs, and printers. *See also* workgroup.

network card Hardware that you insert in a computer to connect the computer to a network.

network adapter A hardware card installed in a computer that enables the computer to communicate on a network.

network ID The portion of an IP address that identifies a group of computers and devices located on the same logical network.

network interface card (NIC) An expansion card or other device used to connect a computer to a LAN.

Network Load Balancing (NLB) A clustering technology included with Microsoft Windows 2000 Advanced Server and Datacenter Server that enhances the scalability and availability of mission-critical, TCP/IP-based services such as Web browsing, Terminal Services, virtual private networking, and streaming media servers. This component runs within cluster hosts as part of Windows 2000 and requires no dedicated hardware support.

Network Name resource The friendly name of a device that exists on a network and is supported as a cluster resource by a resource DLL provided with Cluster Service.

node In LANs, a device that is connected to the network and is capable of communicating with other network devices.

Node Manager A component that handles cluster membership and monitors the health of other nodes in the cluster.

NTFS The file system designed for use with the Windows NT operating system. NTFS supports file system recovery and extremely large storage media, in addition to offering other advantages. It also supports object-oriented applications by treating all files as objects with user-defined and system-defined attributes.

O

Object Manager A component that maintains an in-memory database of entities, or objects (nodes, networks, groups, and so on). Each object has an associated type and a set of methods with which other components can manipulate it. Each cluster object is represented in the Object Manager space. The Object Manager does not differentiate between types of objects.

offline Not connected to a network or the Internet. This term also refers to the state of a resource in Cluster Service.

online Connected to a network or the Internet. This term also refers to the state of a resource in Cluster Service.

online transaction processing (OLTP) An application that automates real-time business activities. OLTP is the distributed version of a transaction program (TP).

overhead, disk The amount of disk space required to store index information.

P

packet A transmission unit of fixed maximum size that consists of binary information representing data and a header containing an ID number, source and destination addresses, and error-control data.

paging file A special file on a PC hard disk. With virtual memory under Windows NT, some of the program code and other information is kept in RAM while other information is temporarily swapped into virtual memory. When that information is required again, Windows NT pulls it back into RAM and, if necessary, swaps other information to virtual memory. Also called a swap file.

parameter In programming, a value that is given to a variable, either at the beginning of an operation or before an expression is evaluated by a program. Until the operation is completed, a parameter is effectively treated as a constant value by the program. A parameter can be text, a number, or an argument name assigned to a value that is passed from one routine to another. Parameters are used as a means of customizing program operation.

parity Redundant information that is associated with a block of information. In Windows NT Server, *stripe sets with parity* means that there is one additional parity stripe per row. As a result, you must use at least three, rather than two, disks to allow for this extra parity information. Parity stripes contain the XOR (the Boolean operation called exclusive OR) of the data in that stripe. Windows NT Server, when regenerating a failed disk, uses the parity information in those stripes in conjunction with the data on the good disks to re-create the data on the failed disk. *See also* fault tolerance; stripe set; stripe sets with parity.

Partition a volume, formatted for an NTFS or FAT file system.

Peripheral Component Interconnect (PCI) A local bus for personal computers that provides a high-speed data path between the processor and peripheral devices.

Physical Disk resource A SCSI-attached disk for shared folders or storage. Physical Disk resources are supported as cluster resources by a resource DLL provided with Cluster Service.

port rules Rules that define how the hosts should distribute the incoming requests on a port or range of ports. They include properties such as port range, protocols, filtering mode, affinity, load percentage, equal load distribution, and handling priority parameters.

Possible Owners Nodes in the cluster that are capable of running that resource. By default, both nodes appear in the Possible Owners list, so the resource can run on either node. In most cases, it is appropriate to use this default setting. If you want the resource to be able to fail over, both nodes must be designated as Possible Owners.

preferred node The node on which you prefer each group to run. For example, the static load balancing model performs best when groups are appropriately balanced between two nodes. When a node fails, the remaining node takes over the groups from the failed node, but performance is diminished. By setting those groups to fail back to their preferred server (the failed node), you automatically restore maximum performance when failback occurs. A group does not fail back if a preferred owner is not selected. You will not always choose a preferred server because it might not matter where the group resides; all that might matter is that the group is still running on one of the two nodes, or the nodes might be equally capable of handling the load required to use some or all of the resources.

Print Spooler resource A printer queue that provides access to a network printer connected to the network by an IP address rather than by an individual name. Print Spooler resources are supported as cluster resources by a resource DLL provided with Cluster Service.

private information store The part of the information store that maintains information in users' mailboxes.

process An object type that consists of an executable program, a set of virtual memory addresses, and one or more threads. When a program starts running, a Windows process is created.

protocol A set of rules and conventions by which two computers pass messages across a network. Networking software usually implements multiple levels of protocols layered one on top of one another. Windows 98 includes NetBEUI, TCP/IP, and IPX/SPX-compatible protocols.

public information store The part of the information store that maintains information in public folders.

Q

Quorum A voting mechanism used to guarantee that specific data necessary for recovery can be maintained consistently between all cluster members. This mechanism involves a special resource called the Quorum resource. The recovery data is stored by the Quorum resource, which is typically a Physical Disk resource that can be owned by one cluster node at any point in time. When the node that owns the Quorum resource fails, the surviving nodes arbitrate to take over its ownership. Each Quorum resource receives one vote, and that vote is transitively passed to the node that currently owns the resource. By default, there is only one Quorum resource per cluster.

Quorum recovery log A log maintained by the Checkpoint Manager that contains node registry information.

Quorum resource The Quorum-capable resource selected to maintain the configuration data necessary for recovery of the cluster. This data contains details of all of the changes that have been applied to the cluster database. The Quorum resource is generally accessible to other cluster resources so that any cluster node has access to the most recent database changes.

R

RAM Random-access memory. RAM can be read from or written to by the computer or other devices. Information stored in RAM is lost when you turn off the computer.

Redundant Array of Independent Disks (RAID) A storage device that uses two or more magnetic or optical disks working in tandem to increase performance and provide various levels of error recovery and fault tolerance. RAID can be implemented in software using standard disk controllers, or it can be designed into the disk controller itself. Software RAID solutions are not supported by Cluster Service.

Registry The database repository for information about a computer's configuration. The Registry supersedes use of separate INI files for all system components and applications that know how to store values in the Registry.

Registry checkpoint files Files that contain node-independent storage of cluster configuration and state data.

remote administration Administration of one computer by an administrator located at another computer and connected to the first computer across the network.

Remote Procedure Call (RPC) A message-passing facility that allows a distributed program to call services available on various computers in a network. Used during remote administration of computers, RPC provides a procedural view, rather than a transport-centered view, of networked operations.

reparse point information about the file that may need to be accessed without recalling the file from storage.

resource A physical or logical entity managed by a cluster node. A resource provides a service to clients in a client/server environment.

Resource DLL A DLL containing an implementation of the Resource API for a specific type of resource. The Resource DLL is loaded into the address space of its Resource Monitor.

Resource Manager A component that makes all resource and resource group management decisions and initiates appropriate actions such as startup, restart, and failover.

Resource Monitor A cluster software component that facilitates communication between a node's Cluster Service and one or more of its resources.

rolling upgrade A planned process that takes one node offline to be upgraded while the second node assumes full responsibility for the resources in the cluster.

routing The process of transferring and delivering messages.

S

scope The full, consecutive range of possible IP addresses for a network. DHCP services can be offered to scopes, which typically define a single physical subnet on a network. DHCP servers primarily use scopes to manage network distribution and assignment of IP addresses and any related configuration parameters.

SCSI Small Computer Standard Interface. An I/O bus designed as a method for connecting several classes of peripherals to a host system without requiring modifications to generic hardware and software.

Secure Sockets Layer (SSL) A protocol that supplies secure data communication through data encryption and decryption. SSL enables communication privacy over networks through a combination of public key cryptography and bulk data encryption.

Server service A service that provides RPC support and file, print, and Named Pipe sharing. *See also* Named Pipes; Remote Procedure Call (RPC).

Shared Device model A cluster implementation model in which software applications running on any node in the cluster can gain access to any hardware in the cluster.

Shared Nothing model A cluster implementation model in which each node owns and manages its local disks. Common devices in the cluster are selectively owned and managed by a single node at any time.

shared resource A type of cluster organization in which some resources are accessible to all nodes in the cluster.

Simple Mail Transport Protocol (SMTP) A protocol used for exchanging mail on the Internet.

socket A software object used by a client to connect to a server; basic components include the port number and the network address of the local host.

SQL Server Enterprise Manager A graphical application that allows for easy, enterprise-wide configuration and management of SQL Server and SQL Server objects. You can also use SQL Server Enterprise Manager to manage logins, permissions, and users; create scripts; manage devices and databases; back up databases and transaction logs; and manage tables, views, stored procedures, triggers, indexes, rules, defaults, and user-defined data types. SQL Server Enterprise Manager is installed by SQL Server Setup as part of the server software on Windows NT–based computers and as part of the client software on Windows NT–based and Windows 95/98–based computers. Because SQL Server Enterprise Manager is a 32-bit application, it cannot be installed on computers running 16-bit operating systems.

SQL Mail A component of SQL Server that includes extended stored procedures and allows SQL Server to send and receive mail messages through the built-in Windows NT mail application programming interface (MAPI). A mail message can consist of a short text string, the output from a query, or an attached file.

SQL Profiler A SQL Server tool that captures a continuous record of server activity in real-time. SQL Server Profiler can monitor many different server events and event categories, filter these events with user-specified criteria, and output a trace to the screen, a file, or another SQL Server.

SQL Query Analyzer A SQL Server utility that allows you to enter Transact-SQL statements and stored procedures in a graphical user interface. Query Analyzer also provides the ability to graphically analyze queries.

SQL Server Agent A SQL Server utility that is used to create and manage local or multiserver jobs, alerts, and operators. Job schedules are defined in the Job Properties dialog box. SQL Server Agent communicates with SQL Server to execute the job according to the job's schedule.

static load balancing The ability to manually move a group between two nodes to balance the load between the nodes. Cluster Service supports static load balancing.

stripe set A method of saving of data across identical partitions on different drives. A stripe set by itself does not provide fault tolerance; however, stripe sets with parity do provide fault tolerance. See also fault tolerance; partition; stripe sets with parity.

stripe sets with parity A method of data protection in which data is striped in large blocks across all the disks in an array. Data redundancy is provided by the parity information. This method provides fault tolerance. *See also* fault tolerance; stripe set.

subnet A portion of a network (which might be a physically independent network segment) that shares a network address with other portions of the network and is distinguished by a subnet number. A subnet is to a network what a network is to the Internet.

subnet mask A 32-bit value that allows the recipient of IP packets to distinguish the network ID portion of the IP address from the host ID.

superscope An administrative grouping of scopes that are used to support multiple, logical IP subnets on the same physical subnet. A superscope contains a list of member scopes (child scopes) that can be activated as a collection.

swap file A hidden file on the hard drive that Windows uses to hold parts of programs and data files that do not fit in memory.

T

Transmission Control Protocol/Internet Protocol (TCP/IP) A set of networking protocols that provide communication across interconnected networks made up of computers with diverse hardware architectures and operating systems. TCP/IP includes standards for how computers communicate and conventions for connecting networks and routing traffic.

Telnet A protocol used for interactive logon to a remote computer.

thread In programming, a process that is part of a larger process or program. In e-mail and Internet newsgroups, a series of messages and replies related to a specific topic.

token ring A type of network architecture that connects clients in a closed ring and uses token passing to enable clients to use the network. *See also* Ethernet; Fiber Distributed Data Interface (FDDI).

Trivial File Transfer Protocol (TFTP) A file transfer protocol that transfers files to and from a remote computer running the TFTP service. TFTP, which is defined in RFC 1350, among others, was designed with fewer functions than FTP.

trust relationship A link between domains that enables pass-through authentication, in which a trusting domain honors the logon authentications of a trusted domain. With trust relationships, a user who has only one user account in one domain can potentially access the entire network. User accounts and global groups defined in a trusted domain can be given rights and resource permissions in a trusting domain, even though those accounts don't exist in the trusting domain's directory database.

U

unicast mode A configuration setting that instructs NLB to change the MAC address of the cluster adapters to the same value for all hosts in a cluster. This is the default mode of operation.

Uniform Resource Locator (URL) The location of a file. You can use addresses to find files on the Internet and your computer. Internet addresses are also known as URLs.

uninterruptible power supply (UPS) A device connecting a computer (or other electronic equipment) and a power source (usually an outlet receptacle) that ensures that electrical flow to the computer is not interrupted because of a blackout and, in most cases, protects the computer against potentially damaging events such as power surges and brownouts. Each UPS unit is equipped with a battery and a loss-of-power sensor; if the sensor detects a loss of power, it switches over to the battery so that the user has time to save any work and shut off the computer.

Universal Naming Convention (UNC) A way to specify a directory on a file server. UNC names are filenames or other resource names that begin with the string \\, indicating that they exist on a remote computer.

User Datagram Protocol (UDP) A TCP complement that offers a connectionless datagram service that doesn't guarantee delivery or correct sequencing of delivered packets (much like IP). *See also* datagram; Internet Protocol (IP); packet.

V

virtual server A collection of services that gives the appearance of a physical Windows server to clients. A virtual server is typically a group containing all of the resources to run a particular application, including a Network Name resource and an IP Address resource.

W

wide area network (WAN) A communications network that connects geographically separated areas.

Windows Internet Name Service (WINS) A name resolution service that resolves Windows networking computer names to IP addresses in a routed environment. A WINS server, which is a Windows NT Server computer, handles name registrations, queries, and releases.

WINS resource A resource that provides network services to clients. It provides a dynamic database service that can register and resolve NetBIOS names to IP addresses used on your network.

WLBS Microsoft Windows NT Load Balancing Service. An add-on to Windows NT 4 Server that load-balances TCP/IP traffic to and from servers in a WLBS cluster. WLBS was renamed Network Load Balancing (NLB) in Windows 2000.

workgroup For Windows NT, a collection of computers that are grouped for viewing purposes. Each workgroup is identified by a unique name.

Index

A

Test *your* readiness *for the* MCP**exam**

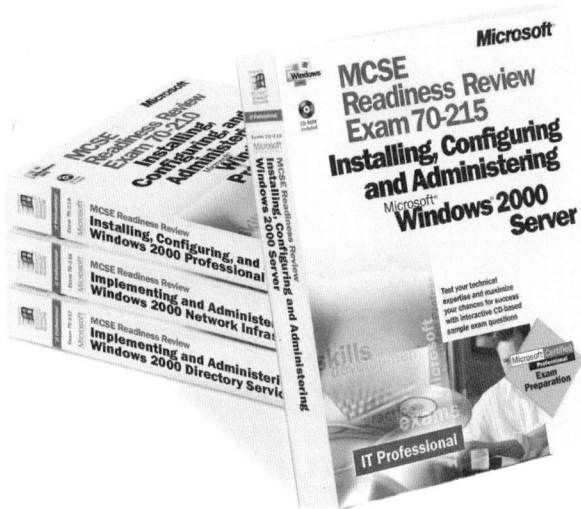

If you took a Microsoft Certified Professional (MCP) exam today, would you pass? With each READINESS REVIEW MCP exam simulation on CD-ROM, you get a low-risk, low-cost way to find out! The next-generation test engine delivers a set of randomly generated, 50-question practice exams covering real MCP objectives. You can test and retest with different question sets each time—and with automated scoring, you get immediate Pass/Fail feedback. Use these READINESS REVIEWS to evaluate your proficiency with the skills and knowledge that you'll be tested on in the real exams.

Comprehensive **technical** *information* and *tools* for deploying and supporting the **Windows 2000 Server** operating system in your organization.

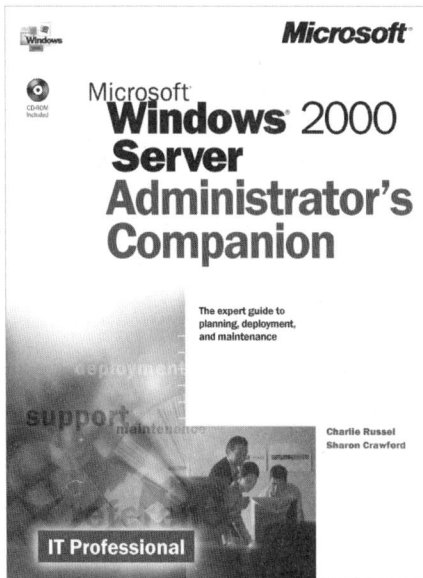

MICROSOFT LICENSE AGREEMENT
Book Companion CD

IMPORTANT—READ CAREFULLY: This Microsoft End-User License Agreement ("EULA") is a legal agreement between you (either an individual or an entity) and Microsoft Corporation for the Microsoft product identified above, which includes computer software and may include associated media, printed materials, and "online" or electronic documentation ("SOFTWARE PRODUCT"). Any component included within the SOFTWARE PRODUCT that is accompanied by a separate End-User License Agreement shall be governed by such agreement and not the terms set forth below. By installing, copying, or otherwise using the SOFTWARE PRODUCT, you agree to be bound by the terms of this EULA. If you do not agree to the terms of this EULA, you are not authorized to install, copy, or otherwise use the SOFTWARE PRODUCT; you may, however, return the SOFTWARE PRODUCT, along with all printed materials and other items that form a part of the Microsoft product that includes the SOFTWARE PRODUCT, to the place you obtained them for a full refund.

SOFTWARE PRODUCT LICENSE

The SOFTWARE PRODUCT is protected by United States copyright laws and international copyright treaties, as well as other intellectual property laws and treaties. The SOFTWARE PRODUCT is licensed, not sold.

1. **GRANT OF LICENSE.** This EULA grants you the following rights:

    a. **Software Product.** You may install and use one copy of the SOFTWARE PRODUCT on a single computer. The primary user of the computer on which the SOFTWARE PRODUCT is installed may make a second copy for his or her exclusive use on a portable computer.

    b. **Storage/Network Use.** You may also store or install a copy of the SOFTWARE PRODUCT on a storage device, such as a network server, used only to install or run the SOFTWARE PRODUCT on your other computers over an internal network; however, you must acquire and dedicate a license for each separate computer on which the SOFTWARE PRODUCT is installed or run from the storage device. A license for the SOFTWARE PRODUCT may not be shared or used concurrently on different computers.

    c. **License Pak.** If you have acquired this EULA in a Microsoft License Pak, you may make the number of additional copies of the computer software portion of the SOFTWARE PRODUCT authorized on the printed copy of this EULA, and you may use each copy in the manner specified above. You are also entitled to make a corresponding number of secondary copies for portable computer use as specified above.

    d. **Sample Code.** Solely with respect to portions, if any, of the SOFTWARE PRODUCT that are identified within the SOFTWARE PRODUCT as sample code (the "SAMPLE CODE"):

        i. **Use and Modification.** Microsoft grants you the right to use and modify the source code version of the SAMPLE CODE, *provided* you comply with subsection (d)(iii) below. You may not distribute the SAMPLE CODE, or any modified version of the SAMPLE CODE, in source code form.

        ii. **Redistributable Files.** Provided you comply with subsection (d)(iii) below, Microsoft grants you a nonexclusive, royalty-free right to reproduce and distribute the object code version of the SAMPLE CODE and of any modified SAMPLE CODE, other than SAMPLE CODE, or any modified version thereof, designated as not redistributable in the Readme file that forms a part of the SOFTWARE PRODUCT (the "Non-Redistributable Sample Code"). All SAMPLE CODE other than the Non-Redistributable Sample Code is collectively referred to as the "REDISTRIBUTABLES."

        iii. **Redistribution Requirements.** If you redistribute the REDISTRIBUTABLES, you agree to: (i) distribute the REDISTRIBUTABLES in object code form only in conjunction with and as a part of your software application product; (ii) not use Microsoft's name, logo, or trademarks to market your software application product; (iii) include a valid copyright notice on your software application product; (iv) indemnify, hold harmless, and defend Microsoft from and against any claims or lawsuits, including attorney's fees, that arise or result from the use or distribution of your software application product; and (v) not permit further distribution of the REDISTRIBUTABLES by your end user. Contact Microsoft for the applicable royalties due and other licensing terms for all other uses and/or distribution of the REDISTRIBUTABLES.

2. **DESCRIPTION OF OTHER RIGHTS AND LIMITATIONS.**

    - **Limitations on Reverse Engineering, Decompilation, and Disassembly.** You may not reverse engineer, decompile, or disassemble the SOFTWARE PRODUCT, except and only to the extent that such activity is expressly permitted by applicable law notwithstanding this limitation.

    - **Separation of Components.** The SOFTWARE PRODUCT is licensed as a single product. Its component parts may not be separated for use on more than one computer.

    - **Rental.** You may not rent, lease, or lend the SOFTWARE PRODUCT.

- **Support Services.** Microsoft may, but is not obligated to, provide you with support services related to the SOFTWARE PRODUCT ("Support Services"). Use of Support Services is governed by the Microsoft policies and programs described in the user manual, in "online" documentation, and/or in other Microsoft-provided materials. Any supplemental software code provided to you as part of the Support Services shall be considered part of the SOFTWARE PRODUCT and subject to the terms and conditions of this EULA. With respect to technical information you provide to Microsoft as part of the Support Services, Microsoft may use such information for its business purposes, including for product support and development. Microsoft will not utilize such technical information in a form that personally identifies you.

- **Software Transfer.** You may permanently transfer all of your rights under this EULA, provided you retain no copies, you transfer all of the SOFTWARE PRODUCT (including all component parts, the media and printed materials, any upgrades, this EULA, and, if applicable, the Certificate of Authenticity), **and** the recipient agrees to the terms of this EULA.

- **Termination.** Without prejudice to any other rights, Microsoft may terminate this EULA if you fail to comply with the terms and conditions of this EULA. In such event, you must destroy all copies of the SOFTWARE PRODUCT and all of its component parts.

3. **COPYRIGHT.** All title and copyrights in and to the SOFTWARE PRODUCT (including but not limited to any images, photographs, animations, video, audio, music, text, SAMPLE CODE, REDISTRIBUTABLES, and "applets" incorporated into the SOFTWARE PRODUCT) and any copies of the SOFTWARE PRODUCT are owned by Microsoft or its suppliers. The SOFT-WARE PRODUCT is protected by copyright laws and international treaty provisions. Therefore, you must treat the SOFTWARE PRODUCT like any other copyrighted material **except** that you may install the SOFTWARE PRODUCT on a single computer provided you keep the original solely for backup or archival purposes. You may not copy the printed materials accompanying the SOFTWARE PRODUCT.

4. **U.S. GOVERNMENT RESTRICTED RIGHTS.** The SOFTWARE PRODUCT and documentation are provided with RESTRICTED RIGHTS. Use, duplication, or disclosure by the Government is subject to restrictions as set forth in subparagraph (c)(1)(ii) of the Rights in Technical Data and Computer Software clause at DFARS 252.227-7013 or subparagraphs (c)(1) and (2) of the Commercial Computer Software—Restricted Rights at 48 CFR 52.227-19, as applicable. Manufacturer is Microsoft Corporation/One Microsoft Way/Redmond, WA 98052-6399.

5. **EXPORT RESTRICTIONS.** You agree that you will not export or re-export the SOFTWARE PRODUCT, any part thereof, or any process or service that is the direct product of the SOFTWARE PRODUCT (the foregoing collectively referred to as the "Restricted Components"), to any country, person, entity, or end user subject to U.S. export restrictions. You specifically agree not to export or re-export any of the Restricted Components (i) to any country to which the U.S. has embargoed or restricted the export of goods or services, which currently include, but are not necessarily limited to, Cuba, Iran, Iraq, Libya, North Korea, Sudan, and Syria, or to any national of any such country, wherever located, who intends to transmit or transport the Restricted Components back to such country; (ii) to any end user who you know or have reason to know will utilize the Restricted Components in the design, development, or production of nuclear, chemical, or biological weapons; or (iii) to any end user who has been prohibited from participating in U.S. export transactions by any federal agency of the U.S. government. You warrant and represent that neither the BXA nor any other U.S. federal agency has suspended, revoked, or denied your export privileges.

DISCLAIMER OF WARRANTY

NO WARRANTIES OR CONDITIONS. MICROSOFT EXPRESSLY DISCLAIMS ANY WARRANTY OR CONDITION FOR THE SOFTWARE PRODUCT. THE SOFTWARE PRODUCT AND ANY RELATED DOCUMENTATION ARE PROVIDED "AS IS" WITHOUT WARRANTY OR CONDITION OF ANY KIND, EITHER EXPRESS OR IMPLIED, INCLUDING, WITHOUT LIMITA-TION, THE IMPLIED WARRANTIES OF MERCHANTABILITY, FITNESS FOR A PARTICULAR PURPOSE, OR NONINFRINGEMENT. THE ENTIRE RISK ARISING OUT OF USE OR PERFORMANCE OF THE SOFTWARE PRODUCT REMAINS WITH YOU.

LIMITATION OF LIABILITY. TO THE MAXIMUM EXTENT PERMITTED BY APPLICABLE LAW, IN NO EVENT SHALL MICROSOFT OR ITS SUPPLIERS BE LIABLE FOR ANY SPECIAL, INCIDENTAL, INDIRECT, OR CONSEQUENTIAL DAM-AGES WHATSOEVER (INCLUDING, WITHOUT LIMITATION, DAMAGES FOR LOSS OF BUSINESS PROFITS, BUSINESS INTERRUPTION, LOSS OF BUSINESS INFORMATION, OR ANY OTHER PECUNIARY LOSS) ARISING OUT OF THE USE OF OR INABILITY TO USE THE SOFTWARE PRODUCT OR THE PROVISION OF OR FAILURE TO PROVIDE SUPPORT SERVICES, EVEN IF MICROSOFT HAS BEEN ADVISED OF THE POSSIBILITY OF SUCH DAMAGES. IN ANY CASE, MICROSOFT'S ENTIRE LIABILITY UNDER ANY PROVISION OF THIS EULA SHALL BE LIMITED TO THE GREATER OF THE AMOUNT ACTUALLY PAID BY YOU FOR THE SOFTWARE PRODUCT OR US$5.00; PROVIDED, HOWEVER, IF YOU HAVE ENTERED INTO A MICROSOFT SUPPORT SERVICES AGREEMENT, MICROSOFT'S ENTIRE LIABILITY REGARDING SUPPORT SERVICES SHALL BE GOVERNED BY THE TERMS OF THAT AGREEMENT. BECAUSE SOME STATES AND JURISDICTIONS DO NOT ALLOW THE EXCLUSION OR LIMITATION OF LIABILITY, THE ABOVE LIMITATION MAY NOT APPLY TO YOU.

MISCELLANEOUS

This EULA is governed by the laws of the State of Washington USA, except and only to the extent that applicable law mandates govern-ing law of a different jurisdiction.

Should you have any questions concerning this EULA, or if you desire to contact Microsoft for any reason, please contact the Microsoft subsidiary serving your country, or write: Microsoft Sales Information Center/One Microsoft Way/Redmond, WA 98052-6399.

System Requirements

To get the most out of the *MCSE Training Kit—Microsoft Windows 2000 Advanced Server Clustering Services*, including the Supplemental Course Materials CD-ROM, you will need two computers, each equipped with the following minimum configuration:

- Pentium II 300-MHz or higher processor
- 256 megabytes (MB) of RAM
- 4GB hard disk
- 256KB L2 cache
- CD-ROM or DVD drive
- Non-ISA network adapter
- Super VGA (SVGA) monitor
- Mouse or other pointing device (recommended)
- Microsoft Windows 2000 Advanced Server with Service Pack 1 applied

In addition to the two computers, you will need:

- 1 external shared storage device, such as a SCSI device, approved for use with a cluster
- 2 Y-cables or self-terminating cables, to connect each node in the cluster to the shared device

To view the electronic version of the book on the companion CD, you will need a browser application such as Microsoft Internet Explorer 4.01 or later. These and other browser applications are available to download over the Internet. A version of Microsoft Internet Explorer 5 that allows you to view the electronic version of the book is supplied on the companion CD. See the README.TXT file on the companion CD for instructions on how to use this supplied version of the Internet Explorer browser to view the electronic version of the book. Microsoft Windows Media Player 7 or later is necessary for viewing the demo files. The Media Player is included on the companion CD.

start faster
go
farther

For information about Microsoft Press®
products, visit our Web site at
mspress.microsoft.com

Microsoft ®